THE CENSUS RETURNS

OF THE

DIFFERENT COUNTIES

OF THE

STATE OF IOWA,

FOR 1856.

SHOWING

IN DETAIL, THE POPULATION, PLACE OF NATIVITY, AGRICULTURAL STATISTICS, DOMESTIC AND GENERAL MANUFACTURES, &c.

PRINTED BY THE AUTHORITY OF THE CENSUS BOARD.

James W. Grimes, Gov.
E. Sells, Secretary of State,
J. Pattee, Auditor of State. } CENSUS BOARD,

IOWA CITY:
CRUM & BOYE, PRINTERS.
1857.

Census Returns.

TABLE,

SHOWING THE POPULATION OF ADAIR COUNTY, FOR 1856.

Townships.	No. dwelling houses.	Number of families.	Number of males.	Number of females.	Colored.	Married.	Widowed.	Native voters.	Naturalized voters.	Aliens.	Militia.	Deaf and Dumb.	Blind.	Insane.	Idiotic.	Owners of land.	Paupers.
Washington	30	29	89	81		61	3	38			36					32	
GrandRiver	21	21	65	56		41	2	14	10		19					22	
Jefferson,	16	16	47	47		31		18	1	1	18	1				19	
Harrison,	24	25	89	64		50	2	37	1		33					29	
Somerset,	21	26	74	51		43		33		1	32					24	
Total, ...	112	117	364	299		226	7	140	12	2	138	1				126	

TABLE,

SHOWING THE AGRICULUURAL STATISTICS OF ADAIR COUNTY, FOR 1856.

Townships.	Acres of improved land.	Acres of unimproved land.	Tons of Hay.	Acres of sp'ng wheat	Bushels Harvested.	Acres of W. Wheat.	Bushels Harvested.	Acres of Oats.	Bushels Harvested.	Acres of Corn.	Bushels Harvested.	Acres of Potatoes.	[illegible]seels Harvested.
Washington	791	7237	232	22	296	3	30	3	40	217	5980	5	
GrandRiver	357	5168	119	40	322	..	...	6	100	146	3775		
Jefferson,	275	2575	84	..	....	..	...	16	80	153	419[illegible]		
Harrison,	352	4382	...	5	....	..	...	..	...	89	3[illegible]		
Somerset,	72	3130	39	18	230	21	550	8	150	150			
Total, ...	1847	22492	474	85	848	24	580	33	370	7[illegible]			

TABLE,

SHOWING THE NUMBER OF HOGS, CATTLE, DOMESTIC AND GENERAL MANUFACTURES OF ADAIR COUNTY, FOR 1856.

TOWNSHIPS.	No. of hogs sold.	Value of hogs sold.	No. of Cattle sold.	Value of Cattle sold.	Pounds of butter made.	Pounds of cheese.	Pounds of Wool.	Value of Domestic Manufacture.	Value of General Manufactures.
Washington, ...	9	41	31	1012	1800	.. .	125	40	....
Grand River, ...	38	152	11	329	1210	20	35	10	20
Jefferson, ...	77	262	21	708	640	....	....	....	....
Harrison, ...	75	760	6	315	300	....	100	....	....
Somerset, ...	41	128	14	415	2125	....	190	40	....
Total, ...	240	1343	83	2779	6075	20	450	90	20

TABLE,

EXHIBITING THE PROFESSIONS, TRADES, OR OCCUPATIONS OF THE INHABITANTS OF ADAIR COUNTY, FOR 1856.

TOWNSHIPS.	Farmers.	Loborers.	Blacksmiths.	Carpenters.	Stone Masons.	Millers.	Shoemakers.	Clergyman.	Cooper.	Surveyor.	Tanner.
Washington, ..	41	....	....	...	...	2	1	...	...	...	...
Grand River,..	15	....	1	2	1	...	...	...	...	...	...
Jefferson, ...	24	....	....	2	...	...	...	...	...	...	...
Harrison, ...	42	1	.	...	...	...	...	1	...	...	...
Somerset, ...	41	....	....	...	..	...	...	...	1	1	1
Total, ...	163	1	1	4	1	2	1	1	1	1	1

TABLE SHOWING THE PLACE OF NATIVITY OF THE INHABITANTS OF ADAIR COUNTY, FOR 1856.

Townships.	Ohio.	Indiana.	Pennsylvania.	Iowa.	New York.	N. Hampshire.	Vermont.	Massachusetts.	Connecticut.	Virginia.	Kentucky.	Illinois.	Michigan.	Arkansas.	N. Carolina.	S. Carolina.	Tennessee.	Missouri.	Georgia.	Maryland.	New Jersey.	England.	Ireland.	Wales.	Germany.
Washington,	18	65	12	28	3	1	1				4	15			9		2	11					1		
Grand River,	19	30		21	9			1	1		3	3	4		3	1	5					2		2	17
Jefferson,	12	32	4	18	1					2		5			14	1					1		4		
Harrison,	13	70	1	12						5	8	20			3	2	1	4	8	1	1		4		
Somerset,	42	10	7	19	7		2	1	4	5	3	11		1			2		1	2	4	1		2	1
Total, ...	104	207	24	98	20	1	3	2	5	12	18	54	4	1	29	4	10	15	9	3	6	3	9	4	18

TABLE SHOWING THE POPULATION OF ADAMS COTNTY, FOR 1856.

Townships.	No. dwelling houses.	Number of families.	Number of males.	Number of females.	Married.	Widowed.	Native voters.	Naturalized voters.	Aliens.	Militia.	Owners of land.
Jasper, ...	40	42	143	105	82		44	3	5	38	45
Quincy, ...	131	142	442	329	272	13	157	23	24	138	121
Total, ...	171	184	585	434	354	15	201	26	29	176	166

AGRICULTURAL STATISTICS OF ADAMS COUNTY, FOR 1856.

Townships	Acres of improved land.	Acres of unimproved land.	Acres of meadow.	Tons of hay.	Acres spring wheat.	Bushels harvested.	Acres winter wheat.	Bushels harvested.	Acres of oats.	Bushels harvested.	Acres of Corn.	Bushels harvested.	Acres of Potatoes.	Bushels harvested.
Jasper,	621	9572		197	32	535	12	125	5	115	433	15720	8	1061
Quincy,	2090	23395	604	3	56	715	49	718	57	1290	758	28755	11	4237
Total,	2711	32967	604	200	88	1250	61	843	62	1405	1191	44475	19	5298

TABLE SHOWING THE NUMBER OF HOGS, CATTE, DOMESTIC AND GENERAL MANUFACTURES OF ADAMS COUNTY, FOR 1856.

Townships.	No. of hogs sold.	Value of hogs sold.	No. of Cattle sold.	Value of cattle sold.	Pounds butter made.	Pounds of cheese.	Pounds of wool.	Value of domestic manufactures.	Value of general manufactures.
Jasper, ...	164	647	169	4948	3125	....	40	....	....
Quincy, ...	149	800	97	2577	4670	200	370	382	691
Total, ...	313	1447	266	7525	7795	200	410	382	691

TABLE

SHOWING THE PLACE OF NATIVITY OF THE INABITANTS OF ADAMS COUNTY, FOR 1856.

Townships.	Ohio.	Indiana.	Pennsylvania.	Iowa.	New York.	Maine.	N. Hampshire.	Vermont.	Massachusetts.	Connecticut.	Virginia.	Kentucky.	Illinois.	Michigan.	NorthCarolina.	Tennessee.	Missouri.	California.	Maryland.	England.	Ireland.	Germany.	France.	Canada.	Switzerland.	Delaware.
Jasper, ...	40	89	20	42	4	1			1		4	7	8		7	4	1	2		2	2	2	11	1		
Quincy, ...	125	215	44	96	31	7	3	6	2	7	39	40	39	2	6	11	14		4	5	6	11	56		1	1
Total, ...	165	304	64	138	35	8	3	6	3	7	43	47	47	2	13	15	15	2	4	7	8	13	67	1	1	1

TABLE

EXHIBITING THE PROFESSIONS, TRADES OR OCCUPATIONS OF THE INHABITANTS OF ADAMS COUNTY, FOR 1856.

Townships.	Farmers.	Laborers.	Blacksmiths.	Carpenters.	Millers;	Sawyers.	Manufacturers.	Merchants.	Druggists.	Hotel keepers.	Physicians.	Lawyers.	Clergymen.	Teachers.	Brick makers.	Jewellers.	Coopers.	Clerks.	Surveyors.	County recorder	Mail carriers.	Constables.	Laundress.	Clerk dis. court.	Pres. Icarian So.	Weavers.	Prairie breakers	Wheelwrights.
Jasper, ...	50			1			1																					
Quincy, ...	105	9	2	12	3	1		4	1	1	3	1	1	2	1	2	1	1	2	1	3	1	1	1	1	1	2	3
Total, ...	155	9	2	13	3	1	1	4	1	1	3	1	1	2	1	2	1	1	2	1	3	1	1	1	1	1	2	3

TABLE, SHOWING THE POPULATION OF ALLAMAKEE COUNTY, FOR 1856.

Townships.	No. dwelling houses.	No. of families.	Number of males.	Number of females.	Colored.	Married.	Widowed.	Native voters.	Naturalized voters.	Aliens.	Malitia,	Deaf and Dumb.	Blind.	Insane.	Idiotic.	Owers of land.	Paupers.
Makee,	152	159	471	372		318	8	152	51	68	290		1			132	
Ludlow,	80	80	232	215		165	8	76	24	10	77					83	
Hanover,	39	39	116	95		76	3	20	9	20	42					43	1
Union Prairie,	104	104	167	234		174	13	77	31	12	102		1			98	2
Post,	90	90	256	254		164	7	88	8	2					1	67	1
Franklin,	90	90	264	227		189	12	103	13		97	4				64	
Jefferson,	138	150	387	334		281	11	137	16	34	145		1			136	
Waterville,	116	116	302	290		214	13	28	66	41	124	1				90	
Linton,	92	109	283	231		182	12	59	57	27	113	1			1	74	
Fairview,	35	35	98	79		64	3	28	13	21	30				1	28	
Taylor,	91	98	257	237		177	6	12	50	35	79					94	
LaFayette,	91	93	248	223		167	19	23	42	41	82	1				3	
Lansing,	123	123	351	287	3	234	19	94	55	30	20					102	
Iowa,	23	23	71	57		38	4	11	4		20	1				15	
Union City,	30	30	68	70		49	2	17	9	6	25	1				27	1
French Creek,	49	55	144	134		102	5	17	17	23	41	1		1		47	
Centre,	78	87	212	186		164	8	20	11	136	68				1	76	2
Waterloo,	32	32	83	74		47	5	18	8	13	31					28	1
Total,	1453	1513	4110	3599	3	2805	158	980	484	519	1386	10	3	1	4	1207	8

2

TABLE,

SHOWING THE NUMBER OF HOGS, CATTLE, DOMESTIC AND GENERAL MAUFACTURES OF ALLAMAKEE CO., FOR 1856.

Townships.	Acres of improved land.	Acres of unimproved land.	Acres of meadow.	Tons of hay.	Bushels of grass seed.	Acres of spring wheat	Bushels harvested.	Acres of Winter Wheat.	Bushels harvested.	Acres of oats	Bushels harvested	Acres of Corn	Bushels harvested	Acres of Potatoes.	Bushels harvested
Makee,	2516	13968	6	....	...	732	12980	...	...	155	5817	701	27570	49	7021
Ludlow,	1964	9699	139	117	...	574	11543	...	...	196	6535	561	18939	28	3466
Hanover,	441	3784		353	...	49	718	...	...	9	565	81	2749	9	891
Union Prairie,	4395	9412	45	812	3	642	11573	...	...	329	14752	623	24490	49	5981
Post,	3401	7167	221	560	6	754	13633	...	...	341	12877	856	34570	½	1828
Eranklin,	1280	8387	797	545		51	468	...	...	22	1060	117	4880	...	....
Jefferson,	2046	10083	325	473	1	460	8088	...	...	124	5465	468	18065	21	1788
Waterville,	1096	4694	133	444	3	345	6459	28	176	81	2511	263	8060	19	1725
Linton,	1370	9211	61	51	4	127	2068	23	178	47	993	307	10959	38	3010
Fairview,	405	3498	9	3	...	31	425	1	30	15	325	47	1805	1	920
Taylor,	681	4735	220	425	...	222	4579	...	...	22	799	134	4595	42	3722
LaFayette,	403	2292		9	...	241	4207	...	...	23	417	145	5950	16	2040
Lansing,	340	1430	3	....	8	71	1330	37	534	18	680	76	2700	1	600
Iowa,	101	20	35	130	...	8	100	...	...	....	.....	67	1500	3	80
Union City,	676	4634	74	190	...	39	1682	...	...	20	750	153	4200	8	632
French Creek,	495	5018	80	80	...	51	756	...	...	18	286	186	9130	16	1531
Centre,	698	8573	94	26	...	188	2709	6	22	39	872	178	5470	17	1813
Waterloo,	383	4098		....	...	30	600	...	...	20	800	95	4180	2	150
Total,	22591	110703	2242	4819	26	4638	83918	95	947	1479	55104	5053	189812	321	37199

TABLE,

SHOWING THE NUMBER AND VALUE OF HOGS, CATTLE, DOMESTIC AND GENERAL MANUFACTURES OF ALLAMAKEE COUNTY, FOR 1856.

TOWNSHIPS.	No. of Hogs sold.	Value of Hogs sold.	No. of Cattle sold.	Value of Cattle sold.	Pounds of Butter made.	Pounds of Cheese.	Pounds of Wool	Value of Dom. Manufactures.	Value of Gen'l Manufactures.
Makee, ...	182	1141	161	6289	1[illegible]5	1690	82	....	.....
Ludlow, ...	122	1249	71	2432	6[illegible]2	150	145	15	.....
Hanover, ...	11	46	33	1000	[illegible]0	.....	27	1725	.....
Union Prairie	376	2743	125	4456	8[illegible]95	290	99	....	.....
Post, ...	521	4468	48	[illegible]52	4[illegible]0	.....	927	160	2600
Franklin, ...	129	567	28	932	[illegible]0	900	.....	....	.....
Jefferson, ...	178	1773	123	4804	7[illegible]3	250	75	1245	1500
Waterville, ..	68	610	44	1189	3[illegible]5	114	226	....	.....
Linton, ...	110	713	35	1135	3[illegible]6	60	26	413	.....
Fairview, ...	33	308	9	242	1[illegible]5	.....	70	25	.....
Taylor, ...	95	967	13	772	1[illegible]5	200	32	....	150
La Fayette, ..	67	674	16	640	2[illegible]0	75	70	....	23000
Lansing, ...	37	362	8	295	[illegible]5	.....	.....	....	7750
Iowa, ...	....	.....	....	.....	....	.....	.....	....	.....
Union City, .	95	371	10	465	[illegible]0	55	.....	....	.....
French Creek	110	668	20	884	3[illegible]0	.....	107	65	.....
Centre, ...	34	258	20	539	3[illegible]0	50	10	....	.....
Waterloo, ...	52	431	8	450	1[illegible]0	.....	.....	....	.....
Total, ...	2220	17351	782	28827	63[illegible]0	3834	1896	3648	35000

TABLE,

EXHIBITING THE PROFESSIONS, TRADES OR OCCUPATIONS OF THE INHABITANTS OF ALLAMAKEE COUNTY, FOR 1856.

Townships.	Farmers.	Laborers.	Blacksmiths.	Carpenters.	Wagon makers.	Bricklayers.	Plasterers.	Stone Masons.	Stone Cutters.	Carriage makers.	Engineers.	Millers.	Sawyers.	Millwright.	Painters.	Cabinet makers.	Chair makers.	Milliners.	Tailors.	Shoemakers.	Harness makers.	Bakers.	Butchers.	Mechanics.	Manufacturers.	Merchants.	Traders.	Druggists.	Hotel keepers.	Clothiers.	Physicians.
Makee,	150	60	9	12				2				2			1	2				1						6			1	1	1
Ludlow,	98	5																						4							2
Hanover,	40	10	3	2										1		1															
Union Prairie,	126	10	1	5										1				2								1					2
Post,	51	4	3	4								1												1		4					1
Franklin,	66	16	3	13						1	2	3	1	2		3				1						3					2
Jefferson,	120	24	6	14		1	1	1					1	1	1					2	1			1		3			1		2
Waterville,	86	5	2									1							1	1											
Linton,	123		1	7		1	1					3	5	5						2											
Fairview,	34		1	2																				3		1			1		
Taylor,	78	13	2	3				4									2	1	1							2					
Lafayette,	81	6	3	5				3				6			1					2						5	1		1		
Lansing,	45	24	4	17	3		3	5	1		1	2		2	2				3	3	3	2	1	2	2	19		3	9		4
Iowa,	21																			1											
Union City,	28			1							1																				1
French Creek,	58	10	1	1				1				1									2										
Centre,	68	14	1										1																		1
Waterloo,	28	3	1	1				1				1	3	1												1					
Total,	1301	204	41	87	3	2	4	17	1	1	4	20	11	13	5	6	2	3	5	13	3	2	1	11	2	45	1	3	11	1	16

TABLE—Continued,

EXHIBITING THE PROFESSIONS, TRADES OR OCCUPATIONS OF THE INHABITANTS OF ALLAMAKEE COUNTY, FOR 1856.

Townships.	Lawyers.	Clergymen.	Teachers.	Printers.	Editors.	Artists.	Daguer'an Artists	Teamsters.	Brick makers.	Jewellers.	Gunsmiths.	Coopers.	Clerks.	Wheelwright.	Surveyors.	Stage drivers.	Tanners.	Miners.	Dress makers.	Lime burners.	Lumbermen.	Tailoresses.	Basket makers.	Pilots.	Shingle makers.	Trappers.	Jobbers.	Servants.	Ferrymen.	Wood chopper.	Barbers.	Weavers.	Brokers.	Stage owners.	Ship builders.	Cradle makers.	Book binders.	Hunters.	Stevedores.
Makee,	1	1	1	..	..	..	1	1	..	..	..	..	2	1	1	1	2	..	..	..	..	..	..	..	..	..	..	..	..	..	..	..	..	..	..	..	..	..	..
Ludlow.	..	1	..	..	..	1	..	..	1	..	..	..	..	..	..	..	..	..	..	..	..	..	..	..	..	..	..	..	..	..	..	..	..	..	..	..	..	..	..
Hanover,	..	..	1	..	..	..	..	..	..	..	..	..	..	..	..	..	..	4	1	..	..	..	..	..	..	..	..	..	..	..	..	..	..	..	..	..	..	..	..
Union Prairie,	..	1	4	..	..	..	..	..	..	..	..	..	..	..	..	..	..	..	..	..	..	..	..	..	..	..	..	..	..	..	..	..	..	..	..	..	..	..	..
Post,	..	..	..	..	..	..	..	1	..	..	..	..	..	..	..	..	..	..	..	..	..	..	..	..	..	..	..	..	..	..	..	..	..	..	..	..	..	..	..
Franklin,	..	2	..	..	..	..	1	..	2	..	..	1	1	..	..	..	..	..	..	1	2	1	..	..	..	..	..	..	..	..	..	..	..	..	..	..	..	..	..
Jefferson,	..	1	2	..	..	..	1	..	..	..	..	1	1	..	..	..	..	..	..	..	..	..	..	..	..	..	..	..	..	..	..	..	..	..	..	..	..	..	..
Waterville,	..	..	2	..	..	..	..	..	..	..	..	..	..	1	..	..	..	..	..	..	..	..	..	..	..	..	..	..	..	..	..	..	..	..	..	..	..	..	..
Linton,	1	1	4	..	..	..	..	..	..	..	..	2	..	..	..	..	..	..	..	..	..	..	..	..	..	..	..	..	..	..	..	..	..	..	..	..	..	..	..
Fairview,	..	..	..	..	..	..	..	..	..	..	..	..	1	..	..	..	..	..	..	..	..	..	1	..	..	..	..	..	..	..	..	..	..	..	..	..	..	..	..
Taylor,	..	..	..	..	..	..	..	..	..	..	..	..	7	..	..	..	..	..	..	..	..	..	..	1	2	1	1	..	..	..	..	..	..	..	..	..	..	..	..
Lafayette,	1	1	..	..	..	..	..	..	..	..	1	..	..	..	..	..	..	..	..	..	..	..	..	..	..	..	..	1	1	2	..	..	..	..	..	..	..	..	..
Lansing,	5	1	1	1	1	..	..	2	2	2	1	3	..	..	..	..	..	..	..	..	4	..	..	1	..	..	..	7	..	..	1	1	1	1	1	3	1	..	..
Iowa,	..	..	..	..	..	..	..	3	..	..	..	..	..	..	..	..	..	..	..	..	..	..	..	..	..	..	..	..	..	..	..	..	..	..	..	..	..	..	..
Union City,	..	..	..	..	..	..	..	..	..	..	..	..	..	..	..	..	..	..	..	..	..	1	..	..	..	..	..	..	..	..	..	1	..	..	..	..	..	1	..
French Creek,	..	..	..	..	..	..	..	..	..	..	..	..	..	..	..	..	..	..	..	..	..	..	..	..	..	..	..	..	..	..	..	..	..	..	..	..	..	..	1
Centre,	..	3	..	..	..	..	..	..	..	..	..	1	..	..	..	..	..	..	..	..	..	..	..	..	..	..	..	..	..	..	..	..	..	..	..	..	..	..	..
Waterloo,	..	..	..	..	..	..	..	..	..	..	..	..	..	..	..	..	..	..	..	..	..	..	..	..	..	..	..	..	..	..	..	..	..	..	..	..	..	..	..
Total,	8	12	15	1	1	1	3	7	5	2	2	8	13	2	1	1	2	4	1	1	6	2	1	2	2	1	1	8	1	2	1	2	1	1	1	3	1	1	1

TABLE,

SHOWING THE PLACE OF NATIVITY OF THE INHABITANTS OF ALLAMAKEE COUNTY, FOR 1856.

Townships.	Ohio.	Indiana.	Pennsylvania.	Iowa.	New York.	Maine.	N. Hampshire.	Vermont.	Massachusetts.	Connecticut.	Rhode Island.	Virginia.	Kentucky.	Illinois.	Michigan.	Arkansas.	Louisiana.	Mississippi.	North Carolina.	Tennessee.	Missouri.	Georgia.
Makee, ...	36	20	58	89	155	98	19	31	42	6	9	1	1	36	1				3	1	2	
Ludlow, ...	49	23	42	45	69	14	8	16	7	5		4		36	3					1		
Hanover, ...	12	8	13	30	23		2		3	1	1	2		16						1		
Union Prairie	43	36	37	52	119	12	2	5	15	21	2	3	7	20				1		1	1	
Post, ...	102	84	25	87	52	11	5	11	4	5		21	10	27	1				1	6	1	1
Franklin, ...	92	23	31	55	106		4	6	6	3		25	3	46					15	2	1	
Jefferson, ...	46	43	211	99	92	5	1	10	13	1		15	3	21	1		2		2		1	
Waterville, ..	21	6	57	106	28			4	3	3	1	18	1	13							1	
Linton, ...	46	21	21	62	69			15	9			26	17	19	1						5	
Fairview, ...	21	5	12	22	13		7	8		2		6	8	3								
Taylor, ...	16	6	31	82	8		4		11			1	8	12		5						
La Fayette, ..	21	3	24	72	41	2	1	2	6		2	3	5	23	3					1	4	
Lansing, ...	42	6	27	80	93	9	6	19	15	5	1	5	8	32	7				4		7	
Iowa, ...	12	1	8	29	20			3	2	1				3							2	
Union City, .	10	4	37	17	6	6				1			1	2	3						1	1
French Creek,	37	1	1	30	27		4	2	3			1	4	30					2	1	1	
Centre, ...	3		17	58	43		4	8	6	2			1	5								
Waterloo, ...	8	4	22	23	19		2	4	2	1			3	5								
Total, ...	617	294	674	1038	983	155	69	153	147	57	16	132	80	349	18	5	2	1	28	14	27	2

TABLE—Continued,

SHOWING THE PLACE OF NATIVITY OF THE INHABITANTS OF ALLAMAKKE COUNTY, FOR 1856.

Townships.	California.	Maryland.	N. Jersey.	England.	Ireland.	Wales.	Scotland.	Germany.	France.	Austria.	Prussia.	Norway.	Sweden.	Holland.	On the Ocean.	Canada.	New Brunswick.	Switzerland.	Denmark.	Hanover.	Saxony.	Wisconsin,	Delaware,	Nova Scotia.	Minnesota.	Oregon.	Unknown.
Makee,......		2	5	11	79			31			4	34				30		17				9		12			1
Ludlow,.....	1	9	4	4	19	1	22	1				3				43	2	1				14				1	
Hanover,....			1	1	30							54				6						7					
Union Prairie,		1	4	5	67	12	3	4				5				9						14					
Post,........			3		3		2	1	4	1	3					14		8				9					7
Franklin, ...		1	2	9	10		8	11								14						11	2		2		3
Jefferson,....		4	1	9	32			18	2		21	36				7					7	10			2		3
Waterville, ..		4	2	5	80		3	28				181	1		1	8		1				12	1		1		2
Linton,.......		4		12	89			10		20	17	2				21		4		2	4	14	3				1
Fairview,....		9	1	2	42			2				1				12		1									
Taylor,......		12		11	184			7		2	1	47			1	67						10					18
La Fayette,..		2	1	30	133		1	14				48				16		3				12					
Lansing,.....		1		23	42	3	4	109	7	3	4	3				17		37				15		3			1
Iowa, ...		1		11	18			9								1						7					
Union City,..				20	20			3								2						6					
French Creek,			5	2	54		2	65	1					1		1						2					1
Centre,......				2	6			47	7			77	83			11		2	6			4					6
Waterloo, ...					21			17				14										11		1			
Total,.....	1	50	29	e57	879	16	45	377	21	26	50	505	84	1	2	279	2	74	6	2	5	167	6	16	5	1	43

SHOWING THE POPULATION OF APPANOOSE COUNTY, FOR 1856.

Townships.	No. dwellinghouses	Number families.	Number of males.	Number females.	Colored.	Married.	Widowed.	Native voters.	Naturalized voters.	Aliens.	Militia.	Deaf and dumb.	Blind.	Insane.	Idiotic.	Owners of land.
Centre,	440	440	1317	1199	....	757	45	435	14	4	359	4	....	....	....	215
Caldwell,	101	101	334	270	....	176	7	89	6	1	74	1	....	....	....	76
Chariton,	103	103	295	252	....	191	10	110	....	....	113	....	....	....	....	74
Independence,	82	82	213	202	....	150	6	83	....	....	75	....	....	....	....	66
Johns,	74	74	207	205	....	151	5	79	2	....	69	2	....	1	2	79
Pleasant,	132	137	403	381	....	247	13	124	10	4	125	....	1	1	....	111
Shoal,	138	154	412	363	1	273	8	150	3	1	126	2	....	....	....	125
Taylor,	116	127	386	336	....	234	14	127	8	1	133	....	....	....	....	106
Union,	115	115	322	326	....	208	13	117	1	....	106	1	....	1	....	82
Wells,	135	135	401	382	9	256	22	153	2	2	131	2	....	....	....	112
Washington,	150	151	460	409	....	237	24	156	7	....	147	1	....	1	....	180
Total,	1586	1619	4750	4325	10	2930	167	1623	53	13	1458	13	1	4	2	1226

TABLE,

SHOWING THE AGRICULTURAL STATISTICS OF APPANOOSE COUNTY, FOR 1856.

Townships.	Acres of improved land.	Acres of unimproved land.	Acres of meadow.	Tons of hay.	Bushels grass seed.	Acres spring wheat.	Bushels harvested.	Acres winter wheat.	Bushels harvested.	Acres of oats.	Bushels harvested.	Acres of corn.	Bushels harvested.	Acres potatoes.	Bushels harvested.
Centre, ...	9695	31140	2728	198	17	613	4942	346	2283	752	21616	2756	85205	20	2224
Caldwell, ...	2103	10614	85	109	9	184	2840	94	1705	289	12065	935	32463	17	2567
Chariton, ...	2412	6827	1	1		148	1426	71	827	180	4409	719	24570	11	1270
Independence, ...	1905	3093	12	2		122	953	102	307	163	4210	990	41300	9	943
Johns, ...	3275	11367	82	30	9	304	2485	68	158	314	8990	1252	39105	3	792
Pleasant, ...	3849	12036	69	42	41	420	14427	159	1555	484	15507	1174	38175	29	3666
Shoal, ...	4662	17962	69	19		285	3188	25	94	327	13485	1458	43740	23	1097
Taylor, ...	4049	10427	105	114	80	495	5306	126	971	666	12586	1761	68180	19	1938
Union, ...	1602	7717	43	35	3	112	781	61	507	154	4180	1048	54265	10	745
Wells, ...	3438	12219	54	40	13	275	3988	210	2277	435	12068	1664	61379	18	1924
Washington, ...	5032	17645	185	173	14	531	5635	221	2217	592	16711	1859	69067	27	2451
Total	42052	146066	3428	764	186	3492	45971	1484	12901	4356	125827	15617	557449	189	19617

TABLE,

SHOWING THE NUMBER & VALUE OF HOGS, CATTLE, DOMESTIC AND GENERAL MANUFACTURES OF APPANOOSE COUNTY, FOR 1856.

TOWNSHIPS.	No. of hogs sold.	Value of hogs sold.	No. of Cattle sold.	Value of cattle sold.	Pounds butter made.	Pounds of cheese.	Pounds of wool.	Value of domestic manufactures.	Value of general manufactures.
Centre, ...	1017	6850	336	7476	3300	275	1985	840	....
Caldwell, ...	272	1897	136	3116	5110	27	1073	841	20
Chariton, ...	391	1996	127	3297	2108	350	494	131	....
Independence	474	2702	146	3761	6845	122	828	1071	....
Johns	372	2585	132	2679	12211	133	796	967	....
Pleasant,.....	399	2495	376	6670	11745	340	900	601	130
Shoal,.......	322	2899	227	5245	14698	724	882	583	500
Taylor, ...	753	6131	380	5939	7971	974	1967	1589	229
Union, ...	598	3810	137	3010	6225	957	876	662	402
Wlles	1074	9193	235	5133	8785	2641	1219	1634	....
Washington..	744	4692	350	4692	3880	180	1133	1164	100
Total,......	6416	45252	2582	53277	82878	6975	12213	10073	1381

TABLE,

SHOWING THE PLACE OF NATIVITY OF THE INHABITANTS OF APPANOOSE COUNTY, FOR 1856.

Townships.	Ohio.	Indiana.	Pennsylvania.	Iowa.	New York.	Maine.	N. Hampshire.	Vermont.	Massachusetts.	Connecticut.	Rhode Island.	Virginia.	Kentucky.	Illinois.	Michigan.	Arkansas.	Alabama.	North Carolina.	South Carolina.	Tennessee.	Missouri.	Georgia.	Maryland.	New Jersey.	England.	Ireland.	Wales.	Scotland.	Germany.	France.	Holland.	On the Ocean.	Canada.	Wisconsin.	Delaware.	Dis. Columbia.	Unknown.
Centre, ...	555	591	116	534	45	1	2	4	4	2		128	133	142	5	9	1	57	7	71	36	2	15	6	10	19	6		2				4		5		
Caldwell, ...	191	55	51	146	9					1		19	35	14				6	1	6	34		4	3	2	18			3			1	4	1			
Chariton, ...	101	83	52	162	8		1	7		1		29	28	24				13	1	17	15		3	2													
Indepnedence	39	113	15	97								52	34	18	1			10		10	16		3			2								5			
Johns, ...	34	179	25	61	1	1		1		2	1	25	25	19				7	3	9	5		4	7		2			2								
Pleasant, ...	267	115	76	150	5	1		2	1	4	1	44	24	14			1	16	3	3	4	11	4	1	13	15			3						2	1	
Shoal Creek,	180	90	52	167	18	8	1	4	1			31	49	65	3		1	15		36	11		3	1	8			2	2		1		2		3		
Taylor, ...	41	171	66	149	8							18	33	[illegible]				106		67	8		1	2	2	6			3	1				1	1		
Union, ...	114	127	42	144	3			1		1		37	26	26			1	14		97	6	1	1	1		2								4			
Wells, ...	175	87	32	171	8	1		2	2			68	76	68			1	14	1	42	24		6		1	2		1					1				
Washington,.	124	186	48	206	6					8		63	70	32			3	9	4	78	11	1	5	1		4			5	2				1	1		1
Total	1821	1797	575	1987	111	16	4	21	8	21	2	514	533	483	9	9	8	267	20	436	170	15	49	24	36	70	6	3	20	3	1	1	11	12	12	1	1

TABLE.

EXHIBITING THE PROFESSIONS, TRADES OR OCCUPATIONS OF THE INHABITANTS OF APPANOOSE COUNTY, FOR 1856.

Townships.	Farmers.	Laborers.	Blacksmiths.	Carpenters.	Wagon makers.	Brick layers.	Plasterers.	Stone masons.	Stone cutters.	Engineers.	Millers.	Millwrights.	Painters.	Cabinet makers.	Chair makers.	Tinners.	Milliners.	Tailors.	Shoemakers.	Harness makers.	Mechanics.	Merchants.	Druggists.	Hotel keepers.	Physicians.	Lawyers.	Clergymen.
Centre,	199	103	6	22	1	1	2		2	1	2		1			2		1	3	6		18	3	1	8	5	
Caldwell,	78	7	2	3														1	1			2					
Chariton,	78		4	8																		3			2		
Independence	70	4		3	1									1	1							1			1		
Johns,	90			1							1				1		1					1					
Pleasant,	112	3	1	2				2			2								1		1	2			2		2
Shoal Creek,	142	2		2	1														1	1		2	2		1	1	1
Taylor,	149	14	4	2								1					1	2	1		1	3			2		
Union,	96		2	4	1					1	4					1	1	1	1		2	2			1	1	1
Wells,	116	11	1	5							3			1						1		5			1		
Washington,	134	11	4	7	1	1								1	1		1		1			1			2		
Total,	1264	155	24	59	5	2	2	2	2	2	12	1	1	3	3	3	4	5	6	8	4	40	5	1	20	7	4

TABLE—Continued,

EXHIBITING THE PROFESSIONS, TRADES OR OCCUPATIONS OF THE INHABITANTS OF APPANOOSE COUNTY, FOR 1856.

Townships.	Teachers.	Editors.	Grocers.	Teamsters.	Brick makers.	Gun smiths.	Coopers.	Clerks.	Pedlar.	Salesman.	Book binders.	Potters.	Weavers.
Centre,			2			2		8	1				
Caldwell,	1												
Chariton,							1						
Independence,													
Johns,	1						1						
Pleasant,		1		1									
Shoal,	2									1	1		
Taylor,	2							1					
Union,								1					
Wells,												1	
Washington,	1				1								1
Total,	7	1	2	1	1	2	2	10	1	1	1	1	1

TABLE,

SHOWING THE POPULATION, AGRICULTURAL STATISTICS, HOGS, CATTLE, DOMESTIC AND GENERAL MANUFACTURES, OF AUDUBON COUNTY, FOR 1856.

No. of dwelling houses,	49
No. of families,	50
No. of males,	150
No. of females,	133
Married,	93
Widowed,	5
Native voters,	67
Naturalized voters,	2
Aliens,	2
Militia,	60
Owners of land,	51
Acres of improved land,	701
Acres of unimproved land,	7883
Acres of spring wheat,	115
Bushels harvested,	1971
Acres of oats,	28
Bushels harvested,	1405
Acres of corn,	33½
Bushels harvested,	10720
Acres of potatoes,	12
Bushels harvested,	1927
No. of hogs sold,	223
Value of hogs sold,	1916
No. of Cattle sold,	132
Value of cattle sold,	4376
Pounds of Butter made,	3656
Pounds of wool,	375
Value of general manufactures,	1335

TABLE,

EXHIBITING THE PROFESSIONS, TRADES, OR OCCUPATIONS OF THE INHABITANTS OF AUDUBON COUNTY, FOR 1856.

Farmers,	32
Laborers,	12
Blacksmiths,	1
Carpenters,	5
Machinists,	3

TABLE,

SHOWING THE PLACE OF NATIVITY OF THE INHABITANTS OF AUDUBON COUNTY, FOR 1856.

Ohio,	47
Indiana,	10
Pennsylvania,	7
Iowa,	48
New York,	34
Maine,	1
New Hampshire,	5
Vermont,	4
Massachusetts,	16
Connecticut,	4
Virginia,	17
Kentucky,	17
Illinois,	12
Michigan,	8
Tennessee,	2
Maryland	2
England,	10
Scotland,	1
Germany,	1
Canada,	1
Kansas Territory,	2
Wisconsin,	4
Unknown,	30

TABLE,

SHOWING THE POPULATION OF BENTON COUNTY, FOR 1856.

Townships.	No. dwelling houses.	Number of families.	Number of males.	Number of females.	Married.	Widowed.	Native voters.	Naturalized voters.	Aliens.	Militia.	Deaf and Dumb.	Blind.	Idiotic.	Owners of land.	Paupers.
Taylor,............	200	227	606	572	441	37	340	69		239	..	..	..	91	..
Benton,............	92	93	312	251	158	18	100	6	11	88	..	..	..	64	..
Canton,............	120	130	396	331	234	19	152	3	2	133	..	..	..	125	..
Jackson, ...	59	62	194	168	126	...	....	1	2	....	..	..	..	50	..
Cue,..............	47	48	139	110	87	4	37	10	7	41	1	..	..	44	..
Cedar,.............	62	80	232	160	151	8	99	...	3	93	..	..	..	67	1
Big Grove, ...	41	41	132	107	82	5	58	4	..	54	..	..	..	50	..
Monroe,............	25	25	79	57	57	2	27	2	3	25	1	1	..	29	..
Eden, ...	36	38	112	100	74	2	48	3	4	35	..	..	..	42	..
Iowa,..............	69	69	199	250	141	12	73	12	10	1	..	..	2	65	..
Polk, ...	150	167	485	277	287	24	181	...	5	157	..	..	1	118	1
Le Roy,............	68	68	198	185	122	3	73	2	2	72	..	..	2	52	1
Harrison, ...	65	65	203	151	128	5	73	5	3	64	1	..	..	62	..
Bruce, ...	19	20	65	66	43	1	19	4		16	1	..	..	22	..
Total,...........	1053	1133	3352	2895	2141	140	1280	121	52	1018	4	1	5	881	3

TABLE,

SHOWING THE NUMBER AND VALUE OF HOGS, CATTLE, DOMESTIC AND GENERAL MANUFACTURES OF BENTON COUNTY, FOR 1856.

Townships.	No. of hogs sold.	Value of hogs sold.	No. of cattle sold.	Value of cattle sold.	Pounds of buttermade	Pounds of Cheese.	Pounds of wool.	Value of Gen'l Manufactures.	Value of Dom. Manufactures.
Taylor,.....................	206	1779	80	2621	4600		159	127	.....
Benton, ...	226	1555	85	1718	1195	1195	242	135	......
Canton, ...	317	1982	103	1993	9306	2085	1129	343	325
Jackson,.....................	198	1009	72	2533	4880	400	12	....	......
Cue, ...	6	85	25	1180	2005	1350	60	....	......
Cedar, ...	120	872	139	1614	5130	5290	100	....	......
Big Grove, ...	166	1405	53	1527	7632	825	....	....	......
Monroe,.....................	38	179	15	283	1335	.....	89	....	......
Eden,.......................	30	206	38	1099	2040	30	....	....	......
Iowa,.......................	185	1424	55	1615	2510	135	227	...	25
Polk, ...	656	2976	218	5932	7075	394	708	107	1820
Le Roy,.....................	61	1778	77	767	2550	.....	84	....	......
Harrison, ...	305	2309	121	2467	3084	.....	363	159	......
Bruce, ...	8	14	18	1170	1080	230	....	....	......
Total,......................	2522	17573	1099	27520	54422	12012	3173	871	2170

TABLE,

SHOWING THE AGRICULTURAL STATISTICS OF BENTON COUNTY, FOR 1856.

Townships.	Acres of improved land.	Acres of unimproved land.	Acres of meadow.	Tons of hay.	Bushels grass seed.	Acres spring wheat.	Bushels harvested.	Acres winter wheat.	Bushels harvested.	Acres of oats.	Bushels harvested.	Acres of corn.	Bushels harvested.	Acres potatoes.	Bushels harvested.
Taylor,	2642	8079	560	391	...	492	8027	..	....	230	7355	11038	51400	12	2034
Benton,	2279	3519	53	430	5	309	4290	..	....	114	3323	547	21820	19	3100
Canton,	3903	15075	33	52	10	521	8702	..	....	273	10417	1211	54210	23	4412
Jackson,	1601	6371	2	1004	...	197	3019	..	....	65	2352	582	21450	17	2945
Cue,	774	4724	....	....	...	70	1288	..	....	44	825	201	8290	10	1285
Cedar,	2035	8812	12	799	3	135	3043	5	20	71	2720	966	25727	21	3127
Big Grove,	1397	4685	1	1	3	67	943	..	....	91	1901	363	17925	6	1110
Monroe,	622	3329	....	....	...	7	130	..	....	12	160	248	8000	2	348
Eden,	1355	5699	10	225	...	193	4062	..	....	32	1505	238	8950	8	1120
Iowa,	717	5150	....	326	...	129	1325	..	....	188	6765	427	21253	9	852
Polk,	2886	12817	39	34	...	637	6485	5	200	337	7519	1506	44159	35	4428
Le Roy,	1310	7261	6	237	...	93	1394	3	150	40	931	179	7100	4	790
Harrison,	1621	7087	....	....	9	323	3082	3	13	117	3507	648	28850	10	1802
Bruce,	204	3535	25	205	...	153	413	..	....	1	35	139	2985		368
Total,	23351	96144	739	3734	30	3326	46203	13	382	1617	49315	18290	321519	180	27721

TABLE,

EXHIBITING THE PROFESSIONS, TRADES OR OCCUPATIONS OF THE INHABITANTS OF BENTON COUNTY, FOR 1856.

Townships.	Farmers.	Laborers.	Blacksmiths.	Carpenters.	Wagon makers.	Bricklayers.	Plasterers.	Stone Masons.	Machinists.	Engineers.	Millers.	Sawyers.	Millwright.	Painters.	Cabinet makers.	Chair makers.	Tinners.	Milliners.	Tailors.	Hatters.	Shoemakers.	Harness makers.	Butchers.	Mechanics.	Merchants.	Speculators.	Druggists.	Hotel Keepers.	Physicians.	Dentists.
Taylor,	126	28	12	50	4	1	2	20	2	1	1	5	1	6	4		3	4	3	1	7	2	2		12	1	2	2	6	1
Benton,	69	1	2	6	1		1	4		2	1		2								1				4				3	
Canton,	163		1	12	1		1	1	1				1					1							3				1	
Jackson,	69		1	1																					1					1
One,	49	12																												
Cedar,	112		1	6					1								1								1					
Big Grove,	54	7		2			2												1											
Monroe,	31			4																										
Eden,	46			6									3								1									
Iowa,	110		2	8									1						1		1				1				1	
Polk,	130	2	5	28			1	1		3		1	2		1	1			1		4	2		1	5				4	
Leroy,	63		2	7				2																						
Harrison,	65	1	1	5															1			1							1	
Bruce,	33			1				1																						
Total,	1120	51	27	136	6	1	7	29	4	6	2	6	10	6	5	1	4	5	7	1	14	5	2	1	27	1	2	2	16	2

TABLE—Continued,

EXHIBITING THE PRROFESSIONS, TRADES OR OCCUPATIONS OF THE INHABITANTS OF BENTON COUNTY, FOR 1856

Townships.	Lawyers.	Clergymen.	Teachers.	Printers.	Editors.	Artists.	Daguer'an Artists	Bankers.	Grocers.	Teamsters.	Brick makers.	Watch makers.	Gunsmiths.	Coopers.	Clerks.	Seamstresses.	Basket makers.	Turners.	Stage drivers.	Livery men.	Surveyors.	Ferrymen.	Hunters.	Ostlers.	Shingle makers.	Weavers.	Pilots.	Pensioners.	Tailoresses.	Segar makers.	Prairie breakers.
Taylor,	7	6	5	3	1		3	1	1	12	4	1	1	2	12	7	1	1	4	1	1	1	1	1			1				
Benton,	2	1	1												2										6	1					
Canton,		4	1												2																
Jackson,			1																												
Cass,			1																												
Cedar,						1																						1	2		
Big Grove																														1	1
Monroe,	1																														
Eden,		1																													
Iowa,			2																							1					
Polk,	3	2								1											1					1					
Leroy,																															
Harrison,	1		1																												
Bruce,																															
Total,	14	15	12	3	1		[illegible]	1	1	13	4	1	1	2	16	7	1	1	4	1	2	1	1	1	6	3	1	1	2	1	1

TABLE,

SHOWING THE PLACE OF NATIVITY OF THE INHABITANTS OF BENTON COUNTY, FOR 1856.

TOWNSHIPS.	Ohio.	Indiana.	Pennsylvania.	Iowa.	New York.	Maine.	New Hampshire.	Vermont.	Massachusetts.	Connecticut.	Rhode Island.	Virginia.	Kentucky.	Illinois.	Michigan.	Arkansas.	Alabama.	Mississippi.	North Carolina.
Taylor,	249	200	148	152	106	5	5	17	28	18		48	47	50	13		1	1	2
Benton,	97	77	111	167	20		2	23	4	3		7	31	35	6				5
Canton,	253	90	120	98	57	1		9		2		15	15	26	8				2
Jackson,	91	34	82	18	25		1	15	1	2		25	5	20	8				
Cue,	32	14	20	9	40	8	3			1		3		19	2				3
Cedar,	78	84	18	23	51	6	3	7	2	14		10	3	49	10				2
Big Grove,	51	61	24	20	20	1	1		5			4	5	7					2
Monroe,	23	29	2	13	10		5	10	1	1		6	4	14					
Eden,	57	17	41	14	21		1	3				10	2	25					
Iowa,	131	39	26	35	58	2	2	1	1	1		3	4	24	2				6
Polk,	130	170	89	135	65		11	5	5	3	1	38	29	103	23	3			12
Le Roy,	93	41	49	74	13							5		94					
Harrison,	32	183	17	21	13		3	2	1	1		4	22	17	1				5
Bruce,	40	9	8	7	16			2	1				2	15	3				1
Total,	1347	1048	769	735	527	23	37	93	49	36	1	178	169	498	81	3	1	1	40

TABLE—Continued.

SHOWING THE PLACE OF NATIVITY OF THE INHABITANTS OF BENTON COUNTY, FOR 1856.

Townships.	South Carolina.	Tennessee.	Missouri.	Georgia.	Maryland.	New Jersey.	England.	Ireland.	Wales.	Scotland.	Germany.	France.	Norway.	Holland,	Canada.	Switzerland.	Denmark.	Wisconsin.	Delaware.	Unknown.	Dist. Columbia.
Taylor,	1	3	1	1	14	6	11	23	2	4	11				7	2		5	4		
Benton,		2	1		6		3	9			6				2			6			
Canton,	1	2	1		3	5	5			1	2			2							
Jackson,					9	1	1	5		2	5	8			2			3			
Cue,					1		6	10		9	2		10		7					50	
Cedar,		9	1		6	1	7	1							7						
Big Grove,	1	1			2	5		7			5				1					2	
Monroe,		1			1		6	2											1		1
Eden,					2		6				4				2		1	1	5		
Iowa,	1	42	1			2	1	3			64				10						
Polk,	1	18	3	1	6	3		2				1						3	2		
Le Roy,			4				7	4													
Harrison,	1	8	4				2			7	3				2			4			
Bruce,							7	4		5					10				1		
Total,	9	85	16	2	50	23	62	70	2	28	102	9	10	2	50	2	1	22	13	52	1

TABLE,

SHOWING THE POPULATION OF BLACKHAWK COUNTY, FOR 1856.

Townships.	No. dwelling houses.	Number families.	Number of males.	Number females.	Colored.	Married.	Widowed.	Native voters.	Naturalized voters.	Aliens.	Militia.	Deaf and dumb.	Insane.	Idiotic.	Owners of land.
Lester,	64	72	200	159	8	158	6	70	20	10	78	....	....	1	79
Barclay,	46	52	130	130	....	95	3	45	8	9	46	....	....	1	37
Mt. Vernon,	21	26	51	51	....	43	4	24	2	1	19	....	....	....	22
Washington,	84	94	262	210	....	175	6	115	4	7	93	2	2	....	71
Cedar Falls,	171	171	522	434	1	375	25	231	52	29	278	....	....	....	20
Blackhawk,	21	21	65	56	....	44	2	28	3	4	29	....	....	....	31
Waterloo,	275	293	955	724	....	643	33	448	27	46	529	3	....	1	364
Orange,	38	39	93	90	....	73	2	44	1	....	41	....	....	....	41
Cedar,	37	42	115	97	....	85	7	39	14	9	51	....	....	1	43
Big Creek,	52	55	149	131	....	110	7	68	1	4	64	....	....	....	46
Spring Creek,	96	98	308	262	....	190	12	110	2	3	108	....	....	1	82
Payner's Creek,	59	59	149	130	....	106	4	54	8	2	58	2	....	....	57
Gilbertville,	14	14	43	22	....	23	1	2	13	5	15	....	....	....	16
Total,	978	1036	3042	2496	9	2120	112	1278	155	129	1409	7	2	5	909

TABLE,

SHOWING THE AGRICULTURAL STATISTICS OF BLACKHAWK COUNTY, OF 1856.

Townships.	Acres of improved land.	Acres of unimproved land.	Acres of meadow.	Tons of Hay.	Bush. of grass seed.	Acres of spring wheat.	Bushels harvested.	Acres of Oats.	Bushels harvested.	Acres of Corn.	Bushels harvested.	Acres of Potatoes.	Bushels harvested.
Lester, ...	1622	11693	52	972		49	1167	26	595	303	10998	16	2149
Barclay, ...	634	3507						3	120	31	1730	1	140
Mt. Vernon, ..	324	2653				12	171	4	80	33	2059	1	275
Washington, .	2752	11496	68	768		306	6063	123	4986	932	41836	31	6010
Cedar Falls, ..	801	3512	40	60		66	1640	56	2330	371	18850	7	1230
Black Hawk, .	650	2141		256		62	1269	36	1162	244	10250	10	2000
Waterloo, ...	2159	6084	43	92		233	5740	136	1580	1109	44345	39	4635
Orange, ...	1134	5627				60	1172	61	1747	135	5600	5	1360
Cedar, ...	1607	2496		376		118	2091	103	4518	300	12440	14	2335
Big Creek, ...	935	7069				64	1185	22	1190	222	12000		120
Spring Creek,	355	11494	13	488	14	205	3373	34	[illegible]	331	27345	20	2620
Payners Creek	1606	7166	108			143	2951	63	[illegible]	555	29715	18	2535
Gibertsville, ..		312											
Total, ...	17778	75246	324	3012	14	1366	26821	[illegible]	[illegible]	5231	217168	152	25409

TABLE,

SHOWING THE NUMBER AND VALUE OF HOGS, CATTLE, DOMESTIC AND GENERAL MANUFACTURES OF BLACK HAWK COUNTY, FOR 1856.

Townships.	No. of hogs sold.	Value of hogs sold.	No. of cattle sold.	Value of cattle sold.	Pounds of butter made.	Pounds of Cheese.	Pounds of wool.	Value of Dom. Manufactures	Value of Gen'l Manufactures.
Lester, ...	141	703	135	6042	6776	100			467
Barclay, ...	11	91	9	406	535				
Mt. Vernon, ...			1	85	216				
Washington, ...	353	2321	97	2776	6314	370	345	91	
Cedar Falls, ...	42	344	2	160	241				1500
Black Hawk, ...	7	84	23	987	1500				
Waterloo, ...	312	2048	110	3974	2465	4642			
Orange, ...	6	78	21	333	710	350			
Cedar, ...	23	180	20	605	3375		30		
Big Creek, ...					1450		200		
Spring Creek, ...	294	1940	105	3835	1891	342	133	93	
Payner's Creek, ...	165	2543	131	5363	3776	100	97		
Gilbertsville, ...					25				
Total, ...	1353	9282	704	24826	36567	5904	184	184	1967

TABLE,

EXHIBITING THE PROFESSIONS, TRADES OR OCCUPATIONS OF THE INHABITANTS OF BLACK HAWK COUNTY, FOR 1856.

Townships.	Farmers.	Laborers.	Blacksmiths.	Carpenters.	Wagon makers.	Brick layers.	Plasterers.	Stone masons.	Stone cutters.	Machinists.	Engineers.	Millers.	Sawyers.	Millwrights.	Painters.	Cabinet makers.	Chair makers.	Tinners.	Milliners.	Tailors.	Shoemakers.	Harness makers.	Bakers.	Butchers.	Mechanics.	Merchants.
Lester,	83	6	2	5				2				1							1	3	1					
Barclay,	53	4	2	2	1			1			1			1		1					1					2
Mt. Vernon,	24																									
Washington,	63	16	1	6												2									6	
Cedar Falls,	49	122	8	33		1	2	13	4			4		6	4	1	1	5		3		5	1	2	6	10
Black Hawk,	30	1		3																						
Waterloo,	186	93	5	67	3		6	14	2	6	1	2	12	3	7	3		2	1	3	11	3		2		26
Orange,	32																									
Cedar,	62	13																								
Big Creek,	66		2	6						1				2												1
Spring Creek,	115		2	10	1		1	2					2	1						1	1					1
Payner's Creek,	53		1	3																						
Gilbertsville,	5	1	2	1				5			1			1						1						
Total,	808	256	25	136	5	1	9	37	6	7	3	7	14	14	11	7	1	7	2	11	14	8	1	4	12	40

TABLE—CONTINUED,

EXHIBITING THE PROFESSIONS, TRADES OR OCCUPATIONS OF THE INHABITANTS OF BLACK HAWK COUNTY, FOR 1856.

TOWNSHIPS.	Speculators.	Agents.	Druggists.	B'rd'g-h'se keepers.	Hotel keepers.	Physicians.	Lawyers.	Clergymen.	Teachers.	Printers.	Editors.'	Artists.	Bankers.	Grocers.	Teamsters.	Brick makers.	Jewellers.	Gun smiths.	Coopers.	Clerks.	Hunters.	Locksmith.	Breaker.	Tanner.	Horse farrier.	Sailors.	Students.	Surveyors.	Moulders.	Livery keepers.	Nurserymen.	Loafers.
Lester, ...						1													3		2	1	1									
Barclay, ...						1			1															1	1	1						
Mt. Vernon, ...																	1															
Washington, ...		1				3									1																	
Cedar Falls, ...	1		2		1	4	4	1	1	4		1		3			1	1		7	1						3	5	2	2	2	
Black Hawk, ..								1								2	1											1				
Waterloo, ...		4	1	2	8	7	11	8	8	3	1		2	5	8				3	7								1		1		
Orange, ...																7																
Cedar, ...																																
Big Creek, ...					2	1														1												
Spring Creek, ..						2										1	1															2
Payners Creek,																																
Gilbertsville, ..																			2													
Total, ...	1	5	3	2	11	18	15	10	10	7	1	1	2	8	9	10	4	1	8	15	3	1	1	1	1	1	3	7	2	3	2	2

TABLE SHOWING THE PLACE OF NATIVITY OF THE INHABITANTS OF BLACK HAWK COUNTY, FOR 1856.

STATES.	NAME OF TOWNSHIPS.													
	Lester.	Barclay.	Mt. Vernon.	Washington.	Cedar Falls.	Black Hawk.	Waterloo.	Orange.	Cedar,	Big Creek.	Spring Creek.	Payner's Creek.	Gilbertsuille.	Total.
Ohio	25	23	10	120	165	8	256	38	35	39	89	44	3	855
Indiana,	22	9	4	43	51	4	87	13	17	40	177	63	1	531
Pennsylvania,	66	57	11	14	76	21	213	22	21	28	80	13	1	623
Iowa,	18	17	1	58	82	8	119	5	18	24	64	43	4	461
New York,	72	59	34	88	164	28	326	21	35	37	26	22	5	917
Maine,	1	3	2	3	31	15	15	4	...	5	2	...	...	81
New Hampshire.	1	1	...	1	8	1	28	...	3	1	...	9	...	53
Vermont,	4	2	7	8	37	11	35	13	...	10	2	9	...	138
Massachusetts,	2	4	...	8	21	4	40	2	4	10	4	...	...	99
Connecticut,	4	9	1	7	12	...	34	1	2	1	...	...	...	71
Rhode Island.	...	...	...	...	2	1	6	...	...	4	...	...	...	13
Virginia,	2	...	5	10	15	1	45	...	2	4	23	12	...	119
Kentucky,	...	2	...	...	4	...	10	...	...	2	10	3	...	31
Illinois,	64	1	2	48	53	6	196	14	10	27	28	26	3	516
Michigan,	9	39	13	21	14	2	26	...	3	2	9	...	1	101
Lousiana,	...	...	...	...	...	...	5	...	...	...	...	...	...	5
Mississippi,	...	...	...	...	...	...	1	...	1	...	...	...	...	2
North Carolina,	...	...	...	2	...	...	...	1	...	1	11	6	...	21
South Carolina,	...	...	...	1	...	...	...	...	...	...	...	...	...	1
Tennessee,	...	...	...	2	2	...	1	1	...	7	5	5	...	23
Missouri,	1	...	...	1	...	...	4	...	...	1	3	...	...	10
California,	...	...	...	...	2	...	...	...	...	...	...	...	...	2
Maryland,	...	...	...	...	11	1	20	...	3	...	7	2	...	44
New Jersey,	...	...	1	4	4	...	18	...	...	1	1	6	3	38
England,	23	3	8	14	25	...	41	1	3	4	1	1	...	124
Ireland,	3	8	3	2	62	6	31	10	...	1	...	5	12	143
Wales,	...	...	...	...	3	...	...	...	...	...	...	...	...	3
Scotland,	1	6	...	5	6	...	2	...	...	...	3	4	1	28
Germany,	16	18	...	4	70	...	40	...	13	9	1	3	4	178
France,	2	...	...	...	...	...	6	...	11	...	...	...	1	20
Austria,	...	...	...	...	...	...	1	...	...	...	...	...	...	1
Prussia,	...	...	...	...	...	...	...	1	...	...	...	...	9	10
Norway,	...	...	...	...	2	1	...	...	...	...	...	...	...	3
Sweden,	...	...	...	...	...	...	1	...	1	...	7	...	...	9
Holland,	...	...	...	...	...	...	1	...	...	...	...	...	3	4
On the Ocean,	...	...	...	...	...	...	...	...	...	...	1	...	...	1
Canada,	14	7	...	7	12	...	48	46	15	15	1	1	...	166
New Brunswick,	1	...	...	...	...	...	1	...	...	...	...	...	...	2
Switzerland,	1	...	...	...	...	...	1	...	...	...	...	...	...	2
Hanover,	5	...	...	...	...	...	...	...	...	...	...	...	...	5
Nova Scotia,	...	...	...	...	...	...	1	...	...	...	...	...	...	1
Wisconsin,	...	2	...	...	14	3	15	...	4	...	14	2	...	54
Delaware,	...	...	...	...	3	...	...	...	...	...	...	...	...	3
Isle of Man,	...	...	...	1	1	...	...	...	...	...	...	...	...	2
District of Columbia,	...	...	...	...	1	...	...	...	1	...	...	...	...	2
Prince E. Island,	...	...	...	...	2	...	...	...	...	...	...	...	...	2
Unknown,	2	...	...	...	1	...	4	...	...	7	1	...	4	19

TABLE,

SHOWING THE POPULATION, AMOUNT OF PRODUCE, NUMBER OF HOGS, AND CATTLE SOLD, THE AMOUNT THEY BROUGHT, AND THE CAPITAL EMPLOYED IN DOMESTIC AND GENERAL MANUFACTURES OF BOONE COUNTY, FOR 1856.

POPULATION.	NAME OF TOWNSHIPS.						
	Boone,	Berry,	Dodge,	Pleasant,	Union,	Yell,	Total,
Number of dwelling houses,	210	109	96	148	21	96	680
Number of families,	210	96	96	147	21	100	670
Number of males,	571	235	325	382	81	287	1881
Number of females,	516	217	359	334	59	252	1637
Colored,	....	.....	.....	1	....	.....	1
Married,	398	163	183	263	46	184	1237
Widowed,	22	7	6	26	....	3	64
Native voters,	146	101	103	137	28	109	624
Naturalized voters,	3	1	9	9	4	2	28
Aliens,	....	.....	.....	36	....	13	49
Militia,	236	89	116	135	26	99	701
Deaf and Dumb,	....	.....	.....	1	....	.....	1
Blind,	1	.....	.....	.....	....	.....	1
Owners of land.	274	79	86	44	21	91	495
Paupers,	1	.....	.....	1	....	.....	2
AGRICULTURAL STATISTICS—							
Acres of improved land,	2410	2779	2531	1983	455	1022	12980
Acres of unimproved land,	34137	8252	11688	8942	6666	11013	80699
Acres of meadow,	51	44	.....	40	....	.....	135
Tons of Hay,	1035	64	769	58	140	299	2365
Bushels of grass seed,	8	18	.....	2	....	.....	27
Acres of spring wheat,	483	353	231	113	29	54	1263
Bushels harvested,	5324	3058	3342	1504	435	775	14428
Acres of winter wheat,	28	30	5	17	2	.....	82
Bushels harvested,	400	420	152	199	47	.....	1218
Acres of oats,	283	204	121	99	13	45	765
Bushels harvested,	7953	3014	3455	2810	350	1325	18907
Acres of Corn,	2034	1311	1106	1236	151	624	6462
Bushels harvested,	80045	25250	45900	62120	4280	26430	244025
Acres of Potatoes,	30	18	20	9	6	22	105
Bushels harvested,	5040	1448	1937	1226	468	2456	9575
STATISTICS OF HOGS, CATTLE, &C.—							
Number of hogs sold,	540	187	122	477	35	598	1959
Value of hogs sold,	4366	1117	870	3547	189	3019	13108
Number of cattle sold,	382	126	146	143	250	142	1189
Value of cattle sold,	7686	2588	3174	1077	1145	4113	19783
Pounds of butter made,	4484	5146	4635	3055	1820	8399	27539
Pounds of cheese,	120	50	2000	550	....	.....	2720
Pounds of wool,	482	740	135	898	73	382	2710
Value of Domestic Manufactures,	70	239	40	715	135	377	1576
Value of General Manufactures,	11900	150	....	.....	....	7425	19475

TABLE,

EXHIBITING THE PROFESSIONS, TRADES, OR OCCUPATIONS OF THE INHABITANTS OF BOONE COUNTY, FOR 1856.

OCCUPATIONS.	NAME OF TOWNSHIPS.						
	Boone.	Berry.	Dodge.	Pleasant.	Union.	Yell.	Total.
Farmers,	133	106	103	46	22	87	497
Laborers,	4	....	....	56	....	....	60
Blacksmiths,	6	....	1	7	1	2	17
Carpenters,	28	2	2	19	..	6	57
Wagon Makers,	3	1	....	....	....	....	4
Brick Layers,	....	....	....	2	....	....	2
Plasterers,	1	....	....	....	....	....	1
Stone Masons,	1	....	....	....	1	....	2
Machinists,	....	....	....	....	....	2	2
Engineers,	....	....	....	1	....	1	2
Millers,	9	....	2	....	....	....	11
Sawyers,	2	....	....	....	....	....	2
Millwrights,	1	1	....	5	....	....	7
Cabinet Makers,	2	....	....	2	....	....	6
Chair Makers,	1	....	....	....	....	1	2
Tinners,	1	....	....	1	....	....	2
Milliners,	....	2	....	2	1	....	6
Tailors,	1	....	...	1	....	....	2
Hatters,	....	....	....	....	....	1	1
Shoemakers,	5	....	.	....	1	1	7
Saddle and Harness Makers,	1	....	....	....	....	...	1
Manufacturers,	1	....	....	....	....	1	2
Merchants,	15	1	1	7	....	1	25
Traders,	3	....	...	....	....	....	3
Druggists,	1	....	....	....	....	....	1
Hotel Keepers,	4	....	....	2	....	....	6
Physicians,	5	1	1	1	2	....	10
Lawyers,	2	....	....	....	....	2	4
Clergymen,	1	....	....	1	....	....	2
Teachers,	....	....	1	....	....	1	2
Grocers,	....	....	....	1	....	....	1
Teamsters,	5	....	....	....	....	1	6
Gun Smiths,	1	1	....	....	....	....	2
Coopers,	....	1	....	1	....	1	2
Clerks,	2	....	....	2	....	....	4
Wheelwrights,	....	...	...	1	....	....	1
Tailoresses,	....	....	....	4	....	....	4

TABLE,

SHOWING THE PLACE OF NATIVITY OF THE INHABITANTS OF BOONE COUNTY, FOR 1856.

STATES.	NAME OF TOWNSHIPS						
	Boone.	Berry.	Dodge.	Pleasant.	Union.	Yell.	Total.
Ohio,	234	120	147	80	24	68	673
Indiana,	383	79	173	251	25	166	1077
Pennsylvania,	48	15	22	25	15	34	159
Iowa,	180	84	79	106	21	71	541
New York,	34	17	14	10	7	16	98
Maine,	1	8	1	....	4	1	15
New Hampshire,	....	3	...	1	....	....	4
Vermont,	1	4	1	....	3	2	11
Massachusetts,	2	3	...	2	....	....	7
Connecticut,	5	1	3	....	....	1	10
Rhode Island,	....	....	1	....	....	....	1
Virginia,	26	14	11	16	9	27	103
Kentucky,	47	22	26	28	4	22	149
Illinois,	29	43	16	59	18	69	234
Michigan,	1	14	....	....	....	6	21
Texas,	....	....	1	....	....	....	1
Alabama,	....	....	....	....	1	....	1
North Carolina,	21	9	19	15	3	16	83
South Carolina,	4	1	1	1	....	2	9
Tennessee,	16	1	6	20	....	10	55
Missouri,	3	7	....	29	....	1	40
Maryland,	11	2	2	1	1	1	18
New Jersey,	2	1	5	1	....	10	19
England,	7	....	9	1	1	4	42
Ireland,	13	....	...	1	1	...	15
Scotland,	....	....	....	1	...	....	1
Germany,	4	....	1	6	3	....	14
France,	7	1	5	....	....	....	13
Norway,	....	....	5	14	....	....	19
Sweden.	2	....	13	44	....	11	70
Canada,	2	....	....	1	....	....	3
Switzerland,	4	....	....	....	....	....	4
Wisconsin,	....	....	1	....	....	1	2
Delaware,	....	....	....	2	....	....	2
Unknown,	....	1	2	1	....	....	4

TABLE,

SHOWING THE POPULATION OF BREMER COUNTY, FOR 1856.

Townships.	No. dwelling houses.	Number families.	Number of males.	Number females.	Married.	Widowed.	Native voters.	Naturalized voters.	Aliens.	Militia.	Deaf and dumb.	Blind.	Idiotic.	Owners of land.
Jackson,	185	218	665	511	424	19	228	22	26	248	....	....	....	164
Jefferson,	101	101	312	245	192	9	101	20	6	106	1	....	..	88
Washington,	53	54	163	125	103	3	60	3	1	48	3	1	....	42
Polk,	57	67	194	173	131	7	82	4	....	63	...	....	1	64
Le Roy,	61	63	182	154	138	7	62	14	11	69	....	....	....	71
Frederica,	53	53	136	108	105	8	34	16	17	51	....	....	....	59
Franklin,	40	51	118	112	94	6	34	15	7	41	....	....	....	49
Fremont,														
Total,	550	607	1760	1428	1187	59	609	94	68	526	4	1	1	537

TABLE,

SHOWING THE AGRICULTURAL STATISTICS OF BREMER COUNTY, FOR 1856.

Townships.	Acres of improved land.	Acres of unimproved land.	Acres of meadow.	Tons of hay.	Bushels grass seed.	Acres spring wheat.	Bushels harvested.	Acres winter wheat.	Bushels harvested.	Acres of oats.	Bushels harvested.	Acres of corn.	Bushels harvested.	Acres potatoes.	Bushels harvested.
Jackson,.........															
Jefferson,.......	2194	21275	10	454	33	284	5395	2	25	190	8450	912	38610	23	4110
Washington,......	3073	16872	94	120	5	277	5660	..	....	228	8494	1065	39040	39	6807
Polk,............	1529	5485	6	249	...	84	1427	..	....	49	1575	304	9675	10	2015
Le Roy,..........	1223	9803	....	....	...	56	1253	..	....	32	1074	391	12396	15	1962
Frederica,.......	1168	9767	167	581	...	11	140	..	....	....	......	214	5680	12	1568
Franklin,........	686	1348	25	180	...	74	1662	..	....	8	291	171	7110	9	1540
Fremont,.	831	5395	....	506	...	52	891	..	....	17	750	168	4005	6	825
Total,..........	10702	69945	302	2090	38	839	17428	2	25	525	20634	3225	116516	115	18827

TABLE,

EXHIBITING THE PROFESSIONS, TRADES OR OCCUPATIONS OF THE INHABITANTS OF BREMER COUNTY, FOR 1856.

OCCUPATIONS.	Jackson.	Jefferson	Washington.	Polk.	Le Roy.	Fr'dricka	Franklin.	Fremont.	Total.
Farmers,	78	102	46	61	77	54	64		482
Laborers,	2	21	1	3	10		1		38
Blacksmiths,	10	4	1	2	11	1			22
Carpenters,	45		2	8	5	2			62
Stone Masons,	11	1			1				13
Stone Cutters,					1				1
Machinists,					1				1
Engineers,	1			1	1				3
Millers,	3								3
Sawyers,	1			2					3
Millwrights,	3			1					4
Painters,	3								3
Cabinet Makers,	4								4
Chair Makers,	4								4
Tinners,	3								3
Milliners,									1
Tailors,	2								2
Shoemakers,	7			1		1	2		11
Harness Makers,	3								3
Mechanics,		8							8
Manufacturers,						3			3
Merchants,	22					1			23
Agents,	1								1
Druggists,	1								1
Hotel keepers,	3								3
Physicians,	5				1				6
Lawyers,	4								4
Clergymen,	3			1	1		1		6
Teachers,	2	1			3	2			8
Printers,	3								3
Editors,	1								1
Artists,	1								1
Teamsters,	4								4
Brick Makers,	3								3
Jewellers,	1								1
Coopers,	1			1					2
Clerks,	11			1					12

TABLE,

SHOWING THE NUMBER OF HOGS, CATTLE, DOMESTIC AND GENERAL MANUFACTURES OF BREMER COUNTY, FOR 1856.

TOWNSHIPS.	No. of hogs sold,	Value of hogs sold.	No. of Cattle sold.	Value of Cattle sold.	Pounds of butter made.	Pounds of cheese.	Pounds of Wool.	Value of Domestic Manufacture.	Value of General Manufactures.
Jackson, ...	127	1285	98	3734	6860	200	105	...	11600
Jefferson, ...	359	2136	184	5951	6467	480	770	97	.....
Washington,.....	109	712	67	2129	2800	550	65	75	101
Polk,...........	141	871	71	3336	4145	180	908	92	.....
Le Roy,........	7	44	29	1183	3750	100	....	...	.....
Frederica,.......	31	238	50	2229	3590	75	78	100	.....
Franklin,........	21	85	45	1435	2580	....	....	...	.....
Fremont,...	...	....	...	.....	.....	....	....	...	.....
Total,.........	795	5371	544	19996	31192	1585	1926	363	11701

TABLE,

SHOWING THE PLACE OF NATIVITY OF THE INHABITANTS OF BREMER COUNTY, FOR 1856.

STATES.	NAME OF TOWNSHIPS.								TOTAL.
	Jackson.	Jefferson.	Washington.	Polk.	Le Roy.	Fredericka.	Franklin.	Fremont.	
Ohio,	208	94	62	35	34	21	21		475
Indiana,	80	58	3	41	18	5	6		211
Pennsylvania,	152	43	27	19	11	5	16		273
Iowa,	104	65	33	43	34	19	13		311
New York,	212	2	59	86	67	37	47		577
Maine,	23	6	..	3	3	8	..		39
New Hampshire,	10	5	..	3	5	3	1		28
Vermont,	30	1	1	11	17	2	10		76
Massachusetts,	10	1	1	4	8	6	..		30
Connecticut,	11	13	3	13	1	..	3		31
Rhode Island,	..	10	.	..	..	..	1		13
Virginia,	25	15	2	8	13	1	18		62
Kentucky,	10	81	17	4	1	..	12		48
Illinois,	132	22	55	58	29	39	..		412
Michigan,	18	..	..	3	11	1	..		72
Louisiana,	..	..	..			1	..		1
North Carolina,	3	1	..	2	..	..	..		6
Tennessee,	4	4	..	.	..	..	..		8
Missouri,	2	2	..		3	..	..		10
California,	..	.	..		1	..	..		1
Maryland,	2	1	..	.	1	1	3		8
New Jersey,	5	10	..		..	..	3		18
England,	47	7	6	12	13	.	8		93
Ireland,	23	5	8	.	20	4	10		70
Scotland,	1	5	.	.	2	..	.		8
Germany,	22	29	4	1	9	84	38		187
France,	..	1	.	.	..		1		2
Austria,	..	.	.		..	..	3		3
Norway,	..	.	.		2		..		2
Sweden,	..	.	.	14	4	..	..		4
Canada,	17	2	2	.	22	..	12		69
New Brunswick,	13	.			..		..		13
Wisconsin,	1	1	4	4	7	7	2		24
Delaware,	1	.		1	..	..	..		2
Minnesota,	..	1		.	..	..	..		1

TABLE,

SHOWING THE POPULATION OF BUCHANAN COUNTY, FOR 1856.

Townships.	No. dwelling houses.	No. of families.	Number of males.	Number of females.	Married.	Widowed.	Native voters.	Naturalized voters.	Aliens.	Malitia.	Deaf and Dumb.	Owners of land.	Paupers.
Jefferson,	96	97	273	227	182	12	97	4	10	83	2	88	1
Perry,	48	52	139	118	98	5	46	4	...	42		43	
Liberty,	105	147	439	366	292	7	181	9	3	150	6	100	
Spring and Prairie,	80	80	281	232	164	6	105	5	4	75		79	
Alton,	74	84	260	206	164	15	93	16	5	81		73	
Byron,	48	48	136	131	85	3	49	3		47		44	
Washington,	169	194	611	467	386	32	213	48	57			130	
Newton,	63	70	181	166	126	5	44	21	11	56		68	
Superior,	91	91	222	202	142	9	76	...	2	77	4	79	
Buffalo,	79	89	256	212	169	11	90	10	8	79		89	
Total,	853	952	2798	2327	1808	105	994	120	120	690	12	793	1

TABLE,

SHOWING THE AGRICULTURAL STATISTICS OF BUCHANAN COUNTY, FOR 1856.

Townships.	Acres of improved land.	Acres of unimproved land.	Acres of meadow.	Tons of hay.	Bushels grass seed.	Acres spring wheat.	Bushels harvested.	Acres winter wheat.	Bushels harvested.	Acres of oats.	Bushels harvested.	Acres of Corn.	Bushels harvested.	Acres of Potatoes.	Bushels harvested.
Jefferson,	3231	11717		2	60	254	4114			109	3411	823	26419	24	2202
Perry,	604	3501	30	4		114	1539	15	150	54	1541	305	12235	6	935
Liberty,	3914	17545	40	496	10	627	5830	3	47	261	9136	735	25500	22	4016
Spring and Prairie,	2472	13621	22	664	34	902	5969			181	5994	642	30770	23	3920
Alton,	1611	6510	19	12		218	3989	9	116	70	3066	608	22640	27	5141
Byron,	1313	3690	5	6	12	143	2657			86	3127	257	7865	11	1630
Washington,	1670	5391	97	242		368	7623	12	210	232	7921	506	17390	19	3120
Newton,	1896	8456		617		226	4124			56	1539	488	16875	16	2377
Superior,	1980	9979	2			252	5029			93	2997	432	17465	14	2848
Buffalo,	2531	13831	10	12		163	3724			155	3030	290	7540	15	1760
Total,	21222	94242	226	2055	116	3267	44598	39	523	1270	41762	5088	184699	181	27949

TABLE,

SHOWING THE NUMBER OF HOGS, CATTLE, DOMESTIC AND GENERAL MANUFACTURES OF BUCHANAN COUNTY, FOR 1856.

Townships.	No. of hogs sold,	Value of hogs sold.	No. of Cattle sold.	Value of Cattle sold.	Pounds of butter made.	Pounds of cheese.	Pounds of Wool.	Value of Domestic Manufacture.	Value of General Manufactures.
Jefferson, ...	239	2182	123	2912	4325	360	181	...	...
Perry, ...	138	1078	33	972	2410	200	28	522	...
Liberty, ...	319	2296	77	2676	9404	45	471	50	400
Spring and Prairie,	395	2666	214	4064	7060	969	701	21	..
Alton, ...	95	731	51	1971	7243	100	120	79	...
Byron, ...	78	504	51	1580	4295	179	90	...	...
Washington, ...	152	1356	43	1288	4377	250	151	36	...
Newton, ...	133	1014	61	2065	7745	135	212	129	...
Superior, ...	210	1587	162	4622	6590	300	116	...	...
Buffalo, ...	93	9[illegible]4	141	3879	4750	350	301	...	...
Total, ...	1849	14348	956	26029	58199	2888	2371	837	400

TABLE

EXHIBITING THE PREOFESSIONS, TRADES OR OCCUPATIONS OF THE INHABITANTS OF BUCHANAN COUNTY, FOR 1856,

OCCUPATIONS.	NAME OF TOWNSHIPS.										TOTAL.
	Jefferson.	Percy.	Liberty.	Prairie & Spring.	Alton.	Byron.	Washington.	Newton.	Superior.	Buffalo.	
Farmers,	110	26	113	90	111	51	60	80	86	84	811
Laborers,	5	9	8		4	6	94	9			135
Blacksmiths,	2	1	4	2	2		4	1	2	1	19
Carpenters,		3	16	15	5	1	34	1	7	4	86
Wagon Makers,	1		3	1			1				6
Stone Masons,	1		4	2			18				25
Stone Cutters,							1	1			2
Machinests,			1								1
Engineers,			1	2					1		4
Millers,			2			3	2				7
Sawyers,			4								4
Millwrights,		1	1		1		2				5
Painters,							3				3
Cabinet Makers,	1		3	1			6				11
Chair Makers,							1				1
Tinners,			1				3		1		5
Milliners,			2	1							3
Tailors,			1				3				4
Hatters,							1				1
Shoemakers.	1	1	2				5		2		11
Saddle & Harness Makers,			1				2				3
Butchers,							2				2
Mechanics,	8				2		1				11
Merchants,	2	3	3		3		23		3		37
Agents,			1				1				2
Druggists,			1				4				5
Boarding House Keepers,							1				1
Hotel Keepers,			1								1
Clothiers,				2							2
Physicians,	1	1	2	2	1		5		1		13
Lawyers,			1				9				10
Clergymen,			7				1				8
Teachers,			2		2	2	2	3			11
Printers,							2				2
Editors,							1				1
Artists,				1							1
Bankers,							1				1
Teamsters,			5				6				11
Brick Makers,			1				3				4
Gunsmiths,			1				2				3
Coopers,		1	1	3			2	3	1		11
Clerks,			7				5				12
Wheelrights,	1							1			2
Surveyors,			2				2				4
Domestics,			5								5
Stage Drivers,			2				7				9
Barbers,							2				2
Students,							2				2

TABLE,

SHOWING THE PLACE OF NATIVITY OF THE INHABITANTS OF BUCHANAN COUNTY, FOR 1856.

STATES.	NAME OF TOWNSHIPS.										
	Jefferson.	Percy.	Liberty.	Spring & Prairie.	Alton.	Byron,	Washington.	Newton.	Superior.	Buffalo.	TOTAL.
Ohio, ...	123	32	254	198	83	78	109	35	95	14	1021
Indiana, ...	59	33	17	8	57	..	54	74	9	10	321
Pennsylvania, ..	40	21	17	48	61	26	122	9	48	26	478
Iowa, ...	51	18	96	52	42	31	103	59	30	29	511
New York, ...	73	52	144	90	75	48	215	72	115	162	1001
Maine, ...	....	1	4	....	..	6	13		2	2	28
N. Hampshire,	....	4	....	2	5	1	4		1	14	31
Vermont, ...	15	21	25	6	9	7	38	11	7		139
Massachusetts, .	10	2	20	13	15	..	40	3	9	23	135
Connecticut, ...	3	5	11	5	1	2	10		9	7	53
Rhode Island, ..	5	..	1	3	1	..	1		7		12
Virginia, ...	5	3	9	6	4	1	12	1	3	36	80
Kentucky, ...	1	2	4	1	2	..	5	15	2		32
Illinois, ...	42	13	38	15	41	24	48	14	5	65	305
Michigan, ...	1	2	30	10	16	2	15		1		77
Alabama, ...	....		1	....	..	..				2	3
Florida, ...	....		....	....	..	2					2
North Carolina,	4		....	....	2			1	1	2	10
South Carolina, .	2		....	....	1						3
Tennessee, ...	7		1	1	..			13	1		23
Missouri, ...	....		2	1	1						4
Maryland, ...	1	5	2	6	3	3	4		2		26
New Jersey, ...	....		2	4	1	13	18	4	6		48
England, ...	6	1	9	2	10	..	37	5	12	14	96
Ireland, ...	3		35	1	6	7	53	54	5	12	176
Wales, ...	3		....	....		..	2				5
Scotland, ...	....	2	....	11	1	7	7	10	3		41
Germany, ...	12	10	12	9	12	1	112		5		173
France, ...	..		....	....	2	..	1		7		10
Sweden, ...	13	....	..	....	....	1	1				15
Canada, ...	7	15	3	1	3	3	10	7	33	31	113
Switzerland, ...	....	6	....	....	....	..					6
Wisconsin, ...	14	9	7	17	11	4	36	5	12	19	134
Delaware, ...	....	....	1	2	1						4
Minnesota, ...	....	....	....	....	....						1
Unknown, ...	....	....	...	1	....		7				8

TABLE,

SHOWING THE POPULATION, AMOUNT OF PRODUCE, NUMBER OF HOGS, AND CATTLE SOLD, THE AMOUNT THEY BROUGHT, AND THE CAPITAL EMPLOYED IN DOMESTIC AND GENERAL MANUFACTURES OF BUTLER COUNTY, FOR 1856.

	NAME OF TOWNSHIPS.							
POPULATION.	Butler.	West Point.	Cold Water.	Shell Rock.	Beaver.	Ripley.	Monroe.	TOTAL.
Number of dwelling houses,	130	43	20	63	72	15	19	362
Number of families,	130	43	21	69	72	15	22	372
Number of males,	394	128	90	207	239	56	75	1189
Number of females,	328	102	75	166	191	30	60	952
Married,	266	80	55	144	170	24	41	780
Widowed,	9	....	3	2	6	5	3	28
Native voters,	161	46	34	88	1	11	25	366
Naturalized voters,	5	4	....	1	11	7	2	30
Aliens,	6	....	9	....	8	....	2	25
Militia,	162	47	39	85	52	14	25	424
Deaf and Dumb,	1	....	....	1	2	....	....	4
Idiotic,	....	....	....	....	....	....	1	1
Owners of land.	135	33	30	53	69	15	25	360
Paupers,	1	....	1	3	1	....	...	6
AGRICULTURAL STATISTICS—								
Acres of improved land,	1793	849	736	401	419	122	600	4920
Acres of unimproved land,	5741	2429	3888	2365	157	1151	3165	18876
Acres of meadow,	6	....	81	....	....	...	2	89
Tons of Hay,	3	38	247	....	....	....	435	723
Bushels of grass seed,	3	....	....	....	....	....	....	3
Acres of spring wheat,	160	68	31	....	33	....	15	327
Bushels harvested,	3186	765	410	....	698	....	350	6409
Acres of winter wheat,	60	....	....	....	....	....	....	60
Bushels harvested,		....	....	....	....	....	....	
Acres of oats,	137	8	4	....	10	....	11	170
Bushels harvested,	5485	325	96	....	500	....	500	6906
Acres of Corn,	789	248	674	....	328	97	148	2284
Bushels harvested,	33625	2425	5000	....	8410	945	3200	53605
Acres of Potatoes,	14	9	16	....	12	3	4	58
Bushels harvested,	2060	1066	904	....	2656	275	750	7811
STATISTICS OF HOGS, CATTLE, &c.—								
Number of hogs sold,	113	97	99	....	4	3	7	323
Value of hogs sold,	1594	263	270	....	48	20	20	2215
Number of cattle sold,	17	287	23	....	13	4	20	364
Value of cattle sold,	553	1935	508	....	155	27	715	3893
Pounds of butter made,	2275	1730	886	....	...	195	300	5386
Pounds of cheese,	....	20	8	....	....	....	....	38
Pounds of wool,	....	6	23	....	....	....	100	129
Value of General Manufactures,	....	....	....	....	....	....	200	200

TABLE,

EXHIBITING THE PROFESSIONS, TRADES, OR OCCUPATIONS OF THE INHABITANTS OF BUTTLER COUNTY, FOR 1856.

OCCUPATIONS.	NAME OF TOWNSHIPS.							TOTAL.
	Butler,	West Point.	Cold Water.	Shell Rock.	Beaver.	Ripley.	Monroe,	
Farmers,	89	26	33	42	63	15	13	281
Laborers,	14	11	....	8	....	....	10	43
Blacksmiths,	3	....	1	6	1	...	1	11
Carpenters,	7	1	....	7	5	....	....	20
Wagon Makers,	1	....	....	...	....	....	....	1
Stone Masons,	1	....	....	....	....	....	....	1
Millers,	....	....	....	2	....	....	....	2
Sawyers,	4	...	....	....	....	....	....	4
Millwrights,	1	....	....	3	....	....	1	5
Painters,	....	1	....	1	....	....	....	2
Cabinet Makers,	1	....	....	....	....	....	....	1
Shoemakers,	...	....	....	1	1	....	1	3
Mechanics,	4	...	....	...	....	....	....	4
Merchants,	2	....	....	3	....	....	....	5
Speculators,	2	....	....	....	....	....	....	2
Hotel Keepers,	1	....	....	1	....	....	...	2
Physicians,	1	....	1	1	1	....	.. .	4
Dentist,	....	....	....	1	....	....	....	1
Lawyers,	3	....	....	....	....	....	....	3
Clergymen,	2	....	....	....	....	....	...	2
Teachers,	1	....	....	....	....	....	1	2
Coopers,	....	....	1	....	....	....	....	1
Clerks,	....	....	....	2	....	....	...	2
County Judge,	1	....	....	....	....	....	....	1
Turners,	1	...	....	....	....	....	....	1
Surveyors,		..	....	1	....	....	...	2
Shingle makers,	...	....	....	....	....	...	1	1
Wheelwrights,	....	....	....	.. .	....	....	1	1

TABLE,

SHOWING THE PLACE OF NATIVITY OF THE INHABITANTS OF BUTLER COUNTY, FOR 1856.

OCCUPATIONS.	NAME OF TOWNSHIPS.							TOTAL.
	Butler,	West Point.	Cold Water.	Shell Rock.	Beaver.	Ripley.	Monroe,	
Ohio,	122	82	25	60	53	21	23	386
Indiana,	144	22	62	33	21	18	4	296
Pennsylvania,	79	9	13	29	10	3	10	161
Iowa,	89	28	19	46	28	9	5	224
New York,	82	10	2	79	119	5	25	322
Maine,	7	....	....	4	7	1	1	20
N. Hampshire,	....	....	....	2	6	....	....	8
Vermont,	2	....	1	4	21	2	2	32
Massachusetts,	12	2	2	2	5	10	1	34
Connecticut,	1	....	....	2	8	....	2	13
Rhode Island,	....	....	....	....	....	....	1	1
Virginia,	23	2	6	9	2	1	5	48
Kentucky,	11	1	2	4	1		...	19
Illinois,	81	41	6	52	54	3	29	266
Michigan,	3	10	9	10	3	2	2	39
Mississippi,	....	....	....	....	....	....	4	4
North Carolina,	4	....	....		...	2	..	7
Tennessee,	10	. .	3	1	. . .		3	17
Missouri,	...	2	....	3	....	....	....	5
Georgia,	....	....	....	....	....	....	1	1
Maryland,	2	1	....	1	1	1	....	6
New Jersey,	5	1	....	4	1	....	....	11
England,	10	1	....	6	11	4	1	33
Ireland,	7	....	10	....	15	3	2	37
Scotland,	2	....	....	2	1	....	3	8
Germany,	1	8	....	3	....	2	....	14
Norway,	....	9	....	....	12	....	....	21
Sweden,	....	....	....	....	....	1	1	2
Holland,	....	....	....	2	....	....	....	2
On the ocean,	1	....	....	....	....	....	....	1
Canada,	7	....	5	11	17	....	....	40
Wisconsin,	16	1	....	3	26	....	9	55
Venezuela,	1	....	....	....	....	....	....	1
Nova Scotia,	....	....	....	....	....	6	1	7

TABLE,

SHOWING THE POPULATION, AMOUNT OF PRODUCE, NUMBER OF HOGS, AND CATTLE SOLD, THE AMOUNT THEY BROUGHT, AND THE VALUE OF DOMESTIC AND GENERAL MANUFACTURES OF CALHOUN COUNTY, FOR 1856.

CALHOUN TOWNSHIP.

POPULATION.

No. dwelling houses,	21
Number of families,	24
Number of males,	77
Number of females,	42
Married,	48
Widowed,	3
Native voters,	36
Naturalized voters,	2
Militia,	37

AGRICULTURAL STATISTICS.

Owners of land,	27
Acres of improved land,	509
Acres of unimproved land,	546
Tons of Hay,	218
Acres of Corn,	200
Bushels harvested,	2500
Acres of Potatoes,	1
Bushels harvested,	418

HOGS, CATTLE AND MANUFACTURES.

Number of hogs sold,	10
Value of hogs sold,	50
Number of cattle sold,	92
Value of cattle sold,	2244
Butter made,	2340

TABLE,

EXHIBITING THE PROFESSIONS, TRADES, OR OCCUPATIONS OF THE INHABITANTS OF CALHOUN COUNTY, FOR 1856.

CALHOUN TOWNSHIP.

Farmers,	27
Laborers,	9
Carpenters,	2
Surveyors,	1

TABLE,

SHOWING THE PLACE OF NATIVITY OF THE INHABITANTS OF CALHOUN COUNTY, FOR 1856.

CALHOUN TOWNSHIP.

Ohio,	35
Indiana,	5
Pennsylvania,	2
Iowa,	12
New York,	8
Vermont,	1
Massachusetts,	1
Virginia,	8
Illinois,	1
Michigan,	41
Mississippi,	1
Missouri,	1
England,	1
Prussia,	1
Unknown,	1

TABLE,

SHOWING THE POPULATION, AMOUNT OF PRODUCE, NUMBER OF HOGS AND CATTLE SOLD, THE AMOUNT THEY BROUGHT, AND THE VALUE OF DOMESTIC AND GENERAL MAUFACTURES OF CARROLL COUNTY, FOR 1856.

POPULATION.	NAME OF TOWNSHIPS.		TOTAL.
	Jasper,	Newton,	
Number of dwelling houses,	22	20	42
Number of families,	22	26	48
Number of males,	66	73	139
Number of females,	66	46	112
Married,	19	46	65
Widowed,	3	....	3
Native voters,	27	25	52
Naturalized voters,	....	5	5
Aliens,	....	1	1
Militia,	19	34	53
Deaf and Dumb,	1	....	1
Owners of land.	15	23	38
AGRICULTURAL STATISTICS—			
Acres of improved land,	151	361	512
Acres of unimproved land,	1715	3216	4931
Tons of Hay,	....	164	164
Acres of spring wheat,	....	19	19
Bushels harvested,	....	190	190
Acres of Corn,	87	215	302
Bushels harvested,	3400	3207	6607
Acres of Potatoes,	1	2	3
Bushels harvested,	67	310	377
STATISTICS OF HOGS, CATTLE, &C.—			
Number of hogs sold,	16	68	84
Value of hogs sold,	951	410	1361
Number of cattle sold,	8	9	17
Value of cattle sold,	270	221	491
Pounds of butter made,	675	2464	3139
Pounds of cheese,	....	14	14
Pounds of wool,	60	....	60

TABLE,

EXHIBITING THE PROFESSIONS, TRADES OR OCCUPATIONS OF THE INHABITANTS OF CARROLL COUNTY, FOR 1856.

Townships.	Farmers,	Blacksmiths.	Carpenters,	Brick Layers,	Machinists,	Engineers,	Millers,	Millwrights,	Milliners,	Shoemakers,
Jasper, ...	32	..	....	....	....	....	....	....	....	2
Newton, ...	28	1	1	1	1	1	1	1	5	...
Total, ...	60	1	1	1	1	1	1	1	5	2

TABLE,

SHOWING THE PLACE OF NATIVITY OF THE INHABITANTS OF CARROLL COUNTY, FOR 1856.

Townships.	Ohio,	Indiana,	Pennsylvania,	Iowa,	New York,	Vermont,	Massachusetts.	Connecticut,	Virginia,	Kentucky.	Illinois,	Michigan,	Tennessee,	Missouri,	New Jersey,	England,	Ireland,	Germany,	Delaware,
Jasper, ...	34	27	10	13	12	..	..	2	10	2	12	5	1	3	..	1	..	..	..
Newton, ...	26	14	25	11	14	10	2	..	..	..	1	2	..	1	2	1	5	4	1
Total, ...	60	41	35	24	26	10	2	2	10	2	13	7	1	4	2	2	5	4	1

TABLE,

SHOWING THE POPULATION, AMOUNT OF PRODUCE, NUMBER OF CATTLE AND HOGS SOLD, AMOUNT THEY BROUGHT, AND THE VALUE OF DOMESTIC AND GENERAL MANUFACTURES, OF CASS COUNTY, FOR 1856.

POPULATION.	NAME OF TOWNSHIP.				TOTAL.
	Cass.	Pymosa.	Turkey Grove.	Edna.	
Number of dwelling houses,	82	31	37	6	156
Number of families,	73	29	37	9	148
Number of males,	233	95	97	33	448
Number of females,	182	80	82	23	367
Married,	155	58	71	24	308
Widowed,	9	1	2	....	12
Native voters,	111	38	42	14	205
Naturalized voters,	....	5	5	....	10
Aliens,	....	4	5	....	9
Militia,	102	37	32	....	171
Idiotic,	....	1	1	....	2
Owners of land,	87	35	44	9	175
AGRICULTURAL STATISTICS—					
Acres of improved land,	1343	1033	719	170	3265
Acres of unimproved land,	9048	6627	6967	3486	26128
Acres of meadow,	....	....	5	....	5
Tons ot Hay,	....	....	172	....	172
Bushels of grass seed,	....	....	2	....	2
Acres of spring wheat,	155	202	85	....	442
Bushels harvested,	1771	1105	962	....	3838
Acres of winter wheat,	....	16	27	....	43
Bushels harvested,	....	48	300	....	348
Acres of Oats,	49	125	47	....	222
Bushels harvested,	1067	705	1530	....	3302
Acres of Corn,	741	273	367	36	1417
Bushels harvested,	20367	7855	10121	1670	40013
Acres of Potatoes,	18	10	10	2	40
Bushels harvested,	2710	1974	1210	315	6209
STATITTICS OF HOGS, CATTLE, &C.—					
Number of hogs sold,	194	34	91	....	319
Value of hogs sold,	960	174	549	....	1682
Number of cattle sold,	181	52	84	....	317
Value of cattle sold,	5958	1611	2735	....	10304
Pounds of butter made,	5433	2550	4758	760	13501
Pounds of wool,	89	120	404	....	613
Value of domestic manufactures,	210	....	140	....	350
Value of general manufactures,	50	....	4100	....	4150

TABLE,

EXHIBITING THE PRROFESSIONS, TRADES OR OCCUPATIONS OFTHE INHABITANTS OF CASS COUNTY, FOR 1856.

OCCUPATIONS.	NAME OF TOWNSHIPS.				TOTAL.
	Cass.	Pymosa.	Turkey Grove.	Edna.	
Farmers,	80	43	42	14	179
Laborers,	....	8	....	....	8
Blacksmiths,	6	...	1	....	7
Carpenters,	11	....	3	....	14
Wagon Makers,	....	....	1	..	1
Stone Masons,	2	....	....	....	2
Millers,	1	....	1	....	2
Sawyers,	3	....	1	....	4
Tinners,	1	....	....	....	1
Milliners,	....	....	2	..	2
Shoemakers,	....	....	1	....	1
Saddle and Harness Makers,	2	....	1	...	3
Merchants,	2	...	....	....	2
Agents,	1	....	....	....	1
Traders,	1	....	....	....	1
Physicians,	2	....	1	...	3
Lawyers,	1	....	....	....	1
Clergymen,	1	....	....	....	1
Teamsters,	....	....	1	....	1
Coopers,	....	....	3	....	3
Clerks,	....	....	1	...	1
Surveyors,	1	....	....	....	1
County Judge,	1	..	....	....	1
Weavers,	....	....	1	....	1

TABLE,

SHOWING THE PLACE OF NATIVITY OF THE INHABITANTS OF CASS COUNTY, FOR 1856.

STATES.	NAME OF TOWNSHIP.				TOTAL.
	Cass.	Pymosa.	Turkey Grove.	Edna.	
Ohio,	78	28	36	16	158
Indiana,	67	32	41	8	148
Pennsylvania,	20	16	9	6	51
Iowa,	78	18	37	5	138
New York,	23	3	9	2	37
Maine,	....	....	3	....	3
Vermont,	14	4	.	....	18
Massachusetts,	14	..	....	....	14
Connecticut,	3	5	1	....	9
Virginia,	12	3	6	1	22
Kentucky,	18	9	3	1	31
Illinois,	44	29	8	17	98
Michigan,	1	....	1	....	2
Arkansas,	1	....	....	....	1
Louisiana,	1	....	....	....	1
Mississippi,	1	....	....	....	1
North Carolina,	15	6	5	....	26
South Carolina,	1	....	....	....	1
Tennessee,	3	5	2	....	10
Missouri,	6	....	3	....	9
Maryland,	2	1	...	....	3
New Jersey,	1	....	...	....	1
England,	1	9	....	..	10
Ireland,	...	3	3	..	6
Germany,	5	....	11	.. .	16
Canada,	2	3	1	...	6
Wisconsin,	3	....	....	....	3
Nova Scotia,	1	....	....	....	1
Unknown,	....	1	....	....	1

TABLE,

SHOWING [illegible] OF CEDAR COUNTY, FOR 1856.

Townships.	No. dwelling houses.	No. of families.	Number of males.	Number of females.	Married.	Widowed.	Native voters.	Naturalized voters.	Aliens.	Militia,	Deaf and Dumb.	Blind.	Insane,	Idiotic,	Owners of land.
Cedar,	[illegible]	[illegible]	[illegible]	[illegible]	[illegible]	57	528	31	21	508	2	3			314
Springdale,	[illegible]	[illegible]	[illegible]	[illegible]	[illegible]	29	256	20	14	285				3	217
Linn,	[illegible]	[illegible]	[illegible]	[illegible]	53	4	39	3		37					29
Sugar Creek,	[illegible]	[illegible]	[illegible]	[illegible]	[illegible]	12	97	21	17	144	2				93
Springfield,	[illegible]	[illegible]	[illegible]	[illegible]	[illegible]	16	122	11	8	122					96
Farmington,	[illegible]	[illegible]	[illegible]	[illegible]	[illegible]	3	54		13	45					33
Cass,	[illegible]	[illegible]	[illegible]	[illegible]	[illegible]	12	102	15	8	76	1			5	73
Iowa,	[illegible]	[illegible]	[illegible]	[illegible]	[illegible]	10	167	9	8	169					109
Pioneer,	[illegible]	[illegible]	[illegible]	[illegible]	[illegible]	28	219	20	14	220	1		2		177
Rochester,	[illegible]	[illegible]	[illegible]	[illegible]	[illegible]	17	132	14	6	122	2	1			77
Inland,	44	[illegible]	[illegible]	[illegible]	[illegible]	8	65	2	3	61					46
Red Oak,	69	71	[illegible]	[illegible]	[illegible]	12	51	29	23	72			1		59
Total,	1541	1696	5075	4406	3189	203	1832	175	135	1861	8	4	3	8	1323

TABLE,

SHOWING THE AGRICULTURAL STATISTICS OF CEDAR COUNTY, FOR 1856.

Townships.	Acres of improved land.	Acres of unimproved land.	Acres of meadow.	Tons of hay.	Bushels grass seed.	Acres spring wheat.	Bushels harvested.	Acres winter wheat.	Bushels harvested.	Acres of oats.	Bushels harvested.	Acres of Corn.	Bushels harvested.	Acres of Potatoes.	Bushels harvested.
Cedar, ...	12999	15389	913	1179	131	3009	37407	10	225	770	21363	3201	127070	686	9005
Springdale, ...	5651	9923	132	132	81	1569	24228	70	1220	322	10382	2103	111300	75	9493
Linn, ...	2131	2560	9	12	...	791	13921			75	2761	631	26620	3	170
Sugar Creek, ...	5364	3473	276	340	13	1619	20575			287	10176	1601	78665	41	5598
Springfield, ...	3594	9809	36	1031	4	1171	19306			250	7585	1001	39615	32	4363
Farmington, ...	1991	2860	10	20	...	403	7235			78	1940	370	19080	9	1155
Cass, ...	5041	13242	326	822	15	1278	15130			475	8013	1479	38675	38	4049
Iowa, ...	6340	9712	666	794	97	1933	27100			375	13210	1822	100505	38	5336
Pioneer, ...	7063	11803	349	407	5	1840	34905			410	17704	2011	98526	32	4917
Rochester, ...	4879	6616	552	708	37	1137	14176	10	70	349	10576	1279	60685	26	3624
Inland, ...	2341	5931	47	66	4	506	9409			136	4522	379	11510	9	1258
Red Oak, ...	4465	7426	118	187	9	1666	30885			266	8770	1259	58720	20	3140
Total, ...	61859	98745	3434	5698	397	16922	254277	90	1515	3795	117002	17136	770971	1010	52108

TABLE,

SHOWING THE NUMBER OF HOGS, CATTLE, DOMESTIC AND GENERAL MANUFACTURES OF CEDAR COUNTY, FOR 1856.

Townships.	No. of hogs sold.	Value of hogs sold.	No. of Cattle sold.	Value of Cattle sold.	Pounds of butter made.	Pounds of cheese.	Pounds of Wool.	Value of Domestic Manufacture.	Value of General Manufactures.
Cedar, ...	1956	14923	402	11264	43527	6448	7473	319	82000
Springdale,	1355	9510	221	7389	22789	5600	1985		
Linn, ...	696	5339	41	1302	4900	200	55	92	24
Sugar Creek	873	7845	140	4821	11325	1000	701	39	800
Springfield,	336	2160	133	5247	11095	300	493	177	14
Farmington	232	1797	23	735	850	320			
Cass, ...	1336	8797	157	5177	12588	1200	115	368	5427
Iowa, ...	1417	13451	178	5349	14588	7923	3851	71	
Pioneer.	1589	11791	177	5388	1515	765	996	733	1300
Rochester,	1230	7382	108	2776	11020		1326	202	
Inland, ...	226	1323	82	2887	4479	750		20	75
Red Oak,	1143	9900	151	5128	4130	850			
Total, ...	12389	94218	1813	57463	142797	25356	16995	2021	94640

TABLE,

EXHIBITING THE PROFESSIONS, TRADES OR OCCUPATIONS OF THE INHABITANTS OF CEDAR COUNTY, FOR 1856.

OCCUPATIONS.	NAME OF TOWNSHIPS.													TOTAL.
	Center.	Springdale.	Linn.	Sugar Creek.	Springfield.	Farmington.	Cass.	Iowa.	Pioneer.	Rochester.	Inland.	Red Oak.	Polk.	
Farmers,	235	283	37	102	145	31	106	122	235	61	37	127	...	1521
Laborers,	86	17	4	23	...	...	...	27	1	...	...	...	...	158
Blacksmiths,	11	7	1	4	3	2	4	2	4	2	5	2	...	47
Carpenters,	66	28	4	4	7	10	7	8	24	...	5	4	...	167
Wagon Makers,	5	2	...	...	...	...	4	...	3	1	2	...	...	17
Brick Layers,	2	3	...	...	...	...	1	...	...	...	...	...	...	6
Plasterers,	7	2	...	...	2	...	1	2	1	...	...	...	...	15
Stone Masons,	9	3	...	...	1	...	4	...	2	2	...	...	...	21
Machinists,	1	...	...	...	...	...	...	...	...	...	...	...	...	1
Engineers,	1	...	...	...	...	...	...	1	1	...	...	...	...	3
Millers,	3	...	...	2	...	...	...	1	4	...	...	...	...	10
Millwrights,	4	...	...	...	...	...	...	...	...	...	...	...	...	4
Painters,	11	1	...	1	2	...	...	...	...	...	...	...	...	15
Cabinet Makers,	2	1	...	...	...	...	1	...	1	...	...	...	...	5
Tinners,	4	1	...	...	...	...	1	...	...	...	...	...	...	6
Milliners,	9	2	...	...	...	...	3	...	2	...	2	...	...	18
Tailors,	7	...	...	...	1	...	...	1	2	...	...	...	...	11
Shoemakers.	8	2	...	...	1	1	4	2	3	...	...	...	...	21
Saddle & Harness Makers,	5	...	...	...	1	...	...	...	...	...	...	...	...	6
Butchers,	2	...	...	...	...	...	...	...	...	...	...	...	...	2
Mechanics,	...	1	...	...	...	...	...	1	...	...	...	...	...	2
Merchants,	19	2	...	...	1	1	1	1	4	1	...	...	...	30
Druggists,	6	...	...	...	...	...	...	...	...	...	...	...	...	6
Boarding House Keepers,	1	...	...	...	...	...	...	...	...	...	...	...	...	1
Hotel Keepers,	4	...	...	...	...	...	1	...	1	...	...	...	...	6
Clothiers,	...	...	...	...	...	...	...	...	1	...	...	...	...	1
Physicians,	10	2	...	...	1	1	1	1	2	1	...	...	...	19
Lawyers,	8	...	...	...	...	...	...	...	...	...	...	...	...	8
Clergymen,	8	...	...	2	...	...	1	1	1	...	2	...	...	15
Teachers,	3	3	...	1	7	...	4	...	2	...	1	...	...	21
Printers,	4	...	...	...	1	...	...	...	...	...	...	...	...	5
Editors,	2	...	...	...	...	...	...	...	...	...	...	...	...	2
Daguerrean Artists,	...	1	...	1	...	...	...	...	...	...	...	...	...	2
Bankers,	1	...	...	...	...	...	...	...	...	...	...	...	...	1
Grocers,	3	...	...	...	...	...	...	...	...	...	...	...	...	3
Teamsters,	8	...	...	...	...	...	...	...	1	...	...	...	...	9
Brick Makers,	5	...	...	5	...	...	...	...	...	...	...	...	...	10
Watch Makers,	1	...	...	...	...	...	...	...	...	...	...	...	...	1
Jewelers,	1	...	...	...	...	...	...	...	...	...	...	...	...	1
Gunsmiths,	...	...	...	...	...	...	...	1	...	1	...	...	...	2
Coopers,	...	...	...	...	...	...	1	...	2	...	...	...	...	3
Clerks,	12	1	...	1	...	...	1	...	...	...	...	...	...	15
Furniture Dealers,	2	...	...	...	...	...	...	...	...	...	...	...	...	2
Tailoress,	2	...	...	...	...	...	...	...	...	...	...	...	...	2
Surveyors,	2	...	...	...	...	...	...	...	...	...	...	...	...	2
Lumber Dealers,	1	...	...	...	...	...	...	...	...	...	...	...	...	1
Livery Keepers,	2	...	...	...	...	...	...	...	...	...	...	...	...	2
Peddlars,	2	...	...	...	...	...	...	...	...	...	...	...	...	2
Nurserymen,	...	...	...	...	...	...	...	...	...	...	...	...	...	2

TABLE,

SHOWING THE PLACE OF NATIVITY OF THE INHABITANTS OF CEDAR COUNTY, FOR 1856.

STATES.	NAME OF TOWNSHIPS.													Total.
	Centre.	Springdale.	Linn.	Sugar Creek.	Springfield.	Farmington.	Cass.	Iowa.	Pioneer.	Rochester.	Inland.	Red Oak.	Polk.	
Ohio	687	561	37	128	175	38	172	377	345	235	84	96	...	2935
Indiana,	76	52	13	22	18	7	39	25	57	78	15	6	...	408
Pennsylvania,	504	106	65	185	115	47	125	85	282	98	75	33	...	1720
Iowa,	437	183	48	141	98	27	132	189	208	194	21	109	...	1787
New York,	174	76	8	28	47	17	21	28	54	27	24	30	...	534
Maine,	2	4	...	...	16	2	...	3	...	1	...	1	...	29
New Hampshire.	27	5	...	1	3	2	1	4	3	2	2	8	...	58
Vermont,	57	34	1	1	9	2	4	6	4	1	11	2	...	132
Massachusetts,	20	3	...	7	15	10	1	4	4	7	3	3	...	77
Connecticut,	18	2	...	1	2	27	3	...	5	5	3	...	...	66
Rhode Island.	1	3	...	...	...	...	1	...	...	...	...	...	...	5
Virginia,	127	24	5	61	23	5	17	16	28	56	15	10	...	387
Kentucky,	11	2	...	4	4	1	3	2	5	11	...	3	...	46
Illinois,	34	14	...	2	17	5	16	4	11	13	13	1	...	130
Michigan,	20	5	...	1	11	...	4	2	9	7	1	...	...	60
Lousiana,	...	...	...	...	...	...	1	...	...	...	...	...	...	1
Mississippi,	6	...	...	...	...	...	...	...	...	...	...	...	...	6
North Carolina,	12	3	...	...	...	...	...	...	5	2	...	2	...	24
South Carolina,	1	3	...	...	...	1	...	...	...	...	...	...	...	5
Tennessee,	...	1	6	...	...	1	...	1	...	...	...	...	...	9
Missouri,	7	...	...	3	5	...	7	5	3	2	...	...	...	32
Georgia,	...	...	...	...	...	...	...	...	...	1	...	...	...	1
California,	2	...	...	...	...	...	1	...	...	...	...	...	...	3
Maryland,	33	22	...	5	39	...	1	11	8	14	...	11	...	144
New Jersey,	35	18	...	3	7	2	9	15	11	11	3	...	...	114
England,	16	26	16	8	5	1	3	6	11	...	2	13	...	107
Ireland,	41	33	...	4	13	6	10	13	44	...	1	52	...	217
Scotland,	15	...	4	3	2	...	...	...	...	5	...	43	...	72
Germany,	23	4	1	21	12	13	23	7	3	39	6	...	...	152
France,	...	...	...	...	1	...	...	1	...	6	...	...	...	8
Austria,	...	...	...	...	...	...	1	...	...	...	...	...	...	1
Prussia,	...	4	...	13	1	...	...	...	...	...	...	...	...	18
Holland,	...	...	...	...	...	...	...	...	...	5	...	...	...	5
Canada,	30	43	1	1	12	...	...	5	13	7	...	7	...	119
Switzerland,	...	2	...	13	...	...	3	1	...	...	...	...	...	19
Wisconsin,	4	1	...	6	...	...	...	...	5	...	...	...	...	16
Delaware,	4	2	...	1	...	...	...	7	4	1	...	2	...	21
Italy,	1	...	...	...	...	...	...	...	...	...	...	...	...	1
Unknown,	1	...	4	...	...	...	...	5	...	...	...	...	...	10
District of Columbia,	...	1	...	...	...	...	...	...	...	...	...	...	...	1
Oregon,	...	...	...	...	...	...	...	...	...	1	...	...	...	1

TABLE,

SHOWING THE POPULATION OF CERRO GORDO COUNTY, FOR 1856.

TOWNSHIPS.	No. dwelling houses.	Number families.	Number of males.	Number females.	Married.	Widowed.	Native voters.	Naturalized voters.	Aliens.	Militia.	Owners of land.
Canaan, ...	54	67	178	107	100	10	77	5	4	75	60
Falls, ...	31	37	112	77	66	2	32	3	3	37	41
Lake, ...	27	28	58	46	43	1	32	2	2	31	20
Owen, ...	14	1[illegible]	29	25	28		2		2		5
Total, ...	126	146	377	255	237	13	143	10	11	143	126

TABLE,

CONTAINING THE AGRICULTURAL STATISTICS, CATTLE AND HOGS SOLD THEIR VALUE, AND THE VALUE OF DOMESTIC AND GENERAL MANUFACTURES, OF CERRO GORDO COUNTY, FOR 1856.

AGRICULTURAL STATISTICS.	NAME OF TOWNSHIPS.				TOTAL.
	Canaan,	Falls.	Lake.	Owen.	
Acres of improved land,	802	632	231	....	1665
Acres of unimproved land,	8796	5913	1854	....	16563
Acres of meadow,	....	....	70	....	70
Tons of Hay,	604	308	113	....	1025
Acres of Spring wheat,	18	37	4	....	59
Bushels harvnsted,	435	415	60	....	910
Acres of winter wheat,	...	2	....	....	2
Bushels harvested,	...	26	....	....	26
Acres of Oats,	26	8	13	...	47
Bushels harvested,	500	315	320	....	1135
Acres of Corn,	260	149	118	....	527
Bushels harvested,	6645	2670	2480	....	11795
Acres of potatoes,	11	4	5	...	20
Bushels harvested,	2200	755	890	....	3845
CATTLE, HOGS AND MANUFACTURES—					
Number of hogs sold,	83	31	47	....	161
Value of hogs sold,	216	178	145	....	539
Number of cattle sold,	123	80	30	....	233
Value of cattle sold,	4133	661	918	....	5711
Pounds of butter made,	2229	1585	1725	....	5539
Pounds of cheese,	....	50	250	....	300
Pounds of wool,	32	20	50	....	102
Value of domestic manufactures,	....	20	....	....	20

TABLE,

EXHIBITING THE PRROFESSIONS, TRADES OR OCCUPATIONS OF THE INHABITANTS OF CERRO GORDO COUNTY, FOR 1856.

OCCUPATIONS.	NAME OF TOWNSHIPS.				TOTAL.
	Canaan.	Falls.	Lake.	Owen.	
Farmers,	44	30	21	10	105
Laborers,	9	28	2	....	39
Blacksmiths,	2	....	1	....	3
Carpenters,	11	6	1	....	18
Wagon Makers,	2	....	....	....	2
Stone Masons,	2	....	1	....	3
Machinists,	1	....	1	..	2
Millers,	1	....	....	....	1
Millwrights,	1	....	1	....	2
Cabinet Makers	2	1	1	....	4
Milliners,	3	1	....	....	4
Shoemakers,	2	1	1	....	4
Saddle and Harness Makers,	1	....	....	....	1
Mechanics,	....	1	....	....	1
Merchants,	2	....	2	....	4
Speculators,	2	....	....	....	2
Agents,	1	....	....	....	1
Physicians,	2	....	....	....	2
Lawyers,	2	....	1	....	3
Clergymen,	....	1	....	....	1
Teachers,	1	....	1	....	2
Daguerrean Artists,	1	....	....	....	1
Grocers,	1	....	....	....	1
Surveyors,	1	....	1	....	2
Tanners,	1	....	....	....	1
Nurserymen,	1	....	....	....	1
Moulders,	....	....	1	....	1
Pedlars,	....	....	1	....	1

TABLE,

SHOWING THE PLACE OF NATIVITY OF THE INHABITANTS OF CERRO GORDO COUNTY, FOR 1856.

STATES.	NAME OF TOWNSHIPS.				TOTAL.
	Canaan.	Falls.	Lake.	Owen.	
Ohio,	46	35	23	2	106
Indiana,	38	26	18	....	82
Pennsylvania,	15	2	7	....	24
Iowa,	17	11	10	1	39
New York,	77	37	22	23	159
Maine,	4	6	....	....	10
New Hampshire,	11	....	....	....	11
Vermont,	8	1	....	3	12
Massachusetts,	5	4	1	2	12
Connecticut,	2	8	1	....	11
Virginia,	4	6	2	1	13
Kentucky,	1	1	....	....	2
Illinois,	35	4	8	12	59
Michigan,	3	14	2	4	23
Tennessee,	1	....	....	....	1
New Jersey,	1	1	1	....	3
England,	1	17	....	2	20
Ireland,	2	....	6	1	9
Germany,	2	2	....	1	5
Sweden,	....	1	....	....	1
Canada,	9	1	2	....	12
Wisconsin,	3	12	1	2	18

TABLE,

SHOWING THE POPULATION, AMOUNT OF PRODUCE, NUMBER OF HOGS AND CATTLE SOLD, THE AMOUNT THEY BROUGHT, AND THE VALUE OF DOMESTIC AND GENERAL MAUFACTURES OF CHICKASAW COUNTY, FOR 1856.

POPULATION.	MAME OF TOWNSHIPS.						TOTAL.
	Obispo.	Richland.	Chickasaw.	Durfield.*	Bradford.	Yanke.	
Number of dwelling houses,	86	26	63	56	109	127	467
Number of families,	86	26	66	56	109	127	470
Number of males,	265	62	282	180	314	363	1466
Number of females,	223	49	224	141	273	275	1185
Married,	155	41	198	77	209	255	935
Widowed,	1	5	1	1	9	10	27
Native voters,	57	29	104	84	115	113	452
Naturalized voters,	16	3	15	15	15	21	85
Aliens,	28	....	6	....	17	11	62
Militia,	70	31	101	28	143	106	479
Blind,	....	....	....	....	.....	1	1
Owners of land.	68	37	74	42	96	132	449
AGRICULTURAL STATISTICS—							
Acres of improved land,	463	414	1102	213	1135	1142	4469
Acres of unimproved land,	7311	5679	11062	5730	5083	17477	52342
Acres of Meadow,	....	....	.....	55	61	240	356
Tons of Hay,	320	....	.....	452	420	1832	3024
Bushels of Grass seed,	....	....	.....	....	3	.....	3
Acres of spring wheat,	21	....	36	....	65	80	203
Bushels harvested,	320	....	774	....	1317	1109	3520
Acres of winter wheat,	5	....	.....	....	3	.....	8
Bushels harvested,	150	....	.....	....	21	.....	171
Acres of oats,	8	....	48	....	113	34	203
Bushels harvested,	134	....	1602	....	4319	1229	7284
Acres of Corn,	77	137	337	145	521	262	1479
Bushels harvested,	2530	2175	12505	2770	20665	5023	45668
Acres of Potatoes,	5	4	12	4	26	15	68
Bushels harvested,	820	450	3037	900	4800	1673	11680
STATISTICS OF HOGS, CATTLE, &c.—							
Number of hogs sold,	13	....	50	15	153	25	256
Value of hogs sold,	57	....	459	30	1770	174	2490
Number of cattle sold,	54	...	43	45	45	146	333
Value of cattle sold,	1620	....	1504	856	2405	6060	12445
Pounds of butter made,	570	....	4652	3280	3640	4695	16837
Pounds of cheese,	....	....	550	550	120	.....	1220
Pounds of wool,	150	....	.....	....	341	190	681
Value of Domestic Manufactures,	6	....	.....	....	.....	.....	6

TABLE,

EXHIBITING THE PROFESSIONS, TRADES OR OCCUPATIONS OF THE INHABITANTS OF CHICKASAW COUNTY, FOR 1856.

OCCUPATIONS.	NAME OF TOWNSHIPS.						TOTAL.
	Obispo.	Richland.	Chickasaw.	Durfield.	Bradford.	Yanke.	
Farmers,	80	41	76	34	75	138	444
Laborers	1	1	....	....	13		15
Blacksmiths,	3	1	1	....	2	1	8
Carpenters,	4	....	5	4	15	5	33
Wagon Makers,	....	....	....	....	1	....	1
Stone Masons,	....	....	1	....	3	1	5
Machinists,	....	....	....	....	...	1	1
Engineers,	....	....	....	...	1	....	1
Millwrights,	....	....	....	....	1	....	1
Painters,	1	....	...	....	....	....	1
Tinners,	....	....	....	1	....	1	2
Tailors,	....	....	....	....	1	....	1
Shoemakers,	1	....	....	....	....	....	1
Mechanics,	....	....	....	1	1	1	3
Merchants,	1	....	....	1	4	3	9
Physicians,	....	....	....	....	1	1	2
Lawyers,	....	....	....	....	....	2	2
Clergyman,	....	....	....	....	2	....	2
Teachers,	1	....	....	....	....	....	1
Brickmakers,	....	3	....	....	....	....	3
Coopers,	....	....	....	....	1	....	1
Clerks,	....	....	....	1	2	1	4
Coppersmith,	1	....	....	....	..	....	1
Stage drivers,	....	....	....	....	....	1	1

TABLE,

SHOWING THE PLACE OF NATIVITY OF THE INHABITANTS OF CHICKASAW COUNTY, FOR 1856.

STATES.	Obispo.	Richland.	Chickasaw.	Durfield.	Bradford.	Yanke.	TOTAL.
	NAME OF TOWNSHIPS.						
Ohio,	65	36	49	14	50	72	286
Indiana,	27	....	66	22	35	44	194
Pennsylvania,	46	6	30	25	36	26	169
Iowa,	46	7	37	6	60	....	156
New York,	73	33	95	12	175	173	561
Maine,	....	....	....	....	....	1	1
N. Hampshire,	1	2	6	19	....	6	34
Vermont,	9	....	9	3	8	24	53
Massachusetts,	21	2	16	19	13	22	93
Connecticut,	3	4	4	20	23	15	69
Rhode Island,	....	....	1	....	....	2	3
Virginia,	....	3	7	....	6	3	19
Kentucky,	2	....	1	....	4	5	12
Illinois,	16	7	60	102	46	74	305
Michigan,	14	2	20	10	16	2	64
Arkansas	....	....	1	....	....	....	1
Mississippi,	....	....	..	....	1	....	1
North Carolina,	....	....	1	....	....	....	1
Tennessee,	2	....	5	....	1	1	9
Maryland,	10	....	2	3	1	....	16
New Jersey,	1	1	4	....	2	9	17
England,	6	3	18	9	18	11	65
Ireland,	85	2	16	....	7	65	175
Wales,	....	....	....	....	1	....	1
Scotland,	....	....	2	....	8	5	15
Germany,	1	....	4	14	4	34	57
France,	....	....	....	....	7	....	7
Norway,	18	...	2	....	....	4	24
On the ocean,	1	....	....	....	....	....	1
Canada,	6	....	25	11	51	8	101
New Brunswick,	1	....	....	....	....	....	1
Hanover,	....	....	....	....	1	....	1
Wisconsin,	33	3	25	27	9	32	129
Delaware,	....	....	....	....	1	....	1
Bavaria,	....	....	....	....	1	....	1
District of Columbia,	1	....	....	....	....	....	1
Unknown,	....	....	....	5	2	....	7

TABLE,

SHOWING THE POPULATION OF CLAYTON COUNTY, FOR 1856.

Townships.	No. dwelling houses.	Number of families.	Number of males.	Number of females.	Colored.	Married.	Widowed.	Native voters.	Naturalized voters.	Aliens.	Militia.	Deaf and Dumb.	Blind.	Insane.	Idiotic.	Owners of land.	Paupers.
Boadman,	127	127	417	355	1	260	21	122	26	27	102	1				1	
Buena Vista,	40	40	128	88		71	5	28	24	7	38					21	
Cox Creek,	114	114	307	228		205	9	52	42	34	88					109	
Clayton,	110	115	360	270		235	12	96	32	57	88					91	
Elk,	95	95	289	236	14	178	11	92	19	13	99	1				81	1
Gicord,	108	118	319	262		219	14	63	44	49	113				1	82	
Grand Meadow,	77	80	225	188		154	5	71	3	32	94					57	
Garnavillo,	185	203	578	500		393	18	86	90	87	166	2				163	
Farmersburgh,	144	160	447	389		316	19	157	15	21	119	1	1		1	131	1
Highhland,	80	89	251	209		163	9	63	33	15	90					103	
Jefferson,	365	424	1156	924		825	60	42	216	321	421	2				190	
Lodomillo,	126	136	407	319		263	12	155	13	15	152	1				135	
Monono,	132	144	424	386		268	19	141	43	26	167	1				104	
Millville,	118	127	350	314		228	14	103	27	12	53		1			94	1

Mendon,	132	132	401	301	1	253	14	139	34	34	168				1	77	1
Mallory,	136	136	441	379		245	22	131	20	11	128	1	1		2	104	1
Morasser,	75	78	202	189		154	5	8	27	53	40					77	
Read,	112	125	335	291		241	12	42	55	34	102	1				50	
Sperry,	120	132	322	327		231	14	99	15	15	51					118	
Volga,	99	166	261	272		217	16	43	57	39	74					90	
Wagoner,	90	92	273	248		178	10	83	24	7	93					82	
Cass,	111	111	334	285		234	13	142	16	4	109			1	1	137	
Total,	2696	2884	8227	6960	16	5531	334	1958	875	913	2555	11	3	1	6	2097	5

TABLE,

SHOWING THE NUMBER & VALUE OF HOGS, CATTLE, DOMESTIC AND GENERAL MANUFACTURES OF CLAYTON COUNTY, FOR 1856.

Townships.	No. of hogs sold.	Value of hogs sold.	No. of Cattle sold.	Value of cattle sold.	Pounds butter made.	Pounds of cheese.	Pounds of wool.	Value of domestic manufactures.	Value of general manufactures.
Boardman,	16	140	7	175					
Buena Vista,	66	539	4	115	100			15	
Cox Creek,	128	1121	82	2968	6103		381	450	400
Clayton,	163	1209	44	1534	5806		135		13950
Elk,	215	1852	50	1584	4691		276	90	9550
Gicord,	377	3178	76	2852	2098	345	856	34	
Grand Meadow,	205	2230	34	1281	9075		104		
Garnavillo,	566	4660	119	4604	12475		1414	15	2500
Farmersburgh,	501	3980	183	6322	16488	2580	900	384	
Highland,	171	1309	107	3357	8245	264	364	32	200
Jefferson,	459	3478	110	4203	14199	792	526		4130
Lodomillo,	437	3835	164	5327	14649		833	100	
Monono,	178	1689	67	3136	12620	7620	456	14400	
Millville,	211	1723	58	2104	3617	50	209	30	15
Mendon,	106	739	49	1902	3530	59	397	212	7565
Mallory,	510	4173	149	5188	9386		344	100	513
Morasser,	151	1545	86	2612	8769		178	115	50
Read,	455	3450	173	6809	2345	2166	357	20	
Sperry,	261	1727	110	3666	8864	1170	1789	1295	13
Volga,	180	1476	54	1826	2821		178		
Wagner,	157	1386	45	1796	8730	106	317	38	
Cass,	89	589	209	7761	10650	140	595	790	1900
Total,	5603	46030	1980	71123	165261	15272	10669	18120	40786

TABLE,

SHOWING THE AGRICULTURAL STATISTICS OF CLAYTON COUNTY, FOR 1856.

TOWNSHIPS.	Acres of improved land.	Acres of unimproved land.	Acres of meadow.	Tons of hay.	Bushels of grass seed.	Acres of spring wheat.	Bushels harvested.	Acres of winter wheat.	Bushels harvested.	Acres of Oats.	Bushels harvested.	Acres of corn.	Bushels harvested.	Acres of potatoes.	Bushels harvested.
Boardman,	795	3921	28	80	......	108	1868	......	......	50	1330	140	7700	2	480
Buena Vista,	265	2869	11	18	......	43	600	......	......	9	310	84	3165	12	670
Cox Creek,	1919	13458	126	164	1	392	5940	43	912	77	3822	357	16875	14	2208
Clayton,	1617	3975	130	153	17	585	10013	......	......	239	9097	380	14795	16	1745
Elk,	995	5582	20	25	......	58	755	42	448	26	955	411	20290	22	2029
Gicord,	2563	5696	114	102	16	906	16025	17	140	447	16098	665	24925	39	3615
Grand Meadow,	2726	9355	24	16	......	870	16149	......	......	207	8762	520	23449	18	3019
Garnaville,	6793	9979	871	1219	8	2344	40435	4	40	723	28414	1191	51300	52	4455
Farmersburgh,	5458	12276	525	1266	28	1767	35350	......	......	593	21122	958	37066	49	4814
Highland,	1332	8403	37	797	......	310	5161	......	......	59	2249	423	18590	21	2817
Jefferson,	3579	20366	452	875	16	1302	17644	45	387	431	14847	1054	46146	131	14779
Lodomillo,	3616	11600	10	1021	......	427	8290	9	130	178	7962	720	30029	42	4822
Monono,	2827	13798	71	133	......	1055	19592	5	247	453	18662	727	28494	35	4262
Millville,	1006	8398	89	100	7	158	1984	15	212	57	2275	344	12375	16	2260
Meadon,	827	3973	79	64	5	43	534	79	478	49	1180	206	7566	15	1320
Mallory,	2228	8906	164	196	2	294	4095	177	2100	163	5188	719	33565	27	3438
Morasser,	1391	8737	13	1208	1	609	11457	1	15	48	1659	323	12573	15	2235
Read,	3125	6063	310	578	96	1313	23394	......	......	257	10790	761	32601	34	3091
Sperry,	2144	14390	58	29	25	398	8119	18	290	110	4053	675	28710	39	6053
Volga,	1374	508	71	145	22	483	6778	14	144	67	2495	401	18270	37	3790
Wagoner,	2247	12946	11	......	16	820	14111	......	......	119	4784	462	21270	23	2670
Cass,	1192	16124	3	3	......	245	4541	......	......	143	4788	489	17825	28	3665
Total,	50020	201324	3218	7132	260	14392	252835	470	5603	4505	170842	12112	507579	689	78237

TABLE,

EXHIBITING THE PROFESSIONS, TRADES OR OCCUPATIONS OF THE INHABITANTS OF CLAYTON COUNTY, FOR 1856.

TOWNSHIPS.	Farmers.	Laborers.	Blacksmith.	Carpenters.	Wagon makers.	Brick layers.	Plasterers.	Masons.	Stone cutters.	Carriage makers.	Machinists.	Engineers.	Millers.	Sawyers.	Millwrights.	Painters.	Cabinet makers.	Chair makers.	Tinners.	Milliners.
Boardman,	75		5					2				1	1			1	3	1		
Buena Vista,	21	16		2							1	1		1						
Cox Creek,	98	11	2	5				3												
Clayton,	58	68	5	10	1	2		5	1	1	1	3	1	7	4	2	4	3	3	
Elk,	70	22	6	5	4		2	1					3	2	2		1			1
Giard,	115	21		7									2							
Grand Meadow,	111			6	1												1	1		
Garnavillo,	168	84	10	19	1	3	1						3		2	1				3
Farmersburgh,	148	1	4	2	1					1					2					
Highland,	89	13	3	9				5						1						
Jefferson,	154	215	9	55	4			47				1	7	1		1	4		4	
Lodomillo,	149	1	2	10				1			2			1	1					
Monona,	127	40	2	10	1			1						6			2			
Millville,	89	1	4	8				2					1	3						
Mendon,	73	36	8	16	3		1	2						1		1	1		5	1
Mallory,	119	14	5	2				3	2				5							1
Morasser,	87	3						1												
Read,	49		3	3				1	1											
Sperry,	123	12	2	8									1				1			
Volga,	65		3	3				1				1			1		2			
Wagoner,	92		2	1																
Cass,	115		8	19				1					4			1		1		
Total,	2195	558	83	200	16	5	4	76	4	2	4	7	27	23	12	7	19	6	12	6

TOWNSHIPS.	Tailors.	Shoemakers.	Harness makers.	Bakers.	Butchers.	Mechanics.	Manufacturers.	Merchants.	Agents.	Druggists.	Hotel keepers.	Physicians.	Dentists.	Lawyers.	Clergymen.	Teachers.	Musicians.	Printers.	Daguerre'n artists.
Boardman,		5	1					6				1		1	2			2	
Buena Vista,								1				1				1			
Cox Creek,																			
Clayton,	2	3	2	1	1			6			2	2				1			
Elk,		4													2	4			
Giard,	1														1				
Grand Meadow,	1	1									1								
Garnavillo,	2	7	3			2		7				3		6	3	4		1	
Farmersburgh,		4				15		1				1			3				
Highland,								1			1				3				1
Jefferson,	9	8	2	2	4			22		2	3	4		1		5		2	
Lodomillo,		4					2	4				1		1	2				
Monona,		3	4					9			4	2							
Millville,						7		3				1		1					
Mendon,	2	4	3	1				8	1	1	4	3	1	1		3	1		
Mallory,		2	1									1			1	2		1	
Morasser,		1																	
Read,		2	1												1			2	
Sperry,		3						2				1			1	2			
Volga,		2	3			2		4								1			
Wagoner,		1																	
Cass,	1	3						4				1			2				
Total,	18	57	20	4	5	26	2	78	1	3	15	22	1	11	21	23	1	8	1

TABLE—Continued.

EXHIBITING THE PROFESSIONS, TRADES OR OCCUPATIONS OF THE INHABITANTS OF CLAYTON COUNTY, FOR 1856.

TOWNSHIPS.	Grocers.	Teamsters.	Brick makers.	Watch makers.	Jewellers.	Gun Smiths.	Coopers.	Clerks.	Jailor.	Raftmen.	Fishermen.	Miners.	Hunters.	Turners.	Moulders.	Firemen.	Stage proprietors.	Dress makers.	Wool carders.	Mentua-makers.	Seamstress.	Potters.	Postmasters.	Pedlers.	Surveyors.	Students.
Boardman,					1		4	4	1																	
Buena Vista,							1			2	1	1														
Cox Creek,	1																									
Clayton,		4	2				1	5					1	1	1	1	1	1								
Elk,						3	5												2	1	2					
Giard,					1																	1				
Grand Meadow																										
Garnavillo,			2	1			1	3										1					1	1	1	1
Farmersburgh,																										
Highland,							1	1																	1	
Jefferson,	1	4	1	1			9	3				1	1										1			
Lodomillo,																										
Monono,								2																	1	
Millville,		1					5					1														
Mendon,	6	6	2				6	14										1								
Mallory,			1			1	2					1													1	
Morasser,																										
Read,																					1				1	
Sperry,																									1	
Voiga,																										
Wagoner,																										
Cass,	1	1						1										1					1		1	
Total,	9	16	8	2	2	4	35	33	1	2	1	4	2	1	1	1	1	4	2	1	8	1	1	1	7	1

TOWNSHIPS.	Basket makers.	Nailors.	Shingle makers.	Prairie brakers.	Stage drivers.	Gardeners.	Cigar makers.	Brewers.	Book sellers.	Barbers.	Notary Publics.	Saloon keepers.	Weavers.	Drovers.	Mates.	Ferrymen.	Livery keepers.	Glove makers.	Stewards.	Lumbermen.	Nursreymen.	Bar keepers.	Ship Carpenters.	Tanners.	Showmen.
Boardman,																									
Buena Vista,																									
Cox Creek,																									
Clayton,																									
Elk,																									
Giard,																									
Grand Meadow																									
Garnavillo,																									
Farmersburgh,																									
Highland,	1	1	1	3	1																				
Jefferson,						1	1	2	1	1	1	1													
Lodomillo,																									
Monono,																									
Millville,			3																						
Mendon,					2					1			1	1	1	3	1	1	1	1	1	1			
Mallory,			3										2										2	1	
Morasser,																									
Read,																									
Sperry,																									1
Voiga,																									
Wagoner,																									
Cass,																									
Total,	1	1	7	8	3	1	1	2	1	2	1	1	3	1	1	3	1	1	1	1	1	1	2	1	1

TABLE,

SHOWING THE PLACE OF NATIVITY OF THE INHABITANTS OF CLAYTON COUNTY FOR 1856

STATES.	NAME OF TOWNSHIPS.																						
	Boardman.	Buena Vista.	Cox Creek.	Clayton.	Elk.	Gicord.	Grand Meadow.	Garnavillo.	Farmersburgh.	Highland.	Jefferson.	Lodomillo.	Monono.	Millville.	Mendon.	Mallory.	Morasser.	Read.	Sperry.	Volga.	Wagener.	Cass.	Total.
Ohio,	99	13	29	67	137	56	74	95	33	90	182	98	61	59	71	67	27	46	56	70	115	5	1545
Indiana,	5	10	12	22	21	22	16	15	36	12	13	7	18	20	21	8	10	11	12	4	15	33	844
Pennsylvania,	83	15	35	70	38	21	56	55	126	39	25	64	44	100	66	309	1	61	35	21	31	33	1328
Iowa,	138	42	84	119	92	105	47	206	128	73	372	102	102	177	129	118	83	131	91	90	75	63	2567
New York,	101	25	50	57	34	67	57	65	177	66	28	146	158	63	117	83	4	47	113	29	47	188	1722
Maine,	11		2	2	1	1		2	1		2	7	9	4	2				5	1	14	2	66
N. Hampshire,	1		15	3		3		10	28	1		9	12	2	11	5		3			10	6	119
Vermont,	54	4	28	20	6	27	11	24	117	13	5	32	71	10	20	15	1	19	27		89	18	561
Massachusetts,	8		15	7	2	9	3	15	14	9	5	33	12	8	3	2	1	6	16	1		24	188
Connecticut,	10		13	2	3	2	2	25	12	4	1	7	12	1	4	6		1	8	10	1	2	126
Rhode Island,	3					1			2					3		1			1	1		2	14
Virginia,	8	1	2	4	19	13	10	4	12	1	2	18	11	22	10	21		1	8	24	2	17	210
Kentucky,		3	8	3	10	6	1	9	4		6	5		12	18	15		6	4	4		3	117
Illinois,	31	8	48	25	56	13	21	32	5	25	19	71	30	30	[illegible]	27	5	11	57	9		87	635
Michigan,	6	2	3	11	4	1		14		2	3	34	18	8	4	8	3	7	21	1		15	165
Arkansas,						1								1	1								3
Texas,																						1	1
Alabama,		2																	4				6
Louisiana,	1					1		3			7							5					17
Mississippi,								2			24								1				27
Florida,						2																	2
North Carolina,			1		6				1				3	1					1				13
South Carolina,					1						1			3	1				5				11
Tennessee,			4	7	4	8	1	2	4	2	1	1		6	6	1			6	1			54
Missouri,	14	4	7	2	6	6	6	1	1			1	2	23	5	4	2	2	11	5			102
Nova Scotia,				1																			1
Bavaria,								65			16						2						83
Poland,								1															1
Bohemia,						1									4								5
Georgia,						2																	2
Maryland,	4		4	2	6	2	2	8		2	5		4	3	1	28		2		3	1		72
New Jersey,	10	5			7			1		1		6	8						1	13	1	3	51
England,	37	5	7	6	8	15	5	17	12	26	6	5	26	15	9	4		2	26	1	9	12	253
Ireland,	68	34	75	36	14	16	30	45	19	38	2	28	40	35	25	12	1	100	26	55	10	9	756
Wales,				1									3	1									5
Scotland,	1	1		3		1	8	8	2	24	8		27	9	10	15			1	2	9	2	131
Germany,	82	18	73	113	34	109	6	210	68	5	1161	25	11	9	48	17		156	46	172	40	22	2375
France,	2	1		4	7		9			2	1	1		3		3	8						41
Austria,						13												1					14
Prussia,			18		2	3		33			118	1						2					171
Norway,				3			39		12		1		1		6		142				70		274
Sweden,															13								13
Holland,								1															1
On the Ocean,	1										1							2					4
Canada,	31	7	9	16	2	7		5	14	4	3	19	96	27	21	44			14	1	19	4	343
New Brunswick,	6			1				6				1											14
Switzerland,	1		1	1			1	5		9			2		4		83			13			120
Hanover,			1					65			89												155
Saxony,			2		1			1															4
West Indies,	1																						1
Isle of Man,									1														1
Wisconsin,	1	14	1	21	4	2	10	25	4	12	7	5	26	12	39	4	18	5	42	2	13	11	278
Delaware,	1							2			1	1	7	1									12
Minnissota,	1			1									1	1		1							5
Italy,	2																						2
Dist. Columbia,																1							1
Belgium,											1												1
Unknown,		2						6			14				6	6	1		11			5	51

TABLE,

SHOWING THE POPULATION OF CLARKE COUNTY, FOR 1856.

TOWNSHIPS.	No. dwelling houses.	No. of families.	Number of males.	Number of females.	Colored.	Married.	Widowed.	Native voters.	Naturalized voters.	Aliens.	Militia.	Deaf and Dumb.	Idiotic.	Owners of land.	Paupers.
Liberty,	66	75	212	187	...	143	8	80	1	....	....	...	...	60	....
Fremont,	46	46	136	107	...	86	4	53	...	....	38	...	...	53	....
Washington,	47	47	134	122	...	87	5	52	...	....	39	...	...	34	....
Madison,	34	35	98	108	2	71	3	41	2	2	35	1	1	32	....
Troy,	21	21	65	57	...	40	2	27	1	....	27	...	...	19	....
Oceola,	152	154	467	397	...	303	11	191	8	...	174	...	...	126	....
Jackson,	42	44	122	110	...	83	3	50	2	....	49	...	. .	43	1
Franklin,	54	54	172	145	...	109	10	54	4	2	56	...	...	61	....
Green Bay,	57	61	163	165	...	121	6	68	2	....	58	...	1	57	....
Knox,	69	79	229	198	...	135	4	88	3	....	69	1	1	77	....
Doyle,	91	98	326	258	...	194	5	122	2	....	100	...	1	71	....
Total,	679	714	2124	1854	2	1372	61	826	25	4	645	2	4	633	1

TABLE,

SHOWING THE AGRICULTURAL STATISTICS OF CLARKE COUNTY, FOR 1856.

TOWNSHIPS.	Acres of improved land.	Acres of unimproved land.	Acres of meadow.	Tons of hay.	Bushels grass seed.	Acres spring wheat.	Bushels harvested.	Acres winter wheat.	Bushels harvested.	Acres of oats.	Bushels harvested.	Acres of corn.	Bushels harvested.	Acres of potatoes.	Bushels harvested.
Liberty,	1144	6669	....	....	....	54	269	3	30	29	916	642	17790	10	1733
Fremont,	1090	7490	4	....	....	109	769	....	....	49	1245	409	12635	6	732
Washington,	537	3808	....	....	....	12	61	7	80	53	930	121	3500	....	....
Madison,	741	4149	4	....	....	111	710	....	....	51	947	298	10950	8	666
Troy,	537	3428	....	....	....	6	20	....	....	18	550	222	6490	3	331
Oceola,	2713	20969	....	....	....	100	666	31	332	164	4305	1179	37145	17	1933
Jackson,	930	5872	....	....	....	36	400	....	....	45	660	354	8485	2	245
Franklin,	1653	9092	8	1	5	105	365	8	42	124	2380	513	14435	8	1110
Green Bay,	1402	9786	1	219	....	136	511	20	193	100	2190	868	21570	11	1195
Knox,	2104	7234	1	....	....	258	2066	30	500	150	4155	965	26590	10	1618
Doyle,	2204	12521	12	2	....	168	1995	....	....	88	2425	937	23965	19	2559
Total,	15051	90958	30	222	5	1095	7832	99	1177	871	20703	6508	183555	95	12122

TABLE,

SHOWING THE NUMBER OF HOGS, CATTLE, DOMESTIC AND GENERAL MANUFACTURES OF CLARKE COUNTY, FOR 1856.

TOWNSHIPS.	No. of hogs sold.	Value of hogs sold.	No. of Cattle sold.	Value of Cattle sold.	Pounds of butter made.	Pounds of cheese.	Pounds of Wool.	Value of Domestic Manufacture.	Value of General Manufactures.
Liberty, ...	170	740	75	2508	3121	....	477	260	262
Fremont, ...	95	558	43	1278	2675	50	26	95	....
Washington, ...	3	35	102	2128	1875	28	237	290	....
Madison, ...	62	479	40	1105	3390	10	70	228	400
Troy, ...	18	101	33	951	1315	....	25	....	....
Oceola, ...	436	2647	91	2712	7753	20	355	127	....
Jackson, ...	66	350	61	2018	907	....	130	..	....
Franklin, ...	128	897	81	1895	3821	140	418	362	...
Green Bay, ...	245	1083	101	2491	4315	135	240	190	....
Knox, ...	219	1404	98	1958	4695	326	339	242	..
Doyle, ...	321	2152	148	3736	5819	138	548	....	44
Total, ...	1763	10447	873	22781	39685	847	2865	1794	707

TABLE,

EXHIBITING THE PROFESSIONS, TRADES OR OCCUPATIONS OF THE INHABITANTS OF CLARKE COUNTY, FOR 1856.

TOWNSHIPS.	NAME OF TOWNSHIPS.											TOTAL.
	Liberty.	Fremont.	Washington.	Madison.	Troy.	Oceola.	Jackson.	Franklin.	Green Bay.	Knox.	Doyle.	
Farmers,	95	64	39	41	34	106	44	72	74	101	101	771
Laborers,			7	1		34		2				44
Blacksmiths,	2				1	11		1	1			16
Carpenters,	2	1	4	1	3	13	2	1	4	4	9	44
Wagon Makers,		1										1
Plasterers,						4						4
Stone Masons,							1			1		2
Carriage makers,						1						1
Engineers,	1			2							2	5
Millers,						1					2	3
Painters,						2						2
Cabinet Makers						4	2					6
Chair Makers,						1					1	2
Milliners,						1			1	1	1	4
Tailors,						1		1				2
Shoemakers,	2					2					4	8
Mechanics,	1			3							2	6
Merchants,	1			2		10		2		1	3	19
Druggists,						1						1
Hotel Keepers,						2						2
Physicians,						5			1		3	9
Lawyers,						5			2			5
Clergymen,		1				2					1	6
Teachers,						2						2
Editors,								1				1
Teamsters,								1				1
Watch Makers,											1	1
Jewellers,												1
Coopers,		1				1					1	3
Clerks,						4						4
Nurserymen,			2									2
Surveyors,							1					1
Tailoresses,											2	2
Embroiderers,											1	1

TABLE,

SHOWING THE PLACE OF NATIVITY OF THE INHABITANTS OF CLARKE COUNTY, FOR 1856.

STATES.	NAME OF TOWNSHIPS.											TOTAL.
	Liberty.	Fremont.	Washington.	Madison.	Troy.	Oceola.	Jackson.	Franklin.	Green Bay.	Knox.	Doyle.	
Ohio,	150	58	14	45	37	274	28	70	52	92	133	953
Indiana,	59	75	102	47	37	166	72	88	81	95	137	959
Pennsylvania,	20	8	4	18	6	39	28	22	6	18	33	202
Iowa,	47	34	42	38	11	152	42	62	51	71	64	614
New York,	9	2	4	1	2	15	2	1	11	5	16	68
Maine,	1								6	1		8
New Hampshire,										1		1
Vermont,	1		1	6		3				3	7	21
Massachusetts,						7			1		4	12
Connecticut,		1	1				1	1	4		5	13
Rhode Island,	3									1		4
Virginia,	20	8	8	7	1	55	17	23	14	16	28	197
Kentucky,	36	2	19	7	8	27	2	5	19	33	25	183
Illinois,	14	27	33	4	12	58	14	16	40	53	72	343
Michigan,	2			1						1		4
Arkansas,						1						1
Texas,						1						1
Alabama,				1					1			2
Louisiana,											5	5
Mississippi,											2	2
North Carolina,	6	1	9	1	4	17	4	11	12	5	8	78
South Carolina,	1			1			3	1	2			8
Tennessee,	9	15	13	8	1	11	10	1	8	12	23	111
Missouri,	18	2	2	10		3	2		1		12	50
Maryland,	1	5	2		1	6	2	5	5	1	1	29
New Jersey,	1	3	2	2		6	1		9	9	1	34
England,	1					7	1	2	1			12
Ireland,		1				2	2	6	3		1	15
Scotland,						1		1	1			3
Germany,				9		10		1		5		25
France,					2						1	3
Canada,							1				1	2
Delaware,		1				3		1		5		10
Wisconsin,											4	4

TABLE,

SHOWING THE POPULATION, AMOUNT of PRODUCE, NUMBER OF HOGS AND CATTLE SOLD AND THEIR VALUE, AND THE VALUE OF DOMESTIC AND GENERAL MANUFACTURES, OF CRAWFORD COUNTY, FOR 1856.

POPULATION.	TOWNSHIPS.		TOTAL.
	Milford.	Union.	
Number of dwelling houses,	32	10	42
Number of families,	35	12	47
Number of males,	98	33	131
Number of females,	72	32	104
Married,	62	25	87
Widowed,	4	......	4
Native voters,	41	14	55
Naturlized voters,	3	5	8
Aliens,	1	......	1
Militia,	41	5	46
Owners of land,	42	13	55
AGRICULTURAL STATISTICS—			
Acres of improved land,	334	124	458
Acres of unimproved land,	7514	3010	10524
Acres of spring wheat,	67	15	82
Bushels harvested,	822	56	878
Acres of oats,	14	.....	14
Bushels harvested,	470	......	470
Acres of corn,	210	58	268
Bushels harvested,	9140	1995	11135
Acres of Potatoes,	5	2	7
Bushels harvested,	710	370	1080
HOGS, CATTLE AND MANUFACTURES—			
Number of hogs sold,	122	59	181
Value of hogs sold,	763	274	1037
Number of cattle sold,	77	75	152
Value of cattle sold,	2330	1722	4052
Pounds of butter made,	2892	975	3867
Pounds of cheese,	100	.....	100
Pounds of wool,	185	125	310
Value of domectic manufactures,	50	......	50

TABLE—EXHIBITING THE PROFESSIONS, TRADES, OR OCCUPATIONS OF THE INHABITANTS OF CRAWFORD COUNTY, FOR 1856.

TOWNSHIPS.	Farmers.	Laborers.	Blacksmiths.	Carpenters.	Millers.	Painters.	Milliners.	Shoemakers.	Harness makers.	Physicians.
Milford, ...	28	....	1	3	1	1	1	2	1	1
Union, ...	15	3		....	....	....	....	....	....	....
Total, ...	43	3	1	3	1	1	1	2	1	1

TABLE—SHOWING THE PLACE OF NATIVITY OF THE INHABITANTS OF CRAWFORD COUNTY, FOR 1856.

STATES.	TOWNSHIPS.		TOTAL.
	Milford.	Union.	
Ohio,	21	17	38
Indiana,	1	1	2
Pennsylvania,	8	4	12
Iowa,	37	11	48
New York,	21	2	23
Maine,	1	......	1
New Hampshire,	1	2	3
Vermont,	3	......	3
Massachusetts,	3	......	3
Virginia,	2	......	2
Kentucky,	3	2	5
Illinois,	40	7	47
Michigan,	3	2	5
North Carolina,	1	......	1
Tennessee,	3	1	4
Missouri,	2	2	4
Maryland,	4	......	4
New Jersey,	3	......	3
England,	1	11	12
Ireland,	3	2	5
Scotland,	......	1	1
Germany,	2	......	2
Canada,	2	......	2
Wisconsin,	5	......	5

TABLE—Showing the population of Clinton county, for 1856.

TOWNSHIPS.	No. dwelling houses.	Number families.	Number of males.	Number females	Married.	Widowed.	Native voters.	Naturalized voters.	Aliens.	Militia.	Deaf and Dumb.	Blind.	Insane.	Idiotic.	Owners of land.
Berlin,	26	34	88	62	38	6	18	4	9	23	..		..	1	24
Bloomfield,	161	161	417	374	309	12	158	11	40	136	1	1	..	..	147
Brookfield,	89	89	266	247	184	13	91	8	15	39	..	1	1	..	86
Camanche,	225	252	701	614	431	38	192	60	113	214	..	..	..	..	200
Center,	83	84	262	209	154	11	52	16	55	111	..	..	..	1	73
Clinton,	144	144	562	370	340	12	238	57	77	341	..	..	..	1	157
Deep Creek,	63	65	203	136	120	8	36	12	42	77	..	..		..	73
De Witt,	293	322	896	789	619	44	310	51	54	356	1	.	..	..	250
Eden,	82	82	261	204	178	14	76	14	29	92	..	..	..	..	73
Elk River,	197	208	644	509	378	33	152	68	97	279	..	..	..	..	163
Liberty,	91	91	265	226	90	9	89	22	15	105	1	..	..	..	52
Lyons,	432	454	1521	1028	896	68	355	86	282	346	1	..	..	.	88
Olive,	102	102	291	241	207	11	87	6	31	73	..	..	..	..	93
Orange,	36	36	127	119	85	2	49	4	....	50	..	..	..	..	35
Sharon,	97	97	311	267	206	9	97	9	9	79	..	..	..	1	80
Spring Rock,	68	74	192	167	133	7	59	18	6	66	..	..	..	..	60
Washington,	78	78	225	195	146	6	13	42	2	....	..		..	1	71
Waterford,	85	85	242	213	148	7	48	11	41	45	.	..	..	..	83
Total,	2352	2458	7474	5967	4662	310	2120	499	917	2432	4	2	1	5	1808

TABLE—Showing the agricultural statistics of Clinton County, for 1856.

TOWNSHIPS.	Acres of improved land.	Acres of unimproved land.	Acres of Meadow.	Tons of Hay.	Bushels of Grass seed.	Acres of spring wheat.	Bushels harvested.	Acres of winter wheat.	Bushels harvested.	Acres of oats.	Bushels harvested.	Acres of Corn.	Bushels harvested.	Acres of Potatoes.	Bushels harvested.
Berlin, ...	722	3038	10	10		158	2521	6	45	38	1325	166	6165	6	585
Bloomfield, ..	4345	9362	127	170	58	1755	31982			400	17071	1002	38120	57	6090
Brookfield, ..	4565	8371	173	875	11	1172	20544			243	9512	880	43505	30	3570
Camanche, ..	2371	3209	85	83	3	863	17865			292	11402	828	35765	27	3804
Center, ...	2963	7817	86	671		949	17439	2	26	183	8265	628	22210	47	6765
Clinton, ...	2038	3236	198	498	19	886	13783			285	8422	537	26860	25	4669
Deep Creek, .	2495	7518	176	269	30	799	10921			106	4461	378	15575	19	1465
De Witt, ...	7391	21648	470	1811	48	411	50929	24	390	591	23340	1650	79664	69	9734
Eden, ...	3613	6315	42	35	2	1018	21902	89	1883	286	11115	729	32985	39	4975
Elk River, ..	7237	21458	958	1108	35	2198	35362			826	28455	2134	89475	66	9107
Liberty, ...	2129	5217	19	37	12	410	6429			99	3290	393	20980	6	1170
Lyons, ...	3697	8082	200	288	24	1105	21641	10	110	360	14617	1026	49070	73	10655
Olive, ...	2795	7901	41	1004	35	700	14319	7	97	275	5968	726	28625	28	3907
Orange, ...	1487	2119	73	29	2	605	12684	6	88	61	1650	327	11180	11	1582
Sharon, ...	2947	9347		849		524	9455			100	4043	556	20558	41	3980
Spring Rock,	1966	7230	22	51	8	629	10019	14	360	126	3585	449	16212	11	1105
Washington,	1540	7342		250		455	8589			43	1144	357	11090	26	3140
Waterford, ..	1224		22	34		362	5905	14	304	57	2294	527	22390	22	3092
Total, ...	55444	139210	2702	8072	287	14999	312289	172	3303	4270	159959	13293	570429	603	79395

TABLE,

SHOWING THE NUMBER & VALUE OF HOGS, CATTLE, DOMESTIC AND GENERAL MANUFACTURES OF CLINTON COUNTY, FOR 1856.

TOWNSHIPS.	No. of hogs sold.	Value of hogs sold.	No. of Cattle sold.	Value of cattle sold.	Pounds butter made.	Pounds of cheese.	Pounds of wool.	Value of domestic manufactures.	Value of general manufactures.
Berlin, ...	107	687	32	1190	100				
Bloomfield, ..	353	2678	148	4411	5510	1580	175	23	
Brookfield,...	405	3767	124	4430	10704	400	283		
Camanche,...	280	2621	130	4668	11735	1591	102		540
Center, ...	123	1100	152	5704	7510	62	402		
Clinton, ...	251	3324	151	4258	7730	448	489	255	
Deep Creek, .	167	1365	167	5282	3510	700	324		
De Witt, ...	559	4753	435	12934	21700	2360	967	60	200
Eden, ...	304	2742	108	3600	9188	1090	74		
Elk River, ...	749	6235	301	9933	23570	1755	658	25	
Liberty, ...	128	1081	36	1375	3420	1670	205		3300
Lyons, ...	435	5122	138	5232	11555	1155	538	113	
Olive, ...	111	1145	105	3227	6260	400	359		
Orange, ...	171	1288	30	1108	3830	200	160	500	
Sharon,......	143	1341	194	2989	7941		286		
Spring Rock,.	169	1409	105	3795	3560	685	894	130	
Washington, .	29	175	58	1747					
Waterford,...	170	1823	44	1268	4736		204	70	4123
Total, ...	4654	42656	2458	77351	142659	14096	6120	1176	8163

TABLE,

EXHIBITING THE PROFESSIONS, TRADES OR OCCUPATIONS OF THE INHABITANTS, OF CLINTON CO., FOR 1856.

TOWNSHIPS.	Farmers.	Laborers.	Blacksmiths.	Carpenters.	Wagon Makers.	Brick Layers.	Plasterers.	Stone Masons.	Stone Cutters.	Carriage Makers.	Machinists.	Engineers.	Millers.	Sawyers.	Millwrights.	Painters.	Cabinet Makers.	Tinners.	Milliners.	Tailors.	Shoemakers.	Harness Makers.	Bakers.	Butchers.	Mechanics.	Merchants.	Agents.	Traders.	Druggists.	Board'g H. Keep's.
Berlin,......	34	2		3																										
Bloomfield,..	150		4	5																	1					1				
Brookfield,..	126		2	4				1																						
Camanche,..	104	156	3	31			2	11				1	3	1	1	2	1	2	1	4	6	1	1		5	16			2	1
Center,.....	103	12	3	7			1	1													2			1						
Clinton,....	77	106	3	68				15				3	2			13	1	3		3	7	1	1			18		3	1	
Deep Creek,	111	7	1	1																										
De Witt,....	177	82	14	38			3				1	1	1	2		2		3		1	3					6	1		1	
Eden,.. ..	93	49	2	4												1			1	1					2	1				
Elk River,..	238	88	8	7	1			2				2	5		6															
Liberty,. ..	63		2	10				1					4									1				5				
Lyons,.....	114	236	12	135	3	3	6	18	1	2	10	6	11	2	6	11	6	4	3	7	10	4	3	4	1	43	5		5	
Olive,......	99	15	1	2				3												1						1				
Orange, ...	50	1	1										1																	
Sharon,.....	99		2	7				1									1				1					1				
Spring Rock,	63	2		8	1			6			1		1			2		1	1		1					1				
Washington,	79			1				1																1						
Waterford,..	89	13	2	10				1					8													1				
Total, ..	1879	769	60	341	5	3	12	61	1	2	12	13	36	5	13	31	9	13	6	17	31	7	5	6	8	96	6	3	9	1

TABLE—CONTINUED,

EXHIBITING THE PROFESSIONS, TRADES, OR OCCUPATION OF THE INHABITANTS OF CLINTON CO., FOR 1856.

TOWNSHIPS.	Hotel Keepers.	Physicians.	Dentists.	Lawyers.	Clergymen.	Teachers.	Musicians.	Printers.	Artists.	Bankers.	Grocers.	Teamsters.	Brickmakers.	Watchmakers.	Jewellers.	Gunsmiths.	Coopers.	Clerks.	Seamstresses.	Wheelwrights.	Gardeners.	Postmasters.	Draymen.	Shingle makers.	Railroad Agents.	Livery men.	Weavers.	Brewers.	Dress makers.	Surveyors.	Students.
Berlin, ...																			4	1											
Bloomfield, .	1	1																													
Brookfield, .		2			2	4											1														
Camanche, .	3	5	1	3	3	3			1	1		1	1		1		1	7			2	1	1	1	1	2	1	1			
Centre, ...				1																1											
Clinton, ...	1	4		8	4	11				2		4	3					7	1			1	2		2				1	1	1
Deep Creek,																															
De Witt, ...	3	7		7	3	2		2	1		3		5		1	1	1	6		4						1				1	
Eden, ...																		1	1												
Elk River, ..	1					2											4	3												1	
Liberty, ...	1	1		1		1			1				1			1	1														
Lyons, ...	6	11	1	8	9	2	1	3	1	3	14		10	1	1		3	13					3			3	1				
Olive, ...																															
Orange, ...					1																						1				
Sharon, ...		2															1														
Spring Rock,		1			1																									1	
W shington,																	1			1											
Waterford, .																															
Total, ...	16	34	2	28	19	18	1	5	4	6	17	5	20	1	3	2	13	37	6	7	2	2	6	1	3	6	3	1	1	4	1

TABLE—Continued.

EXHIBITING THE PROFESSIONS, TRADES OR OCCUPATION OF THE INHABITANTS OF CLINTON CO., FOR 1856.

TOWNSHIPS.	Barbers.	Saloon Keepers.	Builders.	Stage Drivers.	Hostlers.	Peddlers.	Sheriffs.	Ferrymen.	Sash Makers.	Distillers.	Broom Makers.	Nurserymen.	Pilots.	R. R. Contractors.	Lumber Dealers.	Stewards.	Pattern Makers.	Moulders.	Editors.	Cooks.	Potters.
Berlin,																					
Bloomfield,																					
Brookfield,																					
Camanche,																					
Center,																					
Clinton,	1	1																			
Deep Creek,																					
De Witt,			1	1	1	3	1	2													
Eden,			1																		
Elk River,																					
Liberty,									1	1											
Lyons,											1	2	1	4	16	1	1	1	2	2	
Olive,								1									1				
Orange,						1															
Sharon,																					
Spring Rock,																					
Washington,																					1
Waterford,																					
Total,	1	1	1	1	1	1	1	3	1	1	1	2	1	4	16	2	1	1	2	2	1

TABLE—SHOWING THE PLACE OF NATIVITY OF THE INHABITANTS OF CLINTON COUNTY, FOR 1856.

STATES.	NAME OF TOWNSHIPS.																		
	Berlin.	Bloomfield.	Brookfield.	Camanche.	Centre.	Clinton.	Deep Creek.	De Witt.	Eden.	Elk River.	Liberty.	Lyons.	Oliver.	Orange.	Sharon.	Spring Rock.	Washington.	Waterford.	TOTAL.
Ohio,	24	86	94	122	30	100	10	298	35	87	140	137	68	14	114	67	12	13	1456
Indiana,	..	13	14	33	10	29	8	66	8	59	36	32	19	13	6	10	15	75	423
Pennsylvania,	23	66	51	125	103	88	10	264	24	120	23	247	22	30	40	19	30	6	1291
Iowa,	10	113	63	195	59	123	40	258	57	215	67	331	71	43	72	55	68	61	1901
New York,	25	257	121	210	34	208	59	195	146	99	76	454	115	58	109	48	26	48	2283
Maine,	..	2	...	16	5	23	6	8	...	...	...	5	...	..	...	6	5	1	77
N. Hampshire,	..	19	3	3	1	32	1	19	3	3	1	26	2	..	4	2	..	..	119
Vermont,	..	53	7	8	3	5	10	36	5	44	6	48	8	2	23	12	1	4	275
Massachusetts,	2	7	5	14	6	25	2	29	2	8	3	94	36	..	3	21	5	1	263
Connecticut,	5	3	2	18	3	13	1	17	14	8	5	43	20	1	3	4	4	1	165
Rhode Island.	..	1	...	...	...	5	..	5	...	1	...	9	13	..	1	2	..	..	37
Virginia,	1	5	34	31	3	10	5	34	1	3	4	19	5	48	5	8	1	4	221
Kentucky,	6	...	8	9	2	2	..	23	1	20	4	20	1	..	3	2	8	13	122
Illinois,	8	16	14	64	7	11	5	65	2	42	17	101	30	8	58	13	2	16	474
Michigan,	..	5	1	7	5	4	6	14	4	1	5	56	...	9	1	2	..	10	130
Arkansas,				3															3
Texas,								1											1
Alabama,								1		1		4							6
Lousiana,								2				2							4
N. Carolina,				1	1					3								1	6
South Carolina										2			1						3
Tennessee,				3				4	1	1		2	3		1		1	11	27
Missouri,				12			2	7	2	12	7	5			2		1		50
Poland,												1							1
Kansas,												1							1
Minnesota,												1							1
Georgia,										2									2
California,										1									1
Maryland,			5	5			3	18	2	5	1	5			1	2	5		52
New Jersey,	1	8	5	13	2	3	1	19	12	5	2	16			3	1	1		92
England,	9	46	13	116	46	34	14	39	94	24	7	124	10	5	6	11	57	14	669
Ireland,	30	21	7	88	44	111	45	87	10	182	55	362	26	3	5	17	127	73	1243
Wales,							1	2	1			7							11
Scotland,	1	1	...	4	...	14	..	24	...	25	1	12	...	..	12	4	4	7	109
Germany,	6	11	26	188	88	48	67	36	8	122	25	243	25	1	27	33	12	18	981
France,				1		2		7				4	33		1			6	54
Austria.	4		5																9
Prussia,						1													1
Norway,						1		2			1	8	7						14
Sweden,									1			23							24
On the Ocean,								1		1									2
Canada,	..	57	32	14	1	15	32	70	80	105	4	69	16	11	76	20	81	64	647
N. Brunswick,						1		17		1		2					1		22
Switzerland,						1		3				3							7
Denmark,			2		18				1										21
Hanover,						5													5
Mexico,												1							1
Wisconsin,			1	6			11	6	1	18	1	37			1		1		82
Delaware,				1				7					1		1				11
Unknown,		1				17		1									2	3	24
Bremen,				4															4

TABLE,—SHOWING THE POPULATION, AMOUNT OF PRODUCE, NUMBER OF HOGS AND CATTLE SOLD, THE AMOUNT THEY BROUGHT, AND THE VALUE OF DOMESTIC AND GENERAL MANUFACTURES OF DALLAS COUNTY, FOR 1856.

POPULATION.	NAME OF TOWNSHIPS.						
	Boone.	Union.	Dallas.	Penoach.	Sug. Grove.	Desmoines.	TOTAL.
Number dwelling houses,	73	143	35	211	60	61	583
Number of families, ...	80	164	41	273	65	60	683
Number of males, ...	260	483	115	872	186	233	2149
Number of females, ...	219	427	90	727	155	224	1842
Married, ...	151	309	69	528	107	155	1319
Widowed, ...	8	15	5	28	5	4	65
Native veters, ...	87	179	39	303	65	91	764
Naturalized voters, ...	3	1	4	14	6	2	30
Aliens, ...	1	2	4	2	1	2	12
Militia, ...	75	121	34	255	48	74	607
Owners of land, ...	72	95	39	141	55	43	445
AGRICULTURAL STATISTICS.							
Acres of improved land,	2915	3445	844	4677	816	1908	14605
Acres unimproved land,.	11338	17112	6920	22750	8126	5338	71584
Acres of meadow,......	46	5	2	23		149	225
Tons of Hay, ...	5	2	2	5		1	15
Bushels of grass seed,. .				120	10	1	131
Acres of spring wheat,..	718	439	43	896	84	391	2571
Bushels harvested, ...	254	2932	273	651	645	46	4801
Acres of winter wheat,..	63			12		8	83
Bushels harvested, ...				63			63
Acres of oats,..........	215	78	9	246	24	241	813
Bushels harvested, ...	226	1478	140	382	321	111	2658
Acres of corn, ...	1194	1454	294	1807	226	777	5752
Bushels harvested, ...	333	35885	8375	2852	10975	525	58945
Acres of potatoes, ...		17	3	162	5	64	252
Bushels harvested, ...	5	2490	507	13	815		3830
STATISTICS OF HOGS, CATTLE &C.							
Number of hogs sold,...	35	193	65	790	·	87	1170
Value of hogs sold,.....	391	980	264	3459	42	554	5690
Number of cattle sold,..	69	87	49	70	13	66	354
Value of cattle sold, ...	2223	3596	1608	1851	290	1137	10705
Pounds of butter made,.	2441	4864	1765	6735	60	3701	19566
Pounds of cheese,......	272	300	200	351		3360	4483
Pounds of wool,........	1791	1014	44	1759	59	589	5256
Value of dom's man.,...	1786	210	39	143		265	2443
Value of general man., .	800	137			2000	66	3003

TABLE,

EXHIBITING THE PROFESSIONS, TRADES OR OCCUPATIONS OF THE INHABITANTS OF DALLAS COUNTY, FOR 1856.

OCCUPATIONS.	NAME OF TOWNSHIPS.						TOTAL.
	Boone.	Union.	Dallas.	Penoach.	Sugar Grove.	Des Moines.	
Farmers,	81	151	39	152	56	67	546
Laborers,		1					1
Blacksmiths,		5	1	7		2	15
Carpenters,	3	11	2	20	2	4	42
Wagon Makers,		2		2			4
Plasterers,	3			3			6
Masons,				1		1	2
Millers,		5		2	1	2	10
Millwrights,		1		2		1	4
Painters,				1			1
Cabinet Makers		1		1			2
Chair Makers,		1					1
Tailors,				2			2
Shoemakers,		1	1	4			6
Saddle & Harness Makers,				3			3
Mechanics,	3	1		13			17
Merchants,	1	4		14		2	21
Druggists,				1			1
Hotel Keepers,				1			1
Physicians,		3		5		1	9
Lawyers,				3			3
Clergymen,				3		1	4
Teachers,	1				1		2
Printers,		1			1		2
Editors,				1			1
Bankers,				1			1
Teamsters,				1			1
Gun Smiths,				1			1
Coopers,		1		1		1	3
Stove Makers				1			1
Surveyors,				2			2
Wheelwrights,						1	1

TABLE,

SHOWING THE PLACE OF NATIVITY OF THE INHABITANTS OF DALLAS COUNTY, FOR 1856.

STATES.	NAME OF TOWNSHIPS.						
	Boone.	Union.	Dallas.	Penoach.	Sugar Grove.	Desmoines.	TOTAL.
Ohio,	72	256	43	341	72	167	951
Indiana,	166	266	19	227	62	67	807
Pennsylvania,	15	38	10	123	23	32	241
Iowa,	74	116	16	156	26	1	389
New York,	3	12	2	109	28	60	214
Maine,			1	3			4
New Hampshire,		2		2		1	5
Vermont,	1	4		20		5	30
Massachusetts,		10	2	14		1	27
Connecticut,	1	2		4		6	13
Rhode Island,			1			1	2
Virginia,	6	55	6	87	17	21	192
Kentucky,	7	43	8	184	44	22	308
Illinois,	72	8	62	28	1	7	178
Michigan,	2	5	1	1		7	16
Alabama,				2			2
Louisiana,			1				1
Mississippi,				1			1
North Carolina,	18	42	3	88	34	1	186
South Carolina,	1	4		14		1	30
Tennessee,	16	30	4	53	2	17	122
Missouri,	3	2	8	6			19
Georgia,	1						1
Maryland,	5	2		23	6	7	43
New Jersey,		6		25	1	4	36
England,			4	30	23	2	59
Ireland,	2	2	7	4		24	39
Wales,			2				2
Scotland,	1		1		1		3
Germany,	11	5	1	24	1		42
France,						1	1
Canada,						1	1
Switzerland,			2	3			5
Delaware,				1		1	2
Unknown,	2		1	26			29

TABLE,

SHOWING THE POPULATION OF DAVIS COUNTY, FOR 1856.

TOWNSHIPS.	No. dwelling houses.	No. of families.	Number of males.	Number of females.	Colored.	Married.	Widowed.	Native voters.	Naturalized voters.	Aliens.	Militia.	Deaf and Dumb.	Blind.	Insane.	Idiotic.	Owners of land.	Paupers.
Salt Creek,	150	152	419	399		261	20	156	3	6	149			1	1	121	3
Lick Creek,	132	134	387	374		238	15	139	3	1	142				1	115	
Soap Creek,	131	132	399	377		242	11	107	12	5	105	3	1	2	2	93	
Marion,	118	125	384	337		232	11	120	8	3	104				1	88	
Fox River,	175	175	560	492		336	26	188	2		170			1		126	
Drakeville,	109	109	275	307	1	205	12	108	4	4	74	3				41	
Bloomfield,	293	298	836	783		454	45	305	10	12	278	1				213	
Perry,	124	124	362	350	3	215	15	124	3	8	110	10	1		1	91	
Union,	179	179	524	485		324	13	181	8	11	164	3	1		1	124	
Roscoe,	42	42	135	103		38	4	40	3	3	42					46	
Prairie,	72	72	199	183		64	7	61	6		61				2	58	
Grove,	119	126	383	349		251	6	140	7		121	2			1	106	
Wycondah,	209	209	600	518		386	20	219			198	2				145	
Fabius,	170	170	521	487		340	11	197	2	4	177					138	
TOTAL,	2023	2047	5984	5544	4	3586	216	2085	71	57	1895	24	3	4	10	1505	3

TABLE,

SHOWING THE AGRICULTURAL STATISTICS OF DAVIS COUNTY, FOR 1856.

TOWNSHIPS.	Acres of improved land.	Acres of unimproved land.	Acres of meadow.	Tons of hay.	Bushels grass seed.	Acres spring wheat.	Bushels harvested.	Acres winter wheat.	Bushels harvested.	Acres of oats.	Bushels harvested.	Acres of corn.	Bushels harvested.	Acres of potatoes.	Bushels harvested.
Salt Creek, ...	3190	9905	446	242	8	210	2477	311	4816	316	9215	1696	65951	42	4098
Lick Creek, ...	2921	10556	205	177	2	270	2498	151	1548	396	10484	1418	64489	26	3498
Soap Creek, ...	4981	9273	365	296	15	368	3207	242	3270	442	11724	1697	72795	22	2744
Marion, ...	3033	6370	115	122	...	155	1217	286	3891	258	9600	1462	74206	5	495
Fox River, ...	5425	19294	196	129	19	409	3878	249	2994	1125	37610	2738	111970	8	1907
Drakeville, ...	2412	4844	193	148	1	257	2969	66	1162	304	9626	964	42685	4	925
Bloomfield, ...	560	11214	313	330		377	7903	240	3562	874	29350	2337	95761	15	1604
Perry, ...	5073	9485	379	305	34	320	2684	289	3057	662	18535	1855	91315	17	2060
Union, ...	4875	7586	649	787	140	531	6049	300	3971	850	26440	1798	78765	22	3214
Roscoe, ...	1681	5853	80	85	6	194	1839	77	858	209	5860	898	38480	4	675
Prairie, ...	2063	8125	149	132	23	371	4438	67	450	395	11968	876	28770	5	505
Grove, ...	4685	13213	110	107	8	395	5422	77	1098	599	22150	1637	68050	12	1197
Wyeondah, ...	8969	18702	263	270	36	562	6306	372	4398	1118	39440	3251	123618	35	2928
Fabins, ...	5585	16714	85	85	14	476	4799	202	2053	938	31224	2740	99900	28	2386
Total, ...	60505	151134	3549	3215	306	4895	55684	2929	39228	8486	273226	25367	1056735	245	28236

TABLE,

SHOWING THE NUMBER OF HOGS, CATTLE, DOMESTIC AND GENERAL MANUFACTURES OF DAVIS COUNTY, FOR 1856.

TOWNSHIPS.	No. of hogs sold.	Value of hogs sold.	No. of Cattle sold.	Value of Cattle sold.	Pounds of butter made.	Pounds of cheese.	Pounds of Wool.	Value of Domestic Manufacture.	Value of General Manufactures.
Salt Creek,	564	4186	185	2621	6195	134	2686	1915	690
Lick Creek,	423	2504	320	9088	12207	127	1843	1758	4560
Soap Creek,	990	7341	223	3747	11151	400	2454	1784	1037
Marion, ..	1280	9684	337	7144	10695		1907	1661	750
Fox River,	1176	9390	393	7816	10478	255	2417	1904	800
Drakerville	775	4127	341	9396	9863	370	660	108	7200
Bloomfield,	859	6903	434	8584	9335	451	1864	680	
Perry, ...	1820	12525	397	7069	7694	413	2545	2973	1350
Union, ...	859	6667	261	4543	7930	50	2409	2209	2680
Roscoe, ...	171	1372	128	1786	2555	1032	504		
Prairie, ...	302	2692	100	1963	2800	170	690	448	
Grove, ...	687	5886	256	6239	8015	100	1512	1500	
Wycondah,	1367	10501	671	15057	17850	438	3713	2743	5750
Fabius, ...	1316	6801	387	9294	14970	255	2840	3485	260
Total,	12589	90579	4433	94347	131738	4195	28044	23168	25077

TABLE,—EXHIBITING THE PROFESSIONS TRADES OR OCCUPATIONS OF THE INHABITANTS OF DAVIS COUNTY, FOR 1856.

OCCUPATIONS.	NANE OF TOWNSHIPS.														
	Salt Creek.	Lick Creek.	Soap Creek.	Marion.	Fox River.	Drakeville.	Bloomfield.	Perry.	Union.	Prairie.	Roscoe.	Grove.	Wycondah.	Fabius.	TOTAL.
Farmers,	114	77	112	153	162	62	148	99	138	61	48	98	230	125	1627
Laborers,	33	117	26	5	61		25	38	2			23		55	388
Blacksmiths,	2	2		1	1	5	9		8		1	2	3	4	38
Carpenters,	4	4		4	2	13	18	3	17	3	1	5	3	5	82
Wagon Makers,	2		1			2	1		1			1			8
Brick Layers,	1						1								2
Plasterers,	1					2	6		2						11
Stone Masons,	2	1				1	1		2			1	2		10
Stone Cutters,						1			1						2
Carriage Makers,							1								1
Machinists,				1								1			1
Engineers,		1	1		1	3	1		2						10
Millers,	1	1	3			1			1	1		1		3	12
Sawyers,					3										3
Millwrights,		1		2					1			2			6
Painters,					1	1	1								3
Cabinet Makers,				1		1	2	1	1	1					7
Milliners,					1								3	1	5
Tailors,	3				1	1	3		1	1					10
Shoemakers.		1		2	2	5	8	1	2			1			22
Saddle & Harness Makers,						6	6		1						13
Mechanics,			7					1					3	2	13
Merchants,			1	1	1	6		1	8			2		1	31
Traders,		1					29		1					2	33
Druggists,							1								1
Boarding House Keepers,							1								1
Hotel Keepers,							–		3						3
Physicians,	1	3			1	3	9	1	3			1	1	1	24
Lawyers,						1	10	1							12
Clergymen,		1			1	2	2		2	1		1	1		11
Teachers,	2	2	1	1	4	2	3	8	4			1		8	26
Bankers,									1						1
Grocers,						1	4								5
Teamsters,							4								4
Brick Makers,		2							3			2			7
Jewelers,							1		1						2
Gunsmiths,												1			1
Coopers,	3	4	1	1			1	1	1			1			13
Clerks,						2	5								7
Turners,		13					4								17
Wheelwright,		1					1								2
Seamstress,					2		2								4
Nurserymen,						1									1
Carders,						1	1							1	3
Magistrates,						2									2

13

TABLE,

SHOWING THE PLACE OF NATIVITY OF THE INHABITANTS OF DAVIS COUNTY, FOR 1856.

STATES.	NAME OF TOWNSHIPS.														
	Salt Creek.	Lick Creek.	Soap Creek.	Marion.	Fox River.	Drakeville.	Bloomfield.	Perry.	Union.	Prairie.	Roscoe.	Grove.	Wyecondah.	Eabius.	Total.
Ohio	205	128	159	123	94	112	209	65	275	55	50	117	119	93	1804
Indiana,	116	222	153	86	166	113	447	184	104	56	14	196	337	198	2392
Pennsylvania,	46	26	39	62	73	43	67	3	82	23	9	24	20	33	550
Iowa,	265	191	215	195	267	136	420	190	8	124	55	186	289	271	2812
New York,	9	24	10	5	15	7	19	12	50	9	5	2	7	6	180
Maine,			2				2	5				2			11
N. Hampshire,			1				6		2				1		10
Vermont,	2		1	1			4	1	17	2					28
Massachusetts,						1	5		1		4		1		12
Connecticut,		1	2	1	1	1	6				1	9			22
Rhode Island,						4	1								5
Virginia,	38	47	26	24	69	26	63	39	140	27	12	22	55	51	639
Kentucky,	43	48	35	81	98	32	129	86	61	9	28	46	104	141	941
Illinois,	24	28	37	41	111	42	64	33	11	20	23	34	49	88	608
Michigan,							3						9		12
Arkansas,	1		1			2								1	5
Texas,													1		1
Alabama,		2	1			2	3		4						12
Louisiana,						1									1
Mississippi,			1											1	2
North Carolina,	5	7	8	1	61	19	16	8	23	1	10	10	26	19	200
South Carolina,		1	2		3	2	1	2				1	2	1	15
Tennessee,	17	4	16	88	23	11	35	45	139	18	6	11	23	39	420
Missouri,	14	15	13	19	55	4	36	18	3	1	5	21	62	41	307
Georgia,	1	1			2		8			8			1		11
Maryland,	6	6	5	21	4	4	12	1	30	8	2	3	10	10	117
New Jersey,	4	1	6	3	1	2	5	1	10		4			2	42
England,	1	4	8	7	6	5	8		1		1			4	40
Ireland,	1		6	3		8	13	5	1		3	1		4	40
Scotland,	1								4	3	11				19
Germany,	13	3	23	5		8	6		27	3	1	23		2	109
France,			5			1	10					1			17
Russia,			5												5
Prussia,							1								1
Norway,						1									1
Holland,							1								1
Canada,	3	2	1			8	13	8		6	2	6		2	46
Switzerland,				5			5	6	9	1		2		1	29
Wisconsin,	1			1			1			2					6
Delaware,	1								7	13		15	1		37
D. Columbia,						2							1		2
Unknown,	1			1			10			8	1				16

TABLE,

SHOWING THE POPULATION OF DECATUR COUNTY, FOR 1856.

TOWNSHIPS.	No. dwelling houses.	No. of families.	No. of males.	No. of females.	Colored.	Married.	Widowed.	Native voters.	Naturalized voters.	Aliens.	Militia.	Deaf and Dumb.	Blind.	Insane.	Idiotic.	Owners of land.	Paupers.
Garden Grove,	70	76	216	166	3	142	6	85	5	5	83	..	1	1	..	68	..
Franklin,	40	40	129	96	..	77	1	44	2	3	32	..	..	..	..	40	..
Long Creek,	80	80	244	211	..	84	1	85	6	..	89	..	..	..	..	75	..
Richland,	55	55	169	138	..	100	....	59	7	1	59	..	1	..	..	53	..
Grand River,	33	33	104	98	..	64	7	41	..	1	38	..	..	..	..	30	..
Decatur,	87	87	264	255	.	152	12	83	1	..	56	..	..	..	..	50	..
Centre,	192	192	623	538	.	373	25	171	10	..	163	3	..	..	..	145	..
High Point,	87	87	282	262	..	163	6	81	1	..	82	..	..	..	..	74	..
Woodland,	68	68	204	208	..	126	6	69	9	..	67		..	..	..	83	.
Eden,	79	79	214	226	..	145	5	71	5	..	76	1	..	..	..	60	..
Burrell,	84	86	242	205	..	159	7	82	5	2	70	..	..	..	..	66	..
Bloomington,	34	37	91	84	..	64	4	42	..	1	37	..	..	..	1	36	..
Buda,	30	30	80	72	..	56	1	30	3	4	32	..	..	..	..	32	..
Hamilton,	87	95	304	243	1	178	7	96	2	..	84	2	..	..	1	78	2
Morgan,	56	56	168	144	..	51	3	62	1	..	53	..	..	..	.	47	..
Total,	1082	1101	3332	2937	4	1934	91	1101	57	17	1021	6	2	1	2	937	2

TABLE,

SHOWING THE AGRICULTURAL STATISTICS OF DECATUR COUNTY, FOR 1856.

TOWNSHIPS.	Acres of improved land.	Acres of unimproved land.	Acres of Meadow.	Tons of Hay.	Bushels of Grass seed.	Acres of spring wheat.	Bushels harvested.	Acres of winter wheat.	Bushels harvested.	Acres of oats.	Bushels harvested.	Acres of Corn.	Bushels harvested.	Acres of Potatoes.	Bushels harvested.
Garden Grove,	2763	10929	207	223	22	145	351	20	125	169	3745	977	30179	23	2890
Franklin,	1065	4732	8	9		74	672	20	221	70	1696	431	10655	5	210
Long Creek,	1380	11464			17	66	898	1	25	64	1570	868	15241	13	791
Richland,	729	7039				24	147			38	375	481	14320	10	1036
Grand River,	408	4472				15	791	2		31	320	239	5400	4	405
Decatur,	1280	6555				163	1779	42	1170	140	3234	678	26605	9	1467
Centre,	3733	12440	27	14		327	1389	35	160	210	4015	1705	40025	20	3166
High Point,	1477	6899	12			68	402	23	196	89	1435	1021	25565	16	2457
Woodland,	2022	12022	7	2		102	836	29	167	110	2211	723	22152	1	1503
Eden,	1664	7120	48	5		71	703	4	9	166	3570	740	17630	7	895
Burrell,	1434	8875		3	1	261	2525	26	116	129	2779	821	27110	16	1003
Bloomington,	765	8345				42	300	3		12	148	407	7485	5	483
Buda,	420	2150				56	172	2		28	666	225	2472	3	210
Hamilton,	2160	8662	25	10	8	120	524	6	33	179	4412	899	15735	19	1589
Morgan,	1152	3290	20			97	444	25	238	101	2156	645	22675	6	610
Total,	22453	114994	354	266	48	1631	11233	237	2460	1536	32332	10860	283249	156	18715

TABLE,

SHOWING THE NUMBER & VALUE OF HOGS, CATTLE, DOMESTIC AND GENERAL MANUFACTURES OF DECATUR COUNTY, FOR 1856.

TOWNSHIPS.	No. of hogs sold.	Value of hogs sold.	No. of Cattle sold.	Value of cattle sold.	Pounds butter made.	Pounds of cheese.	Pounds of wool.	Value of domestic manufactures.	Value of general manufactures.
Garden Grove,	103	754	365	11384	6425	500	561	393	2500
Franklin, ...	58	407	67	1482	1645		164	156	
Long Creek, ..	367	2577	151	3453	225				
Richland, ...	405	1608	93	1586	2588	1000	194	200	20
Grand River, .	45	162	27	624	805		34		5000
Decatur, ...	249	750	454	3302	4505	258	348	187	450
Centre, ...	416	2280	251	5665	18526	355	966	777	725
High Point, ..	253	1876	140	3508	4330	5	954	98	763
Woodland, ...	265	1954	76	1087	6020		619	596	1100
Eden, ...	146	468	194	4865	6150	355	165	25	
Burrell, ...	435	1722	187	4446	3129	120	370	223	
Bloomington, .	133	443	151	4293	380		40		
Buda, ...	13	52	47	1337	1613		157		46
Hamilton, ...	306	1095	249	4577	2830	100	610	475	3515
Morgan, ...	372	1461	129	2597	3789		805	512	
Total, ...	3566	17609	2576	53206	63260	2693	5987	3642	14119

TABLE,

EXHIBITING THE PROFESSIONS, TRADES OR OCCUPATIONS OF THE INHABITANTS, OF DECATUR CO., FOR 1856.

TOWNSHIPS.	Farmers.	Laborers.	Blacksmiths.	Carpenters.	Wagon Makers.	Brick Layers.	Plasterers.	Stone Masons.	Engineers.	Millers.	Millwrights.	Painters.	Cabinet Makers.	Tinners.	Milliners.	Tailors.	Shoemakers.	Harness'Makers.	Merchants.	Speculators.	Droves.	Hotel Keepers.	Physicians.	Lawyers.
GardenGrove,	84	5	2	7				1	2	1					5	1	2		4	1	1		2	
Franklin,	46																							
Long Creek,	84		1	3									1						2				1	
Richland,	65			2						1													1	
Grand River,	25		1	3							2		1			1	1							
Decatur,	66		1	6			1		1		1	1	1						5				3	
Centre,	200	18	6	26	1			1		5		1	1	1		3	1	1	12			2	3	4
High Point,	57		1																					
Woodland,	72			4									1											
Eden,	66			1																				
Burrell,	96	1	1	2		2	3	2		2	2		1											
Bloomington,	41	4		1																				
Buda,	31	1		3		1			1							1								
Hamilton,	67	12	5	5	2			1							2		2		4				2	1
Morgan,	44	4	1	3						1			1											
Total,	1016	45	19	66	3	3	4	5	5	10	4	2	7	1	7	6	6	1	29	1	1	2	12	5

TABLE—CONTINUED,

EXHIBITING THE PROFESSIONS, TRADES OR OCCUPATIONS OF THE INHABITANTS OF DECATUS COUNTY, FOR 1856.

TOWNSHIPS.	Clergymen.	Teachers.	Musicians.	Printers.	Teamsters.	Gun Smiths.	Coopers.	Clerks.	Nurserymen,	Ironmonger,	Wheelwright,	Carder,	Surveyors,	County Judge,	Magistrates,	County Treasurer,	Weaver,	Tobacconists,	Horse Trainer,	Distiller,	Moulder,	Hatter,	Peddler,
Garden Grove,		4						1	1	1													
Franklin,	1																						
Long Creek,																							
Richland,											1												
Grand River,	1																						
Decatur,	1				1							1	1										
Centre,	2				1		1						1	1	1	1							
High Point,																							
Woodland,																	1	2					
Eden,																							
Burrell,						1	2						1										
Bloomington,	2																						
Buda,																			1				
Hamilton,		2	1	1																1			
Morgan,							1					2					3				1	1	1
Total,	7	6	1	1	2	1	4	1	1	1	1	3	3	1	1	1	4	2	1	1	1	1	1

TABLE—SHOWING THE PLACE OF NATIVITY OF THE INHABITANTS OF DECATUR COUNTY, FOR 1856.

STATES.	NAME OF TOWNSHIPS.															
	Garden Grove.	Franklin.	Long Creek.	Richland.	Grand River.	Decatur.	Centre.	High Point.	Woodland.	Eden.	Burrell.	Bloomington.	Buda.	Hamilton.	Morgan.	Total.
Ohio, ...	125	50	92	87	44	87	265	126	64	74	69	51	29	53	65	1281
Indiana, ...	16	46	47	64	34	95	244	110	85	68	96	20	15	99	37	1076
Pennsylvania, ..	15	14	46	8	42	17	29	20	8	23	13	20	20	43	13	331
Iowa, ...	40	29		42	31	116	200	111	87	95	97	32	21	88	49	1038
New York, ...	65	5	31	10	3	6	10	20	2	6	3	7		29	3	195
Maine, ...											1	2		1		4
N. Hampshire, .	3						1	1	1							6
Vermont, ...	1			2	2				18	1	2	1	4	2		33
Massachusetts, .	5	1		1	1		3						1	1		13
Connecticut, ...	7	1						1	1				1	3		14
Virginia, ...	27	19	38	11	12	24	69	38		16	26	4	13	19	26	342
Kentucky, ...	4	8	25	19	6	43	64	14	60	31	36	10	6	25	24	375
Illinois, ...	37	35	17	12		49	83	34	10	15	31	12	16	75	35	461
Michigan, ...	13					3	2	1	2	2	4	1				28
Alabama, ...										3	1					4
Mississippi, ...	1				1	1	7									10
North Carolina,		6	64	2		8	54	2	7	1	7	4		11	7	173
South Carolina, .	1	2				3					2					8
Tennessee, ...	3	3	39	24	3	29	48	19	26	47	18	6	5	22	23	315
Missouri, ...	1			7		19	41	20	26	48	18		2	64	26	272
Maryland, ...			6	2	6		15	12		1	1	3		1	1	48
New Jersey, ...	1	1	11				2			1	2		1	2	1	22
England, ...	8	1	7		1		3		2	1	5					28
Ireland, ...	3		16	13	4		3	1	7		1	1	1	1		51
Wales, ...	1						2									3
Scotland, ...	1					1		3	1	7					1	14
Germany, ...	5	2	8	1	1	3	1	2	2		5		4			34
France, ...	2						1	1								4
Austria, ...				1	2		1				3	1	11			19
Prussia, ...	1										5					6
Norway, ...								3								3
Canada, ...		2		1			4	5						2		14
Switzerland, ...			8													8
Wisconsin, ...						8	8							5		21
Delaware, ...						6	1							1	1	9

TABLE,

SHOWING THE POPULATION OF DELAWARE COUNTY, FOR 1856.

TOWNSHIPS.	No. dwelling houses.	No. of families.	Number of males.	Number of females.	Married.	Widowed.	Native voters.	Naturalized voters.	Aliens.	Militia.	Deaf and Dumb.	Idiotic.	Owners of land.	Paupers
Adams,	38	44	94	65	66	2	19	25	13	49			49	
Coffin's Grove,	58	58	175	148	101	13	59	8	7	44	3		34	
Cold Water,	64	73	183	173	134	6	76	9	9	55			66	
Colony,	200	204	593	551	380	25	175	54	27	215	2		156	
Delhi,	200	200	623	507	423	28	225	37	37	225			83	
Delaware,	97	97	236	221	189	4	91	11	6	99			82	
Elk,	115	122	354	308	217	16	125	4	7	93	1		109	
Milo,	77	77	205	207	158	7	65	8	6	76			74	4
North Fork,	92	97	280	237	190	15	89	18	26	113			73	
Oneida,	85	85	249	205	171	3	36	20	53	47			86	
Richland,	93	99	275	231	189	6	90	18	6	83			100	
South Fork,	138	152	458	389	296	20	160	17	2	117			149	
Union,	132	132	388	317	225	22	123	23	22	122		1	125	
York,	76	79	223	204	153	3	90	5	8	86			80	
Total,	1465	1519	4336	3763	2892	170	1423	257	229	1424	6	1	1266	4

TABLE,

SHOWING THE AGRICULTURAL STATISTICS OF DELAWARE COUNTY, FOR 1856.

TOWNSHIPS.	Acres of improved land.	Acres of unimproved land.	Acres of meadow.	Tons of hay.	Bushels grass seed.	Acres spring wheat.	Bushels harvested.	Acres winter wheat.	Bushels harvested.	Acres of oats.	Bushels harvested.	Acres of corn.	Bushels harvested.	Acres of potatoes.	Bushels harvested.
Adams, ...	714	6576		651	...	124	2340	....	....	11	438	186	4175	13	1650
Coffin's Grove, ...	1299	6856	37	47	...	214	4954	....	....	106	4056	419	15190	20	3186
Cold Water, ...	2099	9215	273	502	7	455	7712	....	....	253	9382	799	19435	23	2795
Colony,.........	7323	5551	790	1349	79	1138	18339	....	....	585	21443	1792	55995	54	6789
Delhi, ...	2316	8320	115	219	29	205	4316	4	34	99	3925	677	29730	16	2480
Delaware, ...	1919	11423	87	665	...	449	9558	30	520	333	10451	659	26720	33	5594
Elk, ...	3710	11704	195	996	3	670	10367	10	90	293	8530	901	22928	38	5352
Milo, ...	1640	8880	35	44	...	325	5484	....	....	131	4923	384	11946	18	2038
North Fork, ...	2386	13508	311	196	12	527	9116	212	3	403	8578	1274	30463	26	2899
Oneida, ...	2255	11072	42	31	...	502	9463	....	....	144	5336	573	15829	16	2126
Richland, ...	2540	15063	1867	1343	23	270	3820	2	48	258	8632	758	15922	37	5872
South Fork, ...	4172	18583	600	1421	200	766	12854	5	70	390	12033	1129	50716	49	5605
Union, ...	4877	13949	93	102	22	640	12889	....	....	264	8672	1412	40701	64	7875
York,...........	1584	8300	419	640	207	306	5703	1	20	202	7348	452	12520	24	3107
Total, ...	38836	149002	4861	8207	582	6591	116915	264	785	3472	113747	21416	342270	423	57368

TABLE,

SHOWING THE NUMBER OF HOGS, CATTLE, DOMESTIC AND GENERAL MANUFACTURES OF DELAWARE COUNTY, FOR 1856.

TOWNSHIPS.	No. of hogs sold.	Value of hogs sold.	No. of Cattle sold.	Value of Cattle sold.	Pounds of butter made.	Pounds of cheese.	Pounds of Wool.	Value of Domestic Manufacture.	Value of General Manufactures.
Adams, ...	64	483	30	1329	2360	.....	35	.....	.....
Coffins Grove,	82	757	62	2572	5660	680	400	.....	.....
Cold Water, .	323	2854	86	3121	5990	100	774	256	650
Colony, ...	1242	9479	194	7622	22585	1098	2840	621	10314
Delhi, ...	455	4993	60	3190	4400	351	735	2241	2000
Delaware, ...	67	558	92	3925	10208	7020	.....	.....	.....
Elk, ...	453	3981	97	3833	10992	822	335	2465	3371
Milo, ...	93	800	71	2647	4560	400	621	90	.....
North Fork, .	834	5516	125	4679	9380	1875	978	557	20500
Oneida, ...	207	2031	79	2059	7192	4890	79	.....	.....
Richland, ...	124	1392	269	4684	8880	805	158	435	4000
South Fork, .	820	6416	350	9289	14103	800	822	142	22961
Union, ...	697	4471	160	5159	13330	572	641	3027	.....
York, ...	143	956	104	4027	6690	130	310	265	.....
Total, ...	5604	44687	1779	58136	126330	19543	8728	10099	63796

TABLE,

EXHIBITING THE PROFESSIONS, TRADES OR OCCUPATIONS OF THE INHABITANTS OF DELAWARE COUNTY, FOR 1856.

TOWNSHIPS.	Farmers.	Laborers.	Blacksmiths.	Carpenters.	Wagon makers.	Brick layers.	Plasterers.	Stone Masons.	Stone cutters.	Carriage makers.	Machinists.	Millers.	Sawyers.	Millwrights.	Painters.	Cabinet makers.	Tinners.	Milliners.	Tailors.	Shoemakers.	Harness makers.	Bakers.	Butchers.	Mechanics.	Manufacturers.	Merchants.	Agents.	Traders.	Hotel keepers.	Physicians.	Lawyers.	Clergymen.
Adams, ...	47	4	2	4				2										1		1												
Coffins Grove,	65		1	9						1																			1			
Cold Water, .	68	2	1	3														2		1												
Colony, ...	115	20	6	16		1	6	3	4	1	1	4		1		1	2	4	5	7	3	1				5		2	2	2		2
Delhi, ...	104	74	11	18	3		3	6		1		2	1			7	1	2	3	5	2		2			13	1		3	4	8	3
Delaware, ...	109																							23		2				3		
Elk, ...	96	15	2	8			1		2			1																		1		1
Milo, ...	84	6		1																				3								
North Fork, .	85	10	4	2				2				2		1	1		1	2	1	5	1			3		5			5	2		
Oneida, ...	96		1	1															1													
Richland,....	113	2	3	3	1			2										4		2						5				1		
South Fork,..	166		4	10								1		2	2											5				2		2
Union, ...	161	15	5	9				2						1		1				1					1	2						1
York,.	1	1	4	9									3													1				1		1
TOTAL, ...	1310	149	44	93	4	1	10	17	6	3	1	10	4	5	3	9	4	15	10	22	6	1	2	29	1	38	1	2	11	16	8	10

TABLE—Continued.

EXHIBITING THE PROFSSIONS, TRADES OR OCCUPATION OF THE INHABITANTS OF DELAWARE CO., FOR 1856.

TOWNSHIPS.	Teachers.	Musicians.	Printers.	Grocers.	Teamsters.	Brick Makers.	Gun Smiths.	Coopers.	Clerks.	Dress Makers.	Glove Makers.	Potters.	Broom Makers.	Stage Drivers.	Deputy Sheriff.	Livery Keepers.	Cooks.	Co. Treasurer.	Surveyors.	Saloon Keepers,	Sea Captain.	Post Masters.	Treasurer.	Gardeners.	Constables.	Ostlers.	Tailoresses.	Brewers.	Architects.	Students.	Shingle Makers.
Adams, ...																															
Coffin's Grove, ...					1			1																							
Cold Water, ...																															
Colony, ...	2			1			1		2	7	1	2	1	2																	
Delhi, ...	2		4	1		1		1	4						1	1	1	1	1	2	1	1	1	1	1						
Delaware, ...									1																						
Elk, ...								1	1																	1					
Milo, ...																															
North Fork, ...	4				7	2		2	3					4													2				
Oneida, ...								1																				1			
Richland, ...	2	3							3																		6				
South Fork, ...						1	1	1																					1		
Union, ...						1																								1	1
York, ...																															
Total, ...	10	3	4	2	8	5	2	7	14	7	1	2	1	6	1	1	1	1	1	2	1	1	1	1	1	1	8	1	1	1	1

TABLE,

SHOWING THE PLACE OF NATIVITY OF THE INHABITANTS OF DELAWARE COUNTY, FOR 1856.

STATES.	NAME OF TOWNSHIPS.														
	Adams.	Coffin's Grove.	Cold Water.	Colony.	Delhi.	Delaware.	Elk.	Milo.	North Fork.	Oneida.	Richland.	South Fork.	Union.	York.	TOTAL.
Ohio,	15	53	43	87	32	17	159	28	38	25	41	118	121	55	851
Indiana,	..	17	42	25	80	20	64	9	38	90	17	12	42	11	467
Pennsylvania,	20	10	46	245	60	29	48	65	68	15	12	103	43	129	1793
Iowa,	11	33	26	260	162	44	104	51	72	34	57	155	140	60	1209
New York,	15	68	72	112	279	165	84	114	66	40	124	136	57	178	1510
Maine,	4	1	..	3	4	...	6	2	10	...	2	9	4	...	45
N. Hampshire,	3	..	..	3	20	5	11	1	1	1	5	1	22	...	73
Vermont,	1	10	2	6	28	24	9	19	10	10	28	42	27	12	228
Massachusetts,	3	11	11	16	35	16	15	9	2	...	13	...	9	14	154
Connecticut,	..	3	3	11	13	5	10	3	1	...	4	15	2	2	72
Rhode Island.	..	1	1	7	2	1	1	2	3	...	...	...	...	...	18
Virginia,	..	..	7	10	21	4	22	4	19	4	10	24	32	...	157
Kentucky,	..	..	2	18	13	3	3	2	6	1	2	15	30	...	96
Illinois,	13	16	20	42	85	18	33	38	26	26	47	89	40	20	463
Michigan,	..	13	25	10	14	34	34	7	5	...	15	6	5	9	177
Alabama,	..	..	..	...	8	...	...	...	..	...	...	...	...	...	8
Lousiana,	..	..	..	...	8	...	...	...	..	...	...	5	...	...	8
Mississippi,	..	..	..	...	...	...	1	...	1	...	...	4	...	...	6
N. Carolina,	..	..	2	2	6	3	...	2	2	7	...	...	1	...	25
South Carolina	..	..	1	2	1	...	...	...	..	1	...	1	...	...	6
Tennessee,	..	..	2	1	20	...	1	...	13	...	...	9	2	...	48
Missouri,	..	..	1	28	5	2	2	...	10	4	3	1	...	...	51
Georgia,	..	..	..	1	...	...	...	...	..	...	...	...	...	...	1
Maryland,	..	..	..	3	7	...	2	...	6	1	1	3	4	...	27
New Jersey,	2	3	..	32	18	8	5	8	1	2	3	2	10	4	98
England,	7	7	5	29	72	7	15	13	75	58	35	31	18	3	374
Ireland,	42	7	6	23	47	9	14	6	20	2	5	56	66	5	316
Wales,	..	..	..	...	2	...	...	...	..	...	...	...	...	1	3
Scotland,	4	..	3	27	24	12	9	1	2	...	4	33	4	...	123
Germany,	1	16	18	68	4	11	...	2	3	116	28	1	13	17	298
France,	..	..	1	3	...	2	...	...	..	3	9	...	2	...	20
Russia.	..	..	..	7	...	...	...	...	..	...	...	...	...	...	7
Prussia,	..	..	..	...	...	...	...	8	..	...	4	...	...	...	12
Norway,	..	..	..	...	...	...	...	...	..	1	...	...	...	...	1
Sweden,	..	..	..	...	1	...	...	...	..	...	13	...	...	...	14
On the Ocean,	..	..	..	...	3	...	...	...	..	...	1	...	...	...	4
Canada,	10	50	2	49	17	14	2	18	9	10	17	22	5	4	229
N. Brunswick,	..	..	..		...	...	...	...	..	...	...	1	...	...	1
Switzerland,	..	..	..	2	...	...	...	...	..	...	...	...	...	...	2
Wisconsin,	6	4	8	12	18	9	4	4	9	3	7	...	6	3	93
Delaware,	2	..	1	...	...	...	...	...	..	...	...	...	...	...	3
Oregon,	..	..	..	...	2	...	...	...	..	...	...	...	...	...	2
Isle of Man,	..	..	..	...	...	...	...	...	1	...	...	...	...	...	1
Prince Edwards Island,	..	..	6	...	...	...	4	...	..	...	...	...	...	...	10

TABLE,

SHOWING THE POPULATION OF DES MOINES COUNTY, FOR 1856

TOWNSHIPS.	No. of dwelling houses.	Number of families.	Number of males.	Number of females.	Colored.	Married.	Widowed,	Native voters.	Naturalized voters.	Aliens.	Malitia.	Deaf and Dumb.	Blind.	Insane.	Idiotic.	Owners of land.	Paupers.
Augusta,	86	86	267	230	....	151	17	84	13	4	71	..	....	....	....	52	....
Burlington,	1291	1547	5494	4189	14	3023	234	1124	414	222	2889	1	....	....	2	839	2
Flint River,	187	199	613	550	....	184	28	188	32	33	181	....	....	....	2	132	....
Huron,	116	116	359	298	....	207	12	129	8	4	122	....	....	....	....	80	...
Pleasant Grove,	168	179	537	481	....	323	27	171	10	19	132	...	....	....	....	114	1
Jackson,	23	· 23	64	55	....	19	9	22	5	....	19	1	....	....	....	12	....
Union,	204	214	682	621	1	413	39	186	39	64	217	1	....	4	2	146	9
Yellow Spring,	218	230	681	571	....	402	26	221	18	28	185	....	1	....	....	156	....
Benton,	187	193	563	485	....	334	22	152	36	28	181	....	....	....	....	113	....
Danville,	250	255	809	752	1	481	39	318	17	18	314	4	2	3	1	147	....
Franklin,	239	239	730	668	....	408	30	198	47	25	147	2	1	....	2	155	....
Washington,	82	87	290	234	....	170	4	87	13	20	88	1	....	....	..	75	....
Total,	3051	3368	11069	9129	16	6115	487	2880	652	465	4546	10	4	7	9	2021	12

TABLE,

SHOWING THE AGRICULTURAL STATISTICS OF DES MOINES COUNTY, FOR 1856.

TOWNSHIPS.	Acres of improved land.	Acres of unimproved land.	Acres of meadow.	Tons of hay.	Bushels of grass seed.	Acres of spring wheat.	Bushels harvested.	Acres of winter wheat.	Bushels harvested.	Acres of Oats.	Bushels harvested.	Acres of corn.	Bushels harvested.	Acres of potatoes.	Bushels harvested.
Augusta, ...	2410	3159	336	448	32	354	5923	85	1597	415	10898	1085	55470	15	1586
Burlington, ...	4574	4460	867	1271	20	267	3927	485	6106	715	30545	1673	88485	65	9198
Flint River, ...	7544	2645	927	1222	125	1415	15443	380	5596	1448	46877	2700	151525	89	7290
Huron, ...	4324	8338	425	359	426	394	4240	393	6699	281	8234	2240	120540	38	4205
Pleasant Grove,	6688	2222	717	796	70	1162	12573	233	2956	1379	45205	2923	133500	29	4920
Jackson, ...	480	1186	....	......	....	149	1976	87	1050	51	830	204	6350	8	462
Union, ...	10458	10950	816	1068	234	1067	18369	1209	23541	1295	47971	3521	191050	54	7415
Yellow Spring,	11628	17932	680	732	27	2082	26789	179	2004	959	33279	3849	204540	40	6450
Benton, ...	4398	6356	434	467	22	831	6637	359	3100	641	20438	1816	82274	41	4787
Danville, ...	14675	8248	2096	2108	76	1483	16724	515	8317	2186	76983	3740	210970	47	5420
Franklin, ...	10350	8899	944	2761	70	2112	30029	243	4786	878	28511	4891	140746	67	9495
Washington, ...	4269	5438	52	42	5	882	12209	30	518	410	10167	1389	71141	21	3265
Total, ...	81799	79833	8297	11274	1109	14599	154839	4198	66270	10660	359938	30033	1456491	514	64493

TABLE,

SHOWING THE NUMBER AND VALUE OF HOGS, CATTLE, DOMESTIC AND GENERAL MANUFACTURES OF DES MOINES COUNTY, FOR 1856.

TOWNSHIPS.	No. of Hogs sold.	Value of Hogs sold.	No. of Cattle sold.	Value of Cattle sold.	Pounds of butter made.	Pounds of cheese.	Pounds of wool.	Value of Domestic Manufactures.	Value of General Manufactures.
Augusta,	725	7410	199	4452	8727	3275	448	379	2000
Burlington,	1044	8561	614	5262	13465	....	740	264	21910
Flint River,	2068	18216	618	20940	18745	1315	1416	708	100
Huron,	3400	29487	522	19686	27141	375	846	573	2000
Pleasant Grove,	2954	27571	445	8989	14735	425	3554	2655	1550
Jackson,	96	480	51	1326	1860	....	209	....	....
Union,	1989	19386	279	7067	27837	210	1236	574	155
Yellow Spring,	3899	37020	365	10430	26875	810	1926	1830	....
Benton,	1352	8366	509	9446	9991	220	1404	1418	15196
Danville,	1942	19451	508	13844	29164	17013	3878	2325	15
Franklin,	1984	28790	537	9254	18993	438	3468	56	60
Washington,	922	9419	154	3984	8493	460	931	522	....
Total,	22375	214160	4801	114680	206026	24541	20056	11810	241176

TABLE,

EXHIBITING THE PROFESSIONS, TRADES OR OCCUPATIONS OF THE INHABITANTS OF DES MOINES CO., FOR 1856.

TOWNSHIPS.	Farmers.	Laborers.	Blacksmiths.	Carpenters.	Wagon Makers.	Brick Layers.	Plasterers.	Masons.	Stone Cutters.	Builders.	Carriage Makers.	Machinists.	Engineers.	Millers.	Sawyers.	Millwrights.	Painters.	Cabinet Makers.	Chair Makers.	Tinners.	Milliners.	Tailors.	Hatters.	Shoemakers.	Harness Makers.	Bakers.	Butchers	Mechanics.	Manufacturers.
Augusta, ...	76	6	3	5	3		3	4						1	1				1	1	1	1	1	2			1		1
Burlington, ...	277	1199	63	193	22		16	93	37	2	7	16	21	19	4	3	19	31		23	4	26	1	53	23	22	34	14	3
Flint River, ...	244	12	3	9								1	1	1														7	
Huron, ...	120	5		1			1	1	1				1					1											
Pleasant Grove,	198	24	1	6	3		1	2										1				1		1					
Jackson, ...	23	6																											
Union, ...	176	116	4	12				2	1							1	1	2				1		1					
Yellow Spring, .	303	4	6	11									1	3	1						1			2					3
Benton, ...	111	131	3	11	2			1			1		1	1	2			1						1					
Danville, ...	356		8	16	1	1							1		2		2					2		6	2				
Franklin, ...	182	16	2	3			1	1						5								1		3				9	
Washington, . . .	82		2	6	1																								
TOTAL, ...	2148	1519	95	273	32	1	22	104	39	2	8	17	26	30	10	4	22	36	1	24	6	32	2	69	25	22	35	30	7

TABLE—Continued,

EXHIBITING THE PROFESSIONS, TRADES OR OCCUPATIONS OF THE INHABITANTS OF DES MOINES COUNTY, FOR 1856.

TOWNSHIPS.	Merchants.	Agents.	Droves.	Traders.	Druggists.	Confectioners.	Boarding House Keepers.	Hotel Keepers.	Physicians.	Dentists.	Lawyers.	Clergymen.	Teachers.	Musicians.	Printers.	Editors.	Artists.	Daguerrean Artists.	Bankers.	Grocers.	Teamsters.	Chandlers.	Brick Makers.	Watch Makers.	Gun Smiths.	Coopers.	Clerks.	Gardeners.	Moulders.	Bar Keepers.	Cistern Builders.
Augusta,......	3							1	1						1						1										
Burlington,....	88	12	2	18	6	4	15	11	24	2	31	15	19		19	3	1	2	8	45	100	2	5	9	5	68	112	11	33	20	5
Flint River,....									1			3	1													2					
Huron,........	1								1																	2					
Pleasant Grove,	1								1			1	1															1			
Jackson,.......																															
Union,........												1	2												1	2		1			
Yellow Spring,.	7								3			6	3								1				1	1					
Benton,.......	1		1	2								1											1			8		1			
Danville,......	4			3					2			5	1	1							1	1			1	2	3				
Franklin,......	2								2			2	3								1				2						
Washington,...	1																														
Total,......	108	12	3	23	6	4	15	12	35	2	31	34	30	1	20	3	1	2	8	45	104	3	6	9	10	85	115	14	33	20	5

TABLE—Continued,

EXHIBITING THE PROFESSIONS, TRADES OR OCCUPATIONS OF THE INHABITANTS OF DES MOINES COUNTY, FOR 1856.

TOWNSHIPS.	Steam Boat Captains.	Firemen.	Governor.	Servants.	Cigar Makers.	Hyde Park Keepers.	Coffee House Keepers.	Peddlers.	Porters.	Upholsterers.	Gamblers.	Boatmen.	Gass Fillers.	Fishermen.	Post Master.	City & County Treasurers.	Barbers.	Undertakers.	Pilots.	Ostlers,.	Finishers.	Bookbinders.	Engravers.	Brewers.	Boiler Makers.	Livery Stable Keepers.	Architects.	Stage Drivers.	Magistrates.	Vinegar Makers.	Professors.
Augusta, ...												1																			
Burlington, ...	1	1	1	31	15	1	2	9	14	2	2	6	4	6	1	3	8	1	3	7	13	4	3	11	3	4	3	1	1	4	1
Flint River, ...																															
Huron, ...																															
Pleasant Grove,																															
Jackson, ...																															
Union, ...														1			1														
Yellow Spring, .																															2
Benton, ...																															
Danville, ...								1																							
Franklin, ...																															
Washington, ...																															
Total, ...	1	1	1	31	15	1	2	10	14	2	2	7	4	7	1	3	9	1	3	7	13	4	3	11	3	4	3	1	1	4	3

TABLE—Continued,

EXHIBITING THE PROFESSIONS, TRADES OR OCCUPATIONS OF THE INHABITANTS OF DES MOINES CO., FOR 1856.

TOWNSHIPS.	Unknown.	Contracters.	Constables.	Hackman.	Auctioneers.	Sextons.	Speculators.	Billiard Saloon Keepers.	Land Dealers.	Sheriffs.	Soldiers.	Conductors.	Carvers.	Pork Packers.	Brass Founders.	Foundry.	Plough Makers.	Assessors.	Lathe Machines,	Rope Makers,	Baggage Masters.	Clerk Court.	Tanners.	Weavers.	Dairymen.	Colperteur.	Woodsmen.	Miners.	Nurserymen.	Carders.	President of the College.	Students.	Potters.
Augusta,......																							2										
Burlington,....	115	8	1	1	3	1	2	1	1	2	1	3	1	1	1	1	3	1	1	2	1	1	3										
Flint River,....																								1	1								
Huron,.... ...																										1	1						
Pleasant Grove,																												3					
Jackson,.......																								1									
Union,.... ...											1																		2				
Yellow Spring,.																														1	1	15	
Benton, ...																																	
Danville,......																																3	2
Franklin,......																																	
Washington,...																																	
Total, ...	115	8	1	1	3	1	2	1	1	2	2	3	1	1	1	1	3	1	1	2	1	1	5	2	1	1	1	3	2	1	1	18	2

TABLE—SHOWING THE PLACE OF NATIVITY OF THE INHABITANTS OF DES MOINES COUNTY, FOR 1856.

STATES.	NAME OF TOWNSHIPS.												
	Augusta.	Burlington.	Flint River.	Huron.	Pleasant Grove.	Jackson.	Union.	Yellow Spring.	Benton.	Danville.	Franklin.	Washington.	TOTAL.
Ohio,	106	1129	191	137	143	10	188	306	115	289	153	83	2850
Indiana,	23	312	63	72	126	20	87	123	113	80	88	82	1189
Pennsylvania,	65	650	106	42	83	7	143	169	66	227	244	43	1845
Iowa,	172	1834	374	237	349	31	130	331	330	451	441	133	5113
New York,	10	377	22	21		8	16	41	23	60	39	11	628
Maine,		54		5	2	1	3		2	10	1		78
New Hampshire	3	43	7	4			4	3	1	6	1	13	85
Vermont,	3	59	6	15	2	1	17	14	8	5	3		133
Massachusetts,		110	8	3	2	1	2	6		9	2	1	144
Connecticut,	1	57	4	1	4		2	3	2	46	6	1	127
Rhode Island,		11	1		1			1	75	8	2		99
Virginia,	27	225	82	19	57	9	75	36		208	68	16	822
Kentucky,	6	215	32	39	68	5	28	48	20	24	64	9	558
Illinois,	9	234	24	17	44	8	22	32	25	18	29	21	483
Michigan,		37		2			1			3	1		44
Arkansas,		3					1			1			5
Texas,										2			2
Alabama,		7											7
Louisiana,		6						1					7
Mississippi,		4											4
Florida,		1											1
North Carolina,	12	11	14		7	2	6	1	6	9	11	2	81
South Carolina,		2			7		1	3	2		3	4	22
Tennessee,	4	35	18	3	8	1	14	4	5	13	14	16	125
Missouri,	15	135	7	5	6	1	5	3	4	1	2	7	191
Georgia,	1	5	1										7
Maryland,	8	69	14	2	4		19	3	7	30	5	4	165
New Jersey,	1	57	7	1	11		7	6	4	6	29	1	130
England,	10	217	39	5	2	1	16	21	8	4	26	6	355
Ireland,	1	873	8	6	6		8	59	28	27	63	13	1092
Wales,		37	2					21	9		9	30	108
Scotland,		35	2	3	1		8	12		4		1	66
Germany,	10	2226	118	3	70	13	112	5	180	13	81	9	2843
France,	7	54	1		2		1						65
Russia,		3			3		9				1		16
Prussia,		8	8		1		2			1			23
Norway,		2											2
Sweden,		173		3			39		11	1			227
Holland,		23								1			24
On the Ocean,		5	2				2						9
Canada,	1	46		8			1		1	1	1		59
N. Brunswick,		4		1									5
Switzerland,		13											13
Denmark,		24			1		14						39
Hanover,		3											3
Saxony,		1					12						13
Wisconsin,		26							2	3	1		32
Delaware,	1	15	2	3	5		8		1		2	7	44
District Columbia,		2										1	3
Italy,		4											4
Unknown,	1	204											205

TABLE,

SHOWING THE POPULATION OF DUBUQUE COUNTY, FOR 1856.

TOWNSHIPS.	No. dwelling houses.	Number of families.	Number of males.	Number of females.	Colored.	Married.	Widowed.	Native voters.	Naturalized voters.	Aliens.	Militia.	Deaf & Dumb.	Blind.	Insane.	Idiotic.	Owners of land.	Paupers.
Washington, ...	115	119	416	360	....	196	18	86	50	29	141	....	....	....	...	119	....
White Water, ...	130	148	407	351	....	263	21	78	56	45	132	...	1	....	....	120	....
Moslem, ...	136	136	433	362	2	239	35	30	85	93	157	1	....	2	3	112	18
Vernon, ...	119	119	453	332	....	215	16	57	69	49	97	4	...	..	...	92	....
Dodge, ...	77	81	218	172	....	162	5	45	10	44	82	..	....	....	1	66	....
Centre, ...	211	225	639	546	....	426	34	94	93	117	208	..	....	1	....	150	....
New Wine, ...	170	194	585	425	....	274	31	97	89	127	224	...	....	....	....	149	....
Jefferson, ...	204	216	609	502	....	392	27	41	110	99	181	2	....	....	....	169	....
Liberty, ...	137	137	443	325	....	103	....	58	59	2	102	....	....	....	....	97	....
Prairie Creek, ...	97	99	340	268	....	165	15	29	62	51	116	....	....	....	....	96	....
Cascade, ...	142	166	485	414	....	318	10	104	30	238	93	....	....	....	2	96	....
Table Mound, ...	155	155	557	568	....	286	10	33	90	82	146	....	....	....	1	44	18
Taylor, ...	156	156	564	411	....	324	26	171	41	72	130	....	....	....	....	154	...
Julien, ...	2188	2345	7166	5657	34	4947	361	1048	1180	1276	1128	2	2	....	6	330	....
Iowa, ...	114	114	370	287	....	220	11	50	41	53	108	....	....	....	....	106	....
Penn, ...	109	121	314	282	....	114	7	14	57	86	124	...	....	....	..	87	...
Concord, ...	115	116	324	286	....	209	5	34	49	55	56	....	....	1	....	99	...
Total, ...	4375	4637	14323	11548	36	8853	632	2069	2171	2518	3325	9	3	4	13	2086	36

TABLE,

SHOWING THE AGRICULTURAL STATISTICS OF DUBUQUE COUNTY, FOR 1856.

TOWNSHIPS.	Acres of improved land.	Acres of unimproved land.	Acres meadow.	Tons of hay.	Bushels grass seed.	Acres of spring wheat.	Bushels harvested.	Acres winter wheat.	Bushels harvested.	Acres of oats.	Bushels harvested.	Acres of corn.	Bushels harvested.	Acres of potatoes.	Bushels harvested.
Washington,..	5157	9659	762	966	17	1629	26784	....	....	557	19496	1068	53235	93	11580
White Water,.	3152	6724	44	49	....	795	11455	....	....	388	13831	1100	34438	46	5660
Moslem, ...	2874	10605	548	884	11	880	12944	563	1644	467	12026	711	29166	164	13395
Vernon, ...	404	11204	473	1831	36	1011	17746	....	....	523	19946	1502	56705	71	8038
Dodge, ...	2235	7693	229	1317	....	481	9073	400	10	385	6135	1177	25782	116	3465
Centre, ...	2940	9046	518	555	15	402	4852	54	415	385	15079	760	30929	64	5614
New Wine, ..	2229	13536	102	128	26	876	16636	....	....	264	12914	792	17490	32	3665
Jefferson, ...	5111	10411	523	730	30	624	9637	47	440	605	14816	911	34957	253	13408
Liberty,......	4317	11219	683	1073	84	2443	26061	5	212	494	14932	2048	32809	80	7845
Prairie Creek,	430	12655	301	344	5	1050	14581	....	....	931	18607	1180	43263	77	8044
Cascade, ...	3065	11559	227	567	25	722	12060	4	38	418	13800	993	69737	48	5579
Table Mound,	3307	6277	588	1070	30	763	15134	44	913	776	13359	1168	32217	420	9070
Taylor, ...	2805	1779	325	587	....	982	19331	....	....	510	18698	1240	49246	33	4285
Julien,......	1406	5396	718	590	33	251	5924	....	....	350	9840	342	11320	35	3850
Iowa,........	4798	6876	676	823	....	944	14709	11	41	443	13355	1275	53940	70	7202
Peru,........	1774	7908	366	500	....	88	972	101	732	386	8174	414	11188	76	7025
Concord, ...	2786	13290	454	765	5	758	11888	19	298	304	11099	603	27814	54	6732
Total,......	48792	155838	7538	12779	317	14700	229187	1248	4743	8087	236188	17284	564236	1731	124457

TABLE,

SHOWING THE NUMBER OF HOGS, CATTLE, DOMESTIC AND GENERAL MANUFACTURES OF DUBUQUE COUNTY, FOR 1856.

TOWNSHIPS.	Number of hogs sold.	Value of hogs sold.	Number of cattle sold	Value of cattle sold.	Pounds of butter made.	Pounds of Cheese.	Pounds of Wool.	Value of domestic manufactures.	Value of general manufactures.
Washington, ...	509	4550	143	6077	25880	20	519	180	200
White Water, ...	554	5796	160	6077	8890	1000	141	....	....
Moslem, ...	452	2277	565	4851	13271	2369	347	110	100
Vernon, ...	851	6979	302	9103	13468	1065	584	312	....
Dodge, ...	555	2474	215	7027	4215	9150	562	....	....
Centre, ...	493	3395	414	3868	8694	352	874	318	788
New Wine, ...	346	2670	149	4473	3033	1510	318	2015	720
Jefferson, ...	532	2933	267	6833	10486	485	376	15	....
Liberty, ...	437	3292	323	3570	5103	150	351	220	....
Prairie Creek, ...	566	5165	95	3939	12470	200	661	132	....
Cascade, ...	760	5368	119	7866	10694	1785	909	78	....
Table Mound, ...	333	3499	167	3124	24105	400	60	....	....
Taylor, ...	396	3329	149	5157	6208	828	558	207	100
Julien, ...	61	635	61	1805	5407	20	90	....	....
Iowa, ...	809	7854	181	2996	11630	700	804	294	10000
Peru, ...	60	446	56	1973	5510	200	270	....	....
Concord, ...	427	3776	95	3762	9510	100	191	91	....
TOTAL, ...	8141	63438	3461	82501	178574	20334	7615	3882	11908

TABLE,

EXHIBITING THE PROFESSIONS, TRADES OR OCCUPATIONS OF THE INHABITANTS OF DUBUQUE COUNTY, FOR 1856.

TOWNSHIPS.	Farmers.	Laborers.	Blacksmiths.	Carpenters.	Wagon makers.	Brick layers.	Plasterers.	Stone Masons.	Stone cutters.	Builders.	Carriage makers.	Machinists.	Engineers.	Millers.	Sawyers.	Millwrights.	Painters.	Cabinet makers.	Chair makers.	Tinners.	Milliners.	Tailors.	Waiters & porters	Shoemakers.	Harness makers.	Bakers.	Butchers.	Mechanics.	Manufacturers.	Merchants.
Washington,.	109	28	5	8											1	1						1								1
White Water,	103	25	5	3		1		3						4		3	1			3				4						6
Moslem, ...	112	70		10		1		2										1				1		3						2
Vernon, ...	140		3	7				1						1						1		2		1		1	1			
Dodge, ...	98		1	1										2		1					3									1
Centre, ...	151	50	6	9				7					1	2	3				1	1		22		6		1				5
New Wine,	92	16	3	19				4					1	1						1				7	1			3		12
Jefferson, ...	208	16	5	2	2		1	1							1							1		2						1
Liberty, ...	126		2												1									1						
Prairie Creek,	69		1	3											1									1						1
Cascade, ...	106	19	7	18	3		1	5						1			2	1		1		2		3	3		1			5
Table Mound,	114	74	2	4				11						4																
Taylor, ...	173	83	2	26		1	2	8					3	1			1							4			1			2
Julien, ...	42	490	55	283	23	40	45	59	30	6	3	13	16	7	7	1	68	13	6	24	20	58	11	46	24	28	23	15	2	155
Iowa,.......	152	4	1	5				2						2	1							1		1				1		
Peru, ...	100		4	4	1			8						1								1		2						
Concord,....	110		3	2	1		1	1						1										3						1
Total,.....	2005	875	105	404	30	43	50	112	30	6	3	13	21	27	15	6	72	15	7	31	24	89	11	84	28	30	26	19	2	192

TABLE—Continued,

EXHIBITING THE PROFESSIONS, TRADES OR OCCUPATIONS OF THE INHABITANTS OF DUBUQUE CO., FOR 1856.

TOWNSHIPS.	Speculators.	Agents.	Wood dealers.	Traders.	Druggists.	Confectioners.	B'rding H.keepers	Hotel keepers.	Clothiers.	Physicians.	Dentists.	Lawyers.	Clergymen.	Teachers.	Musicians.	Printers.	Editors.	Artists.	Bankers.	Grocers.	Teamsters.	Chandlers.	Brick makers.	Watch makers.	Jewellers.	Gun smiths.	Coopers.	Clerks.	Rope makers.	Gardeners.	Miners.	Shepherds.
Washington,.										1			2																			
White Water,	1				2			1		3			1	1													7	3				
Moslem, ...										1				1							1						1		1	2	8	1
Vernon,.....										2			7										1				1			1		
Dodge, ...													2																			
Centre, ...								1		1										1	4							2			1	
New Wine,..					1			2		4			2																	1		
Jefferson, ...										1			3															1				
Liberty,.....																																
Prairie Creek,														2																		
Cascade, ...										2			2								2						3	1				
Table Mound,													3			1															4	
Taylor, ...				1				1		2				2						1	5											
Julien,......	8	1	2	16	18	7	21	19	2	22	5	38	14	8	8	21	4	4	19	47	56	5	9	10	9	3	15	155		23	208	
Iowa, ...																																
Peru, ...																														2		
Concord,....																										1						
Total, ...	9	1	2	17	21	7	21	24	2	39	5	38	36	14	8	22	4	4	19	49	68	5	10	10	9	4	27	162	1	29	221	1

TABLE—Continued.

EXHIBITING THE PROFESSIONS, TRADES OR OCCUPATIONS OF THE INHABITANTS OF DUBUQUE COUNTY, FOR 1856.

TOWNSHIPS.	Pedlers.	Boatmen.	Sailors.	Surveyors.	Wheelwrights.	Dress makers.	Barbers.	Weavers.	Hammer makers.	Well diggers.	Horticulturists.	Stage drivers.	Gentlemen.	Sup. Ind't of R. R	Nurserymen.	Iron Founders.	Saloon keepers.	Cobblers.	Leather dealers.	Liquor dealers.	Draymen.	Cigar makers.	Sash makers.	Turners.	Pilots.	Lock smiths.	Finishers.	Moulders.	Broom makers.	Tel. Operators.	Umbrella makers	Usurers.	Smelters.
Washington,...																																	
White Water,..																																	
Moslem, ...	1	2																															
Vernon, ...			1	1	2																												
Dodge, ...																																	
Centre, ...				2	1	2																											
New Wine,....							1	1																									
Jefferson, ...									1																								
Liberty,.......																																	
Prairie Creek, .										1																							
Cascade,......																																	
Table Mound, .																																	
Taylor, ...	1										1	4	1	3	1	1																	
Julien, ...	2	15		22	1	7	12								2		10	7	1	4	17	1	6	8	10	3	4	3	5	1	3	2	8
Iowa, ...					3																												
Peru,.........																																	
Concord,......																																	
Total,.......	4	17	1	25	7	9	13	1	1	1	1	4	1	3	3	1	10	7	1	4	17	1	6	8	10	3	4	3	5	1	3	2	8

TABLE,—CONTINUED.

SHOWING THE PROFESSIONS, TRADES, OR OCCUPATIONS OF THE INHABITANTS OF DUBUQUE COUNTY, FOR 1856.

TOWNSHIPS.	Book sellers.	Glass makers.	Book binders.	Architects.	Potters.	Collectors.	Liv'ry keepers.	Gamblers.	Upholsterers.	Seamstresses.	Pump makers.	Carvers.	Roofers.	Cooks.	Barkeepers.	Brewers.	Fruit dealers.	Auctioneers.	Farriers.	Patt'rn makers.	Land brokers.	Basket makers.	Book keepers.	Brokers.	Founders.	Actors.	Professors.	Gass fitters.	Sextons.	Milk men.	Sculptors.	Stewards.	Tanners.
Washington,..																																	
White water, .																																	
Moslem.																																	
Vernon, ...																																	
Dodge, ...																																	
Centre, ...																																	
New Wine, .																																	
Jefferson, ...																																	
Liberty, ...																																	
Prairie Creek,.																																	
Cascade, ...																																	
Table Mound,.																																	
Taylor, ...																																	
Julien, ...	3	2	2	1	1	1	6	2	6	17	1	1	1	1	7	11	2	7	2	2	7	3	6	3	4	8	1	2	1	1	2	1	1
Iowa, ...				1																													
Peru, ...																																	
Concord, ...																																	
Total, ...	3	2	2	2	1	1	6	2	6	17	1	1	1	1	7	11	2	7	2	2	7	3	6	3	4	8	1	2	1	1	2	1	1

TABLE—SHOWING THE PLACE OF NATIVITY OF THE INHABITANTS OF DUBUQUE COUNTY, FOR 1856.

STATES.	Washington,	White Water,	Moslem,	Vernon,	Dodge,	Centre,	New Wine,	Jefferson,	Liberty,	Prairie Creek,	Cascade,	Table Mound,	Taylor,	Julien,	Iowa,	Peru,	Concord,	TOTAL.
Ohio,	39	71	19	26	25	44	44	29	16	28	66	17	103	435	37	...	6	1005
Indiana,	7	14	2	8	21	15	12	8	...	...	48	...	19	84	8	...	...	246
Pennsylvania,	226	93	50	43	19	75	26	44	47	40	84	51	131	437	25	...	52	1143
Iowa,	157	161	226	212	84	298	60	320	...	176	201	372	156	2233	222	78	195	5246
New York,	60	85	20	42	40	71	191	51	22	38	75	71	74	1188	33	...	24	2085
Maine,	...	3	3	...	..	5	4	2	...	7	6	6	23	79	7	...	1	146
N. Hampshire	...	3	1	1	2	13	2	4	...	...	5	...	14	65	2	...	9	121
Vermont,	11	5	4	...	6	7	10	1	...	...	3	11	7	119	6	...	3	193
Massachusetts	2	5	3	2	6	6	8	7	...	9	7	4	48	188	2	2	2	296
Connecticut,	...	12	2	1	2	3	18	...	...	2	13	...	2	87	1	...	3	116
Rhode Island,	4	1	...	...	...	...	4	1	...	...	...	...	2	9	...	...	...	21
Virginia,	8	2	...	19	8	22	...	17	15	14	18	...	6	112	3	...	3	277
Kentucky,	2	8	3	30	5	21	11	11	...	6	8	1	7	117	7	...	5	242
Illinois,	11	14	18	50	28	47	22	18	...	14	35	8	68	269	15	...	17	634
Michigan,	2	11	2	1	9	7	3	1	...	...	1	2	19	57	1	...	1	117
Arkansas,	...	...	...	...	...	...	...	...	...	...	...	...	...	1	...	...	...	1
Alabama,	...	2	...	2	...	...	...	1	...	...	...	...	1	1	...	...	...	7
Louisiana,	1	2	3	...	...	...	...	...	...	1	...	...	2	20	6	...	4	39
Mississippi,	...	...	2	...	...	...	4	...	...	...	...	...	...	8	...	...	...	14
Florida,	...	...	1	...	...	...	...	...	...	...	...	...	...	...	...	...	...	1
N. Carolina,	...	2	1	1	4	2	1	1	...	...	4	13	3	6	2	...	...	40
S. Carolina,	...	...	...	...	...	1	4	...	...	...	...	...	...	...	1	...	...	6
Tennessee,	...	...	1	7	..	16	...	3	10	3	5	8	2	20	4	...	8	82
Missouri,	...	8	9	15	2	36	4	8	...	1	2	6	9	166	7	..	10	278
D. Columbia,	...	...	...	...	...	...	...	...	...	...	...	...	5	5	...	...	...	10
Unknown,	...	...	...	...	...	...	...	...	...	...	...	...	...	794	...	51	...	845
S. America,	...	...	...	...	...	...	...	...	...	...	...	...	...	1	...	...	...	1
Australia,	...	...	...	...	...	...	...	6	...	...	...	...	...	1	...	...	...	7
Georgia,	...	...	...	...	...	...	...	...	...	1	...	...	...	3	1	...	...	5
California,	...	...	...	...	...	...	...	...	...	...	1	...	...	...	...	...	...	1
Maryland,	2	12	4	9	..	2	4	2	...	6	8	2	5	96	6	...	2	160
New Jersey	...	7	1	4	..	4	...	2	9	1	3	...	4	46	...	...	1	82
England,	1	20	2	38	83	27	189	89	15	10	59	106	16	568	33	1	25	1282
Ireland,	151	171	108	250	17	138	82	70	150	218	65	271	176	2411	150	4	116	4598
Wales,	...	1	...	...	...	1	...	...	...	5	...	6	2	1	...	...	1	17
Scotland,	...	9	...	1	5	5	4	1	...	3	4	13	18	80	5	...	...	148
Germany,	26	17	272	1	12	150	281	325	467	10	161	88	14	2416	46	142	104	4533
France,	36	4	1	12	..	48	...	19	...	1	9	46	8	36	2	25	...	312
Austria,	...	...	1	...	..	4	...	1	...	...	...	...	1	35	...	9	1	52
Prussia,	...	...	2	...	..	5	9	4	...	...	...	...	...	30	...	76	...	126
Norway,	...	...	...	...	...	...	...	...	...	...	...	...	...	5	3	...	...	8
Sweden,	...	...	1	...	...	...	...	...	...	...	...	...	...	14	...	...	11	26
Holland,	...	...	...	...	...	1	2	...	...	...	...	1	...	25	...	37	...	66
On the Ocean,	...	...	1	...	...	...	...	...	...	...	...	...	...	1	...	...	...	2
Canada,	28	17	2	1	11	46	8	39	10	9	5	14	13	186	17	...	9	415
N. Brunswick	...	...	...	...	...	...	...	...	...	2	...	...	...	1	...	...	...	3
Switzerland,	2	...	2	...	..	16	...	20	...	...	...	...	...	141	3	25	...	209
Denmark,	...	...	...	...	...	...	...	...	...	...	...	...	...	1	...	...	...	1
Hanover,	...	...	...	...	...	4	...	...	7	...	...	...	...	5	...	30	...	16
Saxony,	...	...	...	...	...	2	...	...	...	...	...	...	...	...	...	7	...	9
East Indies,	...	...	...	...	...	...	...	...	...	...	...	...	...	1	...	...	...	1
Wisconsin,	...	2	1	3	..	12	7	6	...	3	3	4	17	110	2	...	2	172
Greece,	...	3	...	...	...	...	...	...	...	...	...	...	...	...	...	...	...	3
Belgium,	...	...	5	...	...	...	...	...	...	...	...	4	...	...	...	...	...	9
Poland,	...	...	10	...	1	...	...	...	...	...	...	...	...	5	...	...	...	16
Delaware,	...	...	...	6	..	...	...	...	...	...	...	...	...	14	...	...	...	20

TABLE,—SHOWING THE POPULATION OF FAYETTE COUNTY, FOR 1856.

TOWNSHIPS.	No. of dwelling houses.	Number of families.	Number of males.	Number of females.	Colored.	Married.	Widowed.	Native voters.	Naturalized voters.	Aliens.	Militia.	Deaf and Dumb.	Blind.	Idiotic.	Owners of land.	Paupers.
Jefferson,	32	34	97	96		60	7	30	4		27				33	
Windsor,	40	40	175	144	1	55	1	19	8	1	7	2			10	
Fairfield,	104	105	308	270		220	6	98	29		96				114	1
Pleasant Valley,	136	138	415	339		268	14	131	16	35	109			1	116	5
Auburn,	125	125	460	386		325	11	162	28	22	147	2	1	1	101	
West Union,	244	267	804	648		519	34	240	42	24	356				228	
Banks,	6	6	33	25		10	3	6		9	15				12	
Eden,	70	70	209	188		148	9	62	16	9	67	1			67	1
Putnam,	50	50	124	101		97	1	49	2	5	43				47	1
Clermont,	101	101	284	235		183	10	83	28	52	113				112	
Richland,	37	39	121	95		69	13	50	3	2	46	1			50	
Dover,	89	96	282	278		189	14	79	17	13	89			2	75	
Westfield,	227	235	653	571	43	358	21	150	21	2	96	3			171	3
Illyria,	101	101	331	279		218	5	107	8	15	101				101	1
Oran,	67	67	205	201		145	5	50	12	5	3				57	
Total,	1456	1493	4501	3856	44	2864	144	1316	234	194	1315	9	1	4	1294	13

TABLE,

SHOWING THE AGRICULTURAL STATISTICS OF FAYETTE COUNTY, FOR 1856.

TOWNSHIPS.	Acres of improved land.	Acres of unimproved land.	Acres of meadow.	Tons of hay.	Bushels of grass seed.	Acres of spring wheat.	Bushels harvested.	Acres of winter wheat.	Bushels harvested.	Acres of Oats.	Bushels harvested.	Acres of corn.	Bushels harvested.	Acres of potatoes.	Bushels harvested.
Jefferson, ...	528	5579	121	201	14	168	2812	....	....	45	1528	238	8460	9	1073
Windsor, ...	825	2659	15	153	....	342	3866	616	350	161	3676	426	5362	16	1220
Fairfield, ...	2573	8172	....	752	....	320	6665	....	....	202	9075	631	26400	9	1430
Pleasant Valley, ...	1557	7456	50	74	....	297	5082	....	125	125	4174	627	29335	22	3895
Auburn, ...	6082	8222	319	954	18	735	9047	....	....	209	8818	465	15210	53	6550
West Union, ...	4748	23176	2307	1287	4	1167	23912	190	....	316	13814	1141	39585	51	5569
Banks, ...	464	711	104	425	....	77	1563	....	....	18	630	152	4700	15	1850
Eden, ...	983	6760	753	1297	....	298	5560	8	....	74	2595	375	15290	31	4532
Putnam, ...	684	7932	....	455	....	63	965	....	....	31	1138	118	4150	9	1216
Clermont, ...	1496	4288	365	653	6	299	5529	....	....	50	250	286	11170	23	3715
Richland, ...	568	7129	....	1076	....	156	2639	....	....	20	659	251	7569	9	893
Dover, ...	1535	3147	21	27	1	464	10246	5	300	147	6716	515	20977	2	370
Westfield, ...	2836	12690	20	2	15	1142	7443	9	180	192	6569	911	48261	40	6410
Illyria, ...	1829	17213	26	13	30	308	6402	....	....	91	4364	792	33295	24	3682
Oran, ...	661	10554	....	563	....	113	1864	....	....	12	380	325	9280	9	1430
Total, ...	57369	125688	4101	6932	87	5949	93615	828	955	1693	64386	7254	279044	323	43835

TABLE,

SHOWING THE NUMBER AND VALUE OF HOGS, CATTLE, DOMESTIC AND GENERAL MANUFACTURES OF FAYETTE COUNTY, FOR 1856.

TOWNSHIPS.	No. of hogs sold.	Value of hogs sold.	No. of Cattle sold.	Value of cattle. sold.	Pounds of butter made.	Pounds of cheese.	Pounds of wool.	Value of domestic manufactures.	Value of general manufactures.
Jefferson, ...	80	815	92	3221	2220	....	30	18	....
Windsor, ...	89	521	17	1382	280	30	14	....	....
Fairfield, ...	229	1488	86	9710	8550	1500	445	158	....
Pleasant Valley, .	300	2989	193	3063	11665	6450	562	483	2104
Auburn, ...	271	2455	226	2791	4943	190	241	40	860
West Union, ...	514	3638	339	11370	12275	55	797	386	4225
Banks, ...	54	625	12	645	1800	1	1207	....	....
Eden, ...	127	683	116	4949	2500	780	154	25	....
Putnam, ...	47	80	62	2553	2790	....	65	....	....
Clermont, ...	145	936	79	2302	4330	180	71	634	1939042
Richland, ...	100	633	211	3461	6932	300	....	......	....
Dover, ...	284	2320	55	1818	825	600	160	224	8503
Westfield, ...	359	3354	84	3113	7935	390	1243	400	1320
Illyria, ...	298	2609	126	3594	9332	80	753	....	....
Oran, ...	58	240	108	5244	230	....	108	40	....
Total, ...	2755	23386	1806	59216	72657	10556	5850	2408	1956054

TABLE,

EXHIBITING THE PROFESSIONS, TRADES, OR OCCUPATIONS OF THE INHABITANTS OF FAYETTE COUNTY, FOR 1856.

TOWNSHIPS.	Farmers.	Laborers.	Blacksmiths.	Carpenters.	Wagon Makers.	Plasterers.	Stone Masons.	Stone Cutters.	Carriage Makers.	Machinists.	Millers.	Sawyers.	Millwrights.	Painters.	Cabinet Makers.	Chair Makers.	Tinners.	Milliners.	Tailors.	Hatters.	Shoemakers.	Harness Makers.	Bakers.	Butchers.	Mechanics.	Manufacturers.	Merchants.	Druggists.	Hotel Keepers.	Clothiers.
Jefferson,.........	33			2																										
Windsor,.........	41		2		2																									
Fairfield,.........	114																1													
Pleasant Valley,...	119		6	11	3	2	2				1	2	1								2						2			1
Auburn,.........	82		6	21			1			1	6	8	1						1		5	1				1	5		2	
West Union,......	174	77	7	37		2	15		6	3	2	1	3	3	1	1	3				7	2		1			22	1	6	
Banks,...........	14			1																					1					
Eden,............	58		3	3							1										1						2			
Putnam,.........	29	2		1			1																							
Clermont,........	58	30	5	11							2			1	1	1				1	2			1		1	4			
Richland,.........	61			4																										
Dover,..........	86	12	2	11							3	3	2	1							1						2		1	
Westfield,.......	137		10	30	2	1	3	1		1	3		1	1	2	2	1	2	1		5		1				7	1		1
Illyria,..........	107	17	3		1		3						4																1	
Oran,...........	57	29	1	2	1								2																	
Total,..........	1170	167	45	134	9	5	25	1	6	5	18	14	14	6	4	4	5	2	2	1	23	3	1	2	1	2	44	2	10	2

TABLE—Continued,

EXHIBITING THE PROFESSIONS, TRADES, OR OCCUPATIONS OF THE INHABITANTS OF FAYETTE COUNTY, FOR 1856.

TOWNSHIPS.	Physician.	Lawyers.	Clergymen.	Teachers.	Printers.	Editors.	Daguerrean Artist	Grocers.	Teamsters.	Brick Makers.	Jewellers.	Gun Smiths.	Coopers.	Clerks.	Carders.	Moulders.	Ostlers.	Wheelwrights.	Potters.	Distillers.	Hame Makers.	Surveyors.	Livery Keepers.	Lime Burners.	Dress Makers.	Tanners.	Stage Drivers.	Wine Makers.	Weavers.	Rope Makers.	Plough Makers.
Jefferson,.........																															
Windsor,..........																															
Fairfield,..... ...																															
Pleasant Valley,....	1	1		2						1			1	1	1																
Auburn,...........	4		1						1				4	3		2	2	1	2												
West Union,.......	4	7	2	11	2	1	1			1	1			5				1		6	2	1	1	1	1						
Banks,............																									1						
Eden,.............										2																					
Putnam,...........				1														1													
Clermont, ...	1							1		2		1			1										1	1	1	1			
Richland, ...				2																					1				1		
Dover,............	1																	1													
Westfield,.........	3		4	4							1			2				1				1			1	1				1	1
Illyria,...........	1			2									1	1																	
Oran,.............														1																	
Total,...........	15	8	7	22	2	1	1	1	1	6	2	1	6	13	2	2	2	5	2	6	2	2	1	1	5	2	1	1	1	1	1

TABLE—SHOWING THE PLACE OF NATIVITY OF THE INHABITANTS OF FAYETTE COUNTY, FOR 1856.

STATES.	NAME OF TOWNSHIPS.															TOTAL.
	Jefferson.	Windsor.	Fairfield.	Pleasant Valley.	Auburn.	West Union.	Banks.	Eden.	Putnam.	Clermont.	Richland.	Dover.	Westfield.	Illyria.	Oran.	
Ohio,	41	76	84	79	93	274	...	94	31	60	30	138	126	149	38	1288
Indiana,	50	12	22	1	40	90	...	4	1	5	18	27	153	26	67	516
Pennsylvania,	3	49	40	117	112	179	...	16	12	14	10	64	78	62	67	823
Iowa,	18	11	89	111	102	158	...	47	15	38	10	78	140	84	29	1930
New York,	23	39	134	89	193	268	1	98	77	90	56	29	223	60	56	1136
Maine,	...	...	1	7	12	6	8	...	...	6	...	...	23	2	3	68
N. Hampshire,	...	...	3	2	8	11	5	2	4	5	4	5	10	3	1	63
Vermont,	2	12	22	12	18	37	3	22	16	36	22	8	32	...	7	1249
Massachusetts,	1	...	19	19	5	12	...	3	22	8	7	5	14	2	1	1118
Connecticut,	1	7	4	3	1	7	...	8	4	7	1	6	25	7	3	84
Rhode Island.	...	2	...	1	1	6	...	...	...	...	2	...	7	...	...	19
Virginia,	6	1	20	26	5	21	...	1	...	4	1	8	15	15	11	134
Kentucky,	8	...	...	6	7	15	...	...	...	4	...	3	12	12	7	69
Illinois,	14	38	21	69	75	88	3	40	15	26	23	16	129	58	45	660
Michigan,	...	4	42	2	9	14	...	...	1	10	...	...	16	15	2	115
Alabama,	...	...	...	...	...	...	...	...	...	...	...	...	3	...	...	3
Lousiana,	...	...	...	...	2	...	...	...	...	1	...	...	...	...	...	3
Mississippi,	...	...	1	...	...	1	...	...	...	...	...	...	1	...	...	3
N. Carolina,	2	...	...	...	...	...	...	...	...	...	...	1	16	...	2	21
South Carolina	...	...	...	1	...	2	...	...	...	...	1	...	1	...	...	5
Tennessee,	...	...	...	1	2	2	...	4	...	1	1	1	4	4	...	20
Missouri,	...	...	...	1	2	...	...	...	2	3	...	1	...	3	3	13
Georgia,	...	...	...	...	...	...	...	...	...	...	...	...	1	1	...	2
Maryland,	1	5	2	...	2	11	...	4	...	1	1	5	8	8	1	49
New Jersey,	...	2	4	4	1	10	15	...	2	1	...	4	7	...	3	53
England,	3	4	4	7	24	38	...	4	4	26	6	7	28	37	9	201
Ireland,	...	11	4	3	5	54	15	47	...	90	...	13	23	6	24	295
Wales,	...	...	...	...	...	...	...	...	...	...	...	...	1	11	...	12
Scotland,	...	9	6	2	2	2	6	5	1	19	...	1	8	6	...	67
Germany,	...	18	18	30	57	38	...	1	10	11	2	3	10	6	4	208
France,	1	5	3	10	20	...	...	...	...	1	...	1	1	...	...	42
Austria,	...	...	...	...	1	...	...	...	...	...	...	...	...	...	...	1
Prussia,	10	...	...	...	...	...	...	...	...	...	...	...	...	...	...	10
Norway,	...	...	...	18	1	1	...	...	...	30	...	87	2	...	...	139
Sweden,	...	...	...	...	...	...	...	...	...	...	...	1	...	...	...	1
On the Ocean,	...	...	...	...	...	...	...	1	...	...	...	...	...	1	...	2
Cánada,	1	8	20	7	5	39	...	2	5	14	2	10	46	4	14	177
N. Brunswick,	...	...	...	3	1	...	...	...	...	...	1	...	...	...	...	5
Switzerland,	...	...	...	57	...	1	...	2	...	...	...	...	...	3	...	63
Saxony,	5	...	...	...	...	...	...	...	...	...	...	...	...	...	...	5
Wisconsin,	2	4	7	46	40	63	62	17	3	7	17	38	61	27	11	345
Wirtemburg,	5	...	...	...	...	...	...	...	...	...	...	...	...	...	...	5
Greenland,	...	2	...	...	...	...	...	...	...	...	...	...	...	...	...	2
Minnesota,	...	1	...	1	...	...	...	...	...	...	...	...	...	...	...	2
Delaware,	...	...	7	...	...	...	4	...	...	...	1	...	...	...	...	42
Unknown,	1	1	1	19	...	...	2	...	...	1	...	...	1	2	...	28

TABLE,

SHOWING THE POPULATION, AMOUNT OF PRODUCE, THE VALUE AND NUMBER OF CATTLE AND HOGS SOLD, OF FLOYD COUNTY, FOR 1856:

	TOWNSHIPS.					
POPULATION.	St. Charles.	Floyd.	Rock Grove.	Union.	Cedar.	TOTAL.
Number of dwelling houses,	155	77	53	99	28	412
Number of families, ...	167	82	60	100	28	437
Number of males, ...	533	267	179	282	82	1343
Number of females, ...	439	205	145	224	70	1101
Married, ...	318	166	156	208	58	896
Widowed, ...	16	10	6	8	1	31
Native voters, ...	248	119	68	128	29	592
Naturalized voters, ...	17	6	5	14	7	49
Aliens, ...	13	.....	2	1	.....	16
Militia, ...	231	115	65	117	29	957
Deaf and Dumb, ...	.....	2	.....	.....	.....	2
Insane, ...	1	.....	.....	.....	.....	1
Owners of land, ...	100	79	59	89	31	358
Paupers, ...	.....	1	.....	.....	.....	1
AGRICULTURAL STATISTICS.						
Acres of improved land....	1834	1658	795	1537	203	5427
Acres of unimproved land, .	20746	14524	7762	16285	5726	65044
Tons of hay, ...	1155	738	682	835	432	3842
Acres of spring wheat, ...	135	76	64	97	10	382
Bushels harvested, ...	2016	962	1128	1703	80	5889
Acres of oats, ...	90	27	18	87	2	224
Bushels harvested, ...	3207	1125	597	2800	30	7759
Acres of Corn, ...	388	383	342	577	129	1819
Bushels harvested, ...	14195	12200	12450	21531	3721	64097
Acres of Potatoes, ...	22	20	7	9	8	65
Bushels harvested, ...	3424	2907	960	2530	845	10666
HOGS, CATTLE, &C.—						
Number of hogs sold, ...	93	21	107	103	21	345
Volue of hogs sold, ...	966	193	871	800	52	2882
Number of cattle sold, ...	48	41	40	230	23	382
Value of cattle sold, ...	2713	2248	1540	3693	949	11143
Pounds of butter made, ...	4665	5350	640	4128	...	14783
Pounds of cheese, ...	702	150	.....	328	.....	1180
Pounds of wool, ...	273	.....	.....	93	50	416

TABLE,

EXHIBITING THE PROFESSIONS TRADES OR OCCUPATIONS OF THE INHABITANTS OF FLOYD COUNTY, FOR 1856.

OCCUPATIONS.	TOWNSHIPS.					TOTAL.
	St. Charles.	Floyd.	Rock Grove.	Union.	Cedar.	
Farmers,......	173	94	77	152	31	532
Laborers,......	20	10	4			34
Blacksmiths,......	8	6	4	3	1	22
Carpenters,......	49		2	12	1	64
Wagon Makers,......	2					2
Plasterers,......	2					2
Stone Masons,......	3	2		2	1	8
Stone Cutters,......	1					1
Carriage Makers,......				1		1
Machinists,......		1				1
Engineers,......	2					2
Millers,......	1		1		1	3
Sawyers,......	1	2				3
Millwrights,......		1				1
Painters,......	3					3
Cabinet Makers,......	2			1		3
Chair Makers,......		1				1
Tailors,......	1		1			2
Shoe Makers,......	1	2		1	1	5
Saddle and Harness Makers,......				1		1
Merchants,......	10	3		3		16
Agents,......				1		1
Hotel Keepers,......	1					1
Physicians,......	4		1	1		6
Lawyers......	3					3
Clergymen,......	1					1
Teachers,......	2			1		3
Printers,......	2					2
Editors,......	1					1
Coopers,......	3	1				4
Clerks,......	4					4
Livery Stable Keepers,......	1					1
Peddlers,......	1					1
Surveyors,......	1			1		2

TABLE,

SHOWING THE PLACE OF NATIVITY OF THE INHABITANTS OF FLOYD COUNTY, FOR 1856

STATES.	TOWNSHIPS.					TOTAL.
	St. Charles.	Floyd.	Rock Grove.	Union.	Cedar.	
Ohio	130	50	59	96	5	340
Indiana	42	56	40	47	2	187
Pennsylvania	58	24	12	27	6	127
Iowa	68	39	33	52	10	202
New York	221	100	40	111	48	520
Maine	28	4	8	1	1	42
New Hampshire	6	3		4		12
Vermont	14	34	2	10	4	64
Massachusetts	16	17	3	3		39
Connecticut	5	2	20	22	1	50
Rhode Island		1		1		2
Virginia	28	2	6	7	1	44
Kentucky	7	6	7	2	1	23
Illinois	154	72	25	54	26	331
Michigan	33	3	33	16	10	95
North Carolina	1	5	1	2		9
Tennessee	1		1	3		5
Missouri		1		1		2
Georgia	1	1		1	2	5
Maryland	2			1		3
New Jersey	12		4			16
England	20	11	12	20	11	74
Ireland	31	8		4	7	50
Wales				1		1
Scotland	17	3		1		21
Germany	12			12	8	32
France	1					1
Holland	2					2
Canada	22	20	16	17	1	76
New Brunswick	1					1
Wisconsin	39	10	2	7	3	61
Delaware		1		1	1	3
Unknown					4	4

TABLE,

SHOWING THE POPULATION, AMOUNT OF PRODUCE, THE NUMBER AND VALUE OF HOGS AND CATTLE SOLD, OF FRANKLIN COUNTY, FOR 1856.

POPULATION.	NAME OF TOWNSHIPS.			TOTAL.
	Morgan.	Washington.	Reeve.	
Number of dwelling houses,	15	46	72	133
Number of families,	15	53	81	149
Number of males,	33	158	245	436
Number of females,	33	132	179	344
Married,	25	91	165	281
Widowed,	2		2	4
Native voters,	15	58	87	160
Naturalized voters,	2	1	13	16
Aliens,		2		2
Militia,	16	55	88	159
Deaf and Dumb,	1			1
Idiotic,			1	1
Owners of land,	15	42	81	138
AGRICULTURAL STATISTICS—				
Acres of improved land,	220	885	1372	2477
Acres of unimproved land,	2940	4699	12404	20043
Acres of meadow,			140	140
Tons of hay	92	10	813	915
Acres of spring wheat,	5	25	28	58
Bushels harvested,	50	386	325	761
Acres of oats,		11	72	83
Bushels harvested,		405	1362	1767
Acres of corn,	80	233	362	675
Bushels harvested,	1800	8600	8225	18625
Acres of potatoes,	1	8	14	23
Bushels harvested,	50	1175	2457	3682
HOGS, CATTLE, &C.—				
Number of hogs sold,	5	20	145	170
Value of hogs sold,	12	114	424	550
Number of cattle sold,	83	36	52	171
Value of cattle sold,	1931	1335	1964	5230
Pounds of butter made,	140	2930	1830	4900

TABLE,

EXHIBITING THE PROFESSIONS, TRADES OR OCCUPATIONS OF THE INHABITANTS OF FRANKLIN CO., FOR 1856.

OCCUPATIONS.	TOWNSHIPS.			
	Morgan.	Washington.	Reeve.	TOTAL.
Farmers, ...	12	52	35	149
Blacksmiths, ...	1		1	2
Carpenters, ...			3	3
Wagon Makers,			1	1
Cabinet Makers,			1	1
Tailors, ...			1	1
Shoe Makers, ...	1			1
Harness Makers	1			1
Mechanics, ...			1	1
Traders, ...	1			1
Physicians, ...			3	3
Lawyers, ...		2		2
Gunsmiths, ...			2	2
Coopers, ...			1	1
Surveyors, ...			1	1

TABLE,

SHOWING THE PLACE OF NATIVITY OF THE INHABITANTS OF FRANKLIN COUNTY, FOR 1856.

STATES.	TOWNSHIPS.			
	Morgan.	Washington.	Reeve.	TOTAL.
Ohio, ...	20	63	98	186
Indiana, ...	4	71	76	151
Pennsylvania,	4	13	30	47
Iowa, ...	7	32	31	70
New York, ...	9	40	31	80
Maine, ...		1	1	2
N. Hampshire	1	1		2
Vermont, ...	1	2	12	15
Massachusetts,		2	2	4
Connecticut, ..		2	3	5
Rhode Island,		3	1	4
Virginia, ...	1	8	21	30
Kentucky, ...	4	3	5	12
Illinois, ...	10	18	53	81
Michigan, ...		3	2	5
Arkansas, ...		1		1
N. Carolina, ..		4		4
Tennessee, ...		4	6	10
Missouri, ...		2	1	3
Maryland, ...			3	3
New Jersey, ..	2		3	5
England, ...		2	2	4
Ireland, ...	1		16	17
Scotland, ...	1			1
Germany, ...			14	14
France, ...			1	1
Canada, ...		2		2
Switzerland, ..		2		2
Wisconsin, ...		3	6	9
Unknown, ...	1	4	6	11

TABLE,

SHOWING THE POPULATION OF FREMONT COUNTY, FOR 1856.

TOWNSHIPS.	Number of dwelling houses.	Number of families.	Number of males.	Number of females.	Colored.	Married.	Widowed.	Native voters.	Naturalized voters.	Aliens.	Militia.	Deaf and Dumb.	Blind.	Idiotic.	Owners of land.	Paupers.
Sidney,	166	178	512	452		319	29	74	11	5	141	4		1	106	3
Benton,	29	29	81	67	8	55	2	38	3		35				12	
Monroe,	41	46	113	86		68	10	49	2		47				44	
Scott,	162	164	474	441	2	298	16	185	2	5	158				117	
Franklin,	105	106	324	273		190	19	94	16	12	101			1	73	2
Madison,	63	63	207	182		115	9	61	14	1	62	3			57	2
Fisher,	31	31	79	77		27	11	32		1	31		1		20	1
Total,	597	617	1790	1578	10	1072	96	533	48	24	575	7	1	2	429	8

TABLE,

SHOWING THE AGRICULTURAL STATISTICS OF FREMONT COUNTY, FOR 1856.

TOWNSHIPS.	Acres of improved land.	Acres of unimproved land.	Acres of meadow.	Tons of hay.	Bushels of grass seed.	Acres of spring wheat.	Bushels harvested.	Acres of winter wheat	Bushels harvested.	Acres of oats.	Bushels harvested.	Acres of corn.	Bushels harvested.	Acres of potatoes.	Bushels harvested.
Sidney, ...	3889	17698	239		3	286	364	247	2044	76	1309	1557	70842	23	3774
Benton, ...	803	1712		417		55	148	3	20	22	390	512	18645	7	1014
Monroe, ...	621	15				55	230	11	99	30	102	420	15080	7	760
Scott, ...	4489	12769	10	15	6	398	2239	224	1725	287	2585	1931	76518	45	3915
Franklin, ...	2599	12378	1	513		202	1890	1576	1254	172	3620	1676	81293	21	1877
Madison, ...	2065	8814	3			317	1337	567	520	111	1488	914	40040	11	1554
Fisher, ...	248	707		143		11	40			6	120	81	4040	2	272
Total, ...	14664	54093	253	1088	9	1324	6798	2628	5662	704	9614	7091	306458	116	13166

TABLE,

SHOWING THE NUMBER AND VALUE OF HOGS AND CATTLE SOLD, THE VALUE OF DOMESTIC AND GENERAL MANUFACTURES OF FREMONT COUNTY, FOR 1856.

TOWNSHIPS.	No. of Hogs sold.	Value of Hogs sold.	No. of Cattle sold.	Value of Cattle sold.	Pounds of butter made.	Pounds of cheese.	Pounds of wool.	Value of Domestic Manufactures.	Value of General Manufactures.
Sidney, ...	479	3132	218	3357	6343	444	1130	965	
Benton, ...	162	1321	137	6712	4825	300	270	379	3185
Monroe, ...	130	1252	14	205	110		210	35	
Scott, ...	954	6412	468	11908	17855	190	1947	2137	2240
Franklin, ...	553	3904	229	3599	8355	2833	1593	1294	90
Madison, ...	475	3722	306	7306	7312		523	380	
Fisher, ...	35	220	74	4958	1006		6		500
Total, ...	2788	20263	1446	38045	45806	3767	5679	4190	6015

TABLE,—SHOWING THE OCCUPATIONS OF THE INHABITANTS OF FREMONT COUNTY, FOR 1856.

Occupations.	NAME OF TOWNSHIPS.							Total.
	Sidney,	Benton.	Monroe.	Scott.	Franklin.	Madison.	Fisher.	
Farmers,	153	43	41	156	114	60	1	568
Laborers,	1		5	23	10		4	43
Blacksmiths,	5	1	1	4	3	1	1	16
Carpenters,	6		2	11	2	1		22
Wagon makers,	2						1	3
Plasterers,					1			1
Stone masons,				2	1		1	4
Carriage makers,							2	2
Machinists,				1				1
Engineers,					1			1
Millers,	1			3				4
Millwrights,					1			1
Painters,	1							1
Cabinet makers.	1				1			2
Chair makers,							2	2
Tinners,	1							1
Milliners,							2	2
Tailors,	1			2	1			4
Shoe makers,	2	1	1	1	2			7
Saddle & harness makers,	2				1			3
Mechanics,	1		1			3		5
Merchants,	5	1						6
Hotel keepers,	2							2
Physicians,	4	1	2	2	2	2	1	14
Lawyers,	5							5
Clergymen,			1	2	1			4
Teachers,	1				1		1	3
Brick makers.	2				2			4
Gunsmiths,	3							3
Coopers,				1	1			2
Clerks,	7							7
Tanners,	1	1						2
Wheelwrights,	1			1				2
Seamstresses,							3	3
Sheriffs,	1							1
Peddlers,	1							1
Authoresses,		1						1
Dress makers,				1				1
Well diggers,				1				1

TABLE,

SHOWING THE PLACE OF NATIVITY OF THE INHABITANTS OF FREMONT COUNTY, FOR 1856.

STATES,	TOWNSHIPS.							
	Sidney.	Benton.	Monroe.	Scott.	Franklin.	Madison.	Fisher.	TOTAL.
Ohio,	147	23	81	208	55	43	23	530
Indiana,	178	4	31	141	91	31	6	482
Pennsylvania,	36	5	10	18	13	13	2	97
Iowa,	169	16	35	170	124	103	32	649
New York,	15	19	12	29	11	18	28	132
Maine,	....	....	....	2	1	1	2	6
New Hampshire,	1	2	1	1	....	....	3	8
Vermont,	2	....	2	16	....	2	3	25
Massachusetts,	2	9	....	10	....	3	6	30
Connecticut,	3	7	9	4	....	3	1	27
Rhode Island,	....	....	....	....	....	....	1	1
Virginia,	69	17	18	35	22	8	....	169
Kentucky,	74	3	1	62	59	39	3	241
Illinois,	35	8	8	83	69	25	21	249
Michigan,	....	3	....	9	2	3	3	20
Arkansas,	....	....	....	7	1	5	....	13
Alabama,	....	....	....	....	....	....	1	1
North Carolina,	34	....	6	23	12	2	1	78
South Carolina,	1	....	....	2	1	....	....	4
Tennessee,	15	1	3	10	28	2	6	65
Missouri,	95	13	84	103	58	54	9	361
Georgia,	1	1	....	....	2	....	....	4
Maryland,	1	1	....	....	2	1	....	5
New Jersey,	4	....	2	....	2	1	....	9
England,	3	3	....	14	10	1	1	32
Ireland,	5	1	....	5	8	1	....	20
Scotland,	1	....	....	....	2	2	....	5
Germany,	8	....	2	4	6	3	....	23
France,	....	....	....	....	....	1	....	1
Prussia,	1	....	....	....	1	....	....	2
Sweden,	1	....	....	....	....	....	....	1
Canada,	....	7	....	....	3	18	1	29
N. Brunswick,	1	....	1	....	....	....	....	2
Switzerland,	....	....	3	....	18	....	....	21
Wisconsin,	....	1	....	2	....	....	....	3
Delaware,	1	....	....	....	....	....	....	1
Kansas,	....	4	....	....	4	....	....	8
Nebraska Territory,	....	....	....	1	2	....	1	4
Pawnee Country,	....	....	....	1	....	5	2	8
District Columbia,	1	....	....	....	....	....	....	1
Utah Territory,	....	....	....	....	....	1	....	1

TABLE—SHOWING THE POPULATION, AMOUNT OF PRODUCE, NUMBER AND VALUE OF HOGS AND CATTLE SOLD, &C., OF GREENE CO., FOR 1856.

POPULATION.	NAME OF TOWNSHIPS.			
	Jefferson.	Washington.	Kendrick.	TOTAL.
Number of dwelling houses, ...	79	72	50	201
Number of families, ...	79	72	49	200
Number of males, ...	213	193	154	560
Number of females, ...	205	191	133	529
Married, ...	149	139	91	379
Widowed, ...	9	2	4	15
Native voters, ...	94	60	56	210
Naturalized voters, ...	1	1	3	5
Aliens,...	1		1	2
Militia, ...	70		53	123
Insane, ...	1			1
Idiotic, ...		1		1
Owners of land, ...	79	51	46	176
AGRICULTURAL STATISTICS—				
Acres of improved land, ...	1601	938	565	3104
Acres of unimproved land, ...	17036	10398	7508	34942
Acres of meadow, ...	2			2
Tons of hay, ...	208			208
Acres of spring wheat, ...	16	35	71	122
Bushels harvested,...	259	265	550	1074
Acres of oats,............	62	12	42	116
Bushels harvested,....	580	825	573	1978
Acres of corn,.........	642	503	403	1548
Bushels harvested,................	19020	15560	17748	52328
Acres of potatoes, ...	11	8	11	30
Bushels harvested,................	1307	1219	1018	3544
HOGS, CATTLE, &C.—				
Number of hogs sold,.............	157	59	95	311
Value of hogs sold, ...	2197	275	375	2847
Number of cattle sold, ...	82	23	102	207
Value of cattle sold, ...	3317	749	2693	6759
Pounds of made, ...	1770		3313	5083
Pounds of cheese, ...	66			66
Pounds of wool, ...	136	145	86	367
Value of domestic manufactures, ..	127		40	167

TABLE,

EXHIBITING THE PROFESSIONS, TRADES OR OCCUPATIONS OF THE INHABITANTS OF GREENE COUNTY, FOR 1856.

TOWNSHIPS.	OCCUPATIONS.																							
	Farmers.	Laborers.	Blacksmiths.	Carpenters.	Plasterers.	Carriage Makers.	Machinists.	Engineers.	Sawyers.	Tinners.	Tailors.	Hatters.	Shoemakers.	Mechanics.	Merchants.	Traders.	Physicians.	Lawyers.	Artists.	Coopers.	Basket Makers.	[illegible]	Tanners.	Surveyors.
Jefferson, ...	94	..	1	5	..	1	..	..	2	1	1	1	1	..	3	1	1	2	1	1	1	1	1	1
Washington, ...	63	5	..	2	1	..	..	..	..	..	..	..	..	3	2	..	..	..	..	..	..	..	..	..
Kendrick, ...	42	..	..	..	..	..	1	1	..	..	..	..	..	1	1	..	2	..	..	..	..	..	..	1
Total, ...	199	5	1	7	1	1	1	1	2	1	1	1	1	4	5	1	3	2	1	1	1	1	1	2

TABLE,

SHOWING THE PLACE OF NATIVITY OF THE INHABITANTS OF GREENE COUNTY, FOR 1856.

TOWNSHIPS.	Ohio.	Indiana.	Pennsylvania.	Iowa.	New York.	N. Hampshire.	Vermont.	Massachusetts.	Virginia.	Kentucky.	Illinois.	Michigan	North Carolina.	South Carolina.	Tennessee.	Missouri.	Maryland.	New Jersey.	England.	Ireland.	Wales.	Germany.	Delaware.	Wisconsin.
Jefferson, ...	6	111	19	32	7	3	3	..	42	23	64	5	11	1	13	12	3	2	1	1	1	..	2	..
Washington,	60	129	10	47	18	..	1	1	20	13	52	..	8	1	3	12	..	1	1	1	..	2	..	4
Kendrick, ..	41	111	11	34	12	3	2	..	6	11	19	9	8	..	8	..	..	..	..	12	..	..	..	..
Total, ...	162	351	40	113	37	6	6	1	68	47	135	14	27	2	23	24	3	3	2	14	1	2	2	4

TABLE,

SHOWING THE POPULATION, AMOUNT OF PRODUCE, NUMBER AND VALUE OF HOGS AND CATTLE SOLD, OF GRUNDY COUNTY, FOR 1856.

POPULATION.	NAME OF TOWNSHIPS.		
	Palermo.	Grundy.	TOTAL.
Number of dwelling houses,.... ...	39	22	61
Number of families, ...	39	25	64
Number of males, ...	164	63	227
Number of females, ...	142	66	208
Married, ...	125	48	173
Widowed, ...		3	3
Native voters, ...	78	28	106
Naturalized voters, ...	9	6	15
Aliens, ...	2		2
Militia, ...	68		68
Owners of land,..................	61	18	79
AGRICULTURAL STATISTICS—			
Acres of improved land, ...	1197	164	1361
Acres of unimproved land, ...	8952	2723	11674
Acres of meadow, ...		1028	1028
Tons of hay, ...		322	322
Acres of spring wheat, ...	26	16	42
Bushels harvested, ...	400	250	650
Acres of oats,....................	21	1	22
Bushels harvested, ...	930	20	950
Acres of corn, ...	219	109	328
Bushels harvested,................	5175	1080	6255
Acres of potatoes, ...	5	3	8
Bushels harvested, ...	670	335	1055
HOGS, CATTLE, &C.—			
Number of hogs sold, ...	7	7	14
Value of hogs sold, ...	60		60
Number of cattle sold, ...	10	9	19
Value of cattle sold, ...	386	450	836
Pounds of butter made,............	1700	1490	3190
Pounds of cheese, ...	100	500	600
Pounds of wool, ...	10		10

TABLE,

SHOWING THE PROFESSIONS, TRADES OR OCCUPATIONS OF THE INHABITANTS OF GRUNDY COUNTY, FOR 1856.

TOWNSHIPS.	Farmers.	Carpenters.	Wagon makers.	Engineers.	Physicians.	Brick makers.	Coopers.
Palermo,	72	10	2	1	1	1	1
Grundy,	36	......	......	......	......	......	......
TOTAL,	108	10	2	1	1	1	1

TABLE,

SHOWING THE PLACE OF NATIVITY OF THE INHABITANTS OF GRUNDY COUNTY, FOR 1856.

TOWNSHIPS.	Ohio.	Indiana.	Pennsylvania.	Iowa.	New York.	Maine.	N. Hampshire.	Vermont.	Massachusetts.	Connecticut.	Virginia,	Kentucky,	Illinois.	Michigan.	Louisiana.	Mississippi,	North Carolina.	Tennessee.	Maryland.	New Jersey.	England.	Ireland.	Germany.	Prussia.	Canada.	Wisconsin.
Palermo,	29	67	27	18	43	15	2	6	15	2	7	3	32	9	1	1	4	1	2	2	8	1	5	2	2	2
Grundy,	24	1	5	6	30	1	1	7	..	5	1	..	28	..	..	..	..	..	1	..	1	..	..	..	17	1
TOTAL,	53	68	32	24	73	16	3	13	15	7	8	3	60	9	1	1	4	1	3	2	9	1	5	2	19	3

TABLE—SHOWING THE POPULATION, AMOUNT OF PRODUCE, THE NUMBER AND VALUE OF HOGS AND CATTLE SOLD &c., OF GUTHRIE CO., FOR 1856.

POPULATION.	NAME OF TOWNSHIPS.				TOTAL.
	Cass.	Jackson.	Beer Grove	Dodge.	
Number of dwelling houses,.	135	114	59	47	355
Number of families, ...	160	114	62	49	385
Number of males, ...	457	341	186	177	1161
Number of females, ...	395	281	148	164	988
Married, ...	258	216	122	104	800
Widowed, ...	13	13		8	34
Native voters, ...	159	132	65	61	417
Naturalized voters, ...	9	2	7	3	21
Aliens, ...			2		2
Militia, ...	140	96	70	22	328
Idiotic, ...			1	1	2
Owners of land, ...	128	108	59	56	351
AGRICULTURAL STATISTICS.					
Acres of improved land.....	1834	2288	793	1132	6047
Acres of unimproved land, ..	7163	12895	7761	29682	57501
Acres of meadow, ...	21				21
Tons of hay, ...	248			305	553
Acres of spring wheat, ...	363	673	97	188	1326
Bushels harvested, ...	4775		1265	1370	7410
Acres of winter wheat, ...	6		11		17
Bushels harvested, ...	72		130		202
Acres of oats, ...	60	138	17	14	230
Bushels harvested, ...	1480	2	525	300	2307
Acres of Corn, ...	757	1451	220	464	2892
Bushels harvested, ...	33740		7855	14960	56555
Acres of Potatoes, ...	20		6	9	35
Bushels harvested, ...	2722		1423	1155	5300
HOGS, CATTLE, &c.—					
Number of hogs sold........	164		194	96	454
Volue of hogs sold, ...	1188	76	665	475	2404
Number of cattle sold, ...	77		77	72	226
Value of cattle sold, ...	2375	122	1779	1748	6024
Pounds of butter made, ...	5270		1467	5027	11764
Pounds of cheese, ...	249		60	12	321
Pounds of wool, ...	438	10	62	86	596
Value of dom. manufactures,	151	38	40		229
Value of gen'l manufactures,				450	450

TABLE,

EXHIBITING THE PROFESSIONS TRADES OR OCCUPATIONS OF THE INHABITANTS OF GUTHRIE COUNTY, FOR 1856.

OCCUPATIONS.	TOWNSHIPS.				TOTAL
	Cass.	Jackson.	Beer Grove.	Dodge.	
Farmers,	115	96	59	60	330
Blacksmiths,	4	2	3		9
Carpenters,	2	6		1	9
Brick layers,	1				1
Plasterers,	1				1
Stone Masons,				1	1
Millers,	3			1	4
Sawyers,	1		1		2
Millwrights,		2			2
Cabinet Makers,	1				1
Chair Makers,	1				1
Tailors,			2		2
Shoe Makers,	3	2			5
Saddle and Harness Makers,	1				1
Mechanics,	7			1	8
Traders,	3				3
Hotel Keepers,	3		1		4
Physicians,	6	2		1	9
Lawyers.	1		1	1	3
Clergymen,	2				2
Teachers,				1	1
Teamsters,	1				1
Brickmakers,			1		1
Gunsmiths,			1		1
Coopers,		1			1
Clerks,	6				6
Wheelwrights,	1				1
Seamstresses,	2				2

TABLE,

SHOWING THE PLACE OF NATIVITY OF THE INHABITANTS OF GUTHRIE COUNTY, FOR 1856

STATES.	NAME OF TOWNSHIPS.				TOTAL.
	Cass.	Jackson.	Beer Grove.	Dodge.	
Ohio,	49	139	19	106	313
Indiana,	34	223	3	80	340
Pennsylvania,	15	26	7	12	60
Iowa,		54		41	95
New York,	10	3	11	19	43
Maine,		5	1		6
New Hampshire,		3			3
Vermont,	1	4			5
Connecticut,	1		2		3
Virginia,	12	36	1	15	64
Kentucky,	16	14	2	1	33
Illinois,		39	3	35	77
Michigan,				8	8
North Carolina,	10	20	5	11	46
South Carolina,	1	2			3
Tennessee,	5	7	3	1	16
Missouri,		4			4
Georgia,		1			1
Maryland,	2	5	1	1	9
New Jersey,	6	1	1	6	14
England,	2	2	9		12
Ireland,	6	4		1	11
France,	1				1
Switzerland,	1			3	4
Unknown,	680	30	267		977
Nova Scotia,				1	1

TABLE,

SHOWING THE POPULATION OF HARRISON COUNTY, FOR 1856.

TOWNSHIPS.	No. of dwelling houses.	Number of families.	Number of males.	Number of females.	Married.	Widowed.	Native voters.	Naturalized voters.	Aliens.	Militia.	Insane.	Idiotic.	Owners of land.
Magnolia,	95	95	318	221	180	5	126	15	4	126			75
Lagrange,	61	66	193	163	128	3	74	2	2	65		1	63
Jefferson,	27	28	87	65	55	2	34			19			29
Boyer,	41	41	124	107	78	6	49	8	4	39	1		42
Raylan,	31	31	90	80	70	4	33	1		25			18
Sioux,	28	28	97	86	59	7	36	3	5	19			18
Calhoun,	44	47	145	124	90	6	65	2	6	57			42
Total,	327	336	1054	846	660	33	417	31	21	350	1	1	287

TABLE,

SHOWING THE AGRICULTURAL STATISTICS OF HARRISON COUNTY, FOR 1856.

TOWNSHIPS.	Acres of improved land.	Acres of un-improved land	Acres of meadow.	Tons of hay.	Bushels of grass seed.	Acres of spring wheat.	Bushels harvested.	Acres of winter wheat.	Bushels harvested.	Acres of Oats.	Bushels harvested.	Acres of corn.	Bushels harvested.	Acres of potatoes	Bushels harvested.
Magnolia,.........	1211	8857		637	5	61	907	3	70	13	413	488	21830	17	2640
Lagrange,.........	1306	5757		457		123	1526			61	1242	669	23357	18	3045
Jefferson, ...	587	2770				76	1007			16	290	295	6950	9	1700
Boyer,.	860	7592		551		121	1517			27	611	473	17205	16	2285
Raglan,...........	440	3659	30	385		40	585	4	50			253	6400	9	1030
Sioux, ...	260	6186		163		10	175					234	10780	7	755
Calhoun,..........	642	2212				48	854	6	95	34	1560	232	9395	13	1026
Total, ...	5306	37033	30	2193	5	479	6571	13	215	151	4116	2644	95917	89	12481

TABLE,

SHOWING THE NUMBER AND VALUE OF HOGS, CATTLE, DOMESTIC AND GENERAL MANUFACTURES OF HARRISON COUNTY, FOR 1856.

TOWNSHIPS.	No. of hogs sold.	Value of hogs sold.	No. of Cattle sold.	Value of cattle. sold.	Pounds of butter made.	Pounds of cheese.	Pounds of wool.	Value of domestic manufactures.	Value of general manufactures.
Magnolia, ...	113	841	60	1749	4765		116	58	250
Lagrange, ...	302	2628	88	2259	8794	309	114	7	
Jefferson, ...	213	1058	87	2207	960	50		179	2250
Boyer, ...	244	1570	91	2121	2759	8700	40		150
Raglan, ...	25	192	109	2846	1840	2800			
Sioux, ...	82	822	102	1255	2050				
Calhoun, ...	92	639	259	5655	2750	500	145		6750
Total, ...	1071	7750	796	18092	23909	12359	415	244	9400

TABLE,

EXHIBITING THE PROFESSIONS, TRADES, OR OCCUPATIONS OF THE INHABITANTS OF HARRISON COUNTY, FOR 1856.

TOWNSHIPS.	Farmers.	Laborers.	Blacksmiths.	Carpenters.	Wagon Makers.	Stone Masons.	Engineers.	Millers.	Sawyers.	Millwrights.	Cabinet Makers.	Milliners.	Tailors.	Shoemakers.	Mechanics.	Manufacturers.	Merchants.	Hotel Keepers.	Physicians.	Lawyers.	Clergymen.	Teachers.	Gunsmiths.	Coopers.	Clerks.	Broom makers.	Surveyors.	Lumbermen.	Weavers.	Tailoresses.	Stage drivers.
Magnolia,	129	4	2	12	..	..	2	..	1	..	..	..	..	1	..	..	5	1	2	2	1	..	..	1	5	1	1	1	..	..	..
Lagrange,	78	4	2	2	2	..	..	..	..	..	1	1	..	1	..	1	..	..	..	..	4	2	..	..	..	..	..	..	1	..	..
Jefferson,	26	8	..	..	..	..	..	1	..	1	1	..	..	..	..	..	..	..	..	..	..	..	..	..	..	..	1	..	..	..	..
Boyer,	55	4	1	1	..	1	..	2	..	1	..	..	..	..	..	..	..	..	1	..	..	..	1	..	..	..	..	..	..	..	..
Raglan,	27	..	2	2	..	..	..	..	..	1	..	..	..	..	..	..	..	..	..	..	..	..	..	2	..	..	..	..	..	..	..
Sioux.	41	2	2	2	..	..	..	..	..	..	..	..	..	1	..	..	..	..	1	..	..	2	..	..	..	..	..	..	..	1	..
Calhoun,	39	5	3	5	1	..	1	1	2	1	1	..	1	2	3	..	6	..	..	..	..	3	2	1	1	..	..	..	..	..	2
Total,	395	27	12	24	3	1	3	4	3	4	3	1	1	5	3	1	11	1	4	2	5	7	3	4	6	1	2	1	1	1	2

TABLE,

SHOWING THE PLACE OF NATIVITY OF THE INHABITANTS OF HARRISON COUNTY, FOR 1856.

STATES.	NAME OF TOWNSHIPS.							
	Magnolia	Lagrange.	Jefferson.	Boyer.	Raglan.	Sioux.	Calhoun.	TOTAL.
Ohio,	78	67	39	46	25	35	27	317
Indiana,	97	70	14	28	10	7	51	277
Pennsylvania,	29	13	4	6	3	8	5	68
Iowa,	114	57	17	37	44	43	44	356
New York,	33	10	22	16	8	15	19	123
Maine,		1		1		3	6	11
New Hampshire,	1	1	1		5	1	1	10
Vermont,	11	2		2	10	2	23	50
Massachusetts,	5	3	1	1	1	1	6	18
Connecticut,	1	2	1	1	5	10	3	23
Rhode Island,						3		3
Virginia,	17	20	12	16	2	1	8	76
Kentucky,	20	5		14	11	7	8	65
Illinois,	36	42	24	17	9	18	31	177
Michigan,	5	14	4			1	2	26
Texas,						1		1
Alabama,	2			3				5
North Carolina,	7	6	2	2		2	9	28
South Carolina,	2							2
Tennesssee,	17	16	1	5	6	4	4	53
Missouri,	6	15	8	4		4	6	43
California,							1	1
Maryland,	20							20
New Jersey,	5		1		1	1	1	9
England,	7	7		16	1	10	7	48
Ireland,	3	2		1	12		1	19
Wales,	1							1
Scotland,	3			4	8		1	16
Germany,	9		1			2	2	14
France,						1		1
Sweden,	1				7		1	9
Canada,	8	2		7		1		18
Wisconsin,	1	1		4	2	2		10
Nebraska,							2	

TABLE,

SHOWING THE POPULATION OF HARDIN COUNTY, FOR 1856.

TOWNSHIPS.	No. dwelling houses.	Number of families.	Number of males.	Number of females.	Married.	Widowed.	Native voters.	Naturalized voters.	Aliens.	Militia.	Deaf and Dumb.	Blind.	Owners of land.
Alden,	30	35	93	85	67	1	45	1	2	43			39
Eldora,	146	146	480	425	337	21	234	11	4	222		1	147
Etna,	32	32	112	89	71	3	37	7	10	44			43
Jackson,	58	58	174	152	98	7	65	7		56			50
Hardin,	62	64	261	155	152	8	131		14	120	3		100
Ellis,	17	17	59	49	37	1	24	1		22			18
Pleasant,	68	71	222	173	130	6	77	7	5	76			58
Providence,	81	84	260	219	161	10	97		1	90			94
Clay,	92	100	307	260	192	8	130	6	8	111			108
Union,	75	86	246	212	156	2	98	1	3	92			80
Total,	661	693	2214	1819	1401	67	938	41	47	876	3	1	737

TABLE,

SHOWING THE AGRICULTURAL STATISTICS OF HARDIN COUNTY, FOR 1856.

TOWNSHIPS.	Acres of improved land.	Acres of unimproved land.	Acres of meadow.	Tons of hay.	Bushels of grass seed.	Acres of spring wheat.	Bushels harvested.	Acres of winter wheat	Bushels harvested.	Acres of oats.	Bushels harvested.	Acres of corn.	Bushels harvested.	Acres of potatoes.	Bushels harvested.
Alden,	298	89				16	175			10	500	268	7825	2	380
Eldora,	2609	20750			2	67	836	3	68	114	4160	1040	31945	25	3228
Etna,	927	6392		439		27	465			4	125	287	8600	6	760
Jackson,	416	1393	4			43	415			2	50	263	6150	2	370
Hardin,	1159	17910	80	264		46	775	3	50	6	150	263	8120	9	1620
Ellis,	325	2963		70		20	30					37	500	2	250
Pleasant,	1035	10013		393		9	110			2	80	487	16250	11	1005
Providence,	1832	8813	11	19	20	183	3165			96	3340	871	26085	10	1264
Clay,	2632	5920	121	609		38	686			30	1105	956	32980	10	1445
Union,	1599	7041	3	655		64	1340			72	2030	1071	39265	8	1385
Total,	12832	81285	219	2449	22	513	8038	6	118	336	11540	5483	177720	85	12707

TABLE,

SHOWING THE NUMBER AND VALUE OF HOGS AND CATTLE SOLD, THE VALUE OF DOMESTIC AND GENERAL MANUFACTURES OF HARRISON COUNTY, FOR 1856.

TOWNSHIPS.	No. of Hogs sold.	Value of Hogs sold.	No. of Cattle sold.	Value of Cattle sold.	Pounds of butter made.	Pounds of cheese.	Pounds of wool.	Value of Domestic Manufactures.	Value of General Manufactures.
Alden, ...	81	666	59	1544	500				
Eldora, ...	187	1126	134	4584	8065	150	135		1500
Etna, ...	28	187	43	1545	3875			5	200
Jackson, ...	57	710	21	600	525				
Hardin, ...	39	141	57	1440	1547		25	977	
Ellis, ...	1	3	10	390	415				160
Pleasant, ...	105	549	50	1573	2105	419	23	20	
Providence, ...	266	1907	136	3544	6085	76	814	425	
Clay, ...	392	2943	131	772	7500	15	404		
Union, ...	124	1341	80	2490	6740	80	556	208	
Total, ...	1280	10573	721	18482	37357	740	1957	1635	1860

TABLE,

SHOWING THE PROFESSIONS, TRADES OR OCCUPATIONS OF THE INHABITANTS OF HARDIN COUNTY, FOR 1856.

OCCUPATIONS.	NAME OF TOWNSHIPS.										TOTAL.
	Alden.	Eldora.	Etna.	Clay.	Jackson.	Hardin,	Ellis.	Pleasant.	Providence.	Union.	
Farmers,	27	124	29	103	40	82	20	68	86	107	682
Laborers,	2	11	...	2	...	5	....	6	18	8	52
Blacksmiths,	1	8	1	6	3	5	....	2	1	2	29
Carpenters,	6	28	6	15	7	14	....	5	13	4	98
Wagon Makers,	...	2	...	1	1	1	....	1	....	....	6
Brick Layers,	...	...	...	1	...	...	....	....	....	....	1
Plasterers,	1	...	...	...	1	...	....	....	....	....	2
Stone Masons,	1	3	...	2	...	9	1	....	....	....	16
Stone Cutters,	...	...	...	...	...	1	....	....	....	....	1
Carriage Makers,	...	...	...	...	...	1	....	....	....	....	1
Engineers,	...	1	1	...	...	...	....	....	....	....	2
Millers,	1	3	1	...	...	2	....	....	....	....	7
Sawyers,	...	2	...	1	...	2	....	....	....	....	5
Millwrights,	2	4	...	...	2	1	....	....	....	2	11
Cabinet Makers,	...	8	1	...	2	2	2	....	3	....	18
Chair makers,	...	...	...	...	1	1	....	....	...	....	2
Tinners,	...	1	...	...	...	1	....	....	....	....	2
Milliners,	...	...	...	...	...	...	....	1	....	....	1
Tailors,	...	1	...	...	...	...	....	....	....	....	1
Shoemakers.	1	5	2	1	...	2	....	....	2	1	14
Mechanics,	...	1	...	...	...	1	....	....	....	...	2
Manufacturers,	...	...	...	...	...	3	....	....	....	....	3
Merchants,	1	15	1	1	3	5	....	3	2	....	31
Agents,	...	...	...	...	...	1	....	....	....	....	1
Druggists,	...	1	...	...	...	...	....	....	....	....	1
Hotel Keepers,	1	1	...	...	1	...	....	....	....	....	3
Physicians,	1	5	...	2	2	4	....	2	1	....	17
Lawyers,	...	3	...	...	...	...	....	....	...	....	3
Clergymen,	...	2	...	...	...	...	....	....	....	....	2
Teachers,	1	...	1	1	...	...	....	1	2	....	6
Printers,	...	1	...	...	...	...	....	....	....	....	1
Teamsters,	...	...	...	...	...	2	....	....	2	....	4
Brick Makers,	...	1	...	1	...	2	1	....	....	2	7
Jewelers,	...	1	...	...	...	...	....	....	....	....	1
Coopers,	1	1	1	3	2	...	....	1	1	....	10
Clerks,	1	4	...	1	....	...	....	....	....	....	6
Wheelwright,	1	1	...	....	....	...	....	....	....	....	2
Nurserymen,	...	3	...	....	....	...	....	....	....	....	3
Surveyors,	...	1	...	....	....	2	....	....	....	....	8
Potters,	...	1	...	....	....	...	....	....	....	....	1
Recorders,	...	1	...	....	....	...	....	....	....	....	1
Tailoresses,	...	...	1	....	....	3	....	....	5	....	9
Wool carders,	...	...	...	....	....	1	....	....	....	....	1
Weavers,	...	...	...	....	....	1	5	3	....	....	9
Dress makers,	...	...	...	....	....	2	1	...	....	....	3
Ship builders,	...	...	...	....	....	1	....	....	....	....	1
Broom makers,	...	...	...	....	....	...	1	....	....	....	1

TABLE,

SHOWING THE PLACE OF NATIVITY OF THE INHABITANTS OF HARDIN COUNTY, FOR 1856.

STATES.	TOWNSHIPS.										Total.
	Alden.	Eldora.	Etna.	Clay.	Jackson.	Hardin.	Ellis.	Pleasant.	Providence.	Union.	
Ohio,	25	178	36	137	48	58	25	76	44	89	716
Indiana,	54	91	32	100	61	59	9	92	142	70	710
Pennsylvania,	3	97	20	19	39	39	12	34	8	59	330
Iowa,	24	89	11	72	47	43	6	56	104	66	518
New York,	18	87	16	44	34	98	15	31	7	34	384
Maine,	....	....	....	2	....	1	10	....	....	....	13
New Hampshire	....	13	....	2	1	10	....	....	....	1	27
Vermont,	2	5	4	4	2	14	....	1	....	2	34
Massachusetts,	15	1	1	2	1	7	1	6	....	6	40
Connecticut,	6	3	....	1	1	7	2	....	....	4	24
Rhode Island,	....	1	....	....	1	1	....	....	....	2	5
Virginia,	....	40	4	13	10	5	....	23	7	13	115
Kentucky,	4	40	2	20	4	4	....	8	2	25	109
Illinois,	12	167	25	91	25	21	20	35	21	65	482
Michigan,	1	22	5	17	4	2	....	1	....	3	55
Louisiana,	1	....	....	....	....	....	....	....	....	....	1
Mississippi,	....	2	....	....	....	....	....	....	....	....	2
North Carolina,	....	2	1	13	12	16	....	5	113	6	168
South Carolina,	....	....	....	1	....	....	....	1	....	....	2
Tennessee,	2	9	....	2	1	1	....	4	14	2	35
Missouri,	1	1	1	1	....	....	....	....	....	....	4
Georgia,	....	1	....	1	....	....	....	....	....	....	2
Maryland,	2	7	2	2	2	1	....	2	1	2	21
New Jersey,	....	9	1	1	2	....	....	2	1	2	18
England,	2	9	....	9	2	2	4	....	....	7	35
Ireland,	....	8	5	1	4	3	....	4	....	....	25
Scotland,	....	3	1	....	....	8	1	....	....	....	13
Germany,	2	10	11	10	23	2	....	7	....	....	65
France,	....	1	....	....	....	....	....	....	....	....	1
Prussia,	....	....	1	....	....	....	....	....	2	....	3
Norway,	....	....	....	....	....	1	....	....	....	....	1
Sweden,	....	....	....	1	....	....	....	....	....	....	1
Holland,	....	....	....	....	....	....	....	....	1	....	1
Canada,	1	6	3	1	4	7	....	1	12	....	35
Denmark,	....	....	1	....	....	....	....	....	....	....	1
Hanover,	....	....	17	....	....	....	....	4	....	....	21
Wisconsin,	3	3	1	....	....	4	3	2	....	....	16

TABLE,

SHOWING THE POPULATION OF HENRY COUNTY, FOR 1856.

TOWNSHIPS.	No. dwelling houses.	Number of families.	Number of males.	Number of females	Colored.	Married.	Widowed.	Native voters.	Naturalized voters.	Aliens.	Militia.	Deaf and Dumb.	Blind.	Insane.	Idiotic.	Owners of land.	Paupers.
Baltimore, ...	119	119	325	346		222	16	120	6	11	122					70	
New London, ...	293	327	1013	866	2	585	57	369	32	33	416	1			1	219	
Canaan, ...	25	28	95	96		69	6	38	1	1	36					23	
Scott, ...	64	67	206	169		130	7	63	5		61					57	
Jackson, ...	143	147	441	378		275	23	164	5	10	149			1		131	
Centre, ...	438	517	2642	2097	6	1479	105	1012	130	412	1260	3		4	2	604	1
Marion, ...	142	153	465	434		287	17	161	9	2	144		1			125	
Wayne, ...	76	91	238	199		109	12	103	1	3	87		1		1	67	
Salem, ...	312	319	869	856		542	55	301	24	20	289			1		218	
Tippecanoe, ...	199	199	703	556		371	29	119	14	102	211	7		1		99	
Trenton, ...	210	216	601	630		375	43	223	13	11	200					180	1
Jefferson, ...	190	200	614	556		373	37	224	7	8	202			1	1	160	
Total, ...	2211	2183	8212	7183	8	4817	407	2897	247	613	3177	11	2	8	5	1953	2

TABLE,

SHOWING THE AGRICULTURAL STATISTICS OF HENRY COUNTY, FOR 1856.

TOWNSHIPS.	Acres of improved land.	Acres of unimproved land.	Acres of meadow.	Tons of hay.	Bushels of grass seeds.	Acres of spring wheat.	Bushels harvested.	Acres of winter wheat.	Bushels harvested.	Acres of oats.	Bushels harvested.	Acres of corn.	Bushels harvested.	Acres of potatoes.	Bushels harvested.
Baltimore, ..	2970	6570	366	345	69	345	3926	301	5189	441	12986	1104	54900	29	3398
New London,	11061	4562	1705	1604	371	1777	22143	202	2620	1585	49144	3367	171290	55	6187
Cannan, ...	940	3243	64	73	3	298	4229	35	279	268	9090	502	25340	18	3345
Scott, ...	2871	6913	196	96	104	636	10717	133	2260	272	12087	786	39450	14	2610
Jackson, ...	5053	4371	755	798	1025	1301	16467	177	2860	739	18375	1815	84135	38	3884
Centre, ...	6914	15735	1205	1458	143	1063	12287	447	7624	1247	43707	2766	150235	36	6787
Marion, ...	5633	11922	396	438	18	621	7353	279	3466	748	27478	1941	105470	34	4436
Wayne, ...	2853	4263	291	242	58	627	10018	81	1411	321	10889	892	40190	20	2849
Salem, ...	8499	16402	1443	1641	830	1387	16369	146	3130	1013	37714	2313	120609	21	2144
Tippecanoe, .	5194	11809	602	532	336	633	7055	416	7019	778	26505	1908	92908	33	3782
Trenton, ...	5176	6935	741	727	145	323	4250	645	8282	574	18109	1702	89115	42	4684
Jefferson, ...	7476	14568	790	557	174	1448	13788	147	1600	874	29751	3032	160835	49	4690
Total, ...	64640	108343	8563	8511	3276	10459	129102	3009	45740	8860	295835	22128	1133677	389	48796

TABLE,

SHOWING THE NUMBER AND VALUE OF HOGS, CATTLE, DOMESTIC AND GENERAL MANUFACTURES OF HENRY COUNTY, FOR 1856.

TOWNSHIPS.	No. of hogs sold.	Value of hogs sold.	No. of Cattle sold.	Value of cattle sold.	Pounds of butter made.	Pounds of cheese.	Pounds of wool.	Value of domestic manufactures.	Value of general manufactures.
Baltimore, ...	1030	7086	224	6067	12215	681	1284	4147	10357
New London, ...	1709	17033	233	6830	16980	4920	2979	3723	12665
Canaan, ...	106	747	18	405	5426	475	241	154	500
Scott, ...	687	4716	180	4906	6280		2210	395	50
Jackson, ...	1261	9827	195	5677	17367	1190	1700	857	8375
Centre, ...	1590	15481	378	10119	22655	585	2842	1506	1105
Marion, ...	1037	10389	248	6586	21324	225	1590	1597	
Wayne, ...	509	4930	106	2490	8597	1450	1378	486	28
Salem, ...	2588	15684	276	7249	17680	1730	9017	1455	1800
Tippecanoe, ...	1412	13465	440	12968	18332	367	2943	2602	12190
Trenton, ...	1384	13756	268	6560	19205	450	2698	1616	85
Jefferson, ...	2346	19483	281	7395	18773	1545	2159	1733	
Total, ...	15629	132597	2847	77252	184864	13618	31041	20271	47155

TABLE,

EXHIBITING THE PROFESSIONS, TRADES OR OCCUPATIONS OF THE INHABITANTS OF HENRY COUNTY, FOR 1856.

TOWNSHIPS.	Farmers.	Laborers.	Blacksmiths.	Carpenters.	Wagon Makers	Brick Layers.	Plasterers.	Stone Masons.	Stone Cutters.	Carriage Makers.	Machinists.	Engineers.	Millers.	Sawyers.	Millwrights.	Painters.	Cabinet Makers.	Chair Makers.
Baltimore, ...	121	19	3					1					5		1			
New London,..	166	219	9	30	3	1				2			1		2	1	3	
Canaan, ...	30	1	1				1											
Scott, ...	88	1	1	3			1										1	
Jackson, ...	163	28	2	9	1			1				2	2	2				
Centre, ...	256	425	31	221	9		29	11	10	5	3	34	5	14		17	14	1
Marion, ...	150		4	5					1							2		
Wayne,.... ..	105		1	8				1										
Salem, ...	269	8	9	19	11	4	1			1			1			1	2	
Tippecanoe, ...	187	188	3	28				1				1	11	1	3			
Trenton, ...	178	17	12	20	5	2	4	3					2		2		1	1
Jefferson, ...	159	8	3	15	4		3	1			1	1	1			1	1	
Total, ...	1872	914	79	358	33	7	39	19	11	8	4	38	23	17	8	22	22	2

TABLE—Continued,

EXHIBITING THE PROFESSIONS, TRADES OR OCCUPATIONS OF THE INHABITANTS OF HENRY COUNTY, FOR 1856.

TOWNSHIPS.	Tinners.	Milliners.	Tailors.	Shoemakers.	Saddle & harness makers.	Bakers.	Butchers.	Mechanics.	Manufacturers.	Merchants.	Agents.	Traders.	Druggists.	Hotel Keepers.	Physicians.	Dentists.	Lawyers.	Clergymen.
Baltimore,....				2				13		4					2			
New London,.	1	1	2	7	6	1		2		8	1			1	8		1	5
Canaan,......																		
Scott,........										2					2			
Jackson, ...		1	1	2					3	1					1			1
Centre, ...	11	6	17	13	15	3	8	2		41	5	3	3	8	13	2	46	22
Marion,......							2	1			1							1
Wayne,......		2																1
Salem,.......	5	3	2	5	3	1		3		15				2	10			2
Tippecanoe, ..		1	1	1				1										
Trenton, ...		6	1	5	1		1		2	8		2			1		1	
Jefferson, ...		3		1	1					5				1	4		1	
Total,......	17	23	24	36	26	5	11	22	5	84	7	5	3	12	41	2	49	32

TABLE—Continued,

EXHIBITING THE PROFESSIONS, TRADES OR OCCUPATIONS OF THE INHABITANTS OF BENRY COUNTY, FOR 1856.

TOWNSHIPS.	Teachers.	Musicians.	Printers.	Editors.	Artists.	Daguerrean Artists.	Bankers.	Teamsters.	Brick Makers.	Jewellers.	Gun Smiths.	Coopers.	Clerks.	Potters.	Stage Drivers.	Post Masters.	Weavers.	Nurserymen.
Baltimore,....	1							2					1	4				
New London,..	8		1					1	1	1		2	12		5	1	1	
Canaan,......																		
Scott,.........						1												2
Jackson,......	4											1						
Centre,.......	14	1	8	2	3		3	56	30	3		3	65		19			3
Marion,.......	1											1						
Wayne,.......	1																	
Salem,........	12		1		2			4	3	1		3	4					6
Tippecanoe,...	3	1							1			2	2					
Trenton,......	1										1	2					7	
Jefferson,.....	5							2				3	2					
Total,.. ..	50	2	10	2	5	1	3	65	35	5	1	17	86	4	24	1	8	11

TABLE,—Continued.

SHOWING THE PROFESSIONS, TRADES, OR OCCUPATIONS OF THE INHABITANTS OF HENRY COUNTY, FOR 1856.

TOWNSHIPS.	Glovers.	Miners.	Carders.	Surveyors.	Lumbermen.	Prairie Brakers.	Fariers.	Peddlers.	Fann Mill Makers.	Wheelwrights.	Confectioners.	Barbers.	Waiters.	Liverymen.	Plow Makers.	Tobacconists.
Baltimore,																
New London,																
Canaan,																
Scott,	1	1														
Jackson,																
Centre,			1	3	2		1	5		1	2	3	16	3	1	2
Marion,		1														
Wayne,																
Salem,			1	1	2	1										
Tippecanoe,																
Trenton,							1	1	1							
Jefferson,																
Total,	1	2	2	4	4	1	2	6	1	1	2	3	16	3	1	2

TABLE,

SHOWING THE PLACE OF NATIVITY OF THE INHABITANTS OF HENRY COUNTY, FOR 1856.

STATES.	TOWNSHIPS.												
	Baltimore,	New London	Canaan.	Scott.	Jackson.	Centre.	Marion.	Wayne.	Salem.	Tippecanoe.	Trenton.	Jefferson.	TOTAL.
Ohio,	121	418	83	118	171	1306	224	127	353	274	377	319	3891
Indiana,	87	142	17	9	143	341	108	47	244	173	88	129	1527
Pennsylvania,	45	175	17	53	91	514	93	38	95	68	121	79	1398
Iowa,	220	485	34	65	219	871	236	79	467	312	377	311	3676
New York,	7	104	15	32	17	157	32	22	45	19	23	22	495
Maine,	1	4		1	4	50		1	1	3	3	1	69
N. Hampshire,		2				15		4	4	2			27
Vermont,	10	27	1		13	26	3	1	10	11			102
Massachusetts,	4	15			1	57	11	7	4	3		4	106
Connecticut,	7	7	3	1	1	70	1	4	6	2		3	105
Rhode Island.					1	2			3	2		1	9
Virginia,	28	151		34	38	206	38	53	73	47	63	68	799
Kentucky,	28	39	2	16	13	162	21	13	22	30	17	22	385
Illinois,	27	67	2	6	16	111	52	4	70	35	18	40	448
Michigan,		2	4	16	1	12	1			2		2	40
Alabama,	1					5			7			2	15
Lousiana,		1											1
Mississippi,									6				6
N. Carolina,	11	7		1	25	37	23		99	38	15	13	279
South Carolina	3	1	1			6	1		5	5	5		27
Tennessee,	16	28	1	4	5	84	13	12	24	15	21	35	208
Missouri,	4	3		2	2	21	2	2	14	2	2	5	59
Georgia,	1	2				3			4		1	1	12
California,						1							1
Maryland,	4	25		6	3	39	11	12	17	17	23	26	183
New Jersey,		17			4	52	1	2	26	8	4	16	130
England,	3	36	10		2	90	2	2	48	10	5	18	226
Ireland,	1	78		7	6	335	10	2	8	130	3		580
Wales,	1	9			1	11	2	4			2	16	46
Scotland,		6		1		7	1	1		2		1	19
Germany,	17	15		1	8	88	8		1	13	31	4	181
France,						4			1	4	15	17	41
Austria,						1							4
Russia,						1							1
Prussia,	11					1			2	1	1		16
Norway,					2				8				10
Sweden,		5				3				14	16		38
Holland,									1	1	1		3
On the Ocean,						1							1
Canada,	2	4	1	1	36	16	1		52	8	2	5	128
Switzerland,	1										3		4
Denmark,										1			1
Hanover,						1							1
West Indies,						21							20
Wisconsin,		1				8			1		3		8
Delaware,	1	3		1		14	4		2	7			32
District Columbia,						1			2	1	1		5
Oregon,						1							1
Unknown,					1	31							32

TABLE,

SHOWING THE POPULATION, AMOUNT OF PRODUCE, NUMBER AND VALUE OF HOGS AND CATTLE SOLD, OF HOWARD COUNTY, FOR 1856.

POPULATION.	NAME OF TOWNSHIPS.				TOTAL.
	Vernon Springs.	New Oregon.	Howard.	Jamestown	
Number of dwelling houses, ...			43	51	94
Number of families, ...			43	51	94
Number of males, ...			135	117	252
Number of females, ...			108	84	192
Married, ...			85	89	174
Widowed, ...			8	6	14
Native voters, ...			44	61	105
Naturalized voters, ...			13	3	16
Aliens, ...			5	4	9
Militia, ...			53	53	106
Idiotic, ...			1		1
Owners of land, ...			44		44
AGRICULTURAL STATISTICS—					
Acres of improved land, ...			458		458
Acres of unimproved land, ...			8423		8423
Tons of hay, ...				14	14
Acres of spring wheat, ...				36	36
Bushels harvested, ...				800	800
Acres of oats, ...				4	4
Bushels harvested, ...				180	180
Acres of corn, ...			164	86	250
Bushels harvested, ...			3760	1875	5635
Acres of potatoes, ...			7	4	21
Bushels harvested, ...			900	850	1750
HOGS, CATTLE, &C.—					
Number of hogs sold, ...			8	1	9
Value of hogs sold, ...			20	13	33
Number of cattle sold, ...			38	17	55
Value of cattle sold, ...			1530	613	2143
Pounds of butter made, ...			200	350	550
Pounds of wool, ...				40	40
Value of domestic manufactures, ...				20	20

TABLE,

SHOWING THE PROFESSIONS, TRADES OR OCCUPATIONS OF THE INHABITANTS OF HOWARD COUNTY, FOR 1856.

TOWNSHIPS.	Farmers.	Laborers.	Blacksmiths.	Carpenters.	Stone Masons.	Milliners.	Shoe makers.	Harness makers	Merchants.	Printers.	Surveyors.	Wire drawers.	Shipmasters.
Vernon Springs,	..	..	..	..	..	..	..	..	..	..	..	..	..
New Oregon,	..	..	..	..	..	..	..	..	..	..	..	..	..
Howard,	44	1	..	2	..	1	1	1	2	..	2	1	..
Jamestown,	66	..	1	2	1	..	..	..	1	1	..	..	1
Total,	110	1	1	4	1		1	1	3	1	2	1	1

TABLE,

SHOWING THE PLACE OF NATIVITY OF THE INHABITANTS OF HOWARD COUNTY, FOR 1856.

TOWNSHIPS.	Ohio.	Indiana.	Pennsylvania.	Iowa.	New York.	Maine.	N. Hampshire.	Vermont.	Massachusetts.	Connecticut.	Rhode Island.	Virginia,	Illinois.	Michigan.	Tennessee.	Maryland.	New Jersey.	England.	Ireland.	Scotland.	Germany.	Canada.	Wisconsin.
Vernon Springs,	..	..	..	..	..	..	..	..	..	..	..	..	..	..	..	..	..	..	..	..	..	..	..
New Oregon,	..	..	..	..	..	..	..	..	..	..	..	..	..	..	..	..	..	..	..	..	..	..	..
Howard,	5	5	22	7	76	3	15	..	8	3	..	3	24	3	..	1	4	3	26	3	11	10	11
Jamestown,	19	3	2	3	52	1	16	33	10	5	2	..	8	2	1	..	3	10	3	1	1	7	12
Total,	24	8	24	15	128	4	31	33	18	8	2	3	32	5	1	1	7	13	29	4	12	17	23

TABLE,

SHOWING THE POPULATION OF IOWA COUNTY, FOR 1856.

TOWNSHIPS.	No. of dwelling houses.	Number of families.	Number of males.	Number of females.	Married.	Widowed.	Native voters.	Naturalized voters.	Aliens.	Militia.	Deaf and Dumb.	Blind.	Idiotic.	Owners of land.
Marengo,	162	169	492	419	325	24	194	8	24	205				145
English,	166	185	600	513	383	11	152	21	7	112		1		147
Green,	78	80	261	199	147	10	60	37	17	73	2		1	81
Iowa,	42	42	114	103	79	5	42	7	8	53				42
Cono,	32	32	117	96	54	6	35			35				30
Hartford,	56	74	241	221	148	9	99	12	2	101			5	69
Fillmore,	98	109	317	276	214	14	112	14	11	96				88
Troy,	37	42	117	91	80	6	29	11	7	21				42
Lenox,	48	48	179	133	79	9	16	68		61				5
Honey Creek,	65	69	224	160	131	8	85	9		82				63
Total,	784	850	2662	2211	1640	102	824	187	76	839	2	1	6	712

TABLE,

SHOWING THE AGRICULTURAL STATISTICS OF IOWA COUNTY, FOR 1856.

TOWNSHIPS.	Acres of improved land.	Acres of unimproved land.	Acres of meadow.	Tons of hay.	Bushels of grass seed.	Acres of spring wheat.	Bushels harvested.	Acres of winter wheat	Bushels harvested.	Acres of oats.	Bushels harvested.	Acres of corn.	Bushels harvested.	Acres of potatoes.	Bushels harvested.
Marengo,	2438	12028	16	21		363	5668			239	9397	1195	59960	16	2154
English,	3253	16601	285	51	30	330	5828			156	5148	1099	39655	38	3362
Green,	2018	12601	21	33		383	5205	10	300	110	2799	1367	44987	27	5200
Iowa,	1067	5147	15			63	484			66	2312	369	14280	12	1441
Cono,	1248	4295	38	28	1	170	2117	8	89	126	4000	598	30350	5	694
Hartford,	1556	10972	4	419		153	2675	5	75	45	1480	648	22145	16	2162
Fillmore,	1568	10530	37	13		141	2685	2	45	13	316	604	29620	17	2285
Troy,	500					87	764			44	1970	328	13045	10	1572
Lenox,	760	12113	50	346		99	1590			128	3050	359	18675	20	1715
Honey Creek,	1620	8988	41	27		378	4244	8	100	237	8165	873	46480	14	2142
Total,	16028	93276	507	938	31	2167	31260	33	609	1164	38637	7440	319197	175	22727

TABLE,

SHOWING THE NUMBER AND VALUE OF HOGS AND CATTLE SOLD, THE VALUE OF DOMESTIC AND GENERAL MANUFACTURES OF IOWA COUNTY, FOR 1856.

TOWNSHIPS.	No. of Hogs sold.	Value of Hogs sold.	No. of Cattle sold.	Value of Cattle sold.	Pounds of butter made.	Pounds of cheese.	Pounds of wool.	Value of Domestic Manufactures.	Value of General Manufactures.
Marengo, ...	708	5617	35	1148	9880	320			150
English, ...	615	3975	63	1619	4535	620	1525	1025	
Green, ...	560	4855	82	2563	1950		715	2	
Iowa, ...	175	721	157	2044	2216	35	306	353	600
Cono, ...	413	2545	54	1243	2635	120	105	173	
Hartford, ...	60	471	7	185	210				
Fillmore, ...	211	1668	98	1643	1408	1019	47	32	
Troy, ...	166	1502	30	1123	3041		88		
Lenox, ...	51	448	19	835	2475				
Honey Creek, ...	308	1743	64	1670	3407	143	484	22	1500
Total, ...	3267	23545	609	14073	31807	2257	3270	1607	2250

TABLE,

EXHIBITING THE PROFESSIONS TRADES OR OCCUPATIONS OF THE INHABITANTS OF IOWA COUNTY, FOR 1856.

Townships.	Farmers.	Laborers.	Blacksmiths.	Carpenters.	Wagon makers.	Plasterers.	Stone masons.	Stone Cutters.	Machinists.	Engineers.	Millers.	Sawyers.	Millwrights.	Painters.	Cabinet Makers.	Chair Makers.
Marengo,	152	7	6	25	1		1					4		1		
English,	140	1	5	21	2	1							1	1	1	3
Green,	131	6		4												
Iowa,	32	23	2	1	1	1						1				1
Cono,	30															
Hartford,	51	6	2	15	1		1	1		1	3	1				
Fillmore,	85	22	6	8						5	1				1	
Troy,	55	2	2	2					1			2				
Lenox,	45		1	18	3		6									
Honey Creek,	88	3		11	1		1				4					
Total,	809	70	24	105	9	2	9	1	1	6	8	8	1	2	2	4

TABLE—CONTINUED,

FXHIBITING THE PROFESSIONS, TRADES, OR OCCUPATIONS OF THE INHABITANTS OF IOWA COUNTY, FOR 1856.

TOWNSHIPS.	Tinners.	Milliners.	Tailors.	Shoemakers.	Harness Makers.	Butchers.	Merchants.	Speculators.	Druggists.	Hotel Keepers.	Physicians.	Lawyers.	Clergymen.	Teachers.	Teamsters.	Brick Makers.
Marengo,..............	3		1	1			5	1	2	4	7	6	2			1
English,..............				1			4			1	2		2			1
Green,................																
Iowa,.................		1														1
Cono,.................											1					
Hartford,.............				2							1	1			3	
Fillmore,.............		1		2			5				1			2		3
Troy,.................					3	1										
Lenox,................			1	5	1		3				1			1		
Honey Creek,..........			2	1			2			1				1		
Total,................	3	2	4	12	4	1	19	1	2	6	13	7	4	4	3	6

TABLE—Continued,

EXHIBITING THE PROFESSIONS, TRADES, OR OCCUPATIONS OF THE INHABITANTS OF IOWA COUNTY, FOR 1856.

TOWNSHIPS.	Watch Makers.	Gun Smiths.	Coopers.	Clerks.	Stage Drivers.	Surveyors.	County Judges.	Sheriffs.	Livery Keepers.	Wheelwrights.	Students.	Tailoresses.	Lock Smiths.	Gardeners.	Book Binders.
Marengo,	2			2	1	1	1	1	1						
English,				1											
Green,															
Iowa,															
Cono,															
Hartford,		1								2	1				
Fillmore,			2									1			
Troy,	1			1											
Lenox,	2	1	1										1	1	1
Honey Creek,															
Total,	5	2	3	4	1	1	1	1	1	2	1	1	1	1	1

TABLE,

SHOWING THE PLACE OF NATIVITY OF THE INHABITANTS OF IOWA COUNTY, FOR 1856.

STATES.	TOWNSHIPS.										
	Marengo.	English.	Green.	Iowa.	Cono.	Hartford.	Fillmore.	Troy.	Lenox.	Honey Creek.	TOTAL.
Ohio,	234	435	138	57	77	235	143	65	32	127	1543
Indiana,	199	53	14	30	46	10	75	10	11	51	499
Pennsylvania,	90	84	38	3	14	61	27	11	21	59	418
Iowa,	108	165	79	37	26	42	95	36	31	42	666
New York,	62	78	23	22		8	50	30	20	28	319
Maine,	5		2	1		2	1	5	1	4	22
New Hampshire	1	5	1				1	1		2	11
Vermont,	6	6	2			2	32	3	2	4	47
Massachusetts,	7	3	7	1		23		1		5	47
Connecticut,	4	3	1	2			6	6			22
Rhode Island,					1	1	1				3
Virginia,	14	38	16	2	12	28	22		2		134
Kentucky,	13	36	5	2	10	1	11			9	87
Illinois,	47	46	29	5	1	5	29	1	6	9	178
Michigan,	3	17	7	6			6	1	6	8	54
Alabama,					1						1
Florida,		2									2
North Carolina,	6	1		4			1		3	8	18
South Carolina,	2			1		1	3				7
Tennessee,	9	12	2	8	3	1	11				46
Missouri,	2	3							5		10
Georgia,							1				1
California,	1										1
Maryland,	9	22	1		9	6	3		4	4	58
New Jersey,	2	7				5		1		1	16
England,	15	15	12	11	1	7	7		11	10	89
Ireland,	17	17	80	3		8	45	19	4	11	204
Wales,		1						15			16
Scotland,	4			3		9			2	2	19
Germany,	18	46	1	16		2		1	85	5	174
France,	1	2				3	2		21		28
Prussia,	12								20		32
Norway,	10										10
Holland,		2									2
Canada,	14	10		4	2	3	6	2			41
New Brunswick,							3				3
Switzerland,	1	1							15		17
Saxony,									8		8
Belgium,		3									3
Delaware,			1				1				2
Wisconsin,			1				11		2		14
District of Columbia,						1					1

TABLE,

SHOWING THE POPULATION OF JACKSON COUNTY, FOR 1856.

TOWNSHIPS.	No. dwelling houses	Number of families.	Number of males.	Number of females.	Married.	Widowed.	Native voters.	Naturalized voters.	Aliens.	Militia.	Deaf and Dumb.	Blind.	Insane.	Idiotic.	Owners of land.	Paupers.
Bellevue,,	118	118	335	317	217	21	47	47	45	127		1		2	96	
Farmer's Creek,	178	178	581	515	347	30	213	7		164	1	1			135	1
Fairfield,	107	109	306	286	201	18	103	12	14	92			2		94	
Iowa,	157	162	500	405	296	15	95	41	79	186					156	
Jackson,	97	99	234	287	174	15	101	10	6	93			2		95	
Maquoketa,	222	248	780	655	517	33	296	13	75	279	1	1	1		226	
Monmouth,	177	177	493	436	332	24	169	10	50	157					144	
Otter Creek,	138	139	426	375	246	23	96	45	40	150	1			1	125	
Perry,	193	208	635	528	378	27	218	19	21	173			2		161	
Prairie Spring,	168	171	496	440	274	17	61	57	54	94					131	
Richland,	131	147	406	359	264	19	129	31	22	135					140	
South Fork,	259	266	757	698	516	48	314	9	21	232		1		1	145	
Tete Des Morts,	127	127	373	318	246	8	26	82	118	104				1	101	
Union,	114	114	332	317	352	24	114	25	34	128					52	
Van Buren,	128	151	391	358	283	17	154	5	102	152		2	1		156	
Washington,	111	111	367	321	289	16	94	21	39	85					85	
Total,	2425	2525	7462	6615	4382	350	2230	434	720	2351	3	6	8	5	2042	1

TABLE,

SHOWING THE AGRICULTURAL STATISTICS OF JACKSON COUNTY, FOR 1856.

TOWNSHIPS.	Acres of improved land.	Acres of unimproved land.	Acres of meadow	Tons of hay.	Bushels of grass seed.	Acres of spring wheat.	Bashels harvested.	Acres of winter wheat.	Bushels harvested.	Acres of oats.	Bushels harvested.	Acres of corn,	Bushels harvested.	Acres of potatoes.	Bushels harvested.
Bellevue,.......	3442	17190	514	761	11	774	11654	155	6813	272	6522	943	45460	73	4461
Farmer's Creek,.	3199	11860	235	445	10	415	6295	67	785	309	9052	1165	53418	44	5030
Fairfield,.......	3510	12543	124	877	12	1020	13578	4	28	239	6745	1079	39975	16	2518
Iowa,..........	5161	10148	378	723	8	1791	30476	3	80	493	17764	1103	52015	51	8870
Jackson,........	4583	8656	387	295	19	1765	24035			504	17074	1350	60588	23	2285
Maquoketa,......	3302	10472	364	453	5	709	12526	31	445	354	12045	924	39320	35	3876
Monmouth,.....	3589	10429	146	725	57	594	9335	5	55	348	13187	1653	74165	35	4293
Otter Creek,....	3949	12663	245	257	1	1308	19552			340	9896	1125	55443	67	6172
Perry,.........	6027	12191	779	1243	53	1462	18821	4	30	709	23450	2076	85662	28	4585
Prairie Spring,..	4770	12601	389	549	86	1682	26057	145	2732	445	16301	846	41325	101	11460
Richland,.......	5609	20158	440	510	15	1722	27447			443	16922	1528	71090	77	6030
South Fork,.....	4757	84581	644	1044	53	830	11260	13	439	657	5294	1494	64460	54	4261
Tete Des Morts,.	4483	12753	579	613	15	1734	25466	249	4327	795	20779	1131	51946	88	9746
Union,.........	1309	1623	399	456		464	7145			78	2220	348	15000	10	1170
Van Buren,.....	4712	8904	443	1271	112	1327	16636	2	12	455	15976	1256	47610	51	6550
Washington,....	2719	10024	175	242	5	588	8289			222	5695	612	45935	34	3719
Total,........	55088	256797	6240	10464	462	18185	268572	679	15346	6663	198922	18633	843412	787	85026

TABLE,

SHOWING THE NUMBER AND VALUE OF HOGS, CATTLE, DOMESTIC AND GENERAL MANUFACTURES OF JACKSON COUNTY, FOR 1856.

TOWNSHIPS.	No. of hogs sold.	Value of hogs sold.	No. of Cattle sold.	Value of cattle sold.	Pounds of butter made.	Pounds of cheese.	Pounds of wool.	Value of domestic manufactures.	Value of general manufactures.
Bellevue,.......	586	5268	139	4824	8940	2380	679	6000	
Farmer's Creek,..	537	4304	196	6418	10845	600	371	4284	14850
Fairfield,........	597	3515	160	5110	10480	376	589	355	50
Iowa,...........	669	6258	111	3972	2510		200		
Jackson,.........	897	7195	179	5203	14860	3[illegible]5	1071	657	200
Maquoketa,......	653	4685	165	7503	14655	1935	567	38[illegible]5	20950
Monmouth,......	1504	10312	212	7097	9138	2425	1109	227	40
Otter Creek,.....	951	6480	158	6158	12671	166	682	3336	1560
Perry,..........	1671	22280	332	12372	27170	5651	2552	288	61945
Prairie Spring,...	535	5321	131	3708	17665	1010			
Richland,.......	1266	8340	198	7154	30325	9873	469	192	20
South Fork,......	1323	9657	306	9922	16340	3603	636	63	
Tete Des Morts,..	478	4650	106	4346	15042	440	789	40	732
Union,..........	173	1706	39	1205	1770		265		9700
Van Buren,......	645	3403	241	6589	16025	2980	1745	279	1340
Washington,.....	369	2821	221	7900	3935	114	174	30	
Total,........	12854	105895	2894	99481	213371	31868	11898	19576	111387

TABLE,

SHOWING THE PROFESSIONS, TRADES OR OCCUPATIONS OF THE INHABITANTS OF JACKSON COUNTY, FOR 1856.

TOWNSHIPS.	Farmers.	Laborers.	Blacnsmiths.	Carpenters.	Wagon makers.	Brick layers.	Plasterers.	Stone masons.	Stone Cutters.	Engineers.	Millers.	Sawyers.	Millwrights.	Painters.	Cabinet makers	Chair makers.	Tinners.
Bellevue, ...	108	20	3	5				14									
Farmer's Creek, ...	106	27	4	19	1			4		1	1	3	1		1		1
Fairfield, ...	114	20	3	10													
Iowa, ...	182	6	1	10			1	3									
Jackson, ...	100	1	1	1			1				2	1	1				
Maquoketa, ...	99		10	29	3			14	1	1	3			5	4		1
Monmouth, ...	102	6	2	11	3		2	4			1		1		3		
Otter Creek, ...	181			10	2	1		3			1				1		
Perry, ...	94	5	8	14	2		2	7		1	3	3	2		2	1	
Prairie Spring, ...	185	20	3	6							2						
Richland,..........	132	7	3	10		1					2				1		
South Fork,........	177	67	10	24				7		1	4			2	1		1
Tete Des Morts	130	8	7	3	1					1	3						
Union, ...	19	64	8	18	3	2		2		2	4		1	1	2		2
Van Buren,..	268		3	7	1		1	4									
Washington, ...	116	5	2	4	1	1					3						
Total, ...	2113	256	68	181	18	5	7	62	1	7	29	7	6	8	15	1	5

TABLE—Continued,

EXHIBITING THE PROFESSIONS, TRADES OR OCCUPATIONS OF THE INHABITANTS OF JACKSON COUNTY, FOR 1856.

TOWNSHIPS.	Milliners.	Tailors.	Shoemakers.	Saddle & harness makers.	Bakers.	Butchers.	Mechanics.	Manufacturers.	Merchants.	Speculators.	Traders.	Druggists.	Boarding house Keepers.	Hotel Keepers.	Physicians.	Dentists.	Lawyers.	Clergymen.
Bellevue, ...		1												1				
Farmer's Creek,			3	1				2	4						3		1	1
Fairfield, ...			1	1														
Iowa, ...			1						1									
Jackson, ...			1												1			
Maquoketa, ...		6	4	5	1	1	3		28					2	5	2	5	5
Monmouth, ...			1						3						2			
Otter Creek, .	2		1												1			1
Perry, ...	1	1	6	2					5						3	1	1	1
Prairie Spring,			3						1						2			1
Richland, ...	2	1	8						2									
South Fork, ...	4	4	5	1	2		29	2	10		10		9	2	3		1	1
Tete des Morts,			6															
Union, ...		1	2	3					11			1		4	4			1
Van Buren, ...			2	1					2	2					2		2	
Washington, ..							1		1						1			
Total, ...	9	14	44	14	3	1	33	4	68	2	10	1	9	9	27	3	10	11

TABLE—CONTINUED,

EXHIBITING THE PROFESSIONS, TRADES OR OCCUPATIONS OF THE INHABITANTS OF JACKSON COUNTY, FOR 1856.

TOWNSHIPS.	Teachers.	Musicians.	Printers.	Artists.	Bankers.	Grocers.	Teamsters.	Brick Makers.	Watch Makers.	Jewellers.	Gun Smiths.	Coopers.	Clerks.	Plough boys.	Servants.	Miners.	Washerwomen.	Wheelwrights.
Belleveue, ...			2				1							20	10	1	1	1
Farmer's Creek,											1	16						1
Fairfield, ...	2																	
Iowa, ...	1							2				1						1
Jackson, ...	2	1										1						
Maquoketa, ...	4	1	6		2	4	5	6	1	4		7	4					3
Monmouth, ...												2	1					
Otter Creek, ..	2					1						1						
Perry, ...	1							4			1	1						
Prairie Spring,.	3	1											2					
Richland, ...	2							1										
South Fork, ...	5		2		1						2	1	3					
Tete des Morts,	1																	
Union, ...	1	1		1									1					
Van Buren, ...	2												1					
Washington, ...							1					1						
Total, ...	26	4	10	1	3	5	7	13	1	4	4	31	12	20	10	1	1	6

TABLE—Continued,

EXHIBITING THE PROFESSIONS, TRADES OR OCCUPATIONS OF THE INHABITANTS OF JACKSON COUNTY, FOR 1856.

TOWNSHIPS.	Book keepers	Daguerrean artists.	Printers' devils.	Prairie brakers.	Well diggers.	Seamstresses.	Tailoresses.	Surveyors.	Nurserymen.	Potters.	Dress makers.	Bellows makers.	Boatmen.	Brewers.	Ferrymen.	Mail carriers.	Lumbermen.	Gardeners.
Bellevue, ...	1	1	1															
Farmer's Creek,																		
Fairfield, ...																		
Iowa, ...				1	2													
Jackson, ...						1	1	1										
Maquoketa, ...	1				1	1	7											1
Monmouth, ..								1	1	1								
Otter Creek, ..																		
Perry, ...																		
Prairie Spring,.								1			3							
Richland,.. ...						1	2		1		1	1						
South Fork, ...						1	1				3						1	
Tete des Morts,													3					
Union,..								1						3	1	1	1	1
Van Buren, ...						1	1								1			
Washington, ..															1			
Total, ...	2	1	1	1	3	5	12	4	2	1	7	1	3	3	3	1	2	2

TABLE,—CONTINUED,

SHOWING THE PROFESSIONS, TRADES, OR OCCUPATIONS OF THE INHABITANTS OF JACKSON COUNTY, FOR 1856.

TOWNSHIPS,	Steamboat builders.	Horticulturalists.	Moulders.	Sailors.	Colliers.	Cattle dealers.	Wood Merchants.	Peddlers.	Railroad Agents.	Barbers.	Livery keepers.	Students.	School F. Commis'r.	County collectors.	Staging.	Broom makers.	Constables.	Jailors.
Bellevue, ...																		
Farmer's Creek,																		
Fairfield,......																		
Iowa, ...																		
Jackson, ...																		
Maquoketa, ...					1			1	1	1	2	8						
Monmouth,....																		
Otter Creek,...																		
Perry, ...																1	1	1
Prairie Spring .																		
Richland, ...																		
South Fork, ...													1	1	1			
Tete Des Morts,																		
Union,........	1																	
Van Buren, ...		1	1	1														
Washington, ..					1	1	1											
Total, ...	1	1	1	1	2	1	1	1	1	1	2	8	1	1	1	1	1	1

TABLE,

SHOWING THE PLACE OF NATIVITY OF THE INHABITANTS OF JACKSON COUNTY, FOR 1856.

TOWNSHIPS.	Ohio.	Indiana.	Pennsylvania.	Iowa.	New York.	Maine.	N. Hampshire.	Vermont.	Massachusetts.	Connecticut.	Rhode Island.	Virginia.	Kentucky.	Illinois.	Michigan.	Arkansas.	Texas.	Alabama.	Lousiana.	Mississippi.	N. Carolina.	South Carolina.	Tennessee.	Missouri.	Minnesota.	Georgia.	California.
Billevue,	33	11	85	175	25	..	1	2	2	1	..	9	6	13	..	..	..	..	..	..	10	1	6	9	..	..	..
Brandon,*	....	....	....	....	....	..	..	....	....	..	..	....	....	....	..	..	..	..	..	..	..	..	..	..	..	..	..
Butler,*	....	....	....	....	....	..	..	....	....	..	..	....	....	....	..	..	..	..	..	..	..	..	..	..	..	..	..
Farmer's Creek,	290	46	245	258	57	2	2	16	....	2	1	50	23	39	4	..	..	..	..	..	4	2	..	5	..	..	..
Fairfield,	95	12	134	105	70	3	4	7	4	2	1	26	4	10	7	..	..	..	1	..	..	..	5	5	..	..	..
Iowa,	61	1	28	189	90	3	3	8	5	6	1	14	....	31	5	..	..	5	6	1	..	..	..	5	..	1	..
Jackson,	26	30	240	115	15	..	..	....	....	..	..	40	10	20	1	..	..	..	..	..	7	..	10	7	..	..	..
Maquoketa,	122	68	157	206	326	3	25	72	11	17	2	28	22	62	8	1	..	..	..	..	14	2	2	6	..	..	..
Monmouth,	121	65	85	205	95	7	1	15	7	2	..	24	15	55	5	..	..	..	..	..	2	..	6	2	..	1	..
Otter Creek,	57	7	234	182	40	..	..	2	....	1	3	4	14	24	..	..	..	1	1	..	1	..	2	6	..	..	..
Perry,	102	10	490	225	119	2	13	8	24	2	2	28	6	27	2	..	..	..	1	..	2	..	5	9	2	..	..
Prairie Spring,	43	....	69	200	115	1	3	....	5	10	..	20	6	6	..	..	..	..	1	..	..	..	..	2	..	..	..
Richland,	45	14	60	160	230	8	6	16	5	2	..	....	1	36	8	..	..	..	..	..	..	..	1	2	..	..	..
South Fork,	160	60	175	250	375	..	25	93	21	35	..	5	25	40	4	..	1	..	..	..	1	..	1	1	..	..	2
Tete Des Morts,	11	....	39	222	5	..	..	1	....	2	..	1	6	35	1	..	..	..	..	1	1	..	..	6	..	..	..
Union,	68	12	44	128	118	2	..	19	....	8	..	6	5	29	9	..	..	..	..	..	..	1	1	9	..	..	..
Van Buren,	97	15	50	148	150	..	..	37	14	9	..	5	5	37	20	..	..	..	..	..	..	..	1	4	..	..	..
Washington,	30	29	208	....	22	14	2	1	2	..	..	8	4	47	2	..	..	..	1	..	3	..	3	15	..	..	..
Total,	1361	380	2341	2768	1852	45	85	297	100	99	10	268	152	511	79	1	1	6	11	2	45	6	43	93	2	2	2

* Butler and Brandon Townships come in after the summary was made up.

TABLE,—CONTINUED,

SHOWING THE PLACE OF NATIVITY OF THE INHABITANTS OF JACKSON COUNTY, FOR 1856.

TOWNSHIPS.	Maryland.	New Jersey.	England.	Ireland.	Wales.	Scotland	Germany.	France.	Austria.	Russia.	Prussia.	Sweden.	Holland.	On the Ocean.	Canada.	N. Brunswick.	Switzerland	Denmark.	Hanover.	Nebraska.	West Indies.	D. Columbia.	Wisconsin.	Delaware.	Nova Scotia.	Portugal.	Unknown.
Bellevue,	7	8	5	62	..	16	156	1	..	1	2	..	..	..	5	6	..	..	..	..	..	..	1	..	1	1	....
Brandon,*	..	....	....	....	..	..	....	..	..	..	..	..	..	..	....	..	..	..	..	..	..	..	..	..	..	..	....
Butler,*	..	....	....	....	..	..	....	..	..	..	..	..	..	..	....	..	..	..	..	..	..	..	..	..	..	..	....
Farmer's Creek,	1	7	5	4	..	..	11	..	..	..	..	..	..	..	15	..	..	..	..	..	..	..	7	..	..	..	5
Fairfield,	8	10	12	10	..	2	40	..	..	..	..	..	..	..	17	..	..	..	..	..	..	..	..	..	..	..	4
Iowa,	..	11	113	54	8	2	77	2	..	..	..	..	..	..	137	1	..	17	..	..	..	..	..	..	..	..	....
Jackson,	5	1	14	17	..	3	3	..	..	..	..	4	..	1	....	..	..	..	..	..	..	..	2	..	..	..	....
Maquoketa,	2	11	47	39	1	11	35	2	6	..	2	1	..	1	98	..	4	..	..	..	..	..	7	..	..	..	2
Monmouth,	1	11	9	16	..	2	24	..	85	..	3	1	1	3	55	..	..	..	1	..	..	..	2	..	2	..	....
Otter Ceeek,	12	1	14	168	..	2	11	..	1	..	..	..	..	..	10	..	..	..	..	..	1	..	1	..	..	..	1
Perry,	2	4	20	23	1	..	28	2	..	..	..	..	..	..	3	..	..	..	..	..	..	..	..	1	..	..	....
Prairie Spring,	..	8	5	142	..	9	240	3	..	..	..	..	..	..	45	..	1	..	..	..	..	..	2	..	..	..	....
Richland,	5	17	23	45	..	22	43	..	..	..	6	..	..	..	5	2	..	..	..	..	..	..	2	..	3	..	....
South Fork,	12	10	22	15	..	..	30	..	..	..	1	1	..	..	63	..	..	..	..	1	..	..	6	..	..	..	20
Tete Des Morts,	4	....	....	8	..	..	341	1	..	..	..	..	..	..	1	..	4	..	..	..	..	..	..	1	..	..	....
Union,	8	3	27	34	..	1	68	..	..	..	..	..	..	..	34	1	..	..	..	..	..	1	3	..	..	..	10
Van Buren,	4	8	20	12	..	2	83	..	..	..	..	..	..	..	20	..	3	..	..	..	..	..	3	..	..	..	2
Washington,	4	4	14	41	4	1	85	2	..	..	..	..	..	..	4	1	6	..	..	..	..	..	1	4	.	..	126
Total,	75	108	369	690	14	72	1275	13	92	1	14	7	1	5	512	11	18	17	1	1	1	1	37	6	6	1	170

* Brandon and Butler Townships come in after the summary was made up.

TABLE,

SHOWING THE POPULATION OF JASPER COUNTY, FOR 1856.

TOWNSHIPS.	No. dwelling houses.	Number of families.	Number of males.	Number of females.	Colored.	Married.	Widowed.	Native voters.	Naturalized voters.	Aliens.	Militia.	Deaf and Dumb.	Blind.	Insane.	Idiotic.	Owners of land.
Clear Creek, ..	124	133	387	362		255	17	149	5	1	131			1	1	115
Desmoines, ...	178	184	577	480		387	15	207	9	10	184	2		1	2	180
Elk Creek, ...	87	99	290	233		190	8	99	11		106					87
Fairview, ...	150	155	424	390	1	273	15	143	12	9	120	1			1	108
Linn Grove, ...	94	103	347	284		196	6	108	4	5	109			2	1	97
Newton, ...	518	540	1507	1260		1015	49	640	27	17	644	1		2		476
Powesheik, ...	122	135	393	320		216	13	133		2	132		1		1	95
Rock Creek, ..	44	45	136	100		88	7	45	7		51	1				43
Total, ...	1317	1394	4061	3429	1	2620	130	1524	75	44	1477	5	1	6	6	1201

TABLE,

SHOWING THE AGRICULTURAL STATISTICS OF JASPER COUNTY, FOR 1856.

TOWNSHIPS.	Acres of improved land.	Acres of unimproved land.	Acres of meadow.	Tons of hay.	Bushels of grass seeds.	Acres of spring wheat.	Bushels harvested.	Acres of winter wheat.	Bushels harvested.	Acres of oats.	Bushels harvested.	Acres of corn.	Bushels harvested.	Acres of potatoes.	Bushels harvested.
Clear Creek, . .	2646	18450	26	23		429	7704			87	1870	1234	47865	34	4191
Desmoines, . .	4982	15065	42	464	1	644	9499	5	00	275	8496	2474	136724	33	5061
Elk Creek, . .	2108	4960	1	2		399	6478	46	448	106	4410	894	52655	9	1840
Fairview, . . .	2961	11364	21	511		451	6489			207	7075	1304	73140	19	3760
Linn Grove, .	2345	4337		168		223	3999	80	2600	165	6085	1058	52525	3	270
Newton, ...	7401	61152	32	3		676	11160	11	164	318	12646	2457	120282	68	9080
Poweshiek, . .	3199	12247	3	5		370	7512	9	74	131	5094	1140	52748	19	4175
Rock Creek, .	571	1412				49	850			20	400	266	11000	1	80
Total, ...	26213	128987	125	1176	1	3242	52691	151	3286	1309	46076	10827	547939	186	28457

TABLE,

SHOWING THE NUMBER AND VALUE OF HOGS AND CATTLE SOLD, THE VALUE OF DOMESTIC AND GENERAL MANUFACTURES OF JASPER COUNTY, FOR 1856.

TOWNSHIPS.	No. of Hogs sold.	Value of Hogs sold.	No. of Cattle sold.	Value of Cattle sold.	Pounds of butter made.	Pounds of cheese.	Pounds of wool.	Value of Domestic manufactures.	Value of "general manufactures.
Clear Creek,.....	475	2442	246	7354	9588	65	682	393	
Desmoines,......	1530	9402	282	9564	15566	392	1927	1015	5350
Elk Creek,......	347	2159	140	4480	6940		515	147	
Fairview,... ...	739	4419	224	4091	9560	75	726	600	3000
Linn Grove,.....	506	3875	62	1747	7450		600	703	
Newton,........	1162	7579	648	12570	24353	840	1589	836	6515
Poweshiek, ...	253	2284	0	208	7365	235	522	306	
Rock Creek,....	82	680	42	1332	660		122	118	
Total,.........	5094	32839	1644	41346	81482	1607	6683	4118	14865

TABLE,

SHOWING THE PROFESSIONS, TRADES OR OCCUPATIONS OF THE INHABITANTS OF JASPER COUNTY, FOR 1856.

TOWNSHIPS.	Farmers.	Laborers.	Blacksmiths.	Carpenters.	Wagon Makers	Brick Layers.	Plasterers.	Stone Masons.	Carriage Makers.	Engineers.	Millers.	Sawyers.	Painters.	Cabinet Makers.	Tinners.	Milliners.	Tailors.
Clear Creek, ...	111	20	4	15							1	1				1	1
Desmoines, ...	231	18	3	17						2	2	1					
Elk Creek, ...	128	11	1	3			1	1			1				1		
Fairview, ...	113	14	5	7	1	3	2	1		2	6		1	1			1
Linn Grove, ...	148		2	5							3						
Newton, ...	335	20	16	81	13	2	15	2	1	6	3	6	8	6	4	16	4
Poweshiek, ...	90	67	2	6			2			1		1			1		
Rock Creek, ...	59	15	1	2													
Total, ...	1215	165	34	136	14	5	20	4	1	11	16	9	9	7	6	17	6

TABLE,—Continued,

SHOWING THE PROFESSIONS, TRADES OR OCCUPATIONS OF THE INHABITANTS OF JASPER COUNTY, FOR 1856.

TOWNSHIPS	Shoe makers.	Saddle & harness makers.	Bakers.	Butchers.	Mechanics.	Merchants.	Agents.	Traders.	Boarding house keepers.	Hotel Keepers.	Clothiers.	Physicians.	Dentists.	Lawyers.	Clergymen.	Teachers.	Printers.	Artists.
Clear Creek, ...												1				1		
Desmoines, ...	2				1	5						3				2		
Elk Creek, ...												3					1	
Fairview, ...	2	1	2			8		2		1		3		1	3	1		
Linn Grove, ...						1					2	2				1		
Newton, ...	8	5		1	4	28	3	2	1	5		7	1	9	9	24	5	1
Poweshiek, ...	1					2						1				1		
Rock Creek, .																		
Total, ...	13	6	2	1	5	44	3	4	1	6	2	20	1	10	12	30	6	1

TABLE—Continued,

EXHIBITING THE PROFESSIONS, TRADES, OR OCCUPATIONS OF THE INHABITANTS OF JASPER COUNTY, FOR 1856.

TOWNSHIPS.	Bankers.	Teamsters.	Brick makers.	Watch Makers.	Gun Smiths.	Coopers.	Clerks.	Tailoresses.	Fishermen	Horticulturalists.	Moulders.	Livery Keepers.	Potters.	Barbers.	Hostlers.	Surveyors.	Students.	Sheriffs.
Clear Creek,..		1						3										
Desmoines,...		3	1				1		1									
Elk Creek,...																		
Fairview, . .		7					1											
Linn Grove, .																		
Newton,.....	3	15	6	1	4	2	20	9		2	1	1	1	1	2	1	1	2
Poweshiek,...		1				1	1											
Rock Creek,..																		
Total, ...	3	27	7	1	4	3	23	12	1	2	1	1	1	1	2	1	1	2

TABLE,

SHOWING THE PLACE OF NATIVITY OF THE INHABITANTS OF JASPER COUNTY, FOR 1856.

STATES.	TOWNSHIPS.								TOTAL.
	Clear Creek.	Des moines.	Elk Creek.	Fairview.	Linn Grove.	Newton.	Poweshiek.	Rock Creek.	
Ohio,	151	196	116	160	102	664	194	56	1639
Indiana,	150	231	81	157	164	500	169	58	1570
Pennsylvania,	62	97	34	60	15	231	53	16	568
Iowa,	143	168	84	124	112	361	100	24	1116
New York,	38	32	43	81	10	156	30	8	388
Maine,	2	....	....	1	6	12	3	....	24
New Hampshire	3	3	1	....	1	24	3	4	38
Vermont,	4	4	1	3	2	23	14	2	50
Massachusetts,	1	1	8	5	3	11	6	10	44
Connecticut,	2	4	1	....	1	15	....	1	21
Rhode Island,	....	....	....	....	....	1	....	1	2
Virginia,	29	25	23	58	23	92	21	7	278
Kentucky,	68	57	31	15	31	179	15	16	407
Illinois,	45	84	59	39	89	95	29	12	452
Michigan,	4	2	....	1	1	14	2	1	25
Arkansas.	....	....	....	....	1	2	....	....	3
Alabama,	....	....	....	....	....	1	....	....	1
North Carolina,	8	21	2	8	30	80	8	2	159
South Carolina,	....	1	....	....	2	2	2	....	7
Tennessee,	3	11	5	8	16	118	38	3	201
Missouri,	2	5	3	2	2	25	2	....	41
Georgia,	....	3	....	....	....	4	....	....	7
Maryland,	18	5	6	11	2	15	9	7	73
New Jersey,	5	2	....	18	....	39	4	....	68
England,	12	10	1	7	8	21	....	1	60
Ireland,	5	2	3	5	7	30	2	7	61
Wales,	....	1	....	....	....	1	....	....	2
Scotland,	....	1	....	....	....	3	....	5	9
Germany,	1	28	19	39	2	25	1	....	115
France,	1	1	....	4	....	....	....	....	6
Norway,	1	....	....	....	....	....	....	....	1
Holland,	....	....	1	....	....	....	....	....	1
On the Ocean,	....	....	....	....	....	1	....	....	1
Canada,	3	1	....	2	....	9	....	....	15
West Indies.	....	....	....	....	....	1	....	....	1
Wisconsin,	3	....	1	11	....	5	6	....	26
Delaware,	....	1	....	....	2	6	1	....	10
Unknown.	....	....	....	....	....	1	1	....	2

TABLE,

SHOWING THE POPULATION OF JEFFERSON COUNTY, FOR 1856.

TOWNSHIPS.	No. of dwelling houses.	Number of families.	Number of males.	Number of females.	Married.	Widowed.	Native voters.	Naturalized voters.	Aliens.	Militia.	Deaf and Dumb.	Blind.	Insane.	Idiotic.	Owners of land.	Paupers.
Fairfield, ...	451	468	1444	1372	800	64	398	36	17	411	8			1	186	
Sackridge, ...	305	305	823	798	557	34	212	64	60	293	1	1		1	239	
Walnut, ...	162	162	485	446	293	22	121	59	12	162					134	2
Penn, ...	196	212	621	581	429	27	224			209					161	1
Black Hawk, ...	95	95	258	259	99	9	70	8							67	
Polk, ...	175	175	489	500	309	27	167			156	1			4	123	
Locust Grove, ...	166	170	488	489	311	11	164	3	10	114			3		99	
Des Moines, ...	211	217	648	638	427	24	234	8	1	154			3		165	
Liberty, ...	212	222	643	604	410	37	227	2	8	190		1		1	162	
Cedar, ...	127	127	389	351	236	19	102	21	24	108	1		1		93	
Round Prairie, ...	172	176	507	472	330	17	176	11	4	151	2				133	
Total, ...	2272	2329	6795	6510	4201	291	2095	212	136	1948	13	2	7	7	1562	3

TABLE

SHOWING THE AGRICULTURAL STATISTICS OF JEFFERSON COUNTY, FOR 1856.

TOWNSHIPS.	Acres of improved land.	Acres of unimproved land.	Acres of meadow.	Tons of hay.	Bushels of grass seed.	Acres of spring wheat.	Bushels harvested.	Acres of winter wheat	Bushels harvested.	Acres of oats.	Bushels harvested.	Acres of corn.	Bushels harvested.	Acres of potatoes	Bushels harvested.
Fairfield, ...	9788	19991	1500	1149	900	1991	21060	95	1646	1096	34292	3066	60950	59	7688
Sackridge, ...	6457	18620	763	751	170	950	9411	459	6171	867	7585	2672	143110	54	7415
Walnut, ...	4580	11149	431	359	68	456	3697	403	4738	527	5046	1728	77095	41	3552
Penn, ...	6700	8605	713	535	563	820	5098	138	982	738	19887	2250	112970	36	4479
Black Hawk, .	3190	7441	309	186	182	422	3435	295	522	365	12653	1546	67091	15	2288
Polk, ...	4536	6993	538	224	207	932	8721	18	248	689	21574	2509	135074	31	3803
Locust Grove,	6362	9738	988	1150	32	886	9940	69	1134	879	37020	2906	156175	35	4573
Des Moines, .	7948	7704	954	634	331	1343	14564	113	1895	1116	29797	2939	154302	37	4762
Liberty, ...	7858	15424	1331	933	167	1367	12834	322	5125	1210	31444	2809	48256	51	5555
Cedar, ...	5646	8846	682	532	381	1149	8959	489	7210	864	23237	1707	86890	54	5312
Round Prairie	6711	9893	959	1035	496	1102	12472	94	1578	841	26452	2167	122250	7	2940
Total, ...	69776	124404	8868	7487	3497	11398	110192	2495	31744	9193	248987	26299	1103163	418	52367

TABLE,

SHOWING THE NUMBER AND VALUE OF HOGS, CATTLE, DOMESTIC AND GENERAL MANUFACTURES OF JEFFERSON COUNTY, FOR 1856.

TOWNSHIPS.	No. of hogs sold.	Value of hogs sold.	No. of Cattle sold.	Value of cattle. sold.	Pounds of butter made.	Pounds of cheese.	Pounds of wool.	Value of domestic manufactures.	Value of general manufactures.
Fairfield, ...	1738	4773	335	9362	8006	2195	1464	1144	5211
Sackridge, ...	1951	6736	344	12093	30735	752	3106	3466	32
Walnut, ...	1145	10401	211	5180	9422	130	2284	999	26885
Penn, ...	1915	15585	328	6511	13037	3930	2833	2148	50
Black Hawk, ...	1170	9896	252	3371	14413	1709	1464	16	4730
Polk, ...	1765	13657	289	5598	17502	868	2071	2468	2040
Locust Grove, ...	2491	18498	359	8231	19344	653	2857	1999	4635
Des Moines, ...	1756	14140	421	9275	22433	650	3845	2292	4105
Liberty, ...	1895	15988	1131	8079	29381	520	2295	2310	5740
Cedar, ...	1157	9562	459	7111	13258	2198	2182	975	100
Round Prairie, ...	1554	14501	417	2063	13189	938	2321	2581	21840
Total, ...	18537	138737	4546	76874	190720	14543	26722	20398	75368

TABLE,

EXHIBITING THE PROFESSIONS, TRADES OR OCCUPATIONS OF THE INHABITANTS OF JEFFERSON COUNTY, FOR 1856.

TOWNSHIPS.	Farmers.	Laborers.	Blacksmiths.	Carpenters.	Wagon makers.	Brick Layers.	Plasterers.	Stone masons.	Stone Cutters.	Carriage Makers.	Machinists.	Engineers.	Millers.	Sawyers.	Millwrights.	Painters.
Fairfield, ...	232	91	19	47	7		6	6	2		4		4	3	2	4
Sackridge, ...	230	21	7	14	3		1					2	1	2		2
Walnut, ...	200	15	4	6	2			1					3			
Peen, ...	210		4	20	2	2				3	1	1	3	3		1
Blackhawk, ...	88			2												
Polk, ...	117	5	6	7	3	2										
Locust Grove, ...	128	1	11	8		1							1	1		1
Desmoines, ...	208	18	2	11	2		1					1		1		2
Liberty, ...	258	20	5	12	3		2					1	1	1		
Cedar, ...	128															
Round Prairie, ...	166		7	11	3		2						2			
Total, ...	1965	171	65	138	25	5	12	7	2	3	5	5	15	11	2	10

TABLE—Continued,

EXHIBITING THE PROFESSIONS, TRADES, OR OCCUPATIONS OF THE INHABITANTS OF JEFFERSON COUNTY, FOR 1856.

TOWNSHIPS.	Cabinet Makers.	Chair Makers.	Tinners.	Milliners.	Tailors.	Hatters.	Shoemakers.	Harness Makers.	Bakers.	Butchers.	Mechanics.	Manufacturers.	Merchants.	Agents.	Druggists.	Hotel Keepers.	Physicians.
Fairfield,	7	3	5	3	3		10	7	1	1		2	39	2	1	6	11
Sackridge,	1				2	1	5						4				2
Walnut,			1				3	1					3				
Penn,							3				1		3				1
Blackhawk,											2						
Polk,	2	1					1				1		9				6
Locust Grove,							2						4				2
Desmoines,	2				1		1	1					1				
Liberty,	3			3	3		3	3	1			1	5			1	5
Cedar,																	
Round Prairie,				1	5								5				4
Total,	15	4	6	7	14	1	28	12	2	1	4	3	73	2	1	7	31

TABLE—CONTINUED,

EXHIBITING THE PROFESSIONS, TRADES OR OCCUPATIONS OF THE INHABITANTS OF JEFFERSON COUNTY, FOR 1856.

TOWNSHIPS.	Dentists.	Lawyers.	Clergymen.	Teachers.	Printers.	Artists.	Bankers.	Teamsters.	Brick Makers.	Jewellers.	Coopers.	Clerks.	Colliers.	Stage Drivers.	Students.	Barbers.	Bookbinders.
Fairfield,	1	8	3	2	5		3	17	9	1	1	14	7	3	5	1	1
Sackridge,			4	8													
Walnut,				1							1						
Penn,			1	2				1	1		2						
Blackhawk,				1													
Polk,			1	2				1	1		1						
Locust Grove,			1								1						
Des Moines,			1	4													
Liberty,			4	5	2						4	2					
Cedar,																	
Round Prairie,			3	6		1											
Total,	1	8	18	31	7	1	3	19	11	1	10	16	7	3	5	1	1

TABLE—CONTINUED,

SHOWING THE PROFESSIONS, TRADES OR OCCUPATIONS OF THE INHABITANTS OF JEFFERSON COUNTY, FOR 1856.

TOWNSHIPS.	Hack Drivers.	Livery Keepers.	Carders.	Moulders.	Postmasters.	Peddlers.	Sheriff.	Surveyors.	Professors.	Weavers.	Wheelwrights.	Spinners.	Distillers.	Brewers.	Turners.	Potters.
Fairfield,	1	1	4	1	1	1	1	1	3							
Sackridge,										3	2	1	1			
Walnut,														1	1	
Penn,						1										
Blackhawk,																
Polk,																
Locust Grove,					1						1					
DesMoines,																
Liberty,						2										
Cedar,																1
Round Prairie,																
Total,	1	1	4	1	2	4	1	1	3	3	3	1	1	1	1	1

TABLE,

SHOWING THE PLACE OF NATIVITY OF THE INHABITANTS OF JEFFERSON COUNTY, FOR 1856

STATES.	NAME OF TOWNSHIPS.											TOTAL.
	Fairfield.	Sackridge.	Walnut.	Penn.	Black Hawk.	Polk.	Locust Grove.	Desmoines.	Liberty.	Cedar.	Round Prairie.	
Ohio,	720	203	189	318	129	190	255	217	381	118	190	2908
Indiana,	17[illegible]	76	28	153	41	121	100	166	94	60	75	1097
Pennsylvania,	537	209	131	87	75	123	277	246	149	71	51	1956
Iowa,	581	515	281	390	128	64	100	372	321	223	300	3278
New York,	79	11	5	7	2	22	10	36	24	7	6	209
Maine,	16	23		1			2	1	3		8	54
New Hampshire,	11				4		1	2	7		2	27
Vermont,	16	2	2	2		6	1	2	2		10	43
Massachusetts,	[illegible]3	5	2	2	2		3	6	1		1	55
Connecticut,	8	2		1		1	1	2	1		2	18
Rhode Island,	2								1	1		4
Virginia,	133	70	35	50	11	161	60	80	70	48	95	813
Kentucky,	40	30	19	18	36	116	32	33	47		50	422
Illinois,	101	47	22	47	17	27	37	37	41	31	91	508
Michigan,	5			2					2		2	11
Arkansas,			1	1								1
Texas,											3	1
Alabama,	1										2	3
Louisiana,	1				2		1	1		2		6
Mississippi,										1	1	3
North Carolina,	25	19	6	33	29	31	20	4	9	4	12	192
South Carolina,	2	1	2	3			3	1	1		2	15
Tennessee,	14	27	15	40		57	20	21	11	23	11	229
Missouri,	20	11	4	8				10	5	5	10	63
Georgia,	2	2		1		1					1	7
Maryland,	35	7	5	6	3	23	6	24	20	10	20	169
New Jersey,	28	9	9	6	10	9	3	3	6	7	9	99
England,	43	22		3	14	12	3	5	17	1	10	130
Ireland,	46	6	1	3	2	14	8	11	15	30	6	142
Wales,	2							1				8
Scotland	22	3					7		3	5	2	42
Germany,	8	38	108	15	9	11		3	1		2	195
France,	3	21	4	1			5		7	86		127
Prussia,		5	20						1			26
Sweden,	12	250								1	1	294
On the Ocean,		2										2
Canada,	20	4		1			2		1			28
New Brunswick,	2											2
Switzerland,		1					7					8
Hanover,			15									15
Saxony,			5									5
Wisconsin,	4						2	1		1		8
Delaware,	6			3			2	1				12
Indian Territory,	1											1
Unknown,	32		19								4	55
District of Columbia,	1											4

TABLE,

SHOWING THE POPULATION OF JOHNSON COUNTY, FOR 1856.

TOWNSHIPS.	No. dwelling houses	Number of families.	Number of males.	Number of females.	Colored.	Married.	Widowed.	Native voters.	Naturalized voters.	Aliens.	Militia.	Deaf and Dumb.	Blind.	Insane.	Idiotic.	Owners of land.	Paupers.
Iowa City, ...	982	982	3588	2728	14	1961	172	1308	160	516	1105	10	3		1	616	
Washington, ...	177	182	511	442		349	5	185	66	8	154				1	145	
Pleasant Valley, ...	131	136	452	344	1	273	18	172	4	97	178				1	100	
Big Grove, ...	151	161	472	436		302	20	126	85	31	147					126	
Cedar, ...	96	96	284	242		190	7	78	17	104	88					98	
Penn, ...	152	170	424	403		282	12	102	4	17	45		1	2		79	
Scott, ...	101	106	362	321		213	12	121	18	15	146		1			80	
Union, ...	66	66	189	163		122	12	52	40	18	70	2			1	76	1
Monroe, ...	86	87	251	242		164	11	104	3	4	91	1	1			71	
Jefferson, ...	85	87	272	251	1	154	7	65	10	34	72				1	56	
Oxford, ...	54	54	160	149		106	5	61	13	6	73					61	
Newport, ...	154	167	469	417		318	20	132	46	39	175	1			6	133	
Liberty, ...	100	102	318	285		194	11	69	51	15	89			1	1	102	
Clear Creek, ...	51	51	132	150	2	100	12	50	7	8	60					38	1
Total, ...	2386	2447	7884	6573	18	4728	324	2578	524	941	3486	14	6	3	12	1781	2

TABLE,

SHOWING THE AGRICULTURAL STATISTICS OF JOHNSON COUNTY, FOR 1856.

TOWNSHIPS.	Acres of improved land.	Acres of unimproved land.	Acres of meadow	Tons of hay.	Bushels of grass seed.	Acres of spring wheat.	Bushels harvested.	Acres of winter wheat.	Bushels harvested.	Acres of oats.	Bushels harvested.	Acres of corn,	Bushels harvested.	Acres of potatoes.	Bushels harvested.
Iowa City,......	3031	[illegible]	[illegible]	340		402	7710	30	450	419	14474	1104	46990	28	2987
Washington,....	6024	17108	563	[illegible]	59	1392	17797	30	1030	519	20757	1656	108325	49	7224
Pleasant Valley,	[illegible]	[illegible]	777	245	11	759	13813	25	440	532	20234	2733	143500	29	3460
Big Grove,......	[illegible]	[illegible]	[illegible]	275	20	899	14283	2	10	620	22764	1641	76253	39	5770
Cedar,..........	[illegible]	[illegible]	140	[illegible]	16	630	9672	3	50	339	10669	1264	53540	23	3291
Penn,..........	[illegible]	9364	84	[illegible]	97	1244	19810	14	368	560	19559	1332	68866	47	5151
Scott,.........	[illegible]	7600	110	[illegible]	51	571	8953	10	186	324	9745	1303	63625	33	4365
Union,....	[illegible]	[illegible]	[illegible]	815	7	473	6582	7	205	329	12146	1091	56360	26	3420
Monroe,........	[illegible]	7991	116	101	3	418	5917			194	7737	956	51230	17	2257
Jefferson,......	3929	5559	55	61	9	565	4222	55	1708	289	13247	662	28677	14	1842
Oxford,.	1478	7858	40	525		228	4043			207	5749	582	26040	14	1991
Newport,.......	4584	7679	313	466	16	674	10905	8	95	306	9716	1475	73305	69	11714
Liberty,........	4583	11691	73	507	2	884	12068			685	22241	1771	100080	35	5628
Clear Creek,....	2323	4821	142	174	8	370	4938	2	39	233	7120	589	27620	14	2845
Total,........	55453	135640	3037	5656	299	9559	140713	186	4581	5556	196152	18158	924411	437	61945

TABLE,

SHOWING THE NUMBER AND VALUE OF HOGS, CATTLE, DOMESTIC AND GENERAL MANUFACTURES OF JOHNSON COUNTY, FOR 1856.

TOWNSHIPS.	No. of hogs sold.	Value of hogs sold.	No. of cattle sold.	Value of cattle sold.	Pounds of butter made.	Pounds of cheese.	Pounds of Wool.	Value of domestic Manufactures.	Value of general manufactures.
Iowa City,	1053	8209	91	2814	14610	1095	175	45	400
Washington,	1212	11799	325	6941	24109	1441	1619	1486	......
Pleasant Valley,	3143	29291	912	30637	4350	6135	273	38	......
Big Grove,	962	8825	124	3637	8134	4060	1445	683	2720
Cedar,	1169	7087	135	3543	7296	3[illegible]0	2249	81	132
Penn,	786	7179	182	6013	12843	1428	1064	107	373
Scott,	745	5641	272	4914	10300	410	399	138	....
Union,	893	7597	135	4089	10902	325	411	45	......
Monroe,	648	3740	216	8[illegible]43	4424	200	1042	465	......
Jefferson,	537	4590	67	2009	4680	90	398	428	......
Oxford,	3[illegible]3	1909	55	2795	3890	150	128	......	......
Newport,	9[illegible]7	7158	151	4150	21819	21[illegible]5	2075	281	240
Liberty,	982	8130	131	3836	9849	1605	612	422	2682
Clear Creek,	491	2993	103	2385	6258	929	140	......	......
Total,	13841	114148	2799	86036	143465	20543	12030	4219	6547

TABLE,

SHOWING THE PROFESSIONS, TRADES OR OCCUPATIONS OF THE INHABITANTS OF JOHNSON COUNTY, FOR 1856.

OCCUPATIONS.	NAME OF TOWNSHIPS.														
	Iowa City.	Washington.	Pleasant Valley.	Big Grove.	Cedar.	Penn.	Scott.	Union.	Monroe.	Jefferson.	Oxford.	Newport.	Liberty.	Clear Creek.	TOTAL.
Farmers,	279	119	107	134	121	13	135	87	118	27	80	135	113	50	1518
Laborers,	563	....	90	13	5	....	42	1	9	....	3	22	....	....	748
Blacksmiths,	47	3	....	5	2	1	1	....	2	2	3	2	2	1	71
Carpenters,	273	4	14	11	5	6	4	5	2	4	10	9	6	1	354
Wagon makers,	19	....	....	....	1	....	1	....	....	1	1	....	....	....	23
Brick layers,	55	....	....	....	....	....	....	....	....	....	....	....	....	....	55
Plasterers,	28	....	....	3	....	....	2	....	1	1	....	....	....	....	35
Stone masons,	64	....	....	1	1	2	1	....	2	....	....	1	....	1	73
Stone cutters,	21	....	....	....	....	2	....	....	....	....	....	....	1	....	24
Carriage makers,	25	....	....	....	....	....	1	....	....	....	....	....	....	....	26
Machinists,	5	....	....	....	....	....	....	1	....	....	....	....	....	....	6
Engineers,	13	....	....	....	1	....	....	....	....	....	1	....	....	....	15
Millers,	19	....	1	1	....	1	....	....	....	2	....	....	....	....	24
Sawyers,	....	....	3	....	....	....	....	....	....	....	1	3	....	....	7
Millwrights,	3	....	....	....	....	....	....	....	....	....	....	....	....	....	3
Painters,	33	....	1	....	....	....	....	....	....	....	....	....	....	....	34
Cabinet makers,	18	1	....	....	....	....	1	....	....	....	....	....	1	....	21
Tinners,	30	....	....	....	....	....	....	....	....	....	....	....	....	....	30
Milliners,	9	....	....	3	....	....	1	....	....	....	....	....	....	....	13
Merchant Tailors,	1	....	....	....	....	....	....	....	....	....	....	....	....	....	1
Tailors,	28	....	....	1	1	....	....	....	....	....	....	....	....	....	30
Hatters,	3	....	....	....	....	....	....	....	....	....	....	....	....	....	3
Shoemakers,	35	2	1	2	....	2	1	....	....	....	....	4	....	....	47
Saddle & Harness makers,	20	....	....	....	....	....	....	....	....	....	....	....	....	....	20
Bakers,	15	....	....	....	1	....	....	....	....	....	....	....	....	....	16
Butchers,	14	....	....	....	....	....	....	....	....	....	....	....	....	....	14
Manufacturers,	....	....	....	....	....	....	....	....	....	....	....	2	....	....	2
Merchants,	92	....	....	7	....	....	1	....	....	1	....	....	....	....	101
Agents,	16	....	....	....	....	....	....	....	....	....	....	....	....	....	16
Drovers,	....	....	1	....	....	....	....	....	....	....	....	....	....	....	1
Traders,	58	....	....	....	....	....	....	....	....	....	....	....	....	....	58
Druggists,	8	....	....	....	....	....	....	....	....	....	....	....	....	....	8
Confectioners,	4	....	....	....	....	....	....	....	....	....	....	....	....	....	4
Boarding House keepers,	6	....	....	1	....	....	....	....	....	....	....	....	....	....	7
Hotel keepers,	18	....	....	2	....	....	....	....	....	....	....	1	....	....	21
Physicians,	30	....	1	2	....	....	1	....	1	....	....	....	....	....	35
Dentists,	4	....	....	....	....	....	1	....	....	....	....	....	....	....	5
Lawyers,	36	....	....	....	....	....	....	....	....	....	....	....	....	....	36
Clergymen,	17	1	1	....	1	1	....	....	....	....	....	....	....	....	21
Teachers,	13	....	....	4	....	....	1	....	2	....	....	1	....	....	21
Musicians,	1	....	....	....	1	....	....	....	....	....	....	....	....	....	2
Printers,	18	....	....	....	....	....	....	....	1	....	....	....	....	....	19
Editors,	2	....	....	....	....	....	....	....	....	....	....	....	....	....	2
Daguerrean Artists,	2	....	....	....	....	....	1	....	....	....	....	....	....	....	3
Bankers,	7	....	....	....	....	....	....	....	....	....	....	....	....	....	7
Grocers,	13	....	....	....	....	....	....	....	....	....	....	....	....	....	13
Teamsters,	93	....	2	....	....	....	....	....	....	....	....	2	....	....	97
Chandlers,	1	....	....	....	....	....	....	....	....	....	....	....	....	....	1
Brick makers,	25	....	....	1	....	2	....	....	....	....	....	....	....	....	27
Watch makers,	2	....	....	....	....	....	....	....	....	....	....	....	....	....	2
Jewellers,	8	....	....	....	....	....	....	....	....	....	....	....	....	....	8
Gunsmiths,	3	....	....	....	....	....	....	....	....	....	....	....	....	....	3
Coopers,	4	....	....	2	....	2	....	....	....	....	....	5	....	....	13
Clerks,	131	....	....	2	....	....	....	....	....	....	....	....	....	....	133
Horticulturalists,	2	....	....	....	....	....	....	....	....	....	....	....	....	....	2
Lime burners,	2	....	....	....	....	....	....	....	....	....	....	....	....	....	2
Wheelwrights,	1	....	....	....	....	1	....	....	....	....	....	....	....	....	2
Iron mongers,	1	....	....	....	....	....	....	....	....	....	....	....	....	....	1
Moulders,	5	....	....	....	....	....	....	....	....	....	....	....	....	....	5

TABLE—Continued,

EXHIBITING THE PROFESSIONS, TRADES OR OCCUPATIONS OF THE INHABITANTS OF JOHNSON COUNTY, FOR 1856.

OCCUUATIONS.	NAME OF TOWNSHIPS.														
	Iowa City.	Washington.	Pleasant Valley.	Big Grove.	Cedar.	Penn.	Scott.	Union.	Monroe.	Jefferson.	Oxford.	Newport.	Liberty.	Clear Creek.	Total.
Auctioneers,	4														4
Land Jobbers,	15														15
Professors,	7														7
Lumbermen,	5											2			7
County Judges,	1														1
Livery keepers,	14														14
Brokers,	2														2
Plough makers,	1														1
Book binders,	1														1
Tobacconists,	2														2
Iron founders,	2														2
Sculptors,	2														2
Spinners,	1														1
Draymen,	4														4
Barbers,	5														5
Servants,	86			1											87
Stewards,	2														2
Bar keepers,	1														1
Potters,	2														2
Architects,	2														2
Cooks,	6			1											7
Stage drivers,	9														9
Shoe dealers,	2														2
Carders,	2														2
Surveyors,	2														2
Peddlers,	32														32
Students,	23														28
Fanning mill makers,	2														2
Gardeners,	14		1												15
Railroad contractors,	2														2
Firemen,	3														3
Breakmen,	8														8
Train masters,	1														1
Contractors,	4														4
Miners,	1														1
Book keepers,	2														2
Brewers,	2														2
Weavers,	3			2	1	1						1			8
Treasurer of State,	1														1
Secretary of State,	1														1
Auditor of State,	1														1
Dyers,	1														1
Well diggers,	1														1
County Treasurer,	1														1
Porters,	2														2
Planters,	1														1
Restaurant keepers,	2														2
Prairie breakers,			1												1
Herdsmen,			2												2
Ship Carpenters,			1												1
Seamstresses,				4											4
Grooms,				1											1
Tailoresses,							1				1				2
Oil cloth makers,								1							1
Dairymen,												8			3
Distillers,													2		2

TABLE SHOWING THE PLACE OF NATIVITY OF THE INHABITANTS OF JOHNSON COUNTY, FOR 1856.

STATES.	NAME OF TOWNSHIPS.														
	Iowa City.	Washington.	Pleasant Valley.	Big Grove.	Cedar.	Penn.	Scott.	Union.	Monroe.	Jefferson.	Oxford.	Newport.	Liberty.	Clear Creek.	TOTAL.
Ohio,	1084	325	228	232	119	126	227	56	137	77	85	223	86	42	3047
Indiana,	158	25	58	33	46	23	40	6	63	40	12	66	19	11	600
Pennsylvania,	775	120	154	96	21	383	128	41	46	23	40	97	71	34	2029
Iowa,	845	160	113	221	102	178	113	63	77	55	51	184	154	68	2387
New York,	544	58	64	42	23	28	14	26	32	14	33	42	15	31	966
Maine,	50	2		7	13	1	1	2	7			3			86
New Hampshire,	47			4	10				15						76
Vermont,	80	17	19	2	1	1	2	7	6	1	1	1	1	2	141
Massachusetts,	127	5		7	6	1	2	4	7		1	2		3	165
Connecticut,	52	2	5	10	6	4	9	1	1	1	8	3		2	104
Rhode Island,	3	1								2		1			7
Virginia,	86	21	18	17	9	15	32	7	5	72	10	29	38	12	371
Kentucky,	47	2	7	8	2	1	6		3	27	8	3		2	116
Illinois,	129	10	9	9	6	12	8	2	35	20	6	12	14	13	285
Michigan,	35		5	1	7	1	2	1			2		2		56
Alabama,	5								1	1					7
Louisiana,	11		2					2							15
Mississippi,				4										1	5
Florida,				2				1							3
North Carolina,	14	2	19	1	1	3	3		15	1	1	8		1	69
South Carolina,	1					1						1			3
Tennessee,	27	1	6		3		3	23	7	15	1	6		2	94
Missouri,	33	1	3		1						1	1	1		41
Georgia,	1		3							1		1			6
Maryland,	161	26	8	8	2	4	9		2	6		15	8	2	251
New Jersey,	127	4	19	2	3	2	15	1	2	4		3	12	6	200
England,	141	3	27	2	14	4	24	10	2	4	1	13	3	14	264
Ireland,	681	26	4	5	12	11	24	14	7	6	18	60	14	17	898
Wales,	20	2						31							53
Scotland,	44	1	8	1		6					1	4	2		67
Germany,	650	48	8	100	21	6	20	48	8	2	23	60	55		1049
France,	26	3	1	5	6	4	1					7	62	1	116
Austria,	173		1	73	87				7	149		3			493
Prussia,	12	1				2						5	36		56
Sweden,	4														4
Holland,	4														4
On the Ocean,	1	1			2									1	5
Canada,	45	12	2	10	2	5		1	1		4	2		1	85
New Brunswick,		3													3
Switzerland,	10				1	3			7	1		29			51
Denmark,	7														7
Hanover,	2							2							4
Wisconsin,	14	1	4	3		2		1					4		29
Delaware,	6								1			2	2		11
South America,	8														8
Africa,	4														4
Poland,	2														2
Unknown,	18	70								1			4	16	109

TABLE,

SHOWING THE POPULATION OF JONES COUNTY, FOR 1856.

TOWNSHIPS.	No. dwelling houses.	Number of families.	Number of males.	Number of females.	Colored.	Married.	Widowed.	Native voters.	Naturalized voters.	Aliens.	Militia.	Deaf and Dumb	Blind.	Insane.	Owners of land.	Pauper.
Cass, ...	71	71	222	196	....	155	6	83	6	5	71	....	....	....	65	....
Castle Grove, ..	73	78	206	171	....	148	6	62	14	5	44	...	....	....	70	....
Clay, ...	105	105	304	272	....	215	6	104	21	8	90	....	....	....	81	....
Fairview,.......	259	259	787	661	....	494	31	316	12	12	287	3	....	....	195	....
Greenfield, ...	101	101	334	271	....	196	11	102	4	1	95	3	....	....	91	....
Hale, ...	85	65	266	252	....	181	8	98	3	3	82	....	1	....	73	....
Jackson,.......	71	71	232	202	....	140	3	65	2	1	48	1	....	....	52	...
Madison,.......	73	83	237	199	....	172	4	78	6	9	81	....	....	..	91	....
Monticello, ...	93	102	317	233	....	186	23	109	10	10	108	....	....	1	92	....
Oxford, ...	76	76	200	187	1	140	5	53	8	11	32	....	....	....	54	....
Pierce,........	172	172	495	426	1	346	18	198	10	10	184	3	....	....	153	....
Richland,......	127	127	395	340	3	237	11	69	28	33	116	....	....	....	99	....
Rome, ...	131	131	401	336	....	255	21	157	8	5	140	2	....	1	107	1
Scotch Grove,..	90	91	266	242	....	173	12	104	9	6	78	....	....	....	100	....
Washington,...	143	143	359	413	....	280	22	34	92	79	93	....	....	....	151	....
Wayne,.......	51	56	167	146	....	128	5	80	....	3	58	....	....	....	69	....
Total,.......	1721	1761	5288	4547	5	3446	202	1712	233	201	1607	12	1	2	1543	1

TABLE,

SHOWING THE AGRICULTURAL STATISTICS OF JONES COUNTY, FOR 1856.

TOWNSHIPS.	Acres of improved land.	Acres of unimproved land.	Acres of meadow.	Tons of hay.	Bushels of grass seeds.	Acres of spring wheat.	Bushels harvested.	Acres of winter wheat.	Bushels harvested.	Acres of oats.	Bushels harvested.	Acres of corn.	Bushels harvested.	Acres of potatoes.	Bushels harvested.
Cass, ...	1985	4666	5	472	2	354	6131	....	....	109	3501	512	26789	13	1985
Castle Grove,	2953	10739	57	46	10	399	6324	....	....	208	6769	641	22317	28	4044
Clay, ...	1950	5486	105	162	....	561	9596	....	....	186	7202	774	34035	15	1765
Fairview, ...	5106	9324	272	330	13	1031	15551	16	274	440	15133	1587	62820	32	3999
Greenfield, ..	3514	10979	80	580	12	957	14816	20	350	255	7856	1212	44525	23	2969
Hale, ...	2509	7249	49	351	15	561	10859	....	....	104	3157	1004	38205	27	3792
Jackson, ...	2370	5011	265	484	21	701	10876	....	....	186	4907	971	41670	17	2148
Madison, ...	1475	10191	61	703	....	387	7092	....	....	88	2529	423	15650	23	3270
Monticello, ..	2670	10317	118	872	29	537	9059	7	77	227	8035	726	32213	33	4119
Oxford, ...	1997	4520	30	364	18	257	5405	0	8	64	2189	757	35680	12	1515
Pierce, ...	4002	8408	91	188	20	709	12992	8	400	218	8633	1538	74060	44	6065
Richland, ...	3316	9138	525	887	....	753	17628	....	....	499	19896	938	39746	81	5956
Rome, ...	5211	15136	336	327	22	1299	17994	....	....	416	130306	2026	85364	34	3528
Scotch Grove,	3526	5974	119	51	15	705	13963	44	1013	244	9211	1027	45835	17	2504
Washington, .	3449	18929	928	1229	3	735	10377	4	35	449	15644	1490	63740	85	9040
Wayne, ...	1312	7768	....	763	7	282	5553	....	....	123	3955	343	10645	15	2165
Total, ...	47345	143835	3041	7809	187	10229	174216	99	2157	3815	248923	15969	673294	493	58864

TABLE,

SHOWING THE NUMBER AND VALUE OF HOGS AND CATTLE SOLD, THE VALUE OF DOMESTIC AND GENERAL MANUFACTURES OF JONES COUNTY, FOR 1856.

TOWNSHIPS.	No. of hogs sold.	Value of hogs sold.	No. of Cattle sold.	Value of cattle. sold.	Pounds of butter made.	Pounds of cheese.	Pounds of wool.	Value of domestic manufactures.	Value of general manufactures.
Cass, ...	173	1479	92	2323	3565	260	321	159	....
Castle Grove, ...	514	3061	97	3811	3270	220	1068	32	....
Clay, ...	560	3405	83	3001	5689	1400	763	42	....
Fairview, ...	1097	8856	244	8245	15990	880	2320	740	10000
Greenfield, ...	847	6738	141	4037	6540	2254	803	217	413
Hale, ...	570	3835	95	3060	8221	....	538	378	430
Jackson, ...	762	9620	192	5748	6982	400	1413	195	18
Madison, ...	133	721	217	7745	6365	546	140	142	....
Monticello, ...	708	4683	183	5831	10282	469	539	108	4780
Oxford, ...	377	4125	445	17451	6035	113	233	64	....
Pierce, ...	1087	6420	261	10013	10130	92	349	642	....
Richland, ...	799	7391	429	7292	15730	47000	369	121	....
Rome, ...	1456	12746	375	11567	11545	622	1046	273	8865
Scotch Grove, ...	700	4378	109	3743	7742	455	929	281	....
Washington, ...	1208	9642	61	1951	9785	....	716	279	37
Wayne, ...	67	709	134	4117	3335	658	56	15	....
Total, ...	11058	87809	3158	99941	131206	55369	11603	3688	24543

TABLE,

SHOWING THE PROFESSIONS, TRADES OR OCCUPATIONS OF THE INHABITANTS OF JONES COUNTY, FOR 1856.

TOWNSHIPS.	Farmers.	Laborers.	Blacksmiths.	Carpenters.	Wagon makers.	Plasterers.	Stone Masons.	Stone cutters.	Machinists.	Engineers.	Millers.	Sawyers.	Millwrights.	Painters.	Cabinet makers.	Tinners.	Milliners.	Tailors.
Cass, ...	54	3	2	1	....	....	....	....	....	1	1	....	1	....	....	....	....	1
Castle Grove, ..	65	3	2	1	....	....	....	1	....	....	....	....	....	....	....	....	....	....
Clay, ...	67	....	7	10	....	....	....	....	1	....	1	....	1	....	....	3	....	....
Fairview, ...	123	163	13	13	2	....	17	....	....	4	5	2	2	2	3	4	....	3
Greenfield, ...	56	7	3	....	....	....	....	....	....	....	....	....	....	....	....	....	1	....
Hale, ...	67	19	1	5	....	....	....	....	....	....	1	....	1	....	....	....	3	....
Jackson, ...	67	....	....	4	....	....	1	....	....	....	1	....	....	....	1	....	....	....
Madison, ...	84	9	3	7	....	....	1	....	....	....	....	....	....	....	....	....	1	....
Monticello, ...	76	12	3	7	2	....	....	1	....	....	....	1	....	....	....	....	....	2
Oxford, ...	75	....	....	3	....	....	....	....	....	....	....	....	....	....	....	....	....	....
Pierce, ...	182	2	5	21	....	1	1	....	....	....	....	....	....	....	....	....	11	....
Richland, ...	83	6	1	7	....	....	....	....	....	....	1	....	....	....	....	....	....	....
Rome, ...	87	33	4	14	....	....	3	....	....	....	....	....	....	....	....	....	....	....
Scotch Grove,	68	....	1	2	1	2	....	....	....	....	....	....	....	1	....	....	....	....
Washington, ..	145	88	1	4	....	....	....	....	....	....	....	....	....	....	....	....	....	....
Wayne, ...	74	5	2	....	....	....	1	....	....	....	....	....	....	....	....	....	....	2
Total, ...	1373	350	48	103	5	3	24	2	1	5	10	3	5	3	4	7	16	8

TABLE,—CONTINUED,

SHOWING THE PROFESSIONS, TRADES OR OCCUPATIONS OF THE INHABITANTS OF JONES COUNTY, FOR 1856.

TOWNSHIPS.	Shoe makers.	Harness makers.	Bakers.	Butchers.	Mechanics.	Manufacturers.	Merchants.	Traders.	Druggists.	Confectioners.	Hotel keepers.	Physicians.	Lawyers.	Clergymen.	Teachers.	Printers.	Artists.	Daguerrean artists.
Cass,	....	....	....	....	....	....	1	....	....	....	....	1	....	....	....	....	....	....
Castle Grove,	....	....	....	....	....	....	1	....	....	....	....	....	....	....	....	....	....	....
Clay,	3	....	....	....	....	....	1	....	....	....	....	1	....	....	....	....	....	....
Fairview,	5	4	1	....	24	....	16	....	2	....	2	7	5	1	3	2	1	....
Greenfield,	....	1	....	....	2	1	....	....	....	....	....	1	....	....	....	....	....	....
Hale,	1	....	....	....	....	....	1	1	....	....	....	....	....	1	....	....	....	....
Jackson,	1	....	....	....	....	....	....	....	....	....	....	....	....	3	....	....	....	....
Madison,	....	....	....	....	1	....	1	....	....	....	....	1	....	....	2	....	....	....
Monticello,	1	....	....	1	....	....	2	....	....	....	1	1	1	....	....	....	....	1
Oxford,	....	....	....	....	....	....	....	....	....	....	....	....	....	1	....	....	....	....
Pierce,	6	....	....	....	....	....	5	....	1	....	....	2	....	3	1	....	1	....
Richland,	....	....	....	....	3	....	3	....	....	....	....	....	....	1	1	....	....	....
Rome,	....	....	....	....	1	....	2	....	....	1	....	4	....	....	2	....	....	....
Scotch Grove,	....	....	....	....	....	....	....	....	....	....	....	....	....	1	....	....	....	....
Washington,	1	1	....	....	....	....	....	....	....	....	....	....	....	....	....	....	....	....
Wayne,	....	....	....	....	....	....	....	....	....	....	....	....	....	....	....	....	....	....
Total,	18	6	1	1	32	1	33	1	3	1	3	18	6	11	9	2	2	1

TABLE—Continued,

EXHIBITING THE PROFESSIONS, TRADES, OR OCCUPATIONS OF THE INHABITANTS OF JONES COUNTY, FOR 1856.

TOWNSHIPS.	Grocers.	Teamsters.	Brick makers.	Watch makers.	Coopers.	Clerks.	Weavers.	Sheriff.	Professional.	Potters.	Stage drivers.	Colliers.	Surveyors.	Tobacconists.	Wheelwrights.	Broom makers.	Curriers.	County Judge.
Cass,..			1															
Castle Grove,..																		
Clay,.........					3		1											
Fairview,.....		1			4	6		1	3									
Greenfield, ...					1													
Hale,.					1													
Jackson,......																		
Madison, ...				1						1								
Monticello, ...											1	1	1					
Oxford, ...							1											
Pierce,.......	1					1							1	1	1			
Richland,.....																		
Rome, ...					1	2							1			2		
Scotch Grove,																		
Washington, ..						1											1	
Wayne,.																		1
Total,......	1	1	1	1	10	10	2	1	3	1	1	1	3	1	1	2	1	1

TABLE,

SHOWING THE PLACE OF NATIVITY OF THE INHABITANTS OF JONES COUNTY, FOR 1856.

TOWNSHIPS.	Ohio.	Indiana.	Pennsylvania.	Iowa.	New York.	Maine.	N. Hampshire.	Vermont.	Massachusetts.	Connecticut.	Rhode Island.	Virginia.	Kentucky.	Illinois.	Michigan.	Louisiana.	Mississippi.	N. Carolina.	S. Carolina.
Cass,	100	22	33	82	44	3	6	13	14	6		11	3		5	1		4	
Castle Grove,	41	34	45	53	51	1	35	21	6	3		3	2	11	6			1	
Clay,	95	61	42	99	110	1	4	17	2	2	12	11	12	6			4	1	
Fairview,	306	132	134	285	232	3	10	19	21	16	1	46	35	64	26			4	1
Greenfield,	193	45	95	130	55		1	2	4	2		16	17	11	13			4	
Hale,	139	73	42	75	84		12	6	8	6		33		5	2			2	
Jackson,	158	26		78	74	1		3	3	6	1	20	2	17	2				
Madison,	21	2	82	41	128	4	10	16	4	8		3		37	15				
Monticello,	82	55	41	96	90		20	10	24	2		11	13	31	4			1	
Oxford,	128	29	29	34	50		1	5	6	6	1	2	2	13	3				
Pierce,	245	63	69	157	127	1	13	31	11	19	4	38	14	31	6			1	
Richland,	71	46	36	176	76	1	24	28	5	15	5	1	6	30	1	2	2	2	2
Rome,	289	65	60	151	42	1		6	5	1		49	9	9	8			1	
Scotch Grove,	33	45	107	104	63	1	3	4		2		7	35	16	1			1	
Washington,	22	38	30	218	52	8	1		23	1	5	6	22	23	2	5		1	
Wayne,	51	21	62	29	43		34	9	10		1	1	2	9	3				
Total,	1974	757	907	1808	1321	25	174	190	146	95	30	258	174	313	97	8	6	23	3

TABLE,—CONTINUED,

SHOWING THE PLACE OF NATIVITY OF THE INHABITANTS OF JONES COUNTY, FOR 1856.

TOWNSHIPS.	Tennessee.	Missouri.	Georgia.	Maryland.	New Jersey.	England.	Ireland.	Wales.	Scotland.	Germany.	France.	Austria.	Prussia.	Sweden.	Holland.	On the Ocean.	Canada.	N. Brunswick.	Switzerland.	West Indies.	Wisconsin.	Poland.	Delaware.	Unknown.
Cass,	1	23		1	14	8				5	1						11				7			
Castle Grove,	1		1	1	2	4	41		3	2							7				2			
Clay,	2			7	3	16	49		3	4		1					12							
Fairview,	10	5		10	8	20	7	3	3	16		1	2				13				11	3	1	
Greenfield,	1			2			3	1	3	4					1		2							
Hale,	1			4	3	6	4		2	1							6				2			2
Jackson,	20			9	2	2	1		1	2	4									1			1	
Madison,				1	5	1	4		19	5							30							
Monticello,	1	1		1		11	16			12	5	4		1			11				7			
Oxford,	1			1		15	4		3	50			1			1	1				1			
Pierce,	5	1	2	5	21	20	1		14	9							13							
Richland,		7		2	4	19	109			24	2						3	2	28		5		1	
Rome,				6	3	1	10		1	13							4	1					1	
Scotch Grove,	1	2		2	1		10		16	3							50				1			
Washington,		4		7	1	10	369		1	5	2						12				3		1	
Wayne,							5		3	1							26		1				2	
Total,	44	43	3	59	67	133	633	4	72	156	14	6	3	1	1	1	201	3	29	1	39	3	7	2

TABLE,

SHOWING THE POPULATION OF KEOKUK COUNTY, FOR 1856.

TOWNSHIPS.	No dwelling houses	Number of families	Number of males.	Number of females.	Married.	Widowed.	Native voters.	Naturalized voters	Aliens.	Militia.	Deaf and Dumb.	Blind.	Insane.	Idiotic.	Owners of land.	Paupers.
Richland,	141	242	730	679	466	32	255	7	6	230	2				205	
Jackson,	168	168	522	481	339	18	184	2	6	152	2			2	117	
Benton,	108	120	333	317	212	15	99	14	3	90					88	1
Clear Creek,	105	121	339	339	227	15	94	16	30	66		1			110	
German,	132	141	414	392	268	21	67	58	38	107					125	
Van Buren,	125	125	365	360	231	16	132	9	2	126		2	1	2	104	
Prairie,	21	21	52	53	39		17		1	19					17	
English River,	115	120	341	335	224	19	145	5	11	127				2	115	
Steady Run,	133	133	380	314	242	14	137	6	14	128					101	
Warren,	65	74	217	177	139	10	78	3	1	70	1			2	54	
Lancaster,	194	194	587	523	357	36	222	3	4	195	5			1	149	
La Fayette,	33	36	96	85	59	1	30	9		39					29	5
Sigourney,	174	174	505	429	329	18	203	8	5	180					84	
Washington,	98	102	319	270	187	4	119	4		99	2			1	75	
Adams,	46	49	164	129	97	6	59			55					40	
Liberty,	69	69	202	197	126	5	75	7	2	60	1				62	
Total,	1827	1889	5566	5080	3542	230	1916	141	123	1713	13	3	1	10	1475	6

TABLE,

SHOWING THE AGRICULTURAL STATISTICS OF KEOKUK COUNTY, FOR 1856.

TOWNSHIPS.	Acres of improved land.	Acres of unimproved land.	Acres of meadow	Tons of hay.	Bushels of grass seed.	Acres of spring wheat.	Bushels harvested.	Acres of winter wheat.	Bushels harvested.	Acres of oats.	Bushels harvested.	Acres of corn.	Bushels harvested.	Acres of potatoes.	Bushels harvested.
Richland, ...	6733	13025	593	591	134	930	5680	26	235	763	25467	2915	139360	18	4968
Jackson, ...	5963	6741	248	147	106	1024	5411	21	72	717	19283	3559	190890	33	4247
Benton, ...	3770	10079	184	103	44	559	3892	27	496	441	14340	1738	90690	20	2505
Clear Creek, ...	3994	13046	238	267	6	447	5756	22	261	372	10795	1349	72673	26	3231
German, ...	5008	18360	95	84	6	602	7419	26	252	446	12190	1550	76107	20	1551
Van Buren, ...	2943	9805	153	52	3	555	8620	165	763	250	7613	1541	73263	9	714
Prairie, ...	488	1619	1	66		45	978	2	24	52	560	103	3740	1	274
English River, ..	2708	15799	35	35	2	297	5678	12	350	155	5752	979	47240	17	2245
Steady Run, ...	4577	9679	167	90	7	507	4524	3	5	550	18318	1778	91680	20	3453
Warren, ...	1838	8365	54	45		229	1540			144	3628	994	50757	8	1100
Lancaster, ...	4370	16461	276	510	23	597	2907	30	165	451	11366	2273	123117	18	4433
La Fayette, ...	861	512				21	420	6	120	8	300	138	6250	1	220
Sigourney, ...	3126	9893	75	154		57	975			68	2700	298	12335	31	725
Washington, ...	3745	10276	80	128	4	401	3647	8	70	204	7851	1276	69780	16	2285
Adams, ...	1155	6838	5	3	4	107	1959			51	1805	303	16430	5	925
Liberty, ...	1238	11228				109	1894			41	1129	619	21785	10	1741
Total, ...	52517	163725	2204	2279	339	6488	61300	348	2813	4713	143097	21413	983097	253	34637

TABLE—SHOWING THE NUMBER AND VALUE OF HOGS, CATTLE, DOMESTIC AND GENERAL MANUFACTURES OF KEOKUK COUNTY, FOR 1856.

TOWNSHIPS.	No. of hogs sold.	Value of hogs sold.	No. of cattle sold.	Value of cattle sold.	Pounds of butter made.	Pounds of cheese.	Pounds of Wool.	Value of domestic Manufactures.	Value of general manufactures.
Richland,	2286	14588	530	11673	24191	4035	3810	2177	8370
Jackson,	2389	19981	298	6644	14065	480	2049	1859	2170
Benton,	1443	9697	243	3782	7885	793	1080	935	1100
Clear Creek,	775	5479	388	12679	9736	387	827	529	1050
German,	1629	7540	276	6326	10670	595	1390	1180	15067
Van Buren,	1333	9225	284	7364	10214	187	1166	932	19384
Prairie,	24	256	17	552	1330	150	10	15	
English River,	552	4152	119	3451	1716	130	662	452	
Steady Run,	1342	9721	230	6405	7166	60	1591	1318	1020
Warren,	590	3855	70	1476	4573	9	577	493	616
Lancaster,	1850	13174	330	7749	15561	4379	1785	1983	20
La Fayette,	53	570	24	1549	294	50	50	150	
Sigourney,	216	1747	99	2247	945		100		
Washington,	1235	5284	178	5177	11082	165	1272	1398	
Adams,	153	1252	19	482	4770	650	210	155	
Liberty,	232	1553	60	1834	3530		146	74	
Total,	16102	108073	3165	79390	127728	16070	16725	13650	38697

TABLE,

EXHIBITING THE PROFESSIONS, TRADES OR OCCUPATIONS OF THE INHABITANTS OF KEOKUK COUNTY, FOR 1856.

TOWNSHIPS.	Farmers.	Laborers.	Blacksmiths.	Carpenters.	Wagon makers.	Brick Layers.	Plasterers.	Stone masons.	Stone Cutters.	Carriage Makers.	Machinists.	Engineers.	Millers.	Sawyers.	Millwrights.	Painters.
Richland,	144	23	8	23	5		2			1		2	4	4		
Jackson,	142	81	2	5	2			2								
Benton,	83	12		2												1
Clear Creek,	111	2	2	6	1			2					1	3		
German,	175	26	2	1	1	2							1			
Van Buren,	96		1	2	1	1		4						1		1
Prairie,	15				1											
English River,	113	9	3	13												
Steady Run,	112		3	3			2	1					3	2		
Warren,	66	13		1			1							1		
Lancaster,	188	11	6	22	1	1	1			2	1		4	1	6	1
La Fayette,	33															
Sigourney,	28		10	25	1		4	5	1	1			1			
Washington,	89			11												
Adams,	55	1		3												2
Liberty,	65		2	5											1	
Total,	1515	178	39	122	13	4	10	14	1	4	1	2	14	12	7	5

TABLE—Continued,

SHOWING THE PROFESSIONS, TRADES, OR OCCUPATIONS OF THE INHABITANTS OF KEOKUK COUNTY, FOR 1856.

TOWNSHIPS.	Cabinet makers.	Chair makers.	Tinners.	Milliners.	Tailors.	Hatters.	Shoemakers.	Saddle & harness makers.	Butchers.	Manufacturers.	Merchants.	Druggists.	Hotel Keepers.	Physicians.	Dentists.	Lawyers.	Clergymen.
Richland,........	6	1	2	1	3	1	4	5			6	3	1	6		1	5
Jackson,..........							1	1			3			4			
Benton,..........	1	1	1								1						1
Clear Creek,.......	1		1		4						1			2			
German,..........				2			3				1						
Van Buren,........							1	2	1	1				1			
Prairie,..........																	
English River,.....							1				3	1					1
Steady Run,.......	1										3			1			
Warren,...........								1									
Lancaster,.........	4	2	2	3	1		4	1			7		1	6	1	3	
La Fayette,........																	
Sigourney,.........	4		2		2		6	4			4	1	1	8		6	3
Washington,.......								1			1			5		1	
Adams,...........			2				1					3		1	1		
Liberty,...........																	
Total,.........	17	4	8	6	10	1	21	15	1	1	30	8	3	34	2	11	11

TABLE—Continued,

EXHIBITING THE PROFESSIONS, TRADES OR OCCUPATIONS OF THE INHABITANTS OF KEOKUK COUNTY, FOR 1856.

TOWNSHIPS.	Teachers.	Printers.	Artists.	Daguerrean Ars's.	Bankers.	Grocers.	Teamsters.	Brick makers.	Gunsmiths.	Coopers.	Clerks.	Students.	Tailoresses.	Shingle makers.	Broom makers.	Pump makers.
Richland,	3						3	2			4	2	2	1	2	1
Jackson,	2									3						
Benton,								1		2						
Clear Creek,													2			
German,	1															
Van Buren,		1														
Prairie,																
English River,	2		1							2			4			
Steady Run,	1									2						
Warren,													2			
Lancaster,	4			1	2		1			2	2		6			
La Fayette,																
Sigourney,	1	1				3	4		1		3		1	1		
Washington,											1					
Adams,																
Liberty,																
Total,	14	2	1	1	2	3	8	3	1	12	10	2	17	2	2	1

TABLE—CONTINUED,

SHOWING THE PROFESSIONS, TRADES OR OCCUPATIONS OF THE INHABITANTS OF KEOKUK COUNTY, FOR 1856.

TOWNSHIPS.	Ventailoquists.	Weavers.	Ferrymen.	Wheel Wright.	Brewers.	Lumbermen	Nurserymen.	Sheriffs.	Foreman.	Ostlers.	Surveyors.	Mail Carriers.	Prairie Brakers.	Wind Mill Makers.	Wool Carders.	Distillers.	Stock Dealers.
Richland,............	1	1															
Jackson,............			1														
Benton,............				1													
Clear Creek,.........		1			1												
German,............																	
Van Buren,.........				2		1	1	1									
Prairie,............																	
English River,........									1								
Steady Run,.........																	
Warren,............		2															
Lancaster,..........										2	1	1	1				
La Fayette,.........																	
Sigourney,..........											1			2	1	1	
Washington,........						1											1
Adams,............																	
Liberty,............																	
Total,............	1	4	1	3	1	2	1	1	1	2	2	1	1	2	1	1	1

TABLE—SHOWING THE PLACE OF NATIVITY OF THE INHABITANTS OF KEOKUK COUNTY, FOR 1856.

STATES.	NAME OF TOWNSHIPS.																
	Richland.	Jackson.	Benton.	Clear Creek.	German.	Van Buren.	Prairie.	English River.	Steady Run.	Warren.	Lancaster.	La Fayette.	Sigourney.	Washington.	Adams.	Liberty.	TOTAL.
Ohio,	241	104	255	223	70	109	65	185	131	47	163	68	274	167	104	117	2228
Indiana,	286	194	121	6	82	186	1	180	195	91	332	5	148	87	52	64	2030
Pennsylvania,	76	33	26	91	53	19	2	59	30	13	72	8	80	25	7	20	614
Iowa,	396	280	171	104	223	147	7	93	137	124	275	7	157	148	39	48	2356
New York,	11	6	19	12	3	17	13	18	6	7	19	8	32	25	14	23	228
Maine,	...	...	...	...	...	...	..	5	...	2	...	..	1	...	...	...	8
New Hampshire,	1	...	...	...	...	...	..	1	...	...	4	..	4	...	1	...	11
Vermont,	4	...	2	1	1	8	2	1	1	...	14	..	9	5	4	2	54
Massachusetts,	1	...	1	...	...	...	..	6	3	...	1	8	3	1	10	4	38
Connecticut,	1	1	1	5	1	...	..	1	1	4	1	16	5	3	[illegible]	1	50
Rhode Island,	...	...	...	...	...	...	..	...	...	2	...	..	...	...	...	1	3
Virginia,	34	54	28	22	13	79	4	49	26	15	45	..	35	32	12	57	505
Kentucky,	28	97	22	12	17	27	..	17	40	40	68	..	38	28	8	11	458
Illinois,	37	123	26	23	13	65	5	17	38	22	35	21	63	39	22	34	583
Michigan,	...	...	7	...	...	...	..	...	1	...	1	1	3	5	...	...	18
Arkansas,	...	...	...	...	...	...	..	...	1	...	...	..	...	...	...	...	1
Louisiana,	...	...	...	...	2	...	..	1	...	...	...	..	...	...	...	...	3
Mississippi,	...	...	...	...	...	...	..	2	...	...	...	..	...	...	...	...	2
Florida,	...	...	...	...	...	...	..	...	...	...	...	..	...	...	1	...	1
North Carolina,	107	14	18	3	9	20	..	2	5	5	12	..	15	1	2	...	213
South Carolina,	1	...	...	1	...	2	..	...	...	...	2	..	...	...	...	1	7
Tennessee,	133	52	9	1	6	4	..	2	40	7	18	..	4	3	...	...	279
Missouri,	12	7	1	...	14	1	..	2	6	4	12	..	2	...	...	...	61
Georgia,	...	...	...	...	...	...	..	3	...	...	1	..	...	...	...	1	5
Maryland,	3	11	8	3	3	17	..	19	6	1	7	1	14	2	4	2	96
New Jersey,	9	11	6	1	...	5	..	2	3	2	2	..	8	7	1	...	57
England,	3	...	2	...	...	2	1	...	1	...	1	1	5	3	...	2	21
Ireland,	4	1	...	3	8	9	1	2	12	4	5	12	8	1	2	6	78
Scotland,	3	...	11	...	8	...	..	3	...	1	...	17	2	...	...	...	45
Germany,	14	15	17	165	240	3	..	2	10	1	12	8	17	3	...	3	511
France,	1	...	1	1	...	...	..	1	...	...	...	..	1	...	...	...	5
Russia,	...	...	...	...	1	...	..	...	...	...	...	..	...	...	...	...	1
Prussia,	...	...	...	...	21	...	2	...	...	...	1	..	5	2	...	...	31
Sweden,	1	...	...	...	...	...	..	...	...	...	1	..	...	...	...	...	2
Holland,	...	...	...	...	4	...	..	...	...	...	...	..	...	...	...	...	4
Canada,	1	...	...	...	2	1	..	...	...	...	2	..	...	...	...	1	7
New Brunswick,	...	...	...	1	...	...	..	...	...	...	...	..	...	...	...	1	2
Switzerland,	...	...	...	...	1	...	2	5	...	...	...	..	...	...	...	...	8
Hanover,	...	...	...	...	8	...	..	...	...	...	...	..	...	...	...	...	8
Wisconsin,	1	...	...	...	...	...	..	2	1	...	...	..	...	...	...	...	4
Delaware,	...	...	8	...	3	...	..	...	...	2	3	..	1	2	1	...	15
Africa,	...	...	...	...	...	4	..	...	...	...	...	..	...	...	...	...	4
Unknown,	...	...	...	...	...	...	..	...	...	...	1	..	...	...	...	...	1

TABLE,

SHOWING THE POPULATION, AGRICULTURAL STATISTICS, THE NUMBER AND VALUE OF HOGS AND CATTLE SOLD, &C., OF KOSSUTH COUNTY, FOR 1856.

POPULATION.	TOWNSHIPS. Algona.	Humbolt.	TOTAL.
Number of dwelling houses,	58	22	80
Number of families,	62	26	88
Number of males,	173	64	237
Number of females,	111	49	160
Married,	98	35	133
Widowed,	3	2	5
Native voters,	85	25	110
Naturalized voters,	8	4	12
Aliens,	9		9
Militia,	94	27	121
Owners of land,	....	4	4
AGRICULTURAL STATISTICS—			
Acres of improved land,	696	40	736
Acres of unimproved land,		280	280
Tons of hay,	179	....	179
Bushels of grass seed,	2	....	2
Acres of spring wheat,	50	....	50
Bushels harvested,	680	....	680
Acres of oats,	16	....	16
Bushels harvested,	515	....	515
Acres of corn,	163	....	168
Bushels harvested,	4200	....	4200
Acres of potatoes,	3	....	3
Bushels harvested,	479	....	479
HOGS, CATTLE, &C.—			
Number of hogs sold,	109	....	109
Value of hogs sold,	926	....	926
Number of cattle sold,	26	....	26
Value of cattle sold,	645	....	645
Pounds of butter made,	600	....	600
Pounds of wool,	50	....	50

TABLE,

EXHIBITING THE PROFESSIONS, TRADES, OR OCCUPATIONS OF THE INHABITANTS OF KOSSUTH COUNTY, FOR 1856.

TOWNSHIPS.	Farmers.	Laborers.	Carpenters.	Engineers.	Millers.	Mechanics.	Merchants.	Physicians.	Clergymen.	Teachers.
Algona,	74	10	1	1	..	17	3	1	2	1
Humbolt,	32	..	..	..	2	1	..	1	..	1
Total,	106	10	1	1	2	18	3	2	2	2

TABLE,

SHOWING THE PLACE OF NATIVITY OF THE INHABITANTS OF KOSSUTH COUNTY, FOR 1856.

STATES.	TOWNSHIPS.		TOTAL.
	Algona.	Humbolt.	
Ohio	32	13	45
Indiana,	29	20	49
Pennsylvania,	25	7	32
Iowa,	30	16	46
New York,	21	8	29
Maine,	1	.....	1
New Hampshire,	9	.....	9
Vermont,	12	.....	12
Massachusetts,	23	.....	23
Connecticut,	1	1	2
Rhode Island,	2	.....	2
Virginia,	1	.....	1
Kentucky,	4	1	5
Illinois,	38	29	67
Michigan,	4	.....	4
North Carolina,	2	9	11
South Carolina,	1	.....	1
Tennessee,	.....	3	3
Missouri,	1	.....	1
Maryland,	12	.....	12
New Jersey,	1	.....	1
England,	7	.....	7
Ireland,	7	6	13
Scotland,	7	.....	7
Germany,	8	.....	8
Canada,	3	.....	3
Switzerland,	1	.....	1
Wisconsin,	1	.....	1
Unknown,	1	.....	1

TABLE,

SHOWING THE POPULATION OF LEE COUNTY, FOR 1856.

TOWNSHIPS.	No. dwelling houses.	Number of families.	Number of males.	Number of females.	Colored.	Married.	Widowed.	Native voters.	Naturalized voters.	Aliens.	Militia.	Deaf and Dumb.	Blind.	Insane.	Idiotic.	Owners of land.	Paupers.
Cedar, ...	140	158	440	411	....	305	38	158	10	8	148	....	....	1	1	105	....
Charleston, ...	246	246	683	638	....	431	23	185	50	13	157	....	....	....	....	112	....
Denmark, ...	93	93	418	409	....	302	28	184	11	16	180	....	....	....	2	125	....
Des Moines, ...	203	203	628	506	....	370	18	219	17	18	202	....	1	3	....	89	1
Franklin, ...	244	254	722	683	....	386	20	116	104	60	150	....	1	....	....	176	....
Green Bay, ...	92	92	310	240	....	165	20	96	12	16	93	....	1	....	....	58	....
Harrison, ...	153	164	525	447	....	305	22	153	26	24	176	2	....	....	1	127	....
Jackson, ...	1168	1367	4988	3947	2	2884	216	1719	861	283	2745	6	....	1	4	443	21
Jefferson, ...	110	110	363	284	....	190	28	81	26	21	117	....	....	....	1	81	....
Madison, ...	521	521	1394	1252	....	984	30	275	273	105	460	....	....	....	....	403	....
Marion, ...	197	197	623	563	....	378	23	189	37	11	200	....	....	....	....	152	....
Montrose, ...	322	335	959	838	....	574	33	321	38	23	318	....	....	....	....	42	....
Pleasant, ...	153	169	539	483	....	317	16	155	20	17	148	....	....	....	....	145	....
Van Buren, ...	208	208	593	560	....	376	21	185	15	5	182	....	....	....	....	7	....
Washington, ...	179	186	599	510	....	360	17	200	34	45	227	....	....	....	2	154	....
West Point, ...	291	324	931	787	....	577	44	189	120	82	269	....	....	....	....	232	....
Total, ...	4320	4627	14715	12558	2	8904	587	4426	1654	747	5772	8	3	5	9	2451	22

TABLE,

SHOWING THE AGRICULTURAL STATISTICS OF LEE COUNTY, FOR 1856.

TOWNSHIPS.	Acres of improved land.	Acres of unimproved land.	Acres of meadow.	Tons of hay.	Bushels of grass seed.	Acres of spring wheat.	Bushels harvested.	Acres of winter wheat	Bushels harvested.	Acres of oats.	Bushels harvested	Acres of corn.	Bushels harvested.	Acres of potatoes	Bushels harvested.
Cedar, ...	7547	7378	1022	892	201	1757	22715	58	866	1048	37090	2482	130615	25	3851
Charleston, .	5563	5179	818	899	133	1590	22434	254	5017	1812	42432	2555	110151	69	7142
Denmark, ..	6399	9909	1130	1651	174	845	13424	57	1225	583	17883	1249	69210	21	2818
Des Moines,	8606	2108	708	445	30	1595	25076	42	597	1033	20056	2475	90952	59	6375
Franklin, ...	11335	9745	1516	962	1273	1991	4159	330	13333	1589	146139	3213	209273	83	9043
Green Bay, .	4312	1775	401	512	10	620	8208	656	10706	1705	9308	1699	85560	15	1919
Harrison....	8565	15795	932	1120	318	1177	16634	180	2484	1352	43906	2795	126000	36	4606
Jackson, ..	2016	2398	339	345	....	232	2932	93	1372	216	5710	1493	41425	22	1918
Jefferson, ...	3698	3856	205	165	3	548	6270	151	1880	357	4774	1380	47941	51	5157
Madison, ...	1274	1287	129	167	....	320	1354	209	4151	58	1180	515	21910	6	1110
Marion, ...	12032	8624	1299	1267	1310	2996	33796	135	1741	1903	51545	3472	205504	433	5679
Montrose, ..	8279	7573	948	960	....	1689	23331	130	2108	841	5586	2652	98902	68	8120
Pleasant, ...	9372	8117	1319	1445	271	1994	33542	210	2776	151	52723	3101	171405	33	6011
Van Buren,	2454	2932	356	382	42	831	12960	88	963	630	14697	1399	52259	39	3112
Washington,	9977	14619	1701	1313	145	1676	25904	673	7951	1551	37054	3345	149225	69	7246
West Point,	7640	4623	555	628	113	1341	16882	385	5297	1189	35151	2431	107760	49	5280
Total, ...	109070	105918	13379	13154	4023	21002	269621	3561	62497	15810	525234	36255	1718092	1072	79387

TABLE,

SHOWING THE NUMBER AND VALUE OF HOGS AND CATTLE SOLD, THE VALUE OF DOMESTIC AND GENERAL MANUFACTURES OF LEE COUNTY, FOR 1856.

TOWNSHIPS.	No. of hogs sold.	Value of hogs sold.	No. of cattle sold.	Value of cattle sold.	Pounds of butter made.	Pounds of cheese.	Pounds of Wool.	Value of domestic manufacture.	Value of general manufactures.
Cedar,	1334	1659	311	6303	23893	4062	2706	543	......
Charleston,	1184	11764	313	8257	19396	416	1907	992	2230
Denmark,	702	7267	1280	11187	21861	114023	1703	309	191330
Des Moines,	1425	11713	260	6277	21905	4586	1509	633	65
Franklin,	1358	12741	328	3086	23178	550	6042	417	....
Green Bay,	810	7523	119	3609	9095	600	864	739	....
Harrison,	1826	14928	314	6727	22378	1940	1541	493	3390
Jackson,	465	4259	150	1258	3888	230	165	25	....
Jefferson,	742	4577	243	5094	11780	5000	479	226	....
Madison,	329	2220	24	287	200	....	......	....	....
Marion,	2262	22290	675	10665	28494	2456	3024	1404	4737
Montrose,	833	7394	290	7952	17425	900	782	373	....
Pleasant,	1850	18041	378	7342	32715	8950	2145	1039	130
Van Buren,	555	6860	236	4563	12978	186	1184	482	....
Washington,	1956	15289	794	11193	30861	6776	889	1300	1300
West Point,	1303	12087	316	8522	37110	1100	1261	165	21222
Total,	18934	160612	6031	102322	316957	151775	26201	9140	224404

TABLE,

EXHIBITING THE PROFESSIONS, TRADES OR OCCUPATIONS OF THE INHABITANTS OF LEE COUNTY, FOR 1856.

TOWNSHIPS.	Farmers.	Laborers.	Blacksmiths.	Carpenters.	Wagon makers.	Brick layers.	Plasterers.	Stone Masons.	Stone Cutters.	Builders.	Carriage makers.	Machinists.	Engineers.	Millers.	Sawyers.	Millwrights.	Printers.	Cabinet makers.
Cedar,	144		4	8			1											
Charleston,	154	25	2	2	1													
Denmark,	110	35	6	15								2		5	1			1
Des Moines,	177	43	8	3	1		1	2							1			
Franklin,	170	15	7	11	7	2	4	3				3	2	1	1		1	2
Green Bay,	137	10	2	3				1					1					
Harrison,	223		4	8	1	1	1	2										4
Jackson,	170	648	33	234		25					13	15	42					11
Jefferson,	90	43																
Madison,	13	196	25	66	8	18		6	9			7	7	4		4	7	13
Marion,	210	4	7	4	3													
Montrose,	111	85	12	16	3		1		1					2			2	
Pleasant,	140	10	1	6		1		5					1	1				
Van Buren,	127		5	2	1			5	1					1		1		
Washington,	260	58	5	5	2												1	
West Point,	222	47	10	14	5	1	1	1						1		2		6
Total,	2458	1219	131	397	32	48	9	25	11	....	13	27	53	15	3	7	11	37

TABLE—CONTINUED,

SHOWING THE PROFESSIONS, TRADES OR OCCUPATIONS OF THE INHABITANTS OF LEE COUNTY, FOR 1856.

TOWNSHIPS.	Chair makers.	Tinners.	Milliners.	Merchant tailors.	Tailors.	Hatters.	Shoe makers.	Harness makers.	Bakers.	Butchers.	Mechanics.	Manufacturers.	Merchants.	Speculators.	Agents.	Drovers.	Traders.	Druggists.
Cedar,	....	...	5	....	....	....	2	2	....	....	....	....	3	....	....	....	....	....
Charleston,	...	....	....	....	....	....	....	....	....	....	4	....	10	....	....	....	1	....
Denmark,	....	....	3	....	2	....	1	....	....	....	6	....	....	....	....	....	....	....
Des Moines,	....	....	....	....	....	....	1	....	....	....	1	....	1	....	....	....	....	....
Franklin,	....	....	....	....	3	....	4	3	....	....	....	....	4	....	....	....	....	....
Green Bay,	...	....	2	....	....	....	1	....	....	....	....	....	....	..	....	....	....	....
Harrison,	1	....	1	....	2	...	2	1	....	....	....	1	2	....	....	....	....	....
Jackson,	....	20	11	....	25	4	44	....	25	15	....	3	5	5	19	...	11	22
Jefferson,	....	....	....	....	....	....	....	....	....	....	....	....	....	....	....	....	....	....
Madison,	....	4	....	....	14	....	13	7	4	9	2	1	31	....	....	....	1	4
Marion,	...	....	1	....	....	....	2	....	....	....	....	....	....	....	....	....	....	....
Montrose,	....	....	2	....	1	....	2	....	....	....	....	....	6	....	....	....	....	1
Pleasant,	...	....	1	....	....	....	1	....	....	....	1	....	1	....	....	....	....	....
Van Buren,	...	....	....	....	....	....	2	....	....	....	2	....	....	....	....	....	....	....
Washington,	2	....	....	....	....	....	....	....	....	....	....	....	1	....	....	....	....	....
West Point,	....	3	....	....	7	....	10	....	....	....	....	....	12	....	....	....	....	1
Total,	3	27	26	...	54	4	85	13	29	24	16	5	76	5	19	....	13	28

TABLE—Continued,

SHOWING THE PROFESSIONS, TRADES OR OCCUPATIONS OF THE INHABITANTS OF LEE COUNTY, FOR 1856.

TOWNSHIPS.	Confectioners.	Boarding house keep's.	Hotel keepers.	Clothiers.	Physicians.	Dentists.	Lawyers.	Clergyman.	Teachers.	Musicans.	Printers.	Editors.	Artists.	Daguerrean Artists.	Bankers.	Grocers.	Teamsters.	Chandlers.	Brick makers.	Watch makers.	Jewellers.	Gun Smiths.
Cedar,	....	....	....	....	3	....	....	....	4	....	....	....	....	....	....	....	....	....	....	....	....	....
Charleston,	....	....	2	....	3	....	1	....	7	....	....	....	10	....	....	....	....	....	....	....	....	....
Denmark,	....	....	....	....	....	....	....	4	....	5	....	....	....	....	....	....	....	....	....	....	....	....
Des Moines,	....	....	....	....	1	....	....	1	1	1	....	....	....	....	....	....	....	....	....	....	....	....
Franklin,	....	....	....	....	4	....	....	....	1	....	1	....	....	....	....	....	....	....	2	....	....	....
Green Bay,	....	....	....	....	....	....	....	....	....	....	....	....	....	....	....	....	....	....	....	....	....	....
Harrison,	....	....	2	....	2	....	....	....	4	....	2	....	....	....	....	....	1	....	....	....	....	....
Jackson,	13	3	17	....	....	5	31	...	4	....	1	4	8	....	6	52	35	....	60	....	....	2
Jefferson,	....	....	....	....	....	....	....	....	....	....	....	....	....	....	....	....	....	....	....	....	....	....
Madison,	2	4	1	....	5	2	5	5	....	1	9	....	1	....	2	1	3	....	....	1	2	1
Marion,	....	....	....	....	....	....	....	1	3	....	....	....	....	....	....	....	1	....	3	....	....	....
Montrose,	....	....	2	....	3	....	....	....	....	....	....	....	....	....	....	4	13	....	....	....	....	....
Pleasant,	....	....	....	....	....	....	....	2	7	....	1	....	....	....	....	....	....	....	....	....	....	....
Van Buren,	....	....	....	....	3	....	....	2	....	....	....	....	....	....	....	....	....	....	....	....	....	....
Washington,	....	....	....	....	....	....	....	....	....	....	....	....	....	....	....	....	....	....	6	....	....	....
West Point,	....	2	....	....	4	....	4	6	8	....	....	....	....	....	....	1	....	....	2	....	....	2
Total,	15	9	24	....	28	7	41	21	39	7	4	4	19	....	8	58	103	....	73	1	2	5

TABLE—Continued,

EXHIBITING THE PROFESSIONS, TRADES, OR OCCUPATIONS OF THE INHABITANTS OF LEE COUNTY, FOR 1856.

TOWNSHIPS.	Coopers.	Clerks.	Boat makers.	Weavers.	Gardeners.	Potters	Tanners.	Wheelwrights.	Peddlers.	Cooks	Raftsmen.	Pilots.	Moulders.	Boatmen.	Miners.	Spinners.	Actors.	Architects.	Auctioneers.	Barbers.	Booksellers.	Boiler makers.	Brewers.	Brokers.
Cedar, ...	....	....	1	2	1	....	....	....	....	....	....	....	....	....	....	....	....	....	....	....	....	....	....	....
Charleston, ..	2	....	....	....	....	1	....	....	....	....	....	....	....	....	....	....	....	....	....	....	....	....	....	....
Denmark, ...	....	....	....	....	1	....	1	1	....	....	....	....	....	....	....	....	....	....	....	....	....	....	....	....
Des Moines, ..	14	....	....	....	....	....	....	....	1	1	1	1	....	....	....	....	....	....	....	....	....	....	....	....
Franklin, ...	3	1	....	....	....	....	....	....	....	....	....	....	....	....	....	....	....	....	....	....	....	....	....	....
Green Bay, ..	1	....	....	....	1	....	....	....	....	....	....	....	....	....	....	....	....	....	....	....	....	....	....	....
Har ison, ...	....	4	....	1	....	....	....	....	....	....	....	....	1	1	1	1	....	....	....	....	....	....	....	....
Jackson, ...	16	181	2	....	4	5	....	2	....	5	....	....	....	3	....	....	6	1	4	8	3	1	3	2
Jefferson, ...	4	....	....	....	....	....	....	....	....	....	....	....	....	....	....	....	....	....	....	....	....	....	....	....
Madison, ...	....	6	....	2	....	2	15	....	....	1	....	....	....	....	....	....	....	....	....	2	....	1	1	....
Marion, ...	....	....	....	....	....	....	....	....	....	....	....	....	....	....	....	....	....	....	....	....	....	....	....	....
Montrose, ...	....	2	....	....	....	....	....	....	....	....	....	10	....	2	....	....	....	....	....	....	....	....	....	....
Pleasant, ...	1	....	....	....	....	....	....	....	....	....	....	....	....	....	....	....	....	....	....	....	....	....	....	....
Van Buren, ..	14	1	....	....	....	....	....	....	....	....	....	....	....	....	....	....	....	....	....	....	....	....	....	....
Washington, ..	....	....	....	....	....	....	....	....	....	....	....	....	....	....	....	....	....	....	....	....	....	....	....	....
West Point, ..	....	6	....	....	....	....	....	....	....	....	....	....	....	....	....	....	....	....	....	....	....	....	....	....
Total, ...	55	201	3	5	7	8	16	3	1	7	1	11	1	6	1	1	6	1	4	10	3	2	4	2

TABLE—Continued,

EXHIBITING THE PROFESSIONS, TRADES OR OCCUPATIONS OF THE INHABITANTS OF LEE COUNTY, FOR 1856.

TOWNSHIPS.	County Recorder.	Guards.	Curriers.	Collectors.	City Recorder.	Dyers.	Dairymen.	Engravers.	Founders.	Ferrymen.	Glass cutters.	Gass fitters.	Hackmen.	Hucksters.	Hostlers.	Inspectors.	Judges.	Livery keepers.
Cedar,	....	....	....	....	....	....	....	....	....	....	....	....	....	....	....	....	....	....
Charleston,	....	....	....	....	....	....	....	....	....	....	....	....	....	....	....	....	....	....
Denmark,	....	....	....	....	....	....	....	....	....	....	....	....	....	....	....	....	....	....
Des Moines,	....	....	....	....	....	....	....	....	....	....	....	....	....	....	....	....	....	....
Franklin,	....	....	....	....	....	....	....	....	....	....	....	....	....	....	....	....	....	....
Green Bay,	....	....	....	....	....	....	....	....	....	....	....	....	....	....	....	....	....	....
Harrison,	....	....	....	....	....	....	....	....	....	....	....	....	....	....	....	....	....	....
Jackson,	1	....	1	1	1	3	3	1	20	2	1	1	1	1	5	1	1	9
Jefferson,	....	....	....	....	....	....	....	....	....	....	....	....	....	....	....	....	....	....
Madison,	1	4	....	....	....	....	1	....	....	....	....	....	....	....	....	....	....	2
Marion,	....	....	....	....	....	....	....	....	....	....	....	....	....	....	....	....	....	....
Montrose,	....	....	....	....	....	....	....	....	....	....	....	....	....	....	....	....	....	....
Pleasant,	....	....	....	....	....	....	....	....	....	....	....	....	....	....	....	....	....	....
Van Bnren,	....	....	....	....	....	....	....	....	....	....	....	....	....	....	....	....	....	....
Washington,	....	....	....	....	....	....	....	....	....	....	....	....	....	....	....	....	....	....
West Point,	....	....	....	....	....	....	....	....	....	....	....	....	....	....	....	....	....	....
Total,	2	4	1	1	1	3	4	1	20	2	1	1	1	1	5	1	1	11

TABLE—CONTINUED,

EXHIBITING THE PROFESSIONS, TRADES, OR OCCUPATIONS OF THE INHABITANTS OF LEE COUNTY, FOR 1856.

TOWNSHIPS.	Saloon Keepers.	Domestics.	Students.	Salesmen.	Superintendent of Rail Road.	Stage Driver.	Tobaconists.	Nurserymen.	Lecturers.	Contractor.	Carriers.	Distillers.	County Clerk.	Constables.	County Judges.	Superintendent of Public instructions.	Carders.	Lumbermen.	County Treasurer.	Rope Makers.	Steamboat Hands.	Calkers.	Surveyors.
Cedar,																							
Charleston,																							
Denmark,																							
Des Moines,																							
Franklin,																							
Green Bay,																							
Harrison,																							
Jackson,	3	24	8	1	1	1	10																
Jefferson,																							
Madison,			1				2	1	1	1	1	1	1	1	1	1	1	1	1	1			
Marion,																							
Montrose,							1			1								2		1	2	1	
Pleasant,																							
Van Buren,																							
Washington,																							
West Point,			1																				1
Total,	3	24	10	1	1	1	13	1	1	2	1	1	1	1	1	1	1	3	1	2	2	1	1

TABLE,

SHOWING THE PLACE OF NATIVITY OF THE INHABITANTS OF LEE COUNTY, FOR 1856.

TOWNSHIPS.	Ohio.	Indiana.	Pennsylvania.	Iowa.	New York.	Maine.	New Hampshire	Vermont.	Massachusetts.	Connecticut.	Rhode Island.	Virginia.	Kentucky.	Illinois.	Michigan.	Arkansas.	Texas.	Alabama.	Loiusiana.	Mississippi.	Florida.	North Carolina.	South Carolina.
Cedar,	186	136	116	193	35	1	....	1	1	2	1	40	....	16	4	2	....	5	....	....	....	43	....
Charleston,	211	101	142	361	45	8	3	4	14	1	2	58	35	31	10	....	....	1	....	1	....	5	3
Denmark,	161	14	42	231	64	19	64	16	54	18	....	16	9	39	3	1	....	....	....	....	....	3	2
Desmoines.	165	110	66	321	38	10	3	4	17	8	....	66	58	49	6	6	....	....	....	....	....	7	....
Franklin,	132	39	130	373	18	3	7	16	1	....	....	19	8	17	14	....	....	....	....	....	....	5	....
Green Bay,	92	91	34	155	24	....	....	2	1	..	6	20	7	18	....	....	....	....	....	....	....	4	1
Harrison,	235	35	83	246	70	2	2	8	2	3	....	75	5	20	....	....	....	....	4	....	....	3	6
Jackson,	1179	599	676	1295	640	40	57	45	100	79	9	260	534	325	21	2	5	6	25	4	3	23	6
Jefferson,	87	29	40	190	24	....	....	1	2	2	11	14	27	38	....	....	....	1	....	2	....	8	....
Madison,	278	101	218	605	97	1	8	7	10	20	2	62	35	63	....	....	....	....	4	....	....	6	6
Marion,	197	127	155	260	33	1	10	35	2	10	10	33	9	20	....	....	....	....	....	....	....	48	8
Montrose,	306	140	166	400	140	14	1	17	8	9	....	88	160	100	8	5	....	....	2	....	....	13	3
Pleasant,	245	71	120	260	42	12	4	28	6	10	13	48	5	9	....	....	....	....	....	....	....	10	1
Van Buren,	210	76	81	345	26	....	....	13	6	1	....	126	35	45	....	....	....	....	....	....	....	3	....
Washington,	210	130	113	314	41	4	23	16	20	22	....	32	14	20	....	....	....	....	....	....	....	3	1
West Point,	260	65	173	473	22	2	3	3	8	8	4	38	49	36	6	....	....	....	5	....	....	6	2
Total	4154	1864	2355	6022	1323	117	185	216	252	193	58	995	990	846	72	16	5	13	40	7	3	190	39

TABLE—Continued,

SHOWING THE PLACE OF NATIVITY OF THE INHABITANTS OF LEE COUNTY, FOR 1856.

TOWNSHIPS.	Tennessee.	Missouri.	Georgia.	California.	Maryland.	New Jersey.	England.	Ireland.	Wales.	Scotland.	Germany.	France.	Austria.	Russia.	Prussia.	Norway.	Sweden.	Holland.	On the Ocean.	Canada.	New Brunswick.	Switzerland.	Denmark.	Hanover.	Saxony.	West Indies.	Wisconsin.	Delaware.	District of Columbia.	Minnesota.	Indian Nation.	Unknown.
Cedar,	4	6	2	..	7	6	28	4	..	4	4	...	..	..	...	...	..	...	1	...	..	3	..	..	..	..	..	..	..	..	..	..
Charleston,	8	6	...	..	22	4	8	13	..	...	168	35	..	..	...	...	..	...	..	4	..	3	1	..	..	..	..	7	..	..	..	6
Denmark,	...	5	...	..	4	9	21	....	..	5	26	...	..	..	1	...	..	1	..	2	..	..	..	..	..	..	..	..	..	..	4	..
Des Moines,	21	27	7	..	15	6	3	12	..	7	3	2	..	..	...	38	8	...	..	36	..	..	..	..	..	..	1	2	..	..	..	12
Franklin,	...	6	...	..	5	10	7	10	..	...	545	25	..	..	1	11	..	...	1	...	..	..	..	..	..	..	..	2	..	..	..	..
Green Bay,	4	2	...	.	6	...	9	13	..	...	57	2	..	..	...	...	..	...	..	2	..	..	..	..	..	..	..	..	..	..	..	..
Harrison,	8	4	...	..	8	15	10	27	..	...	76	16	..	..	...	...	..	...	..	5	..	2	..	..	..	..	1	1	..	..	..	..
Jackson,	86	235	13	3	126	21	219	1049	..	66	790	43	4	5	15	1	11	129	2	92	..	7	8	..	1	2	16	20	5	1	2	30
Jefferson,	14	11	...	..	3	1	15	13	..	...	101	...	..	..	...	...	..	7	..	6	..	..	..	..	..	..	.	..	..	..	..	..
Madison,	22	92	...	..	8	7	49	30	..	7	834	10	3	..	44	...	..	9	..	2	..	..	..	3	..	..	..	1	2	..	..	..
Marion,	25	8	...	..	15	6	15	14	..	...	90	9	..	..	30	...	..	...	..	16	..	..	..	..	..	..	..	..	..	..	..	..
Montrose,	43	36	...	1	15	10	45	55	1	2	2	3	..	..	...	18	..	...	..	16	1	..	1	..	..	..	1	3	..	..	..	..
Pleasant,	7	2	5	..	4	3	4	26	.	2	55	12	..	..	...	...	..	...	..	10	..	..	..	..	..	..	..	8	..	..	..	..
Van Buren,	26	31	1	..	14	4	2	18	..	2	56	...	..	..	...	...	..	...	1	15	..	..	..	..	..	..	..	3	..	..	..	13
Washington,	13	4	...	..	2	3	24	9	..	...	67	...	..	..	13	...	..	...	1	1	..	2	..	1	..	..	..	6	..	..	..	..
West Point,	16	15	1	..	19	7	18	10	..	...	438	17	..	..	...	...	..	...	..	2	..	..	..	..	..	..	3	2	2	5	..	..
Total,	297	490	29	4	273	105	477	1303	1	95	3312	174	7	5	104	68	19	146	6	209	1	17	10	4	1	2	22	55	9	6	6	61

TABLE,

SHOWING THE POPULATION OF LINN COUNTY, FOR 1856.

TOWNSHIPS.	No. of dwelling houses	Number of families.	Number of males.	Number of females.	Colored.	Married.	Widowed.	Native voters.	Naturalized voters.	Aliens.	Militia.	Deaf and Dumb.	Blind.	Insane.	Idiotic.	Owners of land.	Paupers.
Brown,	148	159	473	382	....	306	20	184	1	7	153	...	....	....	1	127	....
Buffalo,	97	97	295	231	....	183	10	80	15	18	84	....	....	...	....	86	...
Clinton,	79	79	248	223	...	165	9	97	8	....	90	....	....	....	....	64	....
Franklin,	34	379	1062	970	...	740	55	420	26	27	368	....	....	....	6	207	....
Fayette,	88	88	270	221	....	172	7	96	6	4	72	....	....	....	....	69	....
Jackson,	84	84	253	232	....	170	9	85	6	9	73	....	....	....	....	85	....
Linn,	156	1[illegible]1	475	435	....	3[illegible]9	21	174	13	9	165	....	....	...	....	135	....
Maine,	62	62	197	184	....	134	5	81	2	9	71	....	....	....	....	60	....
Monroe,	106	113	347	287	....	205	19	117	13	4	108	....	....	...	2	79	....
Marion,	481	507	1568	1269	6	984	60	588	32	41	520	..	....	....	4	440	2
Otter Creek,	151	151	405	388	...	279	15	158	6	4	156	....	....	....	....	107	....
Putnam,	159	163	537	459	..	322	17	168	24	17	160	....	....	....	....	129	....
Rapids,	403	403	1285	1085	....	812	47	516	61	60	596	....	1	2	....	78	....
Spring Grove,	39	39	132	100	....	86	4	39	9	....	33	....	....	2	....	42	1
Washington,	117	1[illegible]7	364	322	....	243	9	143	14	6	146	..	....	....	1	116	....
Total,	25[illegible]8	2612	7911	6791	6	5110	307	2946	236	215	2795	....	1	4	14	1824	3

TABLE,

SHOWING THE AGRICULTURAL STATISTICS OF LINN COUNTY, FOR 1856.

TOWNSHIPS.	Acres of improved land.	Acres of unimproved land.	Acres of meadow.	Tons of hay.	Bushels of grass seed.	Acres of spring wheat.	Bushels harvested.	Acres of winter wheat.	Bushels harvested.	Acres of oats.	Bushels harvested.	Acres of corn.	Bushels harvested.	Acres of potatoes.	Bushels harvested.
Brown,........	4312	11002	111	67	10	1379	23907	...	....	497	17280	1695	59560	45	4670
Buffalo,........	2358	10344	10	10	...	490	8261	...	.....	84	2600	763	34335	11	1249
Clinton, ...	2467	5761	34	528	8	501	7244	...	.....	149	5607	660	30930	19	2999
Franklin,.......	9369	11504	1093	1690	90	1961	24989	..	.....	648	24293	3554	168175	44	4960
Fayette, ...	3017	5632	131	153	3	484	6592	2	25	305	8962	2195	51200	13	1598
Jackson,........	3412	7855	74	996	8	498	8592	170	.....	172	6301	937	37790	28	3114
Linn, ...	720	17089	268	1004	49	2422	28501	1	....	609	19747	2929	134230	60	6032
Maine, ...	1837	8844	33	863	6	521	8785	...	.....	235	7128	740	27555	23	2115
Monroe,........	4031	6829	320	394	12	749	7578	...	.....	408	9129	1182	50900	36	5039
Marion, ...	11851	24791	926	1184	44	2210	33548	19	197	968	27616	3762	173367	43	5024
Otter Creek,....	4378	12933	277	499	22	996	13029	52	250	471	14472	1522	60991	29	4082
Putnam,........	6148	12809	147	686	26	1671	27926	5	60	563	20158	1948	87560	32	4820
Rapids,.........	3069	14579	327	257	28	500	8245	...	....	484	9137	972	48070	33	5003
Spring Grove,...	1036	3961	12	118	...	129	2025	...	.....	37	1126	354	12562	10	1204
Washington,....	1145	2058	7	102	...	228	3351	...	.....	225	7118	1038	48650	9	1800
Total,........	66132	155991	3871	8551	306	14739	212573	249	532	5854	180674	24251	1025875	435	53706

TABLE—Showing the number and value of hogs, cattle, domestic and general manufactures of Linn County, for 1856.

TOWNSHIPS.	No. of hogs sold.	Value of hogs sold.	No. of cattle sold.	Value of cattle sold.	Pounds of butter made.	Pounds of cheese.	Pounds of Wool.	Value of domestic Manufactures.	Value of general manufactures.
Brown,	1045	8251	104	2999	14310	1838	608	581	1500
Buffalo,	591	3719	134	4135	7860	225	132	25	......
Clinton,	262	1669	154	1326	4550	650	629	57	40
Franklin,	3289	22918	574	19544	21187	990	2294	900	......
Fayette,	662	5029	128	4269	4125	104	499	261	......
Jackson,	538	3949	128	4304	11785	1525	467	357	......
Linn,	2451	20836	232	6891	17590	680	2179	885	......
Maine,	432	3824	89	2877	5125	705	312	136	......
Monroe,	904	5936	162	4179	13138	1540	1217	1534	7905
Marion,	3974	31275	1094	12641	25677	14998	2767	996	300
Otter Creek,	1045	8328	159	5058	5210	1629	1484	689	......
Putnam,	722	5225	89	2618	9270	150	803	133	......
Rapids,	631	3862	122	4426	9175	562	506	451	202050
Spring Grove,	94	718	34	1138	1294	......	201	193	......
Washington,	325	2403	81	2868	3250	......	45	71	1000
Total,	16965	127942	3284	79273	153646	25596	14143	7269	212795

TABLE,

EXHIBITING THE PROFESSIONS, TRADES OR OCCUPATIONS OF THE INHABITANTS OF LINN COUNTY, FOR 1856.

TOWNSHIPS.	Farmers.	Laborers.	Blacksmiths.	Carpenters.	Wagon makers.	Brick Layers.	Plasterers.	Stone masons.	Stone Cutters.	Builders.	Carriage Makers.	Machinists.	Engineers.	Millers.	Sawyers.	Millwrights.	Painters.	Cabinet makers.
Brown, ...	118	18	3	22	....	....	....	....	1	....	1	....	....	....	1	2	....	1
Buffalo, ...	90	...	...	3	2	....	....	1	....	....	....	....	....	1	....	....	1	1
Clinton, ...	85	...	....	....	....	....	....	....	....	....	....	....	....	....	....	....	....	....
Franklin, ...	287	62	17	50	1	2	6	9	1	....	....	1	3	3	4	2	3	3
Fayette, ...	82	3	4	5	....	....	....	1	....	....	....	....	....	....	....	1	....	....
Jackson, ...	70	1	2	2	....	....	....	....	....	....	....	....	1	1	....	1	....	....
Linn, ...	166	53	5	10	1	....	....	....	....	....	....	1	1	1	....	....	....	....
Maine, ...	99	...	4	2	1	....	....	....	....	....	....	....	....	2	....	....	....	1
Monroe, ...	86	17	1	15	....	....	....	....	....	....	....	....	2	2	6	1	....	....
Marion, ...	307	81	18	70	3	11	8	8	4	....	....	1	3	7	....	2	9	6
Otter Creek, ..	184	39	5	8	....	....	....	....	....	....	....	....	....	....	....	1	....	....
Putnam, ...	160	50	5	13	....	....	....	3	....	....	....	....	1	1	1	....	....	....
Rapids, ...	83	....	28	61	8	...	9	27	1	....	1	3	....	7	2	1	8	4
Spring Grove, .	58	....	...	...	....	....	....	....	....	....	....	....	....	....	....	....	....	....
Washington, ..	126	7	10	18	6	....	1	2	....	....	....	....	1	2	2	3	....	3
Total, ...	2001	431	102	279	22	13	25	51	7	....	2	6	12	27	16	14	21	19

TABLE—Continued,

SHOWING THE PROFESSIONS, TRADES, OR OCCUPATIONS OF THE INHABITANTS OF LINN COUNTY, FOR 8156.

TOWNSHIPS.	Chair makers.	Tinners.	Milliners.	Merchant Tailors.	Tailors.	Hatters.	Shoemakers.	Saddle & harness makers.	Bakers.	Butchers.	Mechanics.	Manufacturers.	Merchants.	Speculators.	Agents.	Drovers.	Traders.	Druggists.
Brown,	...	...	...	...	1	1	3	1	...	...	...	...	2	...	...	...	...	...
Buffalo,	...	...	1	...	1	...	1	...	...	...	...	...	...	...	...	...	...	...
Clinton,	...	...	...	...	...	...	...	...	...	...	...	...	...	...	...	...	...	...
Franklin,	1	4	2	...	4	...	8	5	...	...	...	...	19	...	...	2	1	...
Fayette,	...	...	...	...	...	...	1	...	...	...	...	...	...	...	...	...	...	...
Jackson,	...	...	...	...	...	...	1	...	...	...	...	...	2	...	...	...	...	...
Linn,	...	...	...	...	2	...	1	...	...	...	...	...	...	...	...	...	...	...
Maine,	...	...	...	...	1	...	...	...	...	...	...	...	...	...	...	...	...	...
Monroe,	1	...	...	...	...	...	1	...	...	...	1	...	...	...	...	...	...	...
Marion,	...	3	3	1	6	...	8	5	2	3	1	1	19	...	2	...	...	2
Otter Creek,	...	...	1	...	1	...	...	...	...	...	...	...	3	...	...	...	...	...
Putnam,	...	...	...	...	...	...	2	...	...	...	...	...	...	...	...	...	...	...
Rapids,	4	4	8	...	7	...	1	6	5	...	9	4	38	...	1	...	...	...
Spring Grove,	...	...	...	...	...	...	...	...	...	...	3	...	...	...	...	...	...	...
Washington,	...	...	...	...	2	...	1	...	...	...	...	...	7	1	...	...	...	...
Total,	6	11	15	1	25	1	28	17	7	3	15	5	90	1	3	2	1	2

TABLE—Continued,

EXHIBITING THE PROFESSIONS, TRADES OR OCCUPATIONS OF THE INHABITANTS OF LINN COUNTY, FOR 1856.

TOWNSHIPS.	Confectioners.	Board'g H. keepers.	Hotel keepers.	Clothiers.	Physicians.	Dentists.	Lawyers.	Clergymen.	Teachers.	Musicians.	Printers.	Editors.	Artists.	Daguerrean Artists	Bankers.	Grocers.	Teamsters.	Chandlers.
Brown,	....	....	....	....	2	....	....	1	....	....	....	....	....	....	....	....	....	....
Buffalo,	....	....	....	....	1	....	....	....	....	....	....	....	....	....	....	....	....	....
Clinton,	....	....	....	....	....	....	....	....	....	....	....	....	....	....	....	....	....	....
Franklin,	....	....	5	....	8	....	3	9	9	....	....	1	....	....	....	1	9	....
Fayette,	....	....	....	....	1	....	....	....	....	....	....	....	....	....	....	....	....	....
Jackson,	....	....	....	....	1	....	....	2	....	....	....	....	....	....	....	....	....	....
Linn,	....	....	....	....	1	....	....	2	1	....	....	....	....	....	....	....	....	....
Maine,	....	....	....	....	....	....	....	....	....	....	....	....	....	....	....	....	....	....
Monroe,	....	....	....	....	....	....	....	1	1	....	....	....	....	....	....	....	....	....
Marion,	....	....	2	....	6	....	8	5	4	....	1	1	....	....	2	3	5	....
Otter Creek,	....	....	....	....	....	....	....	....	1	....	....	....	....	....	....	....	1	....
Putnam,	....	....	....	....	....	....	....	1	....	....	....	....	....	....	....	....	....	....
Rapids,	....	....	4	....	16	....	11	7	7	....	....	2	....	....	2	2	....	....
Spring Grove,	....	....	....	....	....	....	....	....	....	....	....	....	....	....	....	....	....	....
Washington,	....	....	2	....	3	....	....	2	7	....	....	....	1	....	....	....	3	....
Total,	....	....	13	....	39	....	22	30	30	....	1	4	1	....	4	6	18	....

TABLE—Continued,

SHOWING THE PROFESSIONS, TRADES OR OCCUPATIONS OF THE INHABITANTS OF LINN COUNTY, FOR 1856.

TOWNSHIPS.	Brick makers.	Watch Makers.	Jewellers.	Gun Smiths.	Coopers.	Clerks.	Shingle makers.	Jacks of all trades.	Surveyors.	Tanners.	Weavers	Mechanics.	Supercargos.	Wheelwrights.	Ferrymen.	Stewards.	Post Masters.	Students.
Brown, ...	....	....	....	....	2	1	1	1	1	....	....	....	....	....	....	....	....	....
Buffalo, ...	....	....	....	....	....	....	....	....	....	1	1	....	....	....	....	....	....	....
Clinton, ...	....	....	....	....	....	....	....	....	....	....	....	17	....	....	....	....	....	....
Franklin, ...	4	1	1	1	4	7	1	....	....	....	3	....	1	3	1	1	1	3
Fayette, ...	....	....	....	1	1	....	....	....	....	....	....	....	....	....	....	....	....	....
Jackson, ...	....	....	....	....	....	....	....	....	1	....	....	....	....	....	....	....	....	....
Linn, ...	1	....	....	....	1	....	....	....	....	....	2	....	....	....	....	....	....	1
Maine, ...	....	....	....	....	....	....	....	....	....	....	....	....	....	....	....	....	....	....
Monroe, ...	....	....	....	....	1	....	....	....	....	....	1	....	....	....	....	....	....	....
Marion, ...	4	....	3	1	1	12	....	....	2	....	....	....	....	....	....	....	....	....
Otter Creek, ...	....	....	....	2	1	....	....	....	....	....	....	....	....	....	....	....	....	....
Putnam, ...	....	....	....	....	1	....	....	....	....	....	....	....	....	....	....	....	....	....
Rapids, ...	....	....	3	....	5	21	....	....	1	....	....	....	....	2	....	....	1	....
Spring Grove, ..	....	....	....	....	....	....	....	....	....	....	....	....	....	....	....	....	....	....
Washington, ...	1	....	....	....	....	....	1	....	1	....	....	....	....	....	....	....	....	....
Total, ...	10	1	7	5	17	41	3	1	6	1	7	17	1	5	1	1	2	4

TABLE—Continued,

SHOWING THE PROFESSIONS, TRADES OR OCCUPATIONS OF THE INHABITANTS OF LINN COUNTY, FOR 1856.

TOWNSHIPS.	Seamstresses.	Stage drivers.	Prairie Brakers.	Lumbermen.	Mariners.	Ferrymen.	Tailoresses.	Constables.	Sheriffs.	School Fund Comm'r	Nurserymen.	County Judges.	Clerks of Court.	Treas'rs & Record'rs	Pensioners.	Livery keepers.	Hostlers.	Wheelwrights.	District Judges.	Operators.	Fence makers.	Gentlemen.	Cooks.	Spinners.	Opticians.	Colliers.	Hunters.
Brown																											
Buffalo																											
Clinton																											
Franklin	2																										
Fayette		3																									
Jackson																											
Linn			1	1																							
Maine					1																						
Monroe						1																					
Marion							1	1	1	1	1	1	1	1	1	1	1	1	[illegible]	1							
Otter Creek	1																				1						
Putnam																											
Rapids	2																					2	1	1	1	1	
Spring Grove																											
Washington																											1
Total	5	3	1	1	1	1	1	1	1	1	1	1	1	1	1	1	1	1	1	1	1	2	1	1	1	1	1

TABLE,—SHOWING THE PLACE OF NATIVITY OF THE INHABITANTS OF LINN COUNTY, FOR 1856.

STATES.	NAME OF TOWNSHIPS.															
	Brown.	Buffalo.	Clinton.	Franklin.	Fayette.	Jackson.	Linn.	Maine.	Monroe.	Marion.	Otter Creek.	Putnam.	Rapids.	Spring Grove.	Washington	TOTAL.
Ohio,	324	148	95	446	174	79	275	37	128	694	267	263	491	104	179	3758
Indiana,	94	24	24	156	39	32	73	77	68	303	73	106	110	38	108	1320
Pennsylvania,	88	61	45	514	42	23	111	17	78	343	81	117	377	4	43	1944
Iowa,	136	89	66	403	74	66	253	66	145	646	184	173	333	...	136	2770
New York,	71	50	122	123	53	92	30	32	28	208	24	33	298	19	26	1209
Maine,	14	1	...	2	1	4	2	47	...	18	...	1	18	...	3	111
New Hampshire,	5	2	...	4	1	16	1	13	1	19	...	...	15	4	2	83
Vermont,	5	5	3	14	1	21	6	2	2	47	6	21	52	1	3	189
Massachusetts,	2	1	4	10	7	29	2	10	2	62	1	...	53	...	5	188
Connecticut,	13	2	3	11	4	12	3	2	2	33	1	4	26	7	1	124
Rhode Island,	...	...	...	2	...	...	...	...	...	...	2	...	2	...	1	7
Virginia,	39	9	10	61	13	1	41	7	18	84	30	42	36	8	37	436
Kentucky,	10	3	2	44	3	5	8	5	9	67	17	9	22	1	37	242
Illinois,	11	21	28	45	33	26	16	16	17	65	44	45	44	14	28	453
Michigan,	3	...	3	6	2	5	13	5	...	20	5	...	19	...	5	86
Alabama,	...	...	...	...	...	...	...	...	...	1	...	...	...	...	...	1
Louisiana,	...	...	...	...	...	...	...	...	...	...	...	...	1	...	1	2
Mississippi,	...	...	...	...	2	...	1	1	...	...	...	...	...	...	...	4
North Carolina,	6	3	...	6	1	3	1	4	5	9	5	3	6	...	7	59
South Carolina,	...	...	...	...	...	...	...	...	...	...	...	2	18	...	3	23
Tennessee,	4	...	1	17	...	...	...	...	2	6	6	12	8	...	4	55
Missouri,	...	...	3	3	...	3	1	1	9	1	1	3	12	...	...	40
Georgia,	...	...	...	...	...	...	...	...	...	...	...	...	2	...	...	2
Maryland,	7	2	2	34	2	3	7	...	2	37	5	13	78	...	8	200
New Jersey,	2	2	20	16	9	6	3	6	19	24	3	8	45	4	11	178
England,	3	6	11	8	2	6	16	4	4	29	...	10	41	14	12	166
Ireland,	8	20	1	46	7	9	12	1	...	19	1	19	46	6	9	204
Wales,	...	...	...	...	...	...	...	...	...	2	...	1	...	1	...	4
Scotland,	1	1	6	3	2	3	16	...	2	6	...	13	19	...	...	72
Germany,	1	9	16	22	2	...	8	14	24	51	27	8	87	2	1	272
France,	1	...	...	1	...	...	1	...	...	3	...	...	5	...	...	11
Austria,	...	39	...	...	...	...	...	...	...	...	...	...	...	...	...	39
Prussia,	...	...	...	...	...	...	...	...	...	1	...	3	1	...	...	5
Norway,	...	...	...	...	...	1	...	...	...	3	...	1	1	...	...	6
Sweden,	...	...	...	...	2	...	...	...	...	...	...	...	...	...	...	2
Holland,	...	...	...	1	...	...	...	...	...	1	...	...	...	...	...	2
On the Ocean,	...	1	...	...	...	...	...	...	...	...	...	...	...	...	...	1
Canada,	4	5	4	7	13	17	7	11	13	15	2	3	31	4	19	155
New Brunswick,	...	...	...	...	...	...	...	2	2	2	...	...	5	...	...	11
Switzerland,	...	...	...	...	...	...	...	...	...	2	...	2	2	...	...	6
Denmark,	...	...	...	1	...	...	...	...	...	...	...	...	...	...	...	1
West Indies,	...	...	...	...	...	...	...	...	...	1	...	...	1	...	...	2
Wisconsin,	3	12	2	5	...	2	1	1	...	4	4	7	9	...	1	51
Delaware,	...	1	...	1	1	...	...	...	...	5	1	...	...	1	...	10
Bohemia,	...	6	...	20	...	...	...	...	...	1	...	67	51	...	...	145
Nova Scotia,	...	6	...	...	1	13	...	...	...	1	1	...	5	...	1	28
Pr. Ed'd's Island,	...	...	...	...	...	8	...	...	...	...	...	...	...	...	...	8
Dis't of Columbia,	...	...	...	...	...	...	2	...	...	2	...	...	...	...	...	4
Unknown,	...	...	...	...	...	...	...	1	...	...	...	...	...	...	...	1
Poland,	...	...	...	...	...	...	...	...	...	1	...	...	...	...	...	1
Moravia,	...	...	...	...	...	...	...	...	...	...	...	6	...	...	...	6
Hungary,	...	...	...	...	...	...	...	...	...	...	...	...	5	...	...	5

TABLE,

SHOWING THE POPULATION OF LOUISA COUNTY, FOR 1856.

TOWNSHIPS.	No dwelling houses	Number of families.	Number of males.	Number of females.	Colored.	Married.	Widowed.	Native voters.	Naturalized voters.	Aliens.	Militia.	Deaf and Dumb.	Blind.	Insane.	Idiotic.	Owners of land.	Paupers.
Columbus City, ...	32[illegible]	355	1057	912	5	647	67	340	44	35	316	....	....	1	....	262	1
Elliott, ...	55	55	170	138	....	92	12	60	9	5	64	1	....	....	....	29	....
Jefferson, ...	89	92	271	180	14	186	14	85	20	38	134	....	....	....	....	31	....
Morning Sun, ...	[illegible]5[illegible]	155	473	392	....	28[illegible]	27	169	12	26	161	....	1	1	....	148	....
Port Louisa, ...	123	144	444	368	....	272	38	143	25	31	166	....	1	....	1	80	....
Wapello, ...	305	333	1045	365	....	653	55	365	71	18	379	....	1	....	....	150	....
Concord, ...	100	100	304	276	....	178	17	116	15	17	89	....	....	....	....	79	1
Grand View, ...	212	212	713	601	12	370	38	165	23	71	166	....	....	1	1	132	....
Marshall, ...	96	102	339	306	....	202	11	124	4	16	81	....	1	....	....	73	....
Oakland, ...	54	64	179	147	....	119	8	57	1	3	66	....	....	....	....	43	....
Union, ...	63	65	211	177	....	117	8	80	2	3	79	....	....	....	....	129	....
Total, ...	1571	1677	5206	4362	31	3117	295	1704	156	263	1701	1	4	3	2	1156	2

TABLE,

SHOWING THE AGRICULTURAL STATISTICS OF LOUISA COUNTY, FOR 1856.

TOWNSHIPS.	Acres of improved land.	Acres of unimproved land.	Acres of meadow.	Tons of Hay.	Bushels of grass seed.	Acres of spring wheat.	Bushels harvested.	Acres of winter wheat.	Bushels harvested.	Acres of Oats	Bushels harvested.	Acres of corn.	Bushels harvested.	Acres of potatoes.	Bushels harvested.
Columbus City,..	10033	8347	766	464	40	714	23438	164	2678	933	29524	3091	166010	45	4300
Elliott, ...	1944	3649	93	113	4	129	882	175	2600	176	4043	1360	74380	31	1527
Jefferson, ...	1280	3531	16	117	....	108	1275	206	3402	168	6119	654	34308	4	815
Morning Sun, ...	7960	13644	754	835	27	1221	16483	314	4127	872	31231	2698	114080	32	5340
Port Louisa, ...	3594	5558	221	213	3	287	4547	472	8420	316	10159	1443	81677	22	3410
Wapello, ...	8026	12168	366	370	23	664	8481	429	1103	825	29525	2955	166220	96	6403
Concord, ...	3422	5077	240	221	1	536	5447	119	1156	400	12619	1866	134612	25	3266
Grand View, ...	8412	8999	713	708	53	1429	17233	420	5241	625	21804	3065	182790	47	6226
Marshall, ...	6253	5411	304	335	60	913	13080	399	5246	420	15429	1462	84520	20	4426
Oakland, ...	2132	4007	14	12	....	330	4550	15	200	102	3550	747	33700	10	1832
Union, ...	2449	6507	64	41	18	513	8649	34	407	241	6408	987	48175	15	2082
Total, ...	55507	769[illegible]0	3553	3429	229	6845	103816	2748	34580	5079	170411	20327	1120472	350	38627

TABLE,

SHOWING THE NUMBER AND VALUE OF HOGS AND CATTLE SOLD, THE VALUE OF DOMESTIC AND GENERAL MANUFACTURES OF LOUISA COUNTY, FOR 1856.

TOWNSHIPS.	No. of hogs sold.	Value of hogs sold.	No. of cattle sold.	Value of cattle sold.	Pounds of butter made.	Pounds of cheese.	Pounds of Wool.	Value of domestic manufacture.	Value of general manufactures.
Columbus City,	2456	21092	280	7133	9600	503	1526	1017	263
Elliot,	921	6226	168	5260	3586	....	554	121	....
Jefferson,	566	4445	84	1913	1575	....	149	....	52
Morning Sun,	2587	36281	500	12358	22400	542	1499	1108	712
Port Louisa,	924	6735	127	3394	9039	300	333	316	75504
Wapello,	3189	24002	568	14004	29133	690	1524	702	1781
Concord,	1284	11426	479	10003	12880	1119	833	1346	10847
Grand View,	2508	22151	1235	30311	22566	911	2533	700	240
Marshall,	961	8890	219	7098	16080	315	245	285	....
Oakland,	1326	4412	62	1184	3405	240	169	15	100
Union,	674	6886	112	3348	7490	....	639	472	400
Total,	17396	152546	3834	96006	137754	4620	10004	6082	89899

TABLE,

EXHIBITING THE PROFESSIONS, TRADES OR OCCUPATIONS OF THE INHABITANTS OF LOUISA COUNTY, FOR 1856.

TOWNSHIPS.	Farmers.	Laborers.	Blacksmiths.	Carpenters.	Wagon makers.	Brick layers.	Plasterers.	Stone Masons.	Stone Cutters.	Builders.	Carriage makers.	Machinists.	Engineers.	Millers.	Sawyers.	Millwrights.	Painters.	Cabinet Makers.
Columbus, City,	265	88	6	26	4	12	1	....	2	....	....	....	1	....	6	....	1	1
Elliott,........	61	9	3	2	....	....	....	....	....	....	....	....	....	....	....	....	1	....
Jefferson,......	69	70	2	9	2	1	....	1	....	....	....	1	2	....	....	....	....	....
Morning Sun,..	130	9	5	10	1	....	1	2	....	....	....	....	1	....	2	....	....	....
Port Louisa,...	150	58	1	6	1	....	....	....	1	....	....	....	1	1	1	2	....	....
Wapello,.......	189	29	17	44	4	1	7	1	5	1	....	3	7	7	....	1	6	3
Concord,.......	97	5	1	1	....	....	....	....	....	....	....	....	....	2	....	....	....	....
Grand View,...	133	85	5	10	5	2	1	....	....	....	....	....	....	4	....	....	....	1
Marshall,......	143	16	2	10	2	....	....	....	....	....	....	....	....	2	2	....	....	2
Oakland,.......	63	8	3	5	....	....	....	....	....	....	....	....	1	....	....	....	....	....
Union,.........	91	3	....	4	1	....	....	....	....	....	....	....	....	....	3	....	....	....
Total,.......	1391	380	45	127	20	16	10	4	8	1	....	4	13	16	14	3	8	7

TABLE—Continued,

SHOWING THE PROFESSIONS, TRADES OR OCCUPATIONS OF THE INHABITANTS OF LOUISA COUNTY, FOR 1856.

TOWNSHIPS.	Chair makers.	Tinners.	Milliners.	Merchant tailors.	Tailors.	Hatters.	Shoe makers.	Harness makers.	Bakers.	Butchers.	Mechanics.	Manufacturers.	Merchants.	Speculators.	Agents.	Drovers.	Traders.	Druggists.
Columbus City,	....	1	6	....	....	....	5	....	....	1	....	....	8	1	....	....	2	1
Elliott,	....	1	2	....	....	1	....	....	....	....	....	....	3	....	....	....	....	....
Jefferson,	....	....	....	....	1	....	....	....	....	....	....	....	5	....	....	....	....	....
Morning Sun,	....	....	1	....	....	....	4	2	....	....	....	....	7	....	....	....	....	....
Port Louisa,	....	....	1	....	1	....	1	....	....	....	....	....	2	....	....	....	....	....
Wapello,	....	1	1	....	8	....	6	3	1	....	1	5	21	6	....	....	....	2
Concord,	....	....	....	....	1	....	....	1	....	....	3	....	1	....	....	....	1	....
Grand View,	....	....	....	....	2	....	1	1	....	1	....	....	6	....	....	....	....	1
Marshall,	....	1	2	....	....	....	....	....	....	....	....	....	....	....	....	....	....	....
Oakland,	....	....	....	....	....	....	1	....	....	....	....	....	1	....	....	....	....	....
Union,	....	....	....	....	....	....	....	....	....	....	1	....	....	....	....	....	....	....
Total,	....	4	13	....	13	1	18	7	1	2	5	5	54	7	....	....	3	4

TABLE—CONTINUED,

EXHIBITING THE PROFESSIONS, TRADES, OR OCCUPATIONS OF THE INHABITANTS OF LOUISA COUNTY, FOR 1856.

TOWNSHIPS.	Confectioners.	Boarding house keep's.	Hotel keepers.	Clothiers.	Physicians.	Dentists.	Lawyers.	Clergyman.	Teachers.	Musicians.	Printers.	Editors.	Artists.	Daguerrean Artists.	Bankers.	Grocers.	Teamsters.	Chandlers.
Columbus City,	....	....	3	4	10	....	2	....	2	....	....	1	....	....	....	3	12	....
Elliott,	....	....	....	....	....	....	....	....	1	....	....	....	....	....	....	....	....	....
Jefferson,	....	....	....	....	1	....	....	....	....	....	....	....	....	....	....	....	....	....
Morning Sun,	....	....	....	....	2	....	....	2	3	....	....	....	....	....	....	....	1	....
Port Louisa,	1	....	....	....	1	....	....	1	2	....	....	....	....	....	....	....	....	....
Wapello,	....	1	2	....	3	1	5	3	7	2	3	1	1	....	....	....	17	....
Concord,	....	1	1	....	1	....	....	....	....	....	....	....	....	1	1	....	....	....
Grand View,	....	....	....	....	3	....	....	2	2	....	....	....	....	....	....	....	....	....
Marshall,	....	....	....	....	....	....	....	2	1	....	....	....	....	....	....	....	....	....
Oakland,	....	....	....	....	1	....	....	....	....	....	....	....	....	....	....	....	....	....
Union,	....	....	....	....	....	....	....	....	2	....	....	....	....	....	....	....	1	....
Total,	1	2	6	4	22	1	7	10	20	2	3	2	1	1	1	3	31	....

TABLE—Continued,

EXHIBITING THE PROFESSIONS, TRADES, OR OCCUPATIONS OF THE INHABITANTS OF LOUISA COUNTY, FOR 1856.

TOWNSHIPS.	Brick makers.	Watch makers.	Jewellers.	Gun Smiths.	Coopers.	Clerks.	Nurserymen.	Weavers.	Shingle Makers.	Contractors.	Ferrymen.	Livery Keepers.	Steamboat Mates.	Potters.	Graziers.	Threshers.	Pedlers.	Lumbermen.	Wood Cutters.	Tobacconists.
Columbus City,	4				4	5	1	2	4	4	1	1	1							
Elliott,					2	1														
Jefferson,					2									1						
Morning Sun,															1	2	1			
Port Louisa,					5	2				1								1	3	
Wapello,			1	1	4	13				3	1	1								
Concord,																				
Grand View,					1	1		1	1											1
Marshall,									1	1										
Oakland,																				
Union,											1									
Total,	4		1	1	18	22	1	3	6	9	3	2	1	1	1	2	1	1	3	1

TABLE,

SHOWING THE PLACE OF NATIVITY OF THE INHABITANTS OF LOUISA COUNTY, FOR 1856.

TOWNSHIPS.	NAME OF TOWNSHIPS.											
	Columbus City.	Elliot.	Jefferson.	Morning Sun.	Port Louisa.	Wapello.	Concord.	Grand View.	Marshall,	Oakland	Union.	TOTAL.
Ohio,	386	77	62	285	149	390	144	329	230	68	91	2211
Indiana,	184	47	31	98	72	153	43	68	26	44	36	802
Pennsylvania,	274	18	19	101	67	209	31	211	96	13	23	1062
Iowa,	419	64	127	201	208	486	137	283	156	76	86	2243
New York,	90	9	25	10	31	86	38	37	18	33	4	381
Maine,	2	1	....	1	5	30	8	5	....	1	....	53
New Hampshire,	9	3	....	....	4	3	....	1	....	1	5	26
Vermont,	47	....	....	2	6	14	3	1	....	....	1	74
Massachusetts,	8	1	2	....	3	11	....	1	....	5	....	31
Connecticut,	5	2	13	2	1	5	....	4	14	....	....	46
Rhode Island,	....	....	....	....	....	....	1	....	1	....	....	2
Virginia,	47	38	37	30	24	63	20	41	25	14	7	346
Kentucky,	27	4	10	13	12	44	9	3	1	29	14	166
Illinois,	50	10	14	15	24	80	37	23	12	5	1	271
Michigan,	6	....	2	....	2	10	6	8	2	7	2	45
Arkansas,	....	....	....	....	....	....	....	....	....	3	....	3
Alabama,	1	....	....	....	....	....	....	....	....	....	....	1
North Carolina,	9	....	4	7	4	9	26	3	1	1	2	66
South Carolina,	3	1	....	11	4	2	1	....	2	....	....	24
Tennessee,	166	....	2	8	9	9	8	1	6	1	103	313
Missouri,	8	....	2	....	3	19	4	11	1	....	....	48
Georgia,	3	....	....	....	2	....	1	....	....	2	....	8
Maryland,	26	4	5	15	8	13	2	27	3	....	1	99
New Jersey,	17	2	4	2	19	23	11	31	6	2	3	120
England,	16	7	3	9	11	15	21	7	25	12	....	126
Ireland,	59	9	83	39	57	49	19	103	15	3	9	445
Wales,	62	....	....	....	....	....	....	....	....	....	....	62
Scotland,	7	....	1	1	....	2	3	3	....	....	....	17
Germany,	22	7	3	2	60	135	6	90	3	....	....	328
France,	3	....	....	....	4	3	....	....	....	....	....	10
Prussia,	1	....	1	....	....	4	....	6	....	....	....	12
Sweden.	1	....	....	....	8	....	....	....	....	....	....	9
Holland,	....	....	....	....	....	5	....	3	....	....	....	8
On the Ocean,	....	....	....	1	....	1	....	....	....	....	....	2
Canada.	4	3	....	5	6	14	1	2	...	2	....	37
New Brunswick,	....	....	....	1	....	....	....	....	....	....	....	1
Switzerland,	....	....	....	....	1	4	....	....	....	1	....	6
Wisconsin,	5	....	....	....	2	3	....	....	....	....	....	10
Delaware,	2	1	1	6	9	5	....	8	2	3	....	37
Minnesota,	....	....	....	....	1	11	....	....	....	....	....	12
Unknown,	....	....	....	....	1	...	....	4	....	....	....	5

TABLE,

SHOWING THE POPULATION OF LUCAS COUNTY, FOR 1856.

TOWNSHIPS.	No. of dwelling houses.	Number of families.	Number of males.	Number of females.	Colored.	Married.	Widowed.	Native voters.	Naturalized voters.	Aliens.	Militia.	Deaf and Dumb.	Blind.	Insane.	Idiotic.	Owners of land.	Paupers.
Chariton,	177	190	528	448	...	349	27	211	8	7	77	1	1	....	....	145	....
Cedar,	94	94	251	217	....	168	9	101	1	....	76	....	....	....	...	73	...
Union,	61	63	175	142	....	106	9	71	....	1	64	....	....	....	....	54	....
Liberty,	48	48	155	133	....	90	8	55	1	1	57	....	....	...	....	48	3
Washington,	35	37	139	132	....	105	6	58	1	1	49	5	....	....	1	53	....
Warren,	64	69	204	161	....	119	6	72	1	3	64	....	....	....	....	58	....
Benton,	53	59	183	173	....	117	6	75	2	1	66	....	....	....	....	55	....
White Breast,	66	66	200	171	....	60	4	84	8	2	87	....	....	....	2	56	....
English,	60	64	173	159	....	118	8	64	....	....	66	....	....	2	....	79	....
Otter Creek,	64	64	167	188	..	125	4	67	1	1	48	1	....	....	...	54	....
Pleasant,	31	31	89	95	....	56	1	32	....	....	32	....	....	....	....	29	....
Jackson,	25	25	66	59	....	50	..	29	1	....	29	1	....	1	...	23	....
Total,	778	810	2330	2078	....	1463	88	919	24	17	715	8	1	3	3	727	3

TABLE,

SHOWING THE AGRICULTURAL STATISTICS OF LUCAS COUNTY, FOR 1856.

TOWNSHIPS.	Acres of improved land.	Acres of unimproved land.	Acres of meadow.	Tons of hay.	Bushels of grass seed.	Acres of spring wheat.	Bushels harvested.	Acres of winter wheat.	Bushels harvested.	Acres of oats.	Bushels harvested.	Acres of corn.	Bushels harvested.	Acres of potatoes.	Bushels harvested.
Chariton, ...	2787	71534	123	206	9	207	1580	43	98	317	9559	1307	38860	13	1630
Cedar, ...	2386	1306	40	5	.	226	1450	70	256	247	6380	940	30525	121	1587
Union, ...	1207	1975	3	...	...	108	566	7	22	83	2035	1265	35180	3	430
Liberty, ...	1101	6069	67	31	...	80	296	29	225	95	2365	650	23381	8	937
Washington, ...	1069	8623	6	13	33	94	688	8	7	86	1960	542	21580	5	1181
Warren, ...	1354	9269	1	....	...	92	644	21	117	142	6420	581	21825	6	675
Benton, ...	1575	8164	10	20	...	247	1456	7	25	141	4271	540	22790	8	785
White Breast, ...	1630	9230	9	7	...	103	1243	26	148	185	5203	634	42875	12	1456
English, ...	1201	8241	16	2	8	226	839	27	542	113	2405	673	24460	10	1081
Otter Creek, ...	1454	8130	....	....	...	48	585	9	118	68	1601	677	22005	...	530
Pleasant, ...	1468	2978	....	....	...	8	87	5	30	16	380	275	11650	2	375
Jackson, ...	650	3982	15	...	...	47	522	8	90	37	758	273	9110	1	300
Total, ...	17883	139501	290	284	50	1489	9956	261	1678	1530	43337	8364	304241	190	10967

TABLE,

Showing the number and value of hogs, cattle, domestic and general manufactures of Lucas County, for 1856.

Townships.	No. of hogs sold.	Value of hogs sold.	No. of cattle sold.	Value of cattle sold.	Pounds of butter made.	Pounds of cheese.	Pounds of Wool.	Value of domestic Manufactures.	Value of general Manufactures.
Chariton, ...	644	2051	346	3035	4803	790	207	612	9319
Cedar, ...	349	3187	91	2539	1472	121	486	162	....
Union, ...	154	1076	38	861	697	30	408	302	....
Liberty, ...	398	1628	116	3332	4714	25	328	1800	....
Washington, ...	118	1269	61	1426	3625	15	510	1115	705
Warren, ...	65	370	144	3134	2450	797	354	119	11
Benton, ...	608	916	769	7957	4754	10	203	4905	....
White Breast, ...	314	2251	279	2823	2678	608	199	53	....
English, ...	239	667	146	2273	4186	160	245	173	340
Otter Creek, ...	269	1380	149	4933	3827	12	134	412	....
Pleasant, ...	80	150	26	772	1900	....	97	10	500
Jackson, ...	44	303	8	170	650	35	252	155	....
Total, ...	3282	15251	2173	33255	35756	2603	3423	9818	10875

TABLE,

EXHIBITING THE PROFESSIONS, TRADES OR OCCUPATIONS OF THE INHABITANTS OF LUCAS COUNTY, FOR 1856.

TOWNSHIPS.	Farmers.	Laborers.	Blacksmiths.	Carpenters.	Wagon makers.	Brick Layers.	Plasterers.	Stone masons.	Stone Cutters.	Builders.	Carriage Makers.	Machinists.	Engineers.	Millers.	Sawyers.	Millwrights.	Painters.	Cabinet makers.
Chariton,......	86		7	33	2	1		3			2			4			1	
Cedar,.........	81	8	1	8	1	1												
Union,.........	82		2		1													
Liberty,......	69			3									2					
Washington,...	60		3	10	1									3				
Warren,.......	64		2	5														
Benton,........	64	7	2	4									1					
White Breast,.	59	23	1	5									2	1		3		
English,........	33	4	1	2			1											
Otter Creek,...	69																	
Pleasant,......	31													1	1			
Jackson,......	26	2	1															
Total,.......	724	44	20	70	5	2	1	3			2		5	9	1	3	1	

TABLE—CONTINUED,

EXHIBITING THE PROFESSIONS, TRADES OR OCCUPATIONS OF THE INHABITANTS OF LUCAS COUNTY, FOR 1856.

TOWNSHIPS.	Chair Makers.	Tinners.	Milliners.	Merchant Tailors.	Tailors.	Hatters.	Shoemakers.	Harness Makers	Bakers.	Butchers.	Mechanics.	Manufacturers.	Merchants.	Speculators.	Agents.	Drovers.	Traders.	Druggists.
Chariton,	....	2	4	....	4	....	1	5	...	....	....	....	12	....	8	....	....	2
Cedar,	....	....	....	....	....	....	....	....	....	....	....	....	....	....	....	....	....	....
Union,	....	....	....	....	....	....	1	....	....	....	....	....	....	....	....	....	....	....
Liberty,	....	....	....	....	....	....	....	....	....	....	....	....	....	....	....	....	....	....
Washington,	....	....	....	....	....	....	1	....	....	....	....	....	1	....	....	....	....	....
Warren,	....	....	....	....	....	....	....	....	....	....	....	....	2	....	....	....	1	....
Benton,	....	....	....	....	1	....	....	....	....	....	....	....	....	....	....	....	....	....
White Breast,	....	....	....	....	....	....	....	....	....	....	....	....	....	....	....	....	....	....
English,	....	....	....	....	....	....	1	....	....	....	....	....	....	....	....	....	....	....
Otter Creek,	....	....	....	....	....	....	....	....	....	....	....	....	....	....	....	....	....	....
Pleasant,	....	....	....	....	....	....	....	....	....	....	....	....	....	....	....	....	....	....
Jackson,	....	....	....	....	....	....	....	....	....	....	....	....	....	....	....	....	....	....
Total,	....	2	4	....	5	....	4	5	....	....	....	....	15	....	8	....	1	2

TABLE—Continued,

EXHIBITING THE PROFESSIONS, TRADES, OR OCCUPATIONS OF THE INHABITANTS OF LUCAS COUNTY, FOR 1856.

TOWNSHIPS.	Confectioners.	Boarding house keepers.	Hotel keeper.	Clothiers.	Physicians.	Dentists.	Lawyers.	Clergymen.	Teachers.	Musicians.	Printers	Editors.	Artists.	Deguerrean Artists.	Bankers.	Grocers.	Teamsters.	Chandlers.
Chariton,			2		5		6	1									1	
Cedar,																		
Union,																		
Liberty,																		
Washington,																		
Warren,																		
Benton,								2	1									
White Breast,					1		2		1									
English,								1	1									
Otter Creek,																		
Pleasant,																		
Jackson,																		
Total,			2		6		8	4	3								1	

TABLE—Continued,

SHOWING THE PROFESSIONS, TRADES OR OCCUPATIONS OF THE INHABITANTS OF LUCAS COUNTY, FOR 1856.

TOWNSHIPS.	Watch Makers.	Jewellers.	Gun Smiths.	Coopers.	Clerks.	Surveyors.	Boat builders.	Hostlers.	Collectors.	Nurserymen.	Notary Public.	Wool Carders.	Register of Land Office.	Weavers.	Jobbers.	Phonographers.	Potters.	Shingle makers.
Chariton,......	1	....	1	....	9	2	1	1	1	1	1	1	1	....	....	....	....	....
Cedar,........	....	....	....	2	....	....	....	....	....	....	....	....	....	....	....	....	....	....
Union,........	....	....	....	....	....	....	....	....	....	....	....	....	....	....	....	....	....	....
Liberty,.......	....	....	....	....	....	....	....	....	....	....	....	....	....	1	....	....	....	....
Washington,...	....	....	....	1	....	....	....	....	....	....	....	....	....	....	....	....	....	....
Warren,.......	....	....	....	....	....	....	....	....	....	....	....	....	....	....	....	....	....	....
Benton,.......	....	....	....	....	....	....	....	....	....	....	....	....	....	1	....	....	....	....
White Breast,..	....	....	....	1	....	....	....	....	....	....	....	....	....	....	1	....	....	....
English,.......	....	....	....	....	....	....	....	....	....	....	....	....	....	....	....	1	1	....
Otter Creek,...	....	....	....	....	....	....	....	....	....	....	....	....	....	....	....	....	....	1
Pleasant,......	....	....	....	....	....	....	....	....	....	....	....	....	....	....	....	....	....	....
Jackson,......	....	....	....	....	....	....	....	....	....	....	....	....	....	....	....	....	....	....
Total,.......	1	....	1	4	9	2	1	1	1	1	1	1	1	2	1	1	1	1

TABLE,

SHOWING THE PLACE OF NATIVITY OF THE INHABITANTS OF LUCAS COUNTY, FOR 1856.

STATES.	NAME OF TOWNSHIPS.												
	Chariton.	Cedar.	Union.	Liberty.	Washington.	Warren.	Benton.	White Breast.	English.	Otter Creek.	Pleasant.	Jackson.	TOTAL.
Ohio,	209	41	57	41	27	72	83	100	70	16	41	24	781
Indiana,	188	200	69	106	100	103	112	120	75	18	23	52	1166
Pennsylvania,	100	20	17	8	16	26	35	23	33	5	13	3	299
Iowa,	146	80	58	53	17	50	41	40	60	....	65	19	649
New York,	49	18	....	1	6	12	11	10	1	....	2	2	112
Maine,	10	....	....	....	4	....	....	....	....	....	....	....	14
New Hampshire,	2	....	1	....	....	....	3	2	....	....	....	....	8
Vermont,	3	1	....	1	....	1	....	2	....	6	....	....	14
Massachusetts,	3	5	....	....	....	1	....	2	....	1	....	1	13
Connecticut,	1	....	....	....	....	2	....	....	....	....	....	....	3
Rhode Island,	....	....	....	....	....	....	1	....	....	....	....	....	1
Virginia,	67	6	64	7	7	36	19	10	14	2	16	2	250
Kentucky,	43	39	10	15	13	14	18	16	10	....	9	8	195
Illinois,	60	22	18	19	13	15	19	12	25	2	8	....	213
Michigan,	2	....	....	....	....	1	....	....	1	....	....	....	4
Texas,	....	....	....	....	....	....	1	....	....	....	....	....	1
Alabama,	....	....	....	2	....	....	....	....	....	....	....	....	2
Mississippi,	....	....	1	....	....	....	....	....	....	....	....	....	1
North Carolina,	16	17	1	1	2	7	3	4	10	8	2	3	74
South Carolina,	....	....	2	....	1	3	....	....	3	1	....	....	10
Tennessee,	4	8	6	2	37	3	4	2	17	9	....	6	98
Missouri,	10	5	6	4	3	5	....	....	2	....	1	....	36
Georgia,	....	1	1	....	....	....	....	....	1	....	....	....	3
Maryland,	8	....	....	25	1	7	....	....	2	....	....	....	43
New Jersey,	3	1	1	....	....	1	1	1	....	1	....	....	9
England,	22	....	....	....	1	....	3	....	....	....	....	....	26
Ireland,	9	1	1	2	1	1	2	6	1	....	....	....	24
Scotland,	6	....	....	....	....	....	....	....	....	....	....	....	6
Germany,	2	....	....	....	1	3	....	5	....	....	....	1	12
Sweden,	3	....	....	....	....	....	....	....	....	....	....	....	3
Canada,	1	....	....	....	....	....	....	3	....	....	....	....	4
New Brunswick,	....	....	....	....	....	....	....	1	....	....	....	....	1
Switzerland,	1	....	....	....	....	....	....	....	....	1	....	....	2
Wisconsin,	3	....	....	....	....	1	....	....	1	....	....	....	5
Delaware,	1	....	1	....	1	....	....	....	4	....	....	....	7
Unknown,	4	3	3	1	....	1	....	12	2	285	4	4	319

TABLE,

SHOWING THE POPULATION OF MADISON COUNTY, FOR 1856.

TOWNSHIPS.	No dwelling houses	Number of families	Number of males.	Number of females.	Colored.	Married.	Widowed.	Native voters.	Naturalized voters.	Aliens.	Militia.	Deaf and Dumb.	Blind.	Insane.	Idiotic.	Owners of land.	Paupers.
Center, ...	283	2[illegible]9	908	786	....	603	37	381	28	1	349	....	2	....	....	95	....
South, ...	149	150	438	403	....	288	23	167	7	14	153	....	....	....	1	110	1
Monroe, ...	74	74	213	195	....	143	7	81	3	1	66	....	....	2	....	68	....
Webster, ...	35	39	87	83	....	62	6	38	2	1	41	2	....	....	2	33	....
Union, ...	93	93	302	259	....	193	9	105	9	8	100	....	....	....	....	87	....
Crawford, ...	69	73	227	198	....	158	4	67	23	9	83	....	....	....	....	80	....
Madison, ...	87	106	332	292	....	214	8	115	5	....	84	1	....	....	....	93	....
Walnut, ...	135	143	421	364	....	240	12	147	3	3	120	1	3	....	....	....	....
Total, ...	925	967	2928	2580	....	1901	106	1101	80	37	996	4	5	2	3	566	1

TABLE,

SHOWING THE AGRICULTURAL STATISTICS OF MADISON COUNTY, FOR 1856.

TOWNSHIPS.	Acres of improved land.	Acres of unimproved land.	Acres of meadow.	Tons of Hay.	Bushels of grass seed.	Acres of spring wheat.	Bushels harvested.	Acres of winter wheat.	Bushels harvested.	Acres of Oats.	Bushels harvested.	Acres of corn.	Bushels harvested.	Acres of potatoes.	Bushels harvested.
Center, ...	4183	13625	143	196	32	456	5664	23	328	256	6731	1646	63800	32	2514
South, ...	3460	19112	51	30	....	429	4194	49	537	227	7120	1327	51426	35	2384
Monroe, ...	1873	12124	3	137	....	74	960	....	.....	51	1100	460	12480	....	1020
Webster, ...	434	4051	....	....	....	61	648	....	.....	22	677	206	7720	....	402
Union, ...	2793	11364	829	29	....	458	5079	2	9	236	6449	962	39205	14	2397
Crawford, ...	1250	11427	....	272	....	129	1436	1	20	37	715	463	11940	13	2337
Madison, ...	3520	19165	29	23	....	632	5873	....	.....	135	4459	1278	49710	....	2014
Walnut, ...	7235	14023	405	4	....	278	3545	2	30	94	1840	1375	63595	9	1508
Total, ...	24748	104891	1460	691	32	2518	27399	77	924	1058	29091	7717	299876	103	14576

TABLE,

SHOWING THE NUMBER AND VALUE OF HOGS AND CATTLE SOLD, THE VALUE OF DOMESTIC AND GENERAL MANUFACTURES OF MADISON COUNTY, FOR 1856.

TOWNSHIPS.	Number of hogs sold.	Value of hogs sold.	Number of cattle sold.	Value of cattle sold.	Pounds of butter made.	Pounds of cheese.	Pounds of wool.	Value of domestic manufactures.	Value of gen'l manufactures.
Center,	531	3481	249	7080	10755	160	1197	278	....
South,	670	4598	164	3134	8805	150	1549	578	....
Monroe,	223	1156	65	1930	3285	6000	313	25	....
Webster,	92	527	34	1145	190	....	30	....	....
Union,	419	2889	273	5994	5980	....	1493	594	....
Crawford,	140	1059	77	1933	3985	....	179	35	100
Madison,	395	2508	103	2750	6356	923	665	....	....
Walnut,	306	2732	117	4823	4610	388	629	77	....
Total,	2776	18950	1082	28789	43966	7621	6055	1587	100

TABLE,

SHOWING THE PROFESSIONS, TRADES OR OCCUPATIONS OF THE INHABITANTS OF MADISON COUNTY FOR 1856.

TOWNSHIPS.	Farmers.	Laborers.	Blacksmiths.	Carpenters.	Wagon makers.	Brick layers.	Plasterers.	Stone masons.	tone cutters.	Builders.	Carriage makers.	Machinists.	Engineers.	Millers.	Sawyers	Millwrights.	Painters.	Cabinet makers.
Center, ...	182	13	11	38	3	....	8	17	5	....	2	....	1	4	2	....	....	5
South, ...	128	26	2	4	....	....	....	....	....	....	....	....	....	....	....	....	....	2
Monroe, ...	97	1	4	....	1	....	....	....	....	....	1	....	....	....	....	....	....	2
Webster, ...	42	1	....	3	....	....	....	....	....	....	....	....	....	....	2	1	....	....
Union, ...	91	32	2	3	....	1	....	....	....	....	....	....	....	2	....	....	....	1
Crawford, ...	87	7	2	7	1	....	....	3	....	....	....	....	2	....	....	1	....	1
Madison, ...	88	39	3	1	....	....	....	....	....	....	....	....	....	....	....	....	....	....
Walnut, ...	136	....	2	2	....	....	1	....	....	....	....	....	....	....	....	....	....	....
Total, ...	851	119	26	58	5	1	9	20	5	....	3	....	4	6	4	2	....	11

TABLE—CONTINUED,

SHOWING THE PROFESSIONS, TRADES, OR OCCUPATIONS OF THE INHABITANTS OF MADISON COUNTY, FOR 1856.

TOWNSHIPS.	Chair makers.	Tinners.	Milliners.	Merchant Tailors.	Tailors.	Hatters.	Shoemakers.	Saddle & harness makers.	Bakers.	Butchers.	Mechanics.	Manufacturers.	Merchants.	Speculators.	Agents.	Drovers.	Traders.	Druggists.
Center, ...	....	4	2	....	5	....	12	3	....	3	1	....	15	....	1	....	1	1
South, ...	....	....	....	....	1	....	1	....	....	....	4	....	4	....	....	....	....	....
Monroe,........	1	....	....	....	....	....	....	....	....	....	....	....	....	....	....	....	....	....
Webster,........	....	....	....	....	....	....	....	....	....	....	....	....	....	....	....	....	....	....
Union,........	....	....	....	....	....	....	2	....	....	....	....	....	....	....	....	....	....	....
Crawford,........	2	....	1	....	1	....	1	1	....	....	....	....	....	....	....	....	....	....
Madison,........	1	....	....	....	....	....	1	....	....	....	....	....	....	....	....	....	....	....
Walnut,........	....	....	....	....	....	....	....	1	....	....	....	....	....	....	....	....	....	....
Total,........	4	4	3	....	7	....	17	5	....	3	5	....	19	....	1	...	1	1

TABLE—Continued,

EXHIBITING THE PROFESSIONS, TRADES OR OCCUPATIONS OF THE INHABITANTS OF MADISON COUNTY, FOR 1856.

TOWNSHIPS.	Confectioners.	Board'g H. keepers.	Hotel keepers.	Clothiers.	Physicians.	Lawyers.	Clergymen.	Teachers.	Printers.	Bankers.	Teamsters.	Watch makers.	Gunsmiths.	Coopers	Clerks.	Barbers.	Carders.	Tailoresses.
Center, ...	....	....	....	....	9	12	2	....	1	1	4	3	1	....	8	1	1	....
South, ...	....	....	....	....	2	....	1	2	....	....	....	....	....	1	....	....	....	....
Monroe, ...	....	....	....	....	....	....	....	....	....	....	....	....	....	....	....	....	....	....
Webster, ...	....	....	....	....	....	....	1	....	....	....	....	....	1	....	....	....	....	1
Union, ...	....	....	....	....	1	....	1	3	....	....	....	....	....	2	....	....	....	....
Crawford, ...	....	....	....	....	....	....	....	....	....	....	....	....	....	....	....	....	....	1
Madison, ...	....	....	....	....	....	....	....	....	....	....	....	....	....	....	....	....	....	....
Walnut, ...	....	....	....	....	....	....	1	....	....	....	....	....	....	....	....	....	....	....
Total, ...	....	....	....	....	13	12	6	5	1	1	4	3	2	3	8	1	1	2

TABLE,

SHOWING THE PLACE OF NATIVITY OF THE INHABITANTS OF MADISON COUNTY, FOR 1856.

STATES.	NAME OF TOWNSHIPS.								TOTAL.
	Center.	South.	Monroe.	Webster.	Union.	Crawford.	Madison.	Walnut.	
Ohio,	351	156	66	39	158	104	164	201	1239
Indiana,	435	214	160	9	129	57	214	192	1410
Pennsylvania,	97	62	11	34	34	25	40	46	349
Iowa,	248	140	38	31	74	43	86	132	792
New York,	33	10	13	15	7	24	1	9	112
Maine,	....	2	3	....	....	....	....	....	5
New Hampshire,	2	....	....	....	....	....	....	....	2
Vermont,	8	....	1	....	2	2	1	....	14
Massachusetts,	19	....	....	....	1	1	....	....	21
Connecticut,	5	....	1	....	....	....	....	1	7
Rhode Island,	1	....	....	....	....	....	....	....	1
Virginia,	77	83	19	5	12	12	21	50	279
Kentucky,	85	41	37	7	28	13	21	34	266
Illinois,	139	28	16	13	27	15	27	43	308
Michigan,	2	1	....	....	4	17	....	....	24
Arkansas,	1	....	....	....	....	....	....	....	1
Texas,	1	....	....	....	....	....	....	....	1
Alabama,	....	3	....	....	....	....	....	....	3
Florida,	....	....	....	....	....	1	....	....	1
North Carolina,	45	14	22	2	5	3	12	17	120
South Carolina,	....	2	3	....	....	....	3	....	8
Tennessee,	18	11	4	....	8	1	7	25	74
Missouri,	28	51	....	....	19	8	12	16	134
California	....	....	....	....	....	....	1	....	1
Maryland,	13	1	1	1	9	6	2	9	42
New Jersey,	10	1	....	4	1	1	3	....	20
England,	29	5	5	1	2	....	....	1	43
Ireland,	5	4	4	1	12	70	8	5	109
Wales,	5	....	....	2	....	....	....	....	7
Scotland,	8	1	....	....	3	....	....	....	12
Germany,	17	7	....	3	15	6	1	4	53
France,	....	1	....	....	....	....	....	....	1
Prussia,	1	....	....	....	....	....	....	....	1
Sweden,	1	....	....	....	....	....	....	....	1
Holland,	....	....	....	....	1	....	....	....	1
Canada,	2	....	1	....	7	2	....	....	12
Wisconsin,	4	2	3	2	2	14	....	....	27
Delaware,	4	1	....	....	1	....	....	....	6
Unknown,	....	....	....	1	....	....	....	....	1

TABLE,

SHOWING THE POPULATION OF MAHASKA COUNTY, FOR 1856.

TOWNSHIPS.	No. of dwelling houses.	Number of families.	Number of males.	Number of females.	Colored.	Married.	Widowed.	Native voters.	Naturalized voters.	Aliens.	Militia.	Deaf and Dumb.	Blind.	Insane.	Idiotic.	Owners of land.	Paupers.
Cedar,	156	163	453	435		299	19	175	4	5	161					100	
Demoine,	84	106	316	272		185	8	104	8	3	89					67	
Scott,	138	153	434	370		261	22	149	3	6	154	2			1	87	
White Oak,	137	137	394	407		226	38	154	2	3	137			1	1	121	
Adams,	74	74	221	189		143	5	68	3		46	2	1			57	
Black Oak,	105	105	318	262		203	18	100	11	21	108	4		1		97	
Prairie,	52	52	160	133	3	100	8	49	4	3	47	1				46	2
Pleasant Grove,	58	53	172	146		112	8	65	7	3	63			2		48	
Harrison,	126	126	425	367		231	17	162	4	3	10				1	90	
Jefferson,	86	92	301	255		169	12	88	1		81				1	66	
Oskaloosa,	686	721	2251	2017		1452	105	836	34	42	935			2		259	1
Monroe,	153	168	447	409		306	22	170	5	3	167		1		1	150	
Madison,	64	68	193	164		123	12	79	1		77					46	
Richland,	171	173	515	443		342	28	210	9	4	294				1	163	
Union,	101	101	292	289		196	6	103	4	1	77					57	
Total,	2191	2297	6892	6158	3	4348	328	2512	100	97	2346	9	2	6	6	1454	3

TABLE,

SHOWING THE AGRICULTURAL STATISTICS OF MAHASKA COUNTY, FOR 1856.

TOWNSHIPS.	Acres of improved land	Acres of unimproved land	Acres of meadow.	Tons of hay.	Bushels of grass seed.	Acres of spring wheat.	Bushels harvested.	Acres of winter wheat.	Bushels harvested.	Acres of oats.	Bushels harvested.	Acres of corn.	Bushels harvested.	Acres of potatoes.	Bushels harvested.
Cedar, ...	5127	10007	512	131	15	1040	5448	2	26	735	26819	2713	153390	25	2977
Demoine, ...	2713	6439	64	49	8	435	1692	21	76	323	7690	1328	75111	15	2571
Scott, ...	4595	10024	193	169	16	907	5296	57	945	423	11226	2339	124550	37	4325
White Oak, ...	3657	11479	307	159	9	554	5027	25	1007	366	10506	1644	81920	24	2997
Adams, ...	2119	8310	25	15		331	4337	40	445	150	4540	951	49890	10	1097
Black Oak, ...	5314	9788	100	61	7	751	9404	24	173	400	13177	1925	91405	33	4530
Prairie	1600	3159	25	20		215	3461	2	20	101	3885	477	24110	1	500
Pleasant Grove, .	1682	4257	7	6	4	233	4159	...	.....	59	1753	876	49665	10	1466
Harrison, ...	6302	10613	748	362	67	829	5327	157	1919	847	19367	2577	176185	35	4019
Jefferson, ...	2684	8300	64	30	1	449	2959	65	524	237	5130	1219	62225	27	2852
Oskaloosa, ...	11547	16388	961	707	26	1510	13047	...	.....	1075	30702	4209	217797	80	7725
Monroe, ...	4324	11766	123	126	50	644	7955	42	358	272	8737	2052	114445	32	4307
Madison, ...	2669	5523	141	51	12	233	2071	14	33	171	4580	1256	68190	10	1377
Richland, ...	4205	13265	85	151	5	854	11955	14	140	166	5152	1624	97505	27	2971
Union, ...	2152	7262	67	40	1	396	5864	11	102	140	4191	1080	61108	19	2157
Total, ...	60690	136590	3482	2078	220	9361	88002	474	4768	5463	157455	26270	1447796	385	45871

TABLE,

SHOWING THE NUMBER AND VALUE OF HOGS, CATTLE, DOMESTIC AND GENERAL MANUFACTURES OF MAHASKA COUNTY, FOR 1856.

TOWNSHIPS.	No. of hogs sold.	Value of hogs sold.	No. of cattle sold.	Value of cattle sold.	Pounds of butter made.	Pounds of cheese.	Pounds of Wool.	Value of domestic Manufactures.	Value of general Manufactures.
Cedar, ...	1699	11256	436	10377	13811	25	2315	2053	5416
Demoine, ...	1352	4832	314	9580	11325	365	728	545	686
Scott, ...	1236	10826	473	11119	19444	1984	1433	598	2600
White Oak, ...	1029	9425	169	4804	11105	894	1460	1276	4946
Adams, ...	596	4669	282	2329	4955	200	1260	720	15
Black Oak, ...	1053	8168	249	7583	10134	10542	1016	1270	....
Prairie, ...	195	1583	26	1044	400	100	280	445	....
Pleasant Grove, ..	801	4766	140	3628	4475	....	258	112	40
Harrison, ...	1641	12808	295	7837	16571	3138	4571	2893	133
Jefferson, ...	664	6528	201	3427	8200	724	955	1165	....
Oskaloosa, ...	2422	22367	482	12238	26380	982	3647	....	126000
Monroe, ...	1478	10389	226	6438	20978	3030	1783	4814	3155
Madison, ...	893	4633	154	3555	4470	110	1123	908	....
Richland, ...	2261	14950	379	7725	11457	1004	1189	1217	16965
Union, ...	748	6175	171	4674	4240	37	483	355	....
Total, ...	18068	133375	3997	96358	167945	23135	22502	18371	159956

TABLE,

EXHIBITING THE PROFESSIONS, TRADES OR OCCUPATIONS OF THE INHABITANTS OF MAHASKA COUNTY, FOR 1856.

TOWNSHIPS.	Farmers.	Laborers.	Blacksmiths.	Carpenters.	Wagon makers.	Brick layers.	Plasterers.	Stone Masons.	Stone Cutters.	Builders.	Carriage makers.	Machinists.	Engineers.	Millers.	Sawyers.	Millwrights.	Painters.	Cabinet Makers.
Cedar, ...	174	8	4	11	3	....	1	1	....	....	....	....	2	3	1	1	....	7
Des Moines, ...	94	....	2	7	....	....	....	....	....	....	....	....	2	3	....	....	....	....
Scott, ...	108	41	3	2	....	....	....	....	....	....	....	....	....	....	....	1	....	....
White Oak, ...	114	34	5	10	....	....	....	....	....	....	....	....	1	1	....	....	....	....
Adams, ...	54	1	....	....	....	....	....	....	....	....	....	....	....	....	....	....	....	....
Black Oak, ...	165	....	2	....	....	....	....	1	....	....	....	....	....	2	....	....	....	....
Prairie, ...	50	....	....	2	....	1	....	....	....	....	....	....	....	1	....	....	....	....
Pleasant Grove,	79	..	....	2	....	....	....	....	....	....	....	....	....	....	....	....	....	....
Harrison, ...	125	....	....	1	....	....	....	1	....	....	....	....	....	....	....	....	....	....
Jefferson, ...	85	....	....	7	....	....	1	1	....	....	....	....	....	....	....	....	....	....
Oskaloosa, ...	425	40	3	20	2	1	5	1	....	....	1	1	4	3	2	....	....	....
Monroe, ...	160	....	3	17	....	....	1	....	....	....	....	....	1	3	....	....	....	1
Madison, ...	54	32	1	3	....	....	....	....	....	....	....	....	....	4	....	....	....	....
Richland, ...	110	32	5	24	3	1	1	3	....	....	....	....	....	3	....	1	1	....
Union, ...	82	....	3	4	....	....	....	2	....	....	....	....	....	3	....	....	....	....
Oskaloosa City,	25	30	22	96	4	21	17	4	8	....	2	....	10	2	....	2	9	18
Total, ...	1904	218	53	206	12	24	26	14	8	....	3	1	20	28	3	5	10	26

TABLE—CONTINUED,

SHOWING THE PROFESSIONS, TRADES OR OCCUPATIONS OF THE INHABITANTS OF MAHASKA COUNTY, FOR 1856.

TOWNSHIPS.	Chair makers.	Tinners.	Milliners.	Merchant tailors.	Tailors.	Hatters.	Shoe makers.	Harness makers.	Bakers.	Butchers.	Mechanics.	Manufacturers.	Merchants.	Speculators.	Agents.	Traders.	Druggists.	Confectioners.
Cedar,	....	....	....	....	....	....	3	2	1	....	....	....	4	....	....	1	1	....
Des Moines,	....	....	....	....	2	....	1	....	....	....	1	....	....	....	....	....	....	....
Scott,	....	....	2	....	....	....	2	....	....	....	20	1	2	....	....	....	....	....
White Oak,	....	....	2	....	....	....	1	....	....	....	....	1	1	....	....	....	....	....
Adams,	....	....	....	....	....	....	....	....	....	....	....	....	....	....	....	....	....	....
Black Oak,	....	....	....	....	....	....	....	....	....	....	....	....	....	....	....	....	....	....
Prairie,	....	....	....	....	....	....	1	....	....	....	....	....	....	....	....	....	....	....
Pleasant Grove,	....	....	....	....	3	....	....	....	....	....	....	....	1	....	....	....	....	....
Harrison,	....	....	....	....	....	....	....	....	....	....	....	....	....	....	....	....	....	....
Jefferson,	1	....	....	....	....	....	....	....	....	....	....	....	....	....	....	....	....	....
Oskaloosa,	1	....	....	....	2	....	1	2	....	....	....	1	....	....	....	....	....	....
Monroe,	1	....	7	....	....	2	1	....	....	....	....	....	5	....	....	....	....	....
Madison,	....	....	2	....	1	....	1	....	....	....	....	....	....	....	....	....	....	....
Richland,	....	....	....	....	....	....	4	....	....	....	....	1	3	....	....	....	....	....
Union,	....	....	....	....	1	....	2	....	....	....	....	....	2	....	....	....	....	....
Oskaloosa, City,	....	10	15	....	7	1	10	13	4	3	....	2	27	....	2	....	2	2
Total,	3	10	28	....	16	3	27	17	5	3	21	6	45	....	2	1	3	2

TABLE—Continued.

SHOWING THE TRADES, PROFESSIONS OR OCCUPATIONS OF THE INHABITANTS OF MAHASKA COUNTY, FOR 1856.

TOWNSHIPS.	Boarding house keep's.	Hotel keepers.	Clothiers.	Physicians.	Dentists.	Lawyers.	Clergyman.	Teachers.	Musicans.	Printers.	Editors.	Artists.	Daguerrean Artists.	Bankers.	Grocers.	Teamsters.	Chandlers.	Brick Makers.
Cedar,		1		3			3	1								4		
Des Moines,				2				4									1	
Scott,		1		3														1
White Oak,				2			2	3										
Adams,		1					1											
Black Oak,							1											
Prairie,								1										
Pleasant Grove,				1		1		1										1
Harrison,					1													
Jefferson,																		
Oskaloosa,						1		10						1		7		2
Monroe,				2			1	9				1						
Madison,																		
Richland,		1		3			1	2					1			2		
Union,				1														1
Oskaloosa City,		5		13	1	20	10	14		13	1	1	5	1	15			
Total,		9		30	2	22	19	45		13	1	2	6	2	15	13	1	5

TABLE—Continued,

EXHIBITING THE PROFESSIONS, TRADES, OR OCCUPATIONS OF THE INHABITANTS OF MAHASKA))JNTY, FOR 1856.

TOWNSHIPS.	Watch makers	Jewellers.	Gun smiths.	Coopers.	Clerks.	Ostlers.	Weavers.	Seamstresses.	Hedgers.	Potters.	Pump makers.	Tanners.	Lime Burners	Lumber men.	Colliers.	Glaziers.	Nursery men.	Carders
Cedar,	....	....	....	1	....	1	2	4	....	....	....	....	....	....	....	....	....	....
Des Moines,	....	....	....	1	....	....	....	....	....	....	....	....	....	....	....	....	....	....
Scott,	....	....	....	3	....	....	....	2	....	....	....	....	....	....	....	....	....	....
White Oak,	....	....	....	....	....	....	....	....	....	....	....	....	....	....	....	....	....	....
Adams,	....	....	....	....	....	....	....	....	....	....	....	....	....	....	....	....	....	....
Black Oak,	....	....	....	....	....	....	....	....	....	....	....	....	....	....	....	....	....	....
Prairie,	....	....	....	....	....	....	....	....	1	....	....	....	....	....	....	....	....	....
Pleasant Grove,	....	....	....	....	1	....	1	1	....	....	....	....	....	....	....	....	....	....
Harrison,	....	....	....	....	....	....	....	....	....	1	....	....	....	....	....	....	....	....
Jefferson,	....	....	....	....	....	....	....	....	....	....	....	....	....	....	....	....	....	....
Oskaloosa,	....	....	1	1	....	....	....	1	....	....	1	1	1	2	1	1	3	1
Monroe,	....	....	....	3	....	....	13	....	6	3	....	....	....	....	....	....	....	....
Madison,	....	....	....	....	....	....	....	1	....	....	....	....	....	....	....	....	....	....
Richland,	....	....	....	3	1	....	1	....	....	....	....	1	....	....	....	....	....	....
Union,	....	....	....	....	....	....	....	....	....	....	....	....	....	....	....	....	....	....
Oskaloosa City,	....	6	2	5	37	2	....	12	3	4	....	....	....	....	....	....	....	3
Total,	....	6	3	17	39	3	17	21	10	8	1	2	1	2	1	1	3	4

TABLE—Continued,

SHOWING THE PROFESSIONS, TRADES OR OCCUPATIONS OF THE INHABITANTS OF MAHASKA COUNTY, FOR 1856.

TOWNSHIPS.	Brewers.	Wheel wrights.	Fruit Growers.	Surveyors.	Miners.	Shingle makers.	Wool spinners.	Shoe binders.	Medical Students.	Segar makers.	Stone quarriers.	Sheriffs.	Hack drivers.	Stage drivers.	Distillers.	Tin peddlers.	Painters.	Furniture dealers.
Cedar,																		
Des Moines,																		
Scott,																		
White Oak,																		
Adams,																		
Black Oak,																		
Prairie,																		
Pleasant Grove,																		
Harrison,																		
Jefferson,																		
Oskaloosa,	1	1																
Monroe,																		
Madison,																		
Richland,		2	1	1														
Union,		1			1	1												
Oskaloosa City,				2			2	1	2	1	1	1	1	12	2	1	3	1
Total,	1	4	1	3	1	1	2	1	2	1	1	1	1	12	2	1	3	1

TABLE—Continued,

EXHIBITING THE PROFESSIONS, TRADES, OR OCCUPATIONS OF THE INHABITANTS OF MAHASKA COUNTY, FOR 1856.

TOWNSHIPS.	Shoe merchants.	County Recorders.	Pump makers.	Livery keepers.	Tobacconists.	Barbers.	Law students.	Stove dealers.	Students.	Colporteurs.	Postmasters.	Music teachers.	Land ladies.	Spring setters.	Draymen.	Peddlers.	Constables.	Insurance officers.
Cedar,	....	....	....	....	....	....	....	....	....	....	....	....	....	....	....	....	....	....
Des Moines,	....	..	....	....	....	....	....	....	....	....	....	....	....	....	....	....	....	....
Scott,	....	....	....	....	....	....	....	....	....	....	....	....	....	....	....	....	....	....
White Oak,	....	....	....	....	....	....	....	....	....	....	....	....	....	....	....	....	....	....
Adams,	....	....	....	....	....	....	....	....	....	....	....	....	....	....	....	....	....	....
Black Oak,	....	....	....	....	....	....	....	....	....	....	....	....	....	....	....	....	....	....
Prairie,	....	....	....	..	....	....	....	....	....	....	....	....	....	....	....	....	....	....
Pleasant Grove,	....	....	....	....	....	....	....	....	....	....	....	....	....	....	....	....	....	....
Harrison,	....	....	....	....	....	....	....	....	....	....	....	....	....	....	....	....	....	....
Jefferson,	....	....	....	....	....	....	....	....	....	....	....	....	....	....	....	....	....	....
Oskaloosa,	....	....	....	....	....	....	....	....	....	....	....	....	....	....	....	....	....	....
Monroe,	....	....	....	....	....	....	....	....	....	....	....	....	....	....	....	....	....	....
Madison,	....	....	....	....	....	....	....	....	....	....	....	....	....	....	....	....	....	....
Richland,	....	....	....	....	....	....	....	....	....	....	....	....	....	....	....	....	....	....
Union,	....	...	...	....	....	....	....	....	....	....	....	....	....	....	....	....	....	....
Oskaloosa City,	1	1	2	3	3	1	2	3	1	1	1	2	4	1	1	2	1	1
Total	1	1	2	3	3	1	2	3	1	1	1	2	4	1	1	2	1	1

TABLE,

SHOWING THE PLACE OF NATIVITY OF THE INHABITANTS OF MAHASKA COUNTY, FOR 1856.

STATES	NAME OF TOWNSHIPS.																TOTAL.
	Cedar.	Des Moines.	Scott.	Whit-Oak.	Adams.	Black Oak.	Prairie.	Pleasant Grove.	Harrison.	Jefferson.	Oskaloosa.	Monroe.	Madison.	Richland.	Union.	Oskaloosa City.	
Ohio,	169	160	201	151	124	107	95	55	214	151	625	220	77	311	146	688	3494
Indiana,	238	76	127	163	83	98	35	119	112	95	318	192	83	93	111	191	2134
Pennsylvania,	38	31	79	19	13	56	44	8	54	51	163	30	24	83	30	262	986
Iowa,	192	147	192	177	63	102	42	43	206	113	450	181	86	159	121	385	2659
New York,	7	19	38	4	15	24	11	...	26	5	24	25	3	18	8	101	328
Maine,	...	1	4	1	...	...	...	...	4	...	2	1	1	15	...	2	31
New Hampshire,	1	...	...	1	...	...	...	...	1	...	26	...	5	4	...	9	47
Vermont,	1	1	5	3	5	4	...	...	7	...	6	7	..	...	1	27	67
Massachusetts,	4	3	3	...	...	1	...	...	3	...	4	1	..	5	2	12	38
Connecticut,	1	...	4	9	...	...	...	...	3	...	2	1	..	15	4	16	55
Rhode Island,	...	2	...	...	...	...	...	...	...	1	6	...	..	2	...	1	12
Virginia,	30	35	34	31	19	9	24	7	34	34	87	33	19	107	19	94	616
Kentucky,	56	29	11	68	52	20	4	41	39	18	56	72	11	23	41	57	598
Illinois,	59	32	36	59	13	26	4	2	21	50	66	40	12	44	32	93	589
Michigan,	...	2	1	1	1	...	...	8	...	...	3	2	4	...	...	4	26
Arkansas,	...	...	...	1	...	...	...	...	...	...	...	...	..	...	...	...	1
Alabama,	...	...	...	2	...	...	...	1	1	...	...	...	..	...	...	1	5
Louisiana,	...	...	...	...	...	...	...	...	...	...	1	...	2	1	...	1	5
Mississippi,	...	...	...	...	...	1	...	...	...	...	...	...	..	...	...	...	1
North Carolina,	12	5	19	17	3	1	2	2	10	3	39	16	12	3	13	25	182
South Carolina,	4	...	...	3	1	...	...	...	1	2	3	...	..	1	...	...	15
Tennessee,	19	8	6	18	3	16	4	4	15	14	19	5	7	11	1	22	202
Missouri,	...	9	5	1	...	1	...	5	4	1	11	...	2	...	...	6	45
Georgia,	1	...	...	...	...	...	...	...	...	...	...	...	..	...	1	2	4
Maryland,	16	4	10	15	9	9	7	2	16	4	25	8	..	33	33	23	214
New Jersey,	4	2	...	1	...	3	8	2	4	...	32	1	1	3	...	29	90
England,	...	7	2	6	2	...	...	3	3	2	12	10	..	3	5	31	86
Ireland,	4	5	5	...	3	3	2	16	9	8	7	10	2	15	3	46	138
Wales,	...	...	...	...	...	...	...	...	...	1	1	...	..	...	1	4	7
Scotland,	...	...	...	...	...	1	1	...	..	1	7	...	..	...	...	3	13
Germany,	22	7	18	5	1	1	5	...	2	...	26	1	..	2	7	57	154
France,	...	...	...	...	...	1	1	...	...	...	...	...	..	...	...	3	5
Prussia,	...	...	...	...	...	...	...	...	...	...	...	...	..	...	...	3	3
Sweden.	...	...	...	...	...	...	...	...	...	1	...	...	..	...	...	...	1
Holland,	...	...	...	...	...	78	...	...	...	...	...	...	..	...	...	1	79
Canada.	...	2	...	1	...	1	1	...	1	1	...	...	..	4	1	5	17
New Brunswick,	2	...	...	...	...	...	...	...	...	...	...	...	1	...	...	...	3
Switzerland,	..	...	...	8	...	...	1	...	...	...	...	...	..	1	...	5	15
Wisconsin,	1	...	2	1	...	...	...	...	2	...	2	2	..	1	1	4	14
Delaware,	6	...	2	1	..	...	...	...	...	...	10	...	5	1	...	5	30
Dist. of Columbia,	1	1	...	...	...	...	...	...	...	...	...	...	..	...	...	1	3
Unknown,	...	...	...	4	...	7	2	..	...	...	4	...	..	...	..	10	27
Netherland,	...	...	...	...	...	10	...	...	...	...	...	...	..	...	...	...	10
Minnesota,	...	...	...	...	...	...	...	...	...	...	...	...	..	...	...	1	1

TABLE,

SHOWING THE POPULATION OF MARION COUNTY, FOR 1856.

TOWNSHIPS.	No. of dwelling houses.	Number of families.	Number of males.	Number of females.	Colored.	Married.	Widowed.	Native voters.	Naturalized voters.	Aliens.	Militia.	Deaf and Dumb.	Blind.	Insane.	Idiotic.	Owners of land.	Paupers.
Clay,	146	149	455	426	....	271	18	159	8	....	144	1	....	1	....	115	....
Dallas,	105	115	300	299	....	115	8	80	22	14	75	1	....	....	....	97	....
Franklin,	33	33	98	78	....	62	7	40	....	4	40	....	....	....	....	32	2
Indiana,	142	146	468	414	....	280	16	165	....	1	155	....	....	....	1	143	1
Knoxville,	481	515	1503	1407	2	953	75	371	24	11	452	1	....	2	....	1354	....
Liberty,	165	165	505	458	....	313	11	175	2	3	147	....	....	....	....	126	....
Lake Prairie,	550	575	1510	1301	....	1035	65	181	260	283	484	....	....	....	....	494	3
Pleasant Grove,	178	178	581	489	....	324	25	204	4	....	178	3	....	....	..	149	1
Perry,	49	49	129	129	....	89	4	43	2	6	37	....	....	....	1	31	....
Polk,	103	106	293	278	....	189	16	97	9	5	78	....	....	....	1	68	1
Red Rock,	147	152	423	400	....	268	21	163	6	5	168	1	....	3	....	90	1
Swan,	103	103	261	240	....	190	9	105	5	2	106	....	....	1	....	56	....
Summit,	124	124	356	280	....	203	17	116	4	....	120	....	....	....	....	97	1
Union,	60	61	195	186	....	116	13	71	3	....	60	1	....	....	....	44	....
Washington,	125	131	348	350	....	120	18	137	3	....	115	....	....	....	....	98	....
Total,	2511	2582	7425	6735	2	4628	323	2107	352	334	2259	8	....	7	3	2994	10

TABLE,

SHOWING THE AGRICULTURAL STATISTICS OF MARION COUNTY, FOR 1856.

TOWNSHIPS.	Acres of improved land.	Acres of unimproved land.	Acres of meadow.	Tons of hay.	Bushels of grass seed.	Acres of spring wheat.	Bushels harvested.	Acres of winter wheat.	Bushels harvested.	Acres of oats.	Bushels harvested.	Acres of corn.	Bushels harvested.	Acres of potatoes.	Bushels harvested.
Clay, ...	4204	11159	124	58	1	603	5001	73	383	420	7878	2112	104160	25	2754
Dallas, ...	2564	7196	69	7	11	383	2125	253	1803	193	4440	1129	35030	20	2343
Franklin, ...	957	2649	9	7	1	128	1157	31	260	17	430	319	9781	6	680
Indiana, ...	3379	1168	184	91	6	5	386	76	114	316	1337	1729	3498	13	2172
Knoxville, ...	10036	25446	149	129	34	1203	14540	98	1200	664	21865	3479	161039	54	6882
Liberty, ...	4139	3044	81	68	4	476	3549	33	257	338	8200	1622	75330	33	3703
Lake Prairie, ...	5074	3334	95	64	...	1286	16654	8	125	471	5862	2891	151362	57	7237
Pleasant Grove, .	4014	14726	55	39	1	530	4901	64	539	203	5904	1943	85045	31	3871
Perry, ...	636	3000	10	8	1	72	835	2	20	38	960	422	20900	7	595
Polk, ...	1908	5052	25	60	...	243	2238	63	559	74	1632	1285	62775	16	2063
Red Rock, ...	1527	9992	44	33	8	192	2787	42	722	121	3445	1033	47180	12	1605
Swan, ...	1904	8254	48	29	8	216	2813	27	467	106	3555	853	38979	16	3191
Summit, ...	4618	6801	191	434	20	1035	10068	16	267	790	9861	1944	102090	32	4322
Union, ...	1481	5961	....	......	...	356	4789	5	236	89	2755	906	40940	11	1427
Washington, ...	2926	8212	64	14	3	300	1942	53	168	217	4994	1419	62280	14	1859
Total, ...	49368	115984	1058	1041	98	7028	73785	844	7120	4057	93119	23086	1000399	347	44702

TABLE,

SHOWING THE NUMBER AND VALUE OF HOGS, CATTLE, DOMESTIC AND GENERAL MANUFACTURES OF MARION COUNTY, FOR 1856.

TOWNSHIPS.	No. of hogs sold.	Value of hogs sold.	No. of cattle sold.	Value of cattle sold.	Pounds of butter made.	Pounds of cheese.	Pounds of Wool.	Value of domestic Manufactures.	Value of general Manufactures.
Clay, ...	1401	10126	732	8460	6970	369	1764	1498	382
Dallas, ...	343	2064	105	2440	6040	95	580	724	2114
Franklin, ...	180	650	31	885	2625	....	198	138	....
Indiana, ...	1071	7184	245	5516	5945	580	2348	2155	....
Knoxville, ...	2669	18429	332	7790	30810	723	3996	3186	24750
Liberty, ...	1301	10261	236	6586	8599	270	1502	1324	....
Lake Prairie, ...	1488	11770	162	4422	13645	4445	158	36	4380
Pleasant Grove, ..	1131	7294	201	4811	10679	522	1714	1286	....
Perry, ...	251	1363	33	827	2000	250	528	400	130
Polk, ...	1074	6464	136	3666	6770	444	702	607	....
Red Rock, ...	664	3757	166	3961	6816	528	697	704	28400
Swan, ...	877	4698	71	1614	6356	840	1289	789	....
Summit, ...	1455	7395	572	9494	14820	875	1368	1460	200
Union, ...	626	3512	138	3346	3203	635	942	515	360
Washington, ...	323	2482	94	2378	9855	665	1574	1722	6580
Total, ...	14854	97449	3254	66196	135070	11241	19360	16544	67296

TABLE,

EXHIBITING THE PROFESSIONS, TRADES OR OCCUPATIONS OF THE INHABITANTS OF MARION COUNTY, FOR 1856.

TOWNSHIPS.	Farmers.	Laborers.	Blacksmiths.	Carpenters.	Wagon makers.	Brick layers.	Plasterers.	Stone Masons.	Stone Cutters.	Builders.	Carriage makers.	Machinists.	Engineers.	Millers.	Sawyers.	Millwrights.	Painters.	Cabinet Makers.
Clay, ...	71	19	2	9	2	....	....	....	....	....	....	....	....	....	....	....	....	1
Dallas, ...	85	....	3	2	1	....	....	....	....	....	....	....	....	....	....	1	....	2
Franklin, ...	54	....	....	....	....	....	....	....	....	....	....	....	....	....	....	1	....	....
Indiana, ...	88	3	4	7	1	....	....	....	....	....	....	....	1	1	2	....	....	....
Knoxville, ...	417	87	12	62	3	6	5	3	....	....	....	1	4	7	6	....	2	4
Liberty, ...	110	....	4	10	....	....		1	....	....	....	....	....	6	....	2	1	6
Lake Prairie, ..	275	146	16	72	5	....	5	20	2	....		....	....	1	2	1	9	10
Pleasant Grove,	219	....	6	17	....	....	....	1	....	....	....	....	2	1	3	....	1	....
Perry, ...	27	8	....	3	....	....	....	....	....	....	....	....	....	....	....	....	....	....
Polk, ...	74	6	....	7	....	....	....	....	....	....	....	....	....	4	....	....	....	2
Red Rock, ...	91	14	7	16	1	....	1	....	....	....	....	....	5	2	7	1	....	4
Swan, ...	76	....	1	3	....	....	....	....	....	....	....	1	....	1	....	....	....	1
Summit, ...	107	15	1	3	....	....	....	....	....	....	....	....	....	....	....	....	2	....
Union, ...	83	6	....	....	....	1	1	....	....	....	....	....	....	....	....	....	....	....
Washington, ..	98	24	2	2	....	....	....	....	....	....	....	....	1	1	....	....	....	....
Total, ...	1875	328	58	213	13	7	12	25	2	....	....	2	13	24	20	6	15	30

TABLE—Continued,

SHOWING THE PROFESSIONS, TRADES, OR OCCUPATIONS OF THE INHABITANTS OF MARION COUNTY, FOR 1856.

TOWNSHIPS.	Chair makers.	Tinners.	Milliners.	Merchant Tailors.	Tailors.	Hatters.	Shoemakers.	Saddle & harness makers.	Bakers.	Butchers.	Mechanics.	Manufacturers.	Merchants.	Speculators.	Agents.	Drovers.	Traders.	Druggists.
Clay,	....	....	2	....	....	....	3	....	....	....	1	....	....	....	....	....	....	....
Dallas,	....	....	....	....	1	....	1	....	....	....	1	....	2	....	....	....	....	....
Franklin,	....	....	....	....	....	....	....	....	....	....	....	....	....	....	....	....	....	....
Indiana,	....	....	1	....	1	....	....	....	1	....	9	....	2	....	....	....	....	....
Knoxville,	4	4	....	....	4	....	3	2	....	....	1	....	25	....	....	....	....	1
Liberty,	....	....	....	....	1	....	2	2	....	....	....	....	2	....	....	....	....	....
Lake Prairie,	1	4	1	....	14	....	20	4	5	2	....	10	23	....	2	....	....	1
Pleasant Grove,	....	....	1	....	1	....	3	....	....	....	....	....	10	....	....	....	....	....
Perry,	....	....	....	....	1	....	....	....	....	....	....	....	....	....	....	....	....	....
Polk,	....	....	....	....	....	....	....	....	....	....	....	....	....	....	....	....	....	....
Red Rock,	....	....	....	....	....	....	2	....	....	....	....	1	7	....	....	....	....	....
Swan,	....	....	....	....	1	....	....	....	....	....	5	....	2	....	....	....	....	....
Summit,	....	....	1	....	1	....	....	....	1	....	5	....	....	....	....	....	....	....
Union,	....	....	....	....	....	....	1	....	....	....	....	....	....	....	....	....	....	....
Washington,	....	....	....	....	....	....	1	1	....	....	4	....	....	....	....	....	....	....
Total,	5	8	6	....	25	....	36	9	7	2	26	11	79	....	2	....	....	2

TABLE—Continued,

EXHIBITING THE PROFESSIONS, TRADES OR OCCUPATIONS OF THE INHABITANTS OF MARION COUNTY, FOR 1856.

TOWNSHIPS.	Confectioners.	Board'g H. keepers.	Hotel keepers.	Clothiers.	Physicians.	Dentists.	Lawyers.	Clergymen.	Teachers.	Musicians.	Printers.	Editors.	Artists.	Daguerrean artists.	Bankers.	Grocers.	Teamsters.	Chandlers.
Clay,	....	....	....	....	....	....	....	....	8	....	....	....	....	....	....	....	....	....
Dallas,	....	....	....	....	1	....	....	....	....	....	....	....	....	....	....	....	....	....
Franklin,	....	....	....	....	1	....	....	....	1	....	....	....	....	....	....	....	....	....
Indiana,	....	....	1	....	1	....	....	2	1	....	....	....	....	....	....	....	....	....
Knoxville,	....	....	1	....	10	1	14	9	8	....	4	1	....	....	....	1	13	....
Liberty,	....	....	....	....	4	....	1	....	1	1	....	....	....	....	....	....	1	....
Lake Prairie,	....	....	3	....	8	....	....	1	6	....	2	1	....	....	....	....	65	....
Pleasant Grove,	....	....	1	....	3	....	....	1	2	....	....	....	....	....	....	....	2	....
Perry,	....	....	....	....	1	....	1	....	....	....	....	....	....	....	....	....	....	....
Polk,	....	....	....	....	....	....	....	....	2	....	....	....	....	....	....	....	....	....
Red Rock,	....	....	2	....	3	....	1	3	1	....	....	....	....	....	....	....	1	....
Swan,	....	....	....	....	....	....	....	....	....	....	....	....	....	....	....	....	....	....
Summit,	....	....	....	....	....	....	....	....	....	....	....	....	....	....	....	....	2	....
Union,	....	....	....	....	....	....	....	....	1	....	....	....	....	....	....	....	....	....
Washington,	....	....	1	....	1	....	....	....	....	....	....	....	....	....	....	....	....	....
Total,	....	....	9	....	33	1	17	16	31	1	6	2	....	....	....	1	84	....

TABLE—Continued,

EXHIBITING THE PROFESSIONS, TRADES, OR OCCUPATIONS OF THE INHABITANTS OF MARION COUNTY, FOR 1856.

TOWNSHIPS.	Brick makers	Watch Makers.	Jewellers.	Gun Smiths.	Coopers.	Clerks.	Shingle makers.	Potters.	Tailoresses.	Surveyors.	Weavers.	Turners.	Wheelwrights.	Horse farriers.	Professors.	P. Masters.	Stage Drivers.	Cigar makers.
Clay,							1											
Dallas,					2													
Franklin,																		
Indiana,								3	1		1		1					
Knoxville,	2	2			1	7												
Liberty,					1	1												
Lake Prairie,	8	2		1	3	5	1	1	2	1		3		2	1	1	1	1
Pleasant Grove						1			3		1							
Perry,				1														
Polk,	1							3	1									
Red Rock,	2			1	1	3	1		1									
Swan,																		
Summit,																		
Union,	1												1					
Washington,																		
Total,	14	4		3	8	17	3	7	8	1	2	3	2	2	1	1	1	1

TABLE—Continued,

SHOWING THE PROFESSIONS, TRADES OR OCCUPATIONS OF THE INHABITANTS OF MARION COUNTY, FOR 1856.

TOWNSHIPS.	Gardners.	City Marshals.	Mayors	Sash makers.	Constables.	Sheriffs.	Coal Diggers.	Nurserymen.	County Judges.	Clerks of Court.	Ferrymen.	Livery keepers.	Carders.	Peddlers.	Lime burners.	Veterinarian.	Domestics.	Colporteurs.
Clay,	....	....	....	....	....	....	....	....	....	....	....	....	....	1	1	....	....	....
Dallas,	....	....	....	....	....	....	....	....	....	....	....	....	....	....	....	....	....	....
Franklin,	....	....	....	....	....	....	....	....	....	....	....	....	....	....	....	....	....	....
Indiana,	....	....	....	....	1	1	....	....	1	1	....	1	....	....	....	....	....	....
Knoxville,	....	....	....	....	....	....	....	....	....	....	....	....	1	....	....	1	....	....
Liberty,	....	....	....	....	....	....	....	....	....	....	....	....	....	....	....	....	....	....
Lake Prairie,	2	1	1	....	....	....	....	2	....	....	....	....	....	....	1	....	33	1
Pleasant Grove,	....	....	....	....	....	....	....	....	....	....	....	....	....	....	....	....	....	....
Perry,	....	....	....	....	....	....	....	....	....	....	....	....	....	....	....	....	....	....
Polk,	....	....	....	1	....	....	1	....	....	....	1	....	2	....	....	....	....	....
Red Rock,	....	....	....	....	....	....	....	....	....	....	....	....	....	....	....	....	....	....
Swan	....	....	....	....	....	....	....	....	....	....	....	....	....	....	....	....	....	....
Summit,	....	....	....	....	....	....	1	....	....	....	....	....	....	....	....	....	1	....
Union,	....	....	....	....	....	....	....	....	....	....	....	....	....	1	....	....	....	....
Washington,	....	....	....	....	....	....	....	....	....	....	....	....	....	....	....	....	....	....
Total,	2	1	1	1	1	1	2	2	1	1	1	1	3	2	2	1	34	1

TABLE,

SHOWING THE PLACE OF NATIVITY OF THE INHABITANTS OF MARION COUNTY, FOR 1856.

STATES.	NAME OF TOWNSHIPS.															TOTAL
	Clay.	Dallas.	Franklin.	Indiana.	Knoxville.	Liberty.	Lake Prairie.	Pleasant Grove.	Perry.	Polk.	Red Rock.	Swan.	Summit.	Union.	Washington.	
Ohio,........	197	131	52	191	702	150	210	234	72	118	211	111	115	122	107	2723
Indiana,......	201	100	26	226	561	178	120	354	44	89	145	147	147	88	170	2596
Pennsylvania,	27	30	4	27	238	55	78	27	15	16	53	31	24	21	28	774
Iowa,........	203	108	41	183	607	269	522	192	59	139	171	84	130	56	129	2903
New York,...	21	10	6	16	70	23	55	12	4	4	21	15	14	2	6	279
Maine,......	8	....	...	...	...	....	2	1	...	...	...	1	...	...	...	12
N. Hampshire,	....	....	2	...	3	....	5	1	...	...	...	...	...	...	...	11
Vermont,....	1	1	3	1	11	3	8	1	...	...	...	1	1	...	...	31
Massachusetts	3	....	2	3	7	5	5	2	...	1	8	...	2	...	1	39
Connecticut, .	....	1	1	...	9	1	6	....	1	...	2	...	...	1	...	22
Rhode Island,	1	....	...	...	1	....	...	....	...	...	...	...	...	1	1	4
Virginia,....	41	17	8	33	25	50	49	49	20	61	56	21	36	29	23	518
Kentucky,...	49	14	2	64	168	75	40	46	6	32	40	18	39	37	90	720
Illinois,......	91	39	4	69	157	65	76	47	4	29	48	4	18	12	71	707
Michigan,....	3	1	...	1	2	....	10	1	...	5	7	1	7	...	1	44
Arkansas,....	....	....	...	...	...	....	...	....	...	...	5	...	...	...	...	5
Texas,.......	....	....	...	...	...	....	1	....	...	...	...	...	...	...	...	1
Alabama,....	....	2	1	...	4	....	...	....	...	...	1	...	...	2	...	10
Louisiana,...	....	....	...	...	...	1	...	....	...	...	...	...	...	...	...	1
Mississippi,...	....	....	...	1	...	1	...	....	...	...	...	...	1	...	...	3
N. Carolina,..	9	12	1	22	42	8	11	25	1	13	7	5	9	1	15	181
S. Carolina,..	....	....	1	5	1	1	2	2	1	...	3	...	5	1	4	26
Tennessee,...	10	10	15	14	51	21	5	32	4	5	11	34	21	1	18	252
Missouri,....	5	4	...	7	12	28	25	6	1	11	6	...	...	...	22	127
Georgia,.....	....	1	6	...	11	....	...	1	...	...	...	...	...	...	...	19
Maryland,...	4	6	...	6	11	3	6	6	...	6	...	5	1	1	5	60
New Jersey, .	14	2	1	11	27	6	5	3	...	3	3	2	11	...	3	91
England,....	3	12	...	..	16	....	19	6	1	...	1	1	...	1	...	60
Ireland,.....	4	3	...	1	26	2	8	2	1	2	4	1	...	...	1	55
Wales,.......	....	....	..	...	6	....	1	....	...	...	...	...	...	...	...	6
Scotland,....	7	....	...	...	4	....	1	....	2	...	...	1	...	1	...	16
Germany,....	....	82	...	1	12	13	36	1	21	1	18	6	2	4	2	199
France,.. ...	....	1	...	..	...	1	7	....	...	...	...	...	...	...	...	9
Prussia,.....	....	....	..	..	1	....	5	....	...	...	...	...	...	...	...	6
Holland,.....	2	....	...	...	1	....	...	....	1	34	...	2	11	...	...	51
Canada,.....	....	9	...	...	7	....	4	1	...	...	1	1	...	...	...	23
Switzerland, .	....	....	...	...	...	....	...	11	...	...	.	4	...	...	...	15
Hanover,....	....	....	...	.	...	....	2	....	...	...	...	...	...	...	...	2
Wisconsin,...	....	....	...	...	1	....	...	....	...	...	...	...	...	...	...	1
Delaware,...	2	3	...	...	5	1	1	3	...	...	...	5	...	...	...	20
Dis. Columbia,	....	....	...	...	1	1	...	....	...	...	...	...	...	...	...	1
Chili, ...	....	....	...	...	1	1	...	....	...	...	...	...	...	...	...	1
Netherlands, .	....	....	...	...	...	....	...	1480	1	...	...	...	...	...	1	1482
California,...	....	....	...	...	...	....	...	....	3	...	...	1	...	...	...	4
Belgium,....	....	....	...	...	...	....	...	6	...	...	...	...	...	...	...	6
Friesland,....	....	....	...	...	...	....	...	....	...	2	..	...	42	...	...	44

TABLE,

SHOWING THE POPULATION OF MARSHALL COUNTY, FOR 1856.

TOWNSHIPS.	No. of dwelling houses.	Number of families.	Number of males.	Number of females.	Colored.	Married.	Widowed.	Native voters.	Naturalized voters.	Aliens.	Militia.	Deaf and Dumb.	Blind.	Insane.	Idiotic.	Owners of land.	Paupers.
Marietta,	103	107	343	283	....	208	6	138	7	3	133	....	....	...	1	81	....
Iowa,	162	168	487	414	....	315	12	193	9	....	198	....	....	...	1	147	1
Marion,	90	98	242	217	....	164	10	84	8	1	84	....	....	....	1	77	....
Legrand,	70	81	228	186	....	159	11	111	5	6	91	....	....	....	1	97	....
Green Castle,	24	27	65	61	....	50	2	29	3	....	24	....	....	....	....	22	....
Jefferson,	58	64	201	172	....	127	6	75	....	....	74	1	1	1	1	51	....
Eden,	37	38	107	88	....	75	....	45	1	1	38	...	....	....	....	37	....
Liberty,	54	66	175	173	....	120	8	62	10	9	60	1	....	....	....	66	....
Bangor,	58	60	184	176	....	114	11	73	2	2	75	....	....	....	....	67	....
Marshall,	112	112	379	279	....	241	13	170	10	10	160	4	1	....	....	92	....
Total,	768	821	2411	2049	....	1567	79	980	55	32	937	6	2	1	5	737	1

TABLE,

SHOWING THE AGRICULTURAL STATISTICS OF MARSHALL COUNTY, FOR 1856.

TOWNSHIPS.	Acres of improved land.	Acres of unimproved land.	Acres of meadow.	Tons of Hay.	Bushels of grass seed.	Acres of spring wheat.	Bushels harvested.	Acres of winter wheat.	Bushels harvested.	Acres of Oats.	Bushels harvested.	Acres of corn.	Bushels harvested.	Acres of potatoes.	Bushels harvested.
Marietta,	1910	8703	4	12	1	138	1892	....	....	59	2105	834	14940	16	2047
Iowa,	4181	20725	14	764	....	282	5412	11	130	180	8250	1537	71940	21	3459
Marion,	1820	12368	33	78	5	98	1358	....	....	123	4338	473	20840	6	755
Legrand,	1657	7081	6	333	....	181	3758	....	....	73	2386	758	26075	19	2010
Green Castle,	374	4274	....	....	....	20	180	....	....	13	185	160	4250	3	165
Jefferson,	1142	11220	3	....	....	111	2058	25	164	76	2615	857	24495	2	400
Eden,	583	7675	....	267	....	16	288	....	....	....	......	239	8670	4	1040
Liberty,	1622	10133	64	509	....	82	697	....	....	69	1340	553	20556	13	1646
Bangor,	1071	2853	6	8	5	113	728	4	12	79	2581	696	20922	5	643
Marshall,	1345	21260	32	547	....	131	3617	....	....	74	3370	488	23340	26	4630
Total,	15704	106292	162	2515	11	1172	19988	40	406	746	27170	6595	246028	115	16795

TABLE,

SHOWING THE NUMBER AND VALUE OF HOGS AND CATTLE SOLD, THE VALUE OF DOMESTIC AND GENERAL MANUFACTURES OF MARSHALL COUNTY, FOR 1856.

TOWNSHIPS.	Number of hogs sold.	Value of hogs sold.	Number of cattle sold.	Value of cattle sold.	Pounds of butter made.	Pounds of cheese.	Pounds of wool.	Value of domestic manufactures.	Value of gen'l manufactures.
Marietta,	270	1409	110	2727	3645	....	143	130	....
Iowa,	413	4315	174	5898	24096	....	1343	1685	2123
Marion,	107	1093	49	1280	700	....	669	....	....
Legrand,	180	1097	71	2090	3772	20	233	363	881
Green Castle,	28	219	23	1063	225	....	60	....	....
Jefferson,	194	2224	83	1974	4473	....	794	496	....
Eden,	24	191	31	1041	2310	....	....	....	....
Liberty,	127	809	70	1319	3370	2450	307	264	8
Bangor,	68	533	69	1328	50	....	168	124	....
Marshall,	166	1743	85	1665	5703	205	388	....	19905
Total,	1577	13633	765	20385	48344	2675	4105	3062	22908

TABLE,

SHOWING THE PROFESSIONS, TRADES, OR OCCUPATIONS OF THE INHABITANTS OF MARSHALL COUNTY FOR 1856.

TOWNSHIPS.	Farmers.	Laborers.	Blacksmiths.	Carpenters.	Wagon makers.	Brick layers.	Plasterers.	Stone masons.	Stone cutters.	Builders.	Carriage makers.	Machinists.	Engineers.	Millers.	Sawyers	Millwrights.	Painters.	Cabinet makers.
Marietta, ...	115	2	4	18	....	....	....	....	....	....	....	....	1	....	1	....	1	4
Iowa, ...	131	22	6	31	3	....	2	1	1	....	....	....	4	....	....	1	1	3
Marion, ...	73	4	1	3	....	....	....	1	....	....	....	....	....	....	1	....	....	....
Legrand, ...	62	28	5	11	3	....	....	1	....	....	....	2	1	1	....	1	....	1
Green Castle, .	29	3	1	....	1	....	....	....	....	....	....	....	....	....	....	....	....	....
Jefferson, ...	92	....	....	5	....	....	....	....	....	....	....	....	....	....	....	....	....	....
Eden, ...	38	....	....	5	....	....	....	....	....	....	....	....	....	....	....	....	....	....
Liberty, ...	61	7	1	4	....	1	....	1	....	....	....	....	1	....	....	1	....	....
Bangor, ...	53	17	3	....	1	..	....	....	....	....	....	....	....	....	....	....	....	....
Marshall, ...	82	16	7	34	....	....	2	3	....	....	1	2	4	5	6	....	1	6
Total, ...	726	99	28	110	8	1	4	7	1	....	1	4	11	6	8	3	3	14

TABLE—Continued,

SHOWING THE PROFESSIONS, TRADES OR OCCUPATIONS OF THE INHABITANTS OF MARSHALL COUNTY, FOR 1856.

TOWNSHIPS.	Chair Makers.	Tinners.	Milliners.	Merchant Tailors.	Tailors.	Hatters.	Shoemakers.	Harness Makers.	Bakers.	Butchers.	Mechanics.	Manufacturers.	Merchants.	Speculators.	Agents.	Drovers.	Traders.	Druggists.
Marietta,	....	....	1	....	1	1	3	1	....	....	....	....	6	....	....	....	....	1
Iowa,	....	1	....	....	4	....	4	1	....	....	1	....	9	....	1	....	....	....
Marion,	....	....	....	....	....	....	1	....	....	....	....	....	2	....	....	....	....	....
Legrand,	....	....	9	....	....	1	....	1	....	2	3	....	1	....	....	....	....	....
Green Castle,	....	....	....	....	....	....	....	....	....	....	....	....	....	....	....	....	....	....
Jefferson,	....	....	....	....	....	....	1	1	....	....	....	....	....	....	....	....	1	....
Eden,	....	....	....	....	....	....	....	....	....	....	....	....	....	....	....	....	....	....
Liberty,	....	....	....	....	....	....	....	1	....	....	....	....	....	....	....	....	....	....
Bangor,	....	....	....	....	....	....	....	....	....	....	2	....	1	....	....	....	....	....
Marshall,	....	2	15	....	2	....	2	1	....	2	5	....	7	....	....	....	3	....
Total,	....	3	25	....	7	2	11	6	....	4	11	....	26	....	1	....	4	1

TABLE—Continued,

EXHIBITING THE PROFESSIONS, TRADES, OR OCCUPATIONS OF THE INHABITANTS OF MARSHALL COUNTY, FOR 1856.

TOWNSHIPS.	Confectioners	Boarding house keepers.	Hotel keeper.	Clothiers.	Physicians.	Dentists.	Lawyers.	Clergymen.	Teachers.	Musicians.	Printers	Editors.	Artists.	Deguerrean Artists.	Bankers.	Grocers.	Teamsters.	Brick makers.
Marietta,					3		4		1						1		3	
Iowa,			2		1		1	1	2		2						2	2
Marion,					1			1	1									
Legrand,									1									
Green Castle,					1													
Jefferson,							1		1									
Eden,									2									
Liberty,																		
Bangor,					2													
Marshall,			2		2		1	1	1								6	1
Total,			4		10		7	3	9		2				1		11	3

TABLE—CONTINUED,

SHOWING THE PROFESSIONS, TRADES, OR OCCUPATIONS OF THE INHABITANTS OF MARSHALL COUNTY, FOR 1856.

TOWNSHIPS.	Coopers	Clerks.	Wheelwrights.	Surveyors.	County Judge.	Recorder.	Shingle makers.	Moulders.	Lumbermen.	Nurserymen.	Peddlers.	Students	Weavers.	Livery stable keepers.	Cloth dressers.	Tobacconists.	Plough makers.
Marietta,	....	5	3	1	1	1	2	2	....	....	....	....	....	....	....	....	....
Iowa,	1	....	....	1	....	....	1	....	2	1	1	1	....	....	....	....	....
Marion,	....	....	....	....	....	....	....	....	....	....	....	....	....	....	....	....	....
Legrand,	2	....	....	....	....	....	....	....	1	....	....	....	1	....	....	....	....
Green Castle,	....	....	....	....	....	....	....	....	....	....	....	....	....	....	....	....	....
Jefferson,	....	....	....	....	....	....	....	....	....	....	....	....	....	....	....	....	....
Eden,	....	....	....	....	....	....	....	....	....	....	....	....	....	....	....	....	....
Liberty,	....	....	1	....	....	....	....	....	....	....	....	....	....	....	....	....	....
Bangor,	....	....	1	....	....	....	4	1	....	....	....	....	3	2	1	2	2
Marshall,	2	1	....	....	....	....	....	....	....	....	....	1	....	....	....	....	....
Total,	5	6	5	2	1	1	7	3	3	1	1	2	4	2	1	2	2

TABLE,

SHOWING THE PLACE OF NATIVITY OF THE INHABITANTS OF MARSHALL COUNTY, FOR 1856.

STATES.	NAME OF TOWNSHIPS.										TOTAL.
	Marietta.	Iowa.	Marion.	Legrand.	Green Castle.	Jefferson.	Eden	Liberty.	Bangor.	Marshall	
Ohio,	259	199	150	192	25	53	35	109	41	178	1241
Indiana,	73	170	57	34	28	41	23	79	140	56	701
Pennsylvania,	52	87	51	25	11	24	16	16	4	106	392
Iowa,	68	143	48	28	14	51	14	30	53	56	505
New York,	53	62	20	14	6	22	17	10	6	83	293
Maine,	....	5	....	....	....	....	1	....	....	4	10
New Hampshire,	....	1	....	....	....	....	....	....	....	1	2
Vermont,	3	8	35	5	....	1	....	....	....	26	78
Massachusetts,	....	6	....	2	....	....	8	2	10	2	30
Connecticut,	2	4	2	2	....	1	4	4	1	9	29
Rhode Island,	....	....	....	....	....	....	....	....	....	1	1
Virginia,	18	11	14	5	....	5	22	7	10	9	101
Kentucky,	5	29	7	7	15	46	9	18	4	6	146
Illinois,	29	100	10	17	13	69	36	20	15	41	350
Michigan,	1	16	13	3	2	3	2	....	....	8	48
Mississippi,	....	1	....	....	....	....	....	....	....	....	1
North Carolina,	14	7	8	2	2	7	....	1	54	4	99
South Carolina,	1	2	....	2	....	2	....	....	1	1	9
Tennessee,	4	21	....	36	1	27	....	....	6	4	99
Missouri,	....	....	6	....	....	....	....	....	....	1	7
Georgia,	....	....	....	1	....	....	....	....	1	8	10
Maryland,	11	1	2	11	....	....	2	1	7	9	44
New Jersey,	1	8	9	....	4	12	3	3	....	2	42
England,	11	5	18	7	....	....	2	2	2	11	58
Ireland,	8	7	2	1	....	8	....	14	....	1	41
Wales,	....	....	2	1	5	....	....	....	....	....	8
Scotland,	....	....	....	1	....	1	....	1	3	1	7
Germany,	1	1	1	14	....	....	....	12	....	14	43
France,	1	....	....	....	....	....	....	13	....	1	15
Holland,	....	....	....	4	....	....	....	....	....	....	4
Canada,	5	3	3	....	....	....	....	3	2	15	31
New Brunswick,	....	1	....	....	....	....	....	....	....	....	1
Wisconsin,	....	....	1	....	....	....	....	2	....	....	3
Delaware,	6	2	....	....	....	....	1	1	....	....	10
Bohemia,	....	1	....	....	....	....	....	....	....	....	1

TABLE,

SHOWING THE POPULATION OF MILLS COUNTY, FOR 1856.

TOWNSHIPS.	No. of dwelling houses.	Number of families.	Number of males.	Number of females.	Colored.	Married.	Widowed.	Native voters.	Naturalized voters.	Aliens.	Militia.	Deaf and Dumb.	Blind.	Insane.	Idiotic.	Owners of land.	Paupers.
West Liberty, ...	162	163	538	437	....	295	26	195	7	1	186	....	....	....	1	150	....
Silver Creek, ...	74	74	260	224	....	157	8	100	1	8	81	....	....	....	....	73	....
Rawls, ...	90	90	278	220	....	167	9	93	3	....	78	1	1	....	....	78	....
Council Bluffs, ...	19	19	67	56	....	44	1	15	3	8	12	....	....	....	....	22	....
Village of St. Marys	35	35	93	61	13	65	4	8	17	35	18	....	....	....	....	43	....
Plattville, ...	54	58	159	150	....	107	7	67	....	....	62	....	....	....	....	35	....
Montgomery, ...	28	31	89	75	....	48	8	28	1	3	27	....	....	....	1	29	....
White Cloud, ...	32	36	117	104	....	62	7	42	1	...	45	....	....	....	....	32	....
Nishnabotny, ...	31	31	95	79	....	62	5	27	1	1	22	....	....	....	....	25	....
Total,	525	537	1696	1406	13	997	75	575	34	51	531	1	1	....	2	487	....

TABLE,

SHOWING THE AGRICULTURAL STATISTICS OF MILLS COUNTY, FOR 1856.

TOWNSHIPS.	Acres of improved land.	Acres of unimproved land.	Acres of meadow.	Tons of hay.	Bushels of grass seeds.	Acres of spring wheat.	Bushels harvested.	Acres of winter wheat.	Bushels harvested.	Acres of oats.	Bushels harvested.	Acres of corn.	Bushels harvested.	Acres of potatoes.	Bushels harvested.
West Liberty, ...	2451	24926	10	410	..	270	3271	88	1131	107	3670	1142	55530	21	3461
Silver Creek, ...	2808	723	1	1	...	257	1338	246	1373	128	2122	1118	37300	21	2765
Rawls, ...	2295	9372	2	...	...	223	2348	82	902	93	1710	1134	43010	13	2478
Council Bluffs, ...	762	4485	16	173	...	145	1516	...	....	68	2140	385	18580	15	1865
Village of St. Mary, .	30	2502	60	...	...	....	......	...	....	...	......	....	......	....	......
Plattville, ...	682	2007	4	...	...	63	270	8	46	...	......	585	22162	13	1460
Montgomery, ...	871	3011	...	...	...	167	1552	1	5	21	380	214	7430	3	418
White Cloud, ...	616	5689	216	...	...	106	1282	6	84	37	675	229	8974	7	1032
Nishnabotny, ...	746	3034	...	...	...	158	1573	8	80	20	322	312	8545	2	543
Total, ...	11261	55749	309	584	...	1329	13150	439	3621	473	11019	5119	201531	95	14022

TABLE,

SHOWING THE NUMBER AND VALUE OF HOGS AND CATTLE SOLD, THE VALUE OF DOMESTIC AND GENERAL MANUFACTURES OF MILLS COUNTY, FOR 1856.

TOWNSHIPS.	Number of hogs sold.	Value of hogs sold.	Number of cattle sold.	Value of cattle sold.	Pounds of butter made.	Pounds of cheese.	Pounds of wool.	Value of domestic manufactures.	Value of gen'l manufactures
West Liberty, ...	437	2256	307	7182	12385	400	499	95	55200
Silver Creek, ...	387	3065	184	5116	86[illegible]5	1180	999	467	....
Rawls, ...	353	2122	296	5440	11955	1555	1514	1186	....
Council Bluffs, ...	120	869	176	2677	1689	10	25	....	....
Village of St. Mary,	....	....	....	....	....	....	....	....	....
Plattville, ...	68	589	76	1738	5715	100	376	....	....
Montgomery, ...	127	800	54	1373	1835	50	127	85	300
White Cloud, ...	148	659	71	1194	2116	12	291	20	....
Nishnabotny, ...	74	633	30	818	1380	600	262	320	....
Total, ...	1714	10993	1194	25538	45690	3907	4093	2173	55500

TABLE,

EXHIBITING THE PROFESSIONS, TRADES OR OCCUPATIONS OF THE INHABITANTS OF MILLS COUNTY, FOR 1856.

OCCUPATIONS.	NAME OF TOWNSHIPS.									TOTAL.
	West Liberty.	Silver Creek.	Rawls.	Council Bluffs.	Village of St. Mary.	Plattville.	Montgomery.	White Cloud.	Nishnabotny.	
Farmers,	101	104	86	29	18	52	28	41	28	487
Laborers,	1	11	2	...	1	2	4	7	1	29
Blacksmiths,	5	2	....	....	2	....	1	2	....	12
Carpenters,	14	2	1	....	4	....	....	1	....	22
Brick Layers,	....	....	....	....	1	....	....	....	....	1
Plasterers,	....	3	....	....	....	....	....	....	....	3
Stone Masons,	....	....	....	....	3	....	....	....	1	4
Machinists,	....	....	....	....	1	1	....	....	....	2
Engineers,	2	....	....	....	1	....	....	....	....	3
Millers,	6	....	....	2	....	6	....	....	....	14
Sawyers,	....	....	....	....	1	....	....	....	....	1
Millwrights,	2	....	1	....	....	1	....	....	....	4
Painters,	2	....	....	....	....	....	....	....	1	3
Cabinet Makers,	1	....	....	....	2	....	....	....	....	3
Tinners,	2	....	....	....	2	....	....	....	....	4
Tailors,	3	....	....	....	1	....	2	....	....	6
Shoemakers,	3	....	....	....	2	....	....	....	....	5
Saddle and harness makers,	1	....	....	....	1	....	....	....	....	2
Butchers,	....	....	....	....	1	....	....	....	....	1
Mechanics,	....	....	....	....	1	....	....	....	....	4
Manufacturers,	....	....	....	....	....	....	....	....	....	1
Merchants,	9	....	....	....	4	....	....	....	....	13
Agents,	....	....	....	1	....	....	....	....	....	1
Traders,	1	....	....	....	1	....	....	....	....	2
Druggists,	3	....	....	....	....	....	....	....	....	3
Hotel keepers,	3	....	....	....	2	....	....	....	....	5
Physicians,	3	1	....	1	....	....	....	....	....	7
Lawyers,	7	....	....	....	....	....	1	....	....	9
Clergymen,	2	1	....	...	....	1	1	....	....	5
Teachers,	2	2	....	....	....	....	....	....	....	4
Printers,	....	1	....	....	....	....	....	....	....	1
Teamsters,	1	....	....	....	1	....	....	....	....	2
Chandlers,	....	....	....	....	1	....	....	....	....	1
Brick makers,	1	....	....	....	1	....	....	....	....	2
Gun Smiths,	4	....	....	....	....	....	....	....	....	4
Coopers,	....	1	....	....	....	1	1	....	....	3
Clerks,	1	....	....	....	4	....	....	....	....	5
Wheelwright,	4	....	....	....	....	....	....	....	....	4
Wool carders,	1	....	....	....	....	....	....	....	....	1
Weavers,	....	....	....	....	1	....	1	....	....	2
Plough makers,	1	....	....	....	....	....	...	....	....	1
Surveyors,	1	....	....	....	1	....	....	....	....	2
Well diggers,	....	....	1	....	....	....	....	....	....	1
Cooks,	....	....	....	....	1	....	....	....	....	1
Pilots,	....	....	....	....	1	....	....	....	....	1
Trappers,	....	....	....	....	1	....	....	....	....	1
Tanners,	....	....	....	....	1	....	....	....	....	1

TABLE,

SHOWING THE PLACE OF NATIVITY OF THE INHABITANTS OF MILLS COUNTY FOR 1856.

STATES.	NAME OF TOWNSHIPS.									TOTAL.
	West Liberty.	Silver Creek.	Rawls.	Council Bluffs.	Village of St. Mary.	Plattville.	Montgomery.	White Cloud.	Nishnabotny.	
Ohio,	159	70	49	13	1	33	47	29	42	443
Indiana,	101	124	47	5	3	54	30	43	7	414
Pennsylvania,	46	36	7	....	1	6	2	1	5	104
Iowa,	126	1	92	30	8	61	31	39	43	431
New York,	47	23	22	1	5	23	9	4	5	138
Maine,	13	....	....	....	....	1	....	....	2	16
New Hampshire,	2	1	....	....	....	2	....	....	....	5
Vermont,	3	5	5	....	....	2	....	....	....	15
Massachusetts,	9	2	3	....	1	13	....	....	....	28
Connecticut,	1	....	....	....	....	5	....	....	....	6
Virginia,	50	33	23	4	....	12	10	25	5	162
Kentucky,	43	28	47	5	7	21	3	19	4	177
Illinois,	89	35	19	10	3	24	11	17	25	233
Michigan,	13	10	1	....	....	....	2	....	....	26
Arkansas,	....	....	17	....	....	....	....	....	....	17
Texas,	....	....	1	....	....	....	....	....	....	1
Alabama,	1	1	1	....	....	....	....	....	....	3
Louisiana,	....	....	....	....	1	....	....	....	....	1
North Carolina,	10	1	10	1	....	4	....	....	5	31
South Carolina,	5	....	....	....	....	1	....	....	....	6
Tennessee,	39	10	36	5	....	11	....	16	2	119
Missouri,	150	71	107	24	8	30	3	25	8	426
Maryland,	15	3	....	....	....	3	....	1	....	22
New Jersey,	7	11	6	....	1	....	6	....	....	32
England,	16	1	3	4	4	2	1	....	....	33
Ireland,	1	1	....	....	....	....	....	....	....	2
Wales,	1	....	....	3	....	....	....	....	....	4
Scotland,	....	1	....	....	....	....	....	1	....	2
Germany,	4	....	1	9	86	....	....	....	....	100
France,	2	....	....	8	3	....	....	....	....	13
Prussia,	....	12	....	....	....	....	....	....	....	12
Norway,	14	....	....	....	....	....	1	....	....	15
Sweden,	1	....	....	....	....	....	....	....	....	1
Canada,	1	....	1	1	1	....	7	1	6	18
New Brunswick,	....	....	....	....	....	....	....	....	1	1
Switzerland,	....	....	....	....	1	....	....	....	....	1
Denmark,	....	....	....	....	1	....	....	....	....	1
Wisconsin,	....	....	....	....	8	....	....	....	6	14
Delaware,	....	....	....	....	....	....	....	....	....	....
Nebraska,	1	....	....	....	6	1	....	....	....	8
Indian Territory,	1	....	....	....	....	....	....	....	....	1
Rocky Mountain,	....	....	....	....	1	....	....	....	....	1
Unknown,	4	4	....	....	....	....	1	....	5	14

TABLE,

SHOWING THE POPULATION, AGRICULTURAL STATISTICS, NUMBER AND VALUE OF HOGS AND CATTLE SOLD, &c., OF MITCHELL CO., FOR 1856.

POPULATION.	NAME OF TOWNSHIPS.					TOTAL.
	Burr Oak.	Mitchell.	Osage.	St. Ansgar.	Wayne.	
No. dwelling houses..	31	80	129	47	62	349
Number of families,..	39	90	129	47	62	367
Number of males,....	116	262	483	135	123	1119
Number of females, ..	98	179	310	98	97	782
Married, ...	75	170	288	84	94	711
Widowed, ...	3	4	14	4	3	28
Native voters,.......	46	108	151	20	43	368
Naturalized voters,...	10	11	22	33	15	91
Aliens, ...	6	9	8	......	4	27
Militia, ...	52	99	164	32	49	396
Idiotic,.............	......	......	1	......	......	1
Owners of land, ...	40	99	140	45	4	328
AGRICULTURAL—						
Acres of improved land	203	1367	1676	435	53	3734
Acres unimprov'd land	9605	12157	10252	11246	......	43260
Acres of meadow, ...	30	......	......	187	......	217
Tons of hay, ...	186	192	512	659	22	1571
Acres of spring wheat,	......	37	103	95	......	235
Bushels harvested,...	......	980	2187	2126	......	5293
Acres of oats, ...	......	5	69	5	......	79
Bushels harvested, ...	......	60	3512	430	......	4002
Acres of corn,.......	20	190	450	70	......	730
Bushels harvested, ...	310	5095	13560	3140	......	22105
Acres of potatoes,....	1	10	22	15	......	48
Bushels harvested, ...	195	2407	4310	1830	......	8742
HOGS, CATTLE, &c.,—						
Number of hogs sold,.	1	5	59	24	......	89
Value of hogs sold, ..	11	40	271	159	......	481
Number of cattle sold,	78	74	85	20	......	257
Value of cattle sold,..	1220	3020	3355	738	......	8333
Pounds of butter made,	600	260	800	5200	......	6860
Pounds of cheese,....	......	......	400	......	......	400
Pounds of wool, ...	......	247	116	225	......	588
Val. domestic manuf's,	......	......	100	6	......	106

TABLE,

EXHIBITING THE PROFESSIONS, TRADES OR OCCUPATIONS OF THE INHABITANTS OF MITCHELL COUNTY, FOR 1856.

OCCUPATIONS.	NAME OF TOWNSHIPS.					TOTAL.
	Burr Oak.	Mitchell.	Osage.	St. Ansgar.	Wayne.	
Farmers,	....	83	104	37	55	279
Laborers,	53	....	65	....	....	118
Blacksmiths,	1	6	7	1	....	15
Carpenters,	4	1	29	1	2	37
Wagon makers,	....	....	1	....	....	1
Plasterers,	....	....	1	....	....	1
Stone masons,	....	1	6	....	....	7
Engineers,	1	....	3	....	....	4
Millers,	....	....	1	....	....	1
Sawyers,	....	5	2	....	....	7
Millwrights,	....	2	5	....	....	7
Painters,	....	....	1	....	....	1
Chair makers,	....	....	1	....	....	1
Milliners,	....	1	....	....	....	1
Hatters,	....	....	1	....	....	1
Shoemakers,	2	2	3	1	....	8
Saddle and harness makers,	....	....	1	....	....	1
Mechanics,	....	21	2	....	1	24
Manufacturers,	....	....	2	....	....	2
Merchants,	....	7	11	2	....	20
Druggists,	....	....	1	....	....	1
Physicians,	....	1	5	....	..	6
Dentists,	....	1	....	....	....	1
Lawyers,	....	5	2	....	....	8
Clergymen,	....	1	2	1	....	4
Teachers,	....	....	1	....	....	1
Printers,	....	....	4	....	....	2
Editors,	....	....	1	....	....	1
Coopers,	....	1	....	....	....	1
Clerks,	....	....	1	....	....	1
Sawyers,	1	....	....	....	....	1
Wheelwrights,	....	....	2	....	....	2
Lumbermen,	....	....	3	....	....	3
Founders,	....	....	1	....	....	1
Mail contractors,	....	....	1	....	....	1
Ship carpenters,	....	....	1	....	....	1

TABLE,

SHOWING THE PLACE OF NATIVITY OF THE INHABITANTS OF MITCHELL COUNTY, FOR 1856.

STATES.	NAME OF TOWNSHIPS.					TOTAL.
	Burr Oak.	Mitchell	Osage.	St. Ansgar.	Wayne.	
Ohio,	11	40	72	....	14	137
Indiana,	4	36	54	....	20	114
Pennsylvania,	30	23	46	....	14	113
Iowa,	9	23	55	15	8	110
New York,	38	121	147	59	45	410
Maine,	....	15	24	....	5	44
New Hampshire,	11	2	21	....	10	44
Vermont,	10	26	51	8	7	102
Massachusetts,	6	2	27	....	2	37
Connecticut,	5	7	4	6	4	26
Rhode Island,	....	....	1	....	....	1
Virginia,	....	6	9	....	1	16
Kentucky,	1	....	5	....	....	6
Illinois,	26	9	72	8	31	146
Michigan,	....	4	31	....	1	36
North Carolina,	....	1	4	....	....	5
Tennessee,	....	3	....	....	...	3
Missouri,	....	....	1	....	....	1
Georgia,	....	....	....	....	1	1
Maryland,	1	....	1	....	1	3
New Jersey,	....	1	5	....	4	10
England,	13	6	3	....	7	29
Ireland,	2	8	5	....	32	47
Wales,	....	1	....	....	....	1
Scotland,	....	12	1	....	....	13
Germany,	28	3	30	....	2	63
Prussia,	....	....	2	....	....	2
Norway,	....	12	61	115	....	188
Sweden,	....	....	....	9	....	9
On the Ocean,	....	....	1	....	....	1
Canada,	....	10	25	....	9	44
New Brunswick,	....	....	2	....	....	2
Denmark,	....	....	1	3	....	4
Wisconsin,	19	70	30	10	2	131
Nova Scotia,	....	....	2	....	....	2

TABLE,

SHOWING THE POPULATION OF MONROE COUNTY, FOR 1856.

TOWNSHIPS.	No. of dwelling houses.	Number of families.	Number of males.	Number of females.	Colored.	Married.	Widowed.	Native voters.	Naturalized voters.	Aliens.	Militia.	Deaf and Dumb.	Blind.	Insane.	Idiotic.	Owners of land.	Paupers.
Pleasant,	160	160	505	461	1	325	19	175	18	10	166	....	....	....	1	121	....
Bluff Creek,	82	82	263	219	....	153	10	81	5	2	71	1	....	....	....	69	....
Union,	111	111	310	307	....	215	5	99	1	....	83	....	....	....	....	78	....
Cedar,	57	57	168	136	....	110	4	53	5	....	44	....	....	....	2	52	....
Wayne,	76	76	223	216	....	145	15	77	2	....	67	....	....	....	....	58	....
Guilford,	95	95	265	269	....	167	11	60	39	....	77	....	....	....	....	83	....
Troy,	198	199	576	516	....	395	23	257	9	....	257	4	....	2	1	139	....
Monroe,	74	74	245	208	....	139	13	85	....	1	76	1	....	....	....	70	....
Mantua,	129	131	355	350	....	233	10	127	2	6	108	....	....	....	....	108	....
Urbana,	111	111	338	331	....	203	19	114	8	2	94	....	....	....	....	95	....
Franklin,	53	53	162	141	....	100	3	55	10	3	45	....	....	....	1	53	....
Jackson,	59	61	163	133	....	114	10	64	1	6	56	....	....	2	....	62	....
Total	1205	1210	3573	3287	1	2299	142	1247	100	31	1144	6	....	4	5	988	....

TABLE,

SHOWING THE AGRICULTURAL STATISTICS OF MONROE COUNTY, FOR 1856.

TOWNSHIPS	Acres of improved land.	Acres of unimproved land.	Acres of meadow.	Tons of Hay.	Bushels of grass seed.	Acres of spring wheat.	Bushels harvested.	Acres of winter wheat.	Bushels harvested.	Acres of Oats.	Bushels harvested.	Acres of corn.	Bushels harvested.	Acres of potatoes.	Bushels harvested.
Pleasant, ...	5531	13441	447	214	88	1100	4849	144	794	665	16181	2412	120860	27	3910
Bluff Creek, ...	3120	9690	50	9	1	510	3089	173	612	334	6136	1316	55640	20	2987
Union, ...	3060	9656	132	13	11	268	732	56	567	203	4434	992	49050	13	1119
Cedar, ...	165[illegible]	8360	13	3	....	119	555	40	306	68	1760	759	40275	9	1629
Wayne, ...	1737	5145	22	18	....	179	601	8	....	116	2830	537	22425	4	463
Guilford, ...	1536	10933	31	29	1	30	180	26	243	152	4265	820	42714	20	2380
Troy, ...	4736	17420	204	41	2	457	1761	112	920	505	14366	1877	80790	22	32[illegible]4
Monroe, ...	3033	6590	90	45	6	346	2788	53	542	359	8296	1226	56700	17	1115
Mantua, ...	3504	11952	125	67	102	562	2867	96	949	408	8225	1636	71050	27	2666
Urbana, ...	3691	7157	158	92	10	560	4647	34	148	381	10755	1337	56266	18	2281
Franklin, ...	1505	8079	561	17	4	130	987	40	254	127	4160	613	24935	10	1270
Jackson, ...	1798	7718	....	....	....	184	874	34	405	138	4055	619	24460	6	746
Total, ...	34972	116141	1833	548	225	4454	25927	816	5440	3356	85463	14044	645165	193	24080

TABLE,

SHOWING THE NUMBER AND VALUE OF HOGS, CATTLE, DOMESTIC AND GENERAL MANUFACTURES OF MONROE COUNTY, FOR 1856.

TOWNSHIPS.	No. of hogs sold.	Value of hogs sold.	No. of cattle sold.	Value of cattle sold.	Pounds of butter made.	Pounds of cheese.	Pounds of Wool.	Value of domestic Manufactures.	Value of general Manufactures.
Pleasant, ...	2420	21379	417	12747	19445	290	2143	1660	44260
Bluff Creek, ...	1310	10531	127	3646	5111	227	1218	1024	....
Union, ...	849	5526	184	4250	3113	1812	1084	1024	....
Cedar, ...	393	2797	70	2115	5275	....	1474	553	300
Wayne, ...	290	2091	59	1253	5710	65	562	538	77
Guilford, ...	485	3836	121	3441	5999	120	697	997	315
Troy, ...	1369	9289	253	5408	14535	101	1295	2302	23359
Monroe, ...	881	6505	162	5370	8730	275	1292	1180	....
Mantua, ...	1025	7858	168	4258	9875	1788	1962	1638	300
Urbana, ...	1010	7196	209	5500	8644	586	1938	1778	2100
Franklin, ...	259	1754	57	1325	4151	174	715	693	....
Jackson, ...	164	1095	98	2847	4783	525	381	382	....
Total, ...	10455	79857	1925	52760	95371	5963	14761	13769	70711

TABLE,

EXHIBITING THE PROFESSIONS, TRADES OR OCCUPATIONS OF THE INHABITANTS OF MONROE COUNTY FOR 1856.

OCCUPATIONS.	NAME OF TOWNSHIPS.												TOTAL.
	Pleasant.	Bluff Creek.	Union.	Cedar.	Wayne.	Guilford.	Troy.	Monroe.	Mantua.	Urbana.	Franklin.	Jackson.	
Farmers,	119	126	79	71	60	72	115	104	105	95	83	82	1111
Laborers,	66	....	....	....	10	....	31	....	1	21	....	2	131
Blacksmiths,	5	....	2	....	2	1	39	....	3	5	2	1	30
Carpenters,	12	4	9	....	6.	....	9	1	6	8	3	4	92
Wagon makers,	2	1	....	....	....	....	1	1	....	....	....	....	5
Brick layers,	1	....	....	....	....	....	1	....	1	1	....	....	4
Plasterers,	1	....	1	....	....	....	4	1	2	2	....	....	11
Stone masons,	2	1	1	....	....	....	4	....	2	....	....	....	10
Stone cutters,	....	...	1	....	....	1	1	....	1	....	....	....	4
Carriage makers,	....	....	....	....	....	....	1	....	....	....	....	....	1
Machinists,	....	....	....	....	....	....	1	....	....	....	....	....	1
Engineers,	2	....	2	....	....	....	....	1	....	1	....	1	7
Millers,	4	....	1	....	....	....	7	....	....	2	....	....	14
Sawyers,	4	....	2	....	....	....	....	....	1	...	....	....	7
Millwrights,	....	....	....	....	....	....	2	....	1	....	....	....	3
Painters,	....	....	....	....	....	....	2	1	....	....	....	....	3
Cabinet makers,	1	....	1	....	....	....	....	....	1	1	....	...	4
Tinners,	....	....	....	....	....	....	3	....	....	....	....	....	3
Milliners,	....	....	....	....	....	....	2	....	5	....	....	....	7
Tailors,	....	....	....	....	....	....	3	....	....	....	....	....	3
Hatters,	....	....	....	....	....	....	1	....	....	....	....	....	1
Shoe makers,	2	....	....	....	2	....	4	....	1	1	1	....	11
Harness makers,	....	....	....	....	....	1	5	....	1	1	....	....	8
Merchants,	2	1	2	....	1	....	25	....	....	1	....	2	34
Druggists,	....	....	....	....	....	....	1	....	....	....	....	....	1
Hotel keepers,	....	....	1	....	....	....	....	....	....	....	....	....	1
Physicians,	....	....	1	1	....	...	6	....	1	2	....	....	11
Lawyers,	....	....	....	....	....	....	7	....	....	1	....	....	8
Clergymen,	3	....	1	1	....	....	4	....	1	....	....	....	10
Teachers,	1	....	....	....	....	....	1	....	4	2	2	....	10
Artists,	....	....	....	....	....	....	3	....	....	....	....	....	3
Teamsters,	....	....	....	....	....	....	....	....	....	3	....	....	3
Brick makers,	....	....	....	....	....	1	....	...	2	....	....	....	3
Jewelers,	....	....	....	....	....	....	1	....	....	....	....	....	1
Gun smiths,	....	....	....	....	1	....	1	....	....	....	....	....	2
Coopers,	4	....	2	1	....	....	1	....	1	1	....	1	12
Clerks,	....	....	....	....	....	....	2	....	....	....	....	....	2
Oculist,	1	....	....	....	....	....	....	....	....	....	....	....	1
Wheel wrights,	....	....	2	....	....	....	....	1	....	....	....	....	3
Ploughmakers,	....	....	....	....	....	....	1	....	....	....	....	....	1
Students,	....	....	....	....	....	....	1	....	....	....	....	1	2
Wool carders,	....	....	....	....	....	....	1	....	....	....	....	....	1
Broom makers,	....	....	....	....	....	....	1	....	....	....	....	....	1
Fan mill makers,	....	....	....	....	....	....	1	....	....	....	....	....	1
Weavers,	....	....	....	....	....	....	1	1	....	1	....	....	3
Nurserymen,	....	....	....	....	....	....	1	....	....	....	...	...	1
Drawing,	....	....	....	....	....	....	....	1	....	....	....	....	1
Tanner & currier,	....	....	....	....	....	....	....	1	....	....	....	....	1
Contractors,	....	....	....	....	....	....	....	....	....	....	....	1	1
Domestics,	....	....	....	....	....	....	....	....	....	1	....	....	1

TABLE,

SHOWING THE PLACE OF NATIVITY OF THE INHABITANTS OF MONROE COUNTY, FOR 1856.

STATES.	NAME OF TOWNSHIPS.												TOTAL.
	Pleasant.	Bluff Creek.	Union.	Cedar.	Wayne.	Guilford.	Troy.	Monroe.	Mantua.	Urbana.	Franklin.	Jackson.	
Ohio,	233	82	84	49	42	89	182	28	182	101	10	38	1120
Indiana,	233	132	156	106	163	107	328	142	55	170	75	95	1762
Pennsylvania,	51	43	25	8	10	29	83	14	47	40	4	4	358
Iowa,	213	97	186	71	87	104	202	87	149	165	44	47	1452
New York,	13	6	3	4	2	2	27	3	18	9	5	11	103
Maine,	2	....	....	....	....	....	1	....	4	....	....	1	8
N. Hampshire,	4	....	....	....	....	....	....	....	3	....	....	1	8
Vermont,	6	1	....	....	....	1	12	....	12	1	1	3	37
Massachusetts	2	....	1	....	....	....	1	1	1	3	1	....	10
Connecticut,	3	....	....	....	....	....	3	2	9	1	....	12	30
Virginia,	39	9	10	9	13	9	42	16	89	33	97	22	377
Kentucky,	34	32	48	21	47	24	97	44	11	61	9	2	450
Illinois,	32	21	32	13	14	28	26	57	14	39	8	....	306
Michigan,	....	....	1	....	....	....	....	....	1	....	....	....	4
Arkansas,	....	....	....	....	....	4	....	....	....	....	....	....	4
Alabama,	1	1	....	....	....	....	....	....	....	....	....	....	2
Louisiana,	....	....	....	....	....	....	....	....	....	....	1	....	1
N. Carolina,	8	11	20	3	27	6	7	12	7	11	2	....	114
S. Carolina,	6	5	....	1	2	....	9	2	40	....	....	....	66
Tennessee,	12	16	20	4	3	4	10	17	6	10	6	3	110
Missouri,	7	1	16	....	21	1	2	1	2	18	....	3	67
Georgia,	....	..	....	....	....	....	1	1	....	1	....	....	3
Maryland,	4	6	3	3	1	....	10	....	6	....	....	4	37
New Jersey,	1	2	....	1	....	....	9	1	5	2	....	4	25
England,	1	1	1	2	....	8	....	....	2	1	1	....	17
Ireland,	38	15	....	3	4	55	14	....	21	3	27	10	190
Wales,	....	....	....	....	....	19	....	....	....	....	....	....	19
Scotland,	2	....	....	....	....	....	....	1	....	....	....	....	3
Germany,	5	1	1	....	....	2	6	10	....	1	....	....	26
France,	....	....	....	1	....	....	....	....	....	....	....	....	1
Sweden,	6	....	....	....	....	....	....	....	9	....	....	3	18
Canada,	1	....	....	1	....	....	1	....	12	1	6	....	22
Switzerland,	....	....	....	....	....	....	....	1	....	....	....	....	1
Wisconsin,	....	....	4	....	2	....	1	....	....	....	....	....	7
Delaware,	9	....	1	1	....	1	7	13	....	....	....	....	32
Unknown,	....	1	....	3	1	41	9	....	....	3	6	....	64

TABLE,

SHOWING THE POPULATION, AGRICULTURAL STATISTICS, NUMBER AND VALUE OF HOGS AND CATTLE SOLD, &c., &c., OF MONONA COUNTY, FOR 1856.

POPULATION.	NAME OF TOWNSHIPS.				TOTAL.
	Ashton.	Belvidere.	Franklin.	Preparation.	
No. dwelling houses........	12	32	14	21	79
Number of families,........	12	32	13	21	78
Number of males,...........	65	95	51	69	280
Number of females,.........	22	71	34	52	179
Married,..................	23	58	17	35	133
Widowed,..................	2	3	7	6	18
Native voters,.............	24	38	10	27	99
Naturalized voters,.........	2	3	1	3	9
Aliens,....................	......	......	8	2	10
Militia,...................	24	33	13	18	88
Deaf & dumb,..............	......	......	......	1	1
Blind,.....................	......	......	......	1	1
Idiotic,...................	......	......	......	1	1
Owners of land,...........	16	14	11	6	47
AGRICULTURAL—					
Acres of improved land......	78	102	236	530	948
Acres of unimproved land..	2734	3011	2990	2260	10995
Tons of hay,...............	......	226	......	......	226
Acres of spring wheat,......	49	88	18	60	215
Bushels harvested,.........	925	1040	220	1000	3185
Acres of winter wheat,.....	......	4	......	25	29
Bushels harvested,.........	......	100	......	350	450
Acres of oats,.............	32	36	......	5	73
Bushels harvested,.........	1800	930	......	100	2830
Acres of corn,.............	146	127	101	234	608
Bushels harvested,.........	8400	4135	2780	10820	26135
Acres of potatoes,..........	8	4	4	8	25
Bushels harvested,.........	1040	306	740	1700	3786
HOGS, CATTLE, &c.,					
Number of hogs sold,.......	46	104	50	40	240
Value of hogs sold,........	225	305	490	100	1120
Number of cattle sold,......	34	50	54	315	453
Value of cattle sold,........	755	993	9 4	6498	9210
Pounds of butter made,......	780	1834	1055	1800	5469
Pounds of cheese,..........	......	......	550	1000	1550
Pounds of wool,...........	50	42	......	550	642
Val. domestic manufactures,	......	13	......	250	263
Val. general manufactures,..	......	10337	......	......	10337

TABLE,

EXHIBITING THE PROFESSIONS, TRADES OR OCCUPATIONS OF THE INHABITANTS OF MONONA COUNTY, FOR 1856.

TOWNSHIPS.	Farmers.	Laborers.	Blacksmiths	Carpenters.	Machinists	Engineers.	Millers.	Cabinet maker	Shoemakers.	Agents.	Hotel keepers	Physicians.	Clergymen	Brick makers	Coopers	Surveyors.	Stage drivers	Shingle maker.	Tailoress.	Seamstress.	Mantua maker.	Weaver.
Ashton,	16	3	1	4	..	1	..	..	..	1	1	..	..	..	..	4	1	..	..	..	..	..
Belvidere,	38	6	2	1	..	..	1	1	1	..	..	1	..	..	1	..	..	..	..	..	..	..
Franklin,	13	..	..	2	..	..	..	..	..	..	..	..	..	..	..	..	..	1	..	..	..	..
Preparation,	27	..	2	1	1	..	..	..	1	..	..	..	1	1	2	..	..	..	1	2	1	1
Total,	95	9	5	8	1	1	1	1	2	1	1	1	1	1	3	4	1	1	1	2	1	1

TABLE,

SHOWING THE PLACE OF NATIVITY OF THE INHABITANTS OF MONONA COUNTY, FOR 1856.

STATES.	TOWNSHIPS.				TOTAL.
	Ashton.	Belvidere.	Franklin	Preparation.	
Ohio,	10	27	8	18	63
Indiana,	5	25	5	14	49
Pennsylvania,	10	6	3	4	23
Iowa,	14	21	17	21	73
New York,	1	14	14	14	43
Maine,	....	13	....	....	13
New Hampshire,	....	1	....	....	1
Vermont,	2	5	2	10	19
Massachusetts,	1	3	....	3	7
Connecticut,	1	....	....	2	3
Virginia,	3	1	2	....	6
Kentucky,	4	4	...	1	9
Illinois,	4	20	6	19	49
Michigan,	....	3	7	....	10
Alabama,	....	1	....	....	1
Mississippi,	....	1	....	....	1
North Carolina,	....	3	....	2	5
Tennessee,	....	1	....	....	1
Missouri,	1	7	1	7	16
Maryland,	....	2	1	....	3
New Jersey,	....	1	....	....	1
England,	3	3	3	2	11
Ireland,	2	....	1	1	4
Wales,	....	....	1	....	1
Germany,	....	....	12	....	12
Canada,	1	3	..	1	5
Switzerland,	....	....	1	....	1
Saxony,	....	....	....	1	1
Wisconsin,	....	1	1	1	3
Minnesota,	2	....	....	....	2
Unknown,	3	....	....	....	3

TABLE—Showing the population, agricultural statistics, number and value of hogs and cattle sold, &c., of Montgomery county, for 1856.

POPULATION.	Name of Townships. Washington.	Jackson.	West.	Total.
Number of dwelling houses,	50	40	56	146
Number of families,	51	43	61	155
Number of males,	148	130	192	470
Number of females,	128	131	143	402
Married,	94	82	108	284
Widowed,	4	3	4	11
Native voters,	63	52	85	200
Naturalized voters,	......	2	.....	2
Aliens,	2	2	1	5
Militia,	57	43	77	177
Owners of land,	49	45	73	167
AGRICULTURAL STATISTICS—				
Acres of improved land,	755	957	678	2390
Acres of unimproved land,	9068	10341	11796	31205
Tons of hay,	......	......	244	244
Bushels of grass seed,	......	......	11	11
Acres of spring wheat,	75	32	18	125
Bushels harvested,	864	154	135	1153
Acres of oats,	30	11	......	41
Bushels harvested,	1020	260	......	1280
Acres of corn,	452	527	323	1302
Bushels harvested,	19480	24535	11945	55960
Acres of potatoes,	7	1	4	12
Bushels harvested,	1545	592	470	2607
HOGS, CATTLE, &c.—				
Number of hogs sold,	271	461	94	826
Value of hogs sold,	2040	3112	414	5566
Number of cattle sold,	210	67	39	316
Value of cattle sold,	4976	1664	917	7557
Pounds of butter made,	4020	2898	3875	10793
Pounds of cheese,	20	50	......	70
Pounds of wool,	231	358	245	834
Value of domestic manufactures,	168	337	130	635
Value of general manufactures,	.....	110	......	110

TABLE,

EXHIBITING THE PROFESSIONS, TRADES, OR OCCUPATIONS OF THE INHABITANTS OF MONTGOMERY COUNTY, FOR 1856.

OCCUPATIONS.	TOWNSHIPS.			
	Washington,	Jackson,	West.	Total
Farmers,....	57	53	45	155
Laborers,...	..	3	46	49
Blacksmiths,	...	....	1	1
Carpenters, .	4	2	....	6
Engineers, . .	1	....	....	1
Millers,.....	...	1	....	1
Millwrights,	....	1	....	1
Shoemakers,	....	...	1	1
Mechanics, . .	1	....	....	1
Merchants, . .	....	1	....	1
Physicians, . .	....	....	1	1
Lawyers, ...	....	....	1	1
Clegymen, . .	....	1	....	1
Teamsters, . .	....	1	....	1
Gun Smiths,	...	1	1	2

TABLE,

SHOWING THE PLACE OF NATIVITY OF THE INHABITANTS OF MONTGOMERY COUNTY, FOR 1856.

STATES.	TOWNSHIPS.			
	Washington.	Jackson.	West.	Total.
Ohio,.........	55	73	15	143
Indiana,......	50	41	240	331
Pennsylvania, .	5	4	....	9
Iowa,.........	36	49	46	131
New York,....	6	3	2	11
Maine,.......	1	..	....	1
N. Hampshire,	2	..	....	2
Vermont,.....	3	..	4	7
Massachusetts,	1	..	....	1
Connecticut, . .	1	..	....	1
Rhode Island, .	..	..	4	4
Virginia,.....	18	4	3	25
Kentucky,....	32	16	8	56
Illinois,......	29	12	8	49
Michigan,.....	2	..	....	2
Arkansas,....	..	..	3	3
N. Carolina,...	12	5	....	17
S. Carolina,...	2	..	....	2
Tennessee,....	3	7	....	10
Missouri,.....	8	40	....	48
Maryland,....	3	1	....	4
New Jersey, . .	2	..	1	3
England,.....	..	1	1	2
Ireland,......	5	..	....	5
Scotland,.....	..	2	....	2
Germany,.....	..	2	....	2
Canada,......	..	1	....	1

TABLE,

SHOWING THE POPULATION OF MUSCATINE COUNTY, FOR 1856.

TOWNSHIPS.	No. of dwelling houses.	Number of families.	Number of males.	Number of females.	Colored.	Married.	Widowed.	Native voters.	Naturalized voters.	Aliens.	Militia.	Deaf and Dumb.	Blind.	Insane.	Idiotic.	Owners of land.	Paupers.
Bloomington,	040	1043	3265	2908	....	2136	148	830	403	219	886	3	....	....	1	293	....
Pike,	98	95	307	259	....	189	11	102	11	12	52	2	....	....	....	91	....
Moscow,	181	160	530	431	....	318	32	115	39	31	131	1	....	....	....	144	....
Cedar,	96	105	280	261	....	159	17	85	18	....	....	....	....	....	....	71	....
Sweetland,	264	277	899	749	....	566	54	333	31	59	290	3	....	....	....	167	....
Montpelier,	141	145	480	413	....	342	24	142	27	53	209	....	....	1	1	132	....
Wapsinonoc,	193	193	602	526	....	384	9	230	7	4	199	....	....	....	....	160	....
Seventy-Six,	106	106	345	345	....	187	20	86	12	10	60	....	2	....	....	93	2
Total,	2119	2124	6707	5862	....	4281	315	1923	548	388	1827	9	2	1	2	1151	2

TABLE,

SHOWING THE AGRICULTURAL STATISTICS OF MUSCATINE COUNTY, FOR 1856.

TOWNSHIPS.	Acres of improved land.	Acres of unimproved land.	Acres of meadow.	Tons of hay.	Bushels of grass seeds.	Acres of spring wheat.	Bushels harvested.	Acres of winter wheat.	Bushels harvested.	Acres of oats.	Bushels harvested.	Acres of corn.	Bushels harvested.	Acres of potatoes.	Bushels harvested.
Bloomington, . .	5838	62097	93	199	25	317	3957	25	400	145	4921	524	21750	5	600
Pike, ...	4150	16353	64	65	26	1097	12546	5	92	564	20807	1800	99990	31	4819
Moscow, ...	7351	10049	581	1407	127	2488	29529	25	625	709	18747	2257	107845	65	7799
Cedar, ...	3957	10654	115	871	10	726	13735	85	2105	356	14910	1120	61575	17	2605
Sweetland, ...	8081	12191	608	948	56	2875	54912	21	325	514	18122	2712	128395	74	8620
Montpelier, . . .	6277	10604	203	209	6	1331	24741	35	700	299	9214	1540	63435	37	4980
Wapsinonoc, . . .	6296	8768	478	761	89	964	16409	10	700	549	16708	2245	117000	31	4445
Seventy-Six, . . .	4792	9676	191	173	. . .	783	13114	121	3013	360	12826	2041	108490	34	4310
Total, ...	46742	140392	2333	4633	339	10581	168943	327	7960	3496	116255	14249	708480	294	38178

TABLE,

SHOWING THE NUMBER AND VALUE OF HOGS AND CATTLE SOLD, THE VALUE OF DOMESTIC AND GENERAL MANUFACTURES OF MUSCATINE COUNTY, FOR 1856.

TOWNSHIPS.	Number of hogs sold.	Value of hogs sold.	Number of cattle sold.	Value of cattle sold.	Pounds of butter made.	Pounds of cheese.	Pounds of wool.	Value of domestic manufactures.	Value of gen'l manufactures.
Bloomington, ...	148	1349	41	1630	....	....	39	....	....
Pike, ...	1272	11650	97	3026	1340	200	325	75	35
Moscow, ...	1283	11698	379	9904	15375	647	880	2043	2565
Cedar,...........	714	6701	92	3166	7000	865	1030	390	....
Sweetland,........	1294	11183	331	12152	26805	108735	2378	709	11075
Montpelier, ...	1250	9642	315	8004	16840	1148	441	250	150
Wapsinonoc,......	1664	16827	209	6725	4305	1200	396	1979	....
Seventy-Six,.......	1088	9665	222	6024	13660	640	1225	341	....
Total,..........	8713	78716	1678	50627	953325	113435	6714	5787	13825

TABLE,

EXHIBITING THE PROFESSIONS, TRADES OR OCCUPATIONS OF THE INHABITANTS OF MUSCATINE COUNTY, FOR 1856.

OCCUPATIONS	NAME OF TOWNSHIPS.								
	Bloomington	Pike.	Moscow.	Cedar.	Sweetland.	Montpelier.	Wapsinonoc,	Seventy-six.	TOTAL.
Farmers,	169	122	187	62	172	148	178	127	1165
Laborers,	216	....	6	...	100	5	3	4	334
Blacksmiths,	42	3	6	....	2	5	3	1	62
Carpenters,	109	7	19	1	23	15	10	1	185
Wagon makers,	15	....	2	....	....	1	2	....	20
Brick Layers,	5	....	....	....	....	....	....	....	5
Plasterers,	11	....	2	....	....	1	1	....	15
Stone Masons,	31	....	5	....	....	1	....	....	37
Ctone Cutters,	2	....	....	....	....	....	....	....	2
Carriage makers,	11	....	....	....	....	....	....	....	11
Machinists,	2	....	1	....	....	....	....	....	3
Engineers,	12	2	....	1	1	....	1	....	17
Millers,	11	....	1	....	1	2	3	....	18
Sawyers,	6	1	1	....	....	....	....	....	8
Millwrights,	4	1	....	....	1	....	2	....	8
Painters,	18	....	....	....	2	....	1	....	21
Cabinet Makers,	18	....	....	....	....	....	1	....	19
Chair makers,	1	....	....	....	....	....	....	....	1
Tinners,	7	....	2	....	....	....	....	....	9
Milliners,	2	....	5	....	....	....	....	....	7
Tailors,	20	....	3	....	....	....	1	....	24
Hatters,	3	....	....	....	....	....	....	....	3
Shoemakers,	33	1	4	.. .	2	....	....	....	40
Saddle and harness makers,	17	....	2	....	....	....	....	....	19
Bakers,	5	....	2	....	....	....	....	....	7
Butchers,	8	....	2	....	....	....	....	....	10
Mechanics,	....	....	....	3	....	1	3	....	7
Manufacturers,	2	....	....	....	1	....	....	....	3
Merchants,	45	....	9	....	9	....	11	....	74
Agents,	2	....	....	....	2	....	....	....	4
Traders,	....	....	1	....	....	....	....	....	1
Druggists,	3	....	....	....	....	....	....	....	3
Confectioners,	1	....	....	....	....	....	....	....	1
Boarding house keepers,	1	....	1	....	....	....	....	....	2
Hotel keepers,	6	....	....	....	1	1	....	....	8
Clothiers,	8	....	....	....	....	....	....	....	8
Physicians,	17	1	6	....	2	1	4	....	31
Dentists,	4	....	....	....	....	....	....	....	4
Lawyers,	15	....	....	....	....	....	1	....	16
Clergymen,	12	....	1	....	1	....	2	....	17
Teachers,	6	....	6	....	4	....	....	....	16
Printers,	10	....	....	....	....	....	....	1	10
Editors,	1	....	....	....	....	....	....	....	1
Artists,	2	....	1	....	....	....	....	....	3
Daguerrean Artists,	2	....	....	....	....	....	....	....	2
Bankers,	4	....	....	....	....	....	....	....	4
Grocers,	19	....	....	...	....	....	....	....	19
Teamsters,	4	...	2	....	5	....	....	....	9
Chandlers,	4	....	1	....	....	....	....	....	5
Brick makers,	14	....	....	....	....	1	....	....	15

TABLE—Continued,

EXHIBITING THE PROFESSIONS, TRADES, OR OCCUPATIONS OF THE INHABITANTS OF MUSCATINE COUNTY, FOR 1856.

OCCUPATIONS.	NAME OF TOWNSHIPS.								Total.
	Bloomington.	Pike.	Moscow.	Cedar.	Sweetland.	Montpelier.	Wapsinonoc.	Seventy-Six.	
Watch makes,	6		1		2				9
Gun Smiths,	3		1						4
Coopers,	27	1			3		2		33
Clerks,	51		2		1		2		56
Segar makers,	1								1
Lumbermen,	3						1		4
Justices of the Peace,	2								2
Dyers,	1								1
Pork Packers,	3								3
Peddlers,	3			1					4
Breakmen,	1								1
Coal diggers,	1								1
Brewers,	1								1
Barbers,	6								6
Shoe Merchants,	2								2
Ship Carpenters,	3								3
Carders and Spinners,	1								1
Ice Dealers,	1								1
Marble Dealers,	2								2
Weavers,	1		2						3
Moulders,	3								3
Rectors,	1								1
Draymen,	1								1
Fruit Dealers,	1								1
Upholsterers,	3								3
Sash and Door Makers,	3								3
Horticulturists,	1								1
Engravers,	1								1
Tanners,	1								1
Livery keepers,	1								1
Auctioneers,	1								1
U. S. Commissioners,	1								1
Tobacconist,	1								1
Booksellers,	1								1
Rope makers,	1								1
County Judge,	1								1
County Treasurer,	1								1
White Washers,	1								1
Potters,	1				10				11
Commission Merchants,	1								1
Cloth Dressers,	1								1
Leather Dealers,	1								1
Hardware Dealers,	2								2
Lime Merchants,	1								1
Furniture Dealers,	2								2
Tailoresses,			4						4
Ferrymen,			1						1
House Keepers,			193						193

TABLE,

SHOWING THE PLACE OF NATIVITY OF THE INHABITANTS OF MUSCATINE COUNTY, FOR 1856.

STATES.	NAME OF TOWNSHIPS.								TOTAL
	Bloomington	Pike.	Moscow.	Cedar.	Sweetland.	Montpelier.	Wapsinonoe.	Seventy-Six.	
Ohio,	848	184	160	154	238	116	138	171	2309
Indiana,	163	37	83	20	161	82	68	65	679
Pennsylvania,	749	98	68	62	224	134	126	49	1510
Iowa,	1115	67	196	147	269	156	211	170	2331
New York,	513	24	37	14	101	57	87	7	840
Maine,	42	1	....	....	40	4	....	....	87
New Hampshire,	63	6	3	....	36	3	....	3	114
Vermont,	62	4	4	22	46	16	6	3	163
Massachusetts,	89	3	6	2	12	7	....	1	120
Connecticut,	100	18	5	6	31	9	2	4	175
Rhode Island,	16	....	....	....	16	....	....	....	32
Virginia,	89	38	27	....	23	36	51	27	291
Kentucky,	70	5	16	3	19	19	26	18	178
Illinois,	103	4	19	4	36	14	18	7	205
Michigan,	19	8	13	5	14	....	3	4	66
Arkansas,	1	....	....	....	....	....	....	....	1
Alabama,	1	....	....	....	2	1	....	....	4
Louisiana,	4	....	1	....	1	....	1	....	7
Mississippi,	8	....	....	....	3	....	....	....	11
Florida,	2	....	....	....	....	....	....	....	2
North Carolina,	12	3	....	25	10	6	2	3	61
South Carolina,	1	....	1	....	1	....	1	2	6
Tennessee,	7	....	1	4	5	1	....	2	20
Missouri,	72	3	6	2	8	4	6	....	101
Georgia	2	....	....	....	....	....	....	....	2
California,	....	....	1	....	2	....	....	....	3
Maryland,	69	2	12	....	22	6	20	9	140
New Jersey,	59	1	4	....	79	5	17	14	179
England,	115	28	12	31	13	11	5	2	217
Ireland,	640	17	7	35	50	22	21	65	857
Wales,	8	....	5	....	....	4	7	....	24
Scotland,	29	4	....	....	7	5	1	....	46
Germany,	819	1	199	2	136	145	3	17	1311
France,	20	....	12	....	2	2	....	14	50
Austria,	1	....	....	....	....	....	....	....	1
Russia,	1	....	....	....	....	....	....	....	1
Prussia,	8	....	5	....	16	10	2	....	41
Sweden,	....	....	1	....	....	1	1	....	3
Holland,	125	....	1	....	....	....	....	....	126
On the Ocean,	1	....	....	....	....	....	....	1	2
Canada,	36	4	4	....	14	3	....	....	61
Switzerland,	64	....	49	....	4	13	....	....	130
Denmark,	....	....	3	....	....	....	....	....	3
Saxony,	....	....	....	....	6	....	....	2...	6
Wisconsin,	12	....	....	1	2	2	1	....	18
Nova Scotia,	3	....	....	....	....	....	....	....	3
Brazil,	2	....	....	....	....	....	....	....	2
Delaware,	7	6	....	....	8	....	2	2	25
Minnesota,	2	....	....	....	....	....	....	....	2

TABLE,

SHOWING THE POPULATION, AGRICULTURAL STATISTICS, NUMBER AND VALUE OF HOGS AND CATTLE SOLD, &c., OF PAGE COUNTY, FOR 1856.

POPULATION.	NAME OF TOWNSHIPS.						TOTAL.
	Nodaway.	Pierce	Amity.	Nebraska.	Buchanan.	Tarkio.	
No. dwelling houses,	114	24	20	99	82	.....	339
Number of families,	123	25	20	105	82	.....	355
Number of males,	364	65	61	278	247	.....	1015
Number of females,	336	59	59	264	231	.....	949
Married,	235	45	38	205	153	.....	676
Widowed,	23	2	4	9	9	.....	47
Native voters,	142	27	24	120	80	.....	393
Naturalized voters,	5	1	.....	1	.....	.....	7
Aliens,	6	.....	.....	1	.....	.....	7
Militia,	135	18	23	107	67	.....	350
Deaf and Dumb,	1	.....	.....	.....	1	.....	2
Insane,	1	.....	.....	.....	.....	.....	1
Idiotic,	2	1	.....	.....	.....	.....	3
Owners of land,	110	16	21	73	61	.....	281
Paupers,	1	.....	.....	1	.....	.....	2
AGRICULTURAL—							
Acres improved land,	2722	476	329	2471	2054	.....	8052
Acres unimprov'd land	16313	1918	4134	12832	8984	.....	41182
Acres of meadow,	.....	.....	.....	9	81	.....	90
Tons of hay,	.....	182	.....	.....	58	.....	240
Bushels of grass seeds,	2	.....	.....	.....	6	.....	8
Acres of spring wheat,	182	28	.....	50	104	.....	624
Bushels harvested,	1686	79	.....	559	162	.....	2486
Acres of winter wheat,	112	8	5	30	102	.....	157
Bushels harvested,	330	100	30	391	493	.....	1344
Acres of oats,	78	11	.....	76	197	.....	362
Bushels harvested,	1180	43	.....	1674	2417	.....	5314
Acres of corn,	1084	213	94	1082	1071	.....	3544
Bushels harvested,	37286	6080	3 50	40915	35746	.....	123197
Acres of potatoes,	16	3	1	11	17	.....	48
Bushels harvested,	1892	670	90	1548	1389	.....	5589
HOGS, CATTLE, &c.—							
No. of hogs sold,	170	48	40	378	465	.....	1101
Value of hogs sold,	1247	272	261	2333	2106	.....	19219
No. of cattle sold,	94	14	17	86	489	.....	760
Value of cattle sold,	2451	332	535	1635	3681	.....	8634
Pounds of butter made,	5759	1210	1675	3192	4195	.....	16034
Pounds of cheese,	511	216	.....	172	1200	.....	2099
Pounds of wool,	621	111	140	835	1087	.....	2794
Val. domestic manuf's,	830	51	95	771	1153	.....	2902
Val. gen. manufactures	500	.....	.....	.....	117	.....	617

TABLE,

EXHIBITING THE PROFESSIONS, TRADES OR OCCUPATIONS OF THE INHABITANTS OF PAGE COUNTY, FOR 1856.

OCCUPATIONS.	NAME OF TOWNSHIPS.						TOTAL.
	Nodaway.	Pierce.	Amity.	Nebraska.	Buchanan.	Ta kio.	
Farmers,	129	26	22	100	81	....	358
Laborers,	....	....	1	....	....	....	1
Blacksmiths,	6	....	1	3	1	....	11
Carpenters,	5	1	1	5	....	....	12
Wagon makers,	1	....	....	1	....	....	2
Stone masons,	2	....	....	....	....	....	2
Millers,	1	....	....	1	....	....	2
Sawyers,	2	....	1	1	....	....	4
Millwrights,	1	....	....	1	....	....	2
Cabinet makers,	....	....	....	1	....	....	1
Tailors,	....	1	....	....	....	....	1
Shoemakers,	....	....	....	2	....	....	2
Mechanics,	....	....	....	2	....	....	2
Merchants,	5	....	1	4	1	....	11
Druggists,	1	....	....	....	....	....	1
Physicians,	5	....	....	2	1	....	8
Clergymen,	1	1	....	1	....	....	3
Gun smiths,	....	....	....	1	....	....	2
Treasurers,	1	....	....	....	....	....	1
Sailors,	....	....	....	1	....	....	1
Wheelwrights,	....	....	....	1	....	....	1

TABLE,

SHOWING THE PLACE OF NATIVITY OF THE INHABITANTS OF PAGE COUNTY, FOR 1856.

STATES.	TOWNSHIPS.						
	Nodaway.	Pierce.	Amity.	Nebraska.	Buchanan.	Tarkio.	TOTAL
Ohio,	211	47	15	56	86	....	415
Indiana,	131	17	16	151	95	....	410
Pennsylvania,	29	6	8	13	9	....	65
Iowa,	122	19	17	79	122	....	359
New York,	10	1	9	10	1	....	31
Maine,	1	...	3	4	....	....	8
New Hampshire,	....	....	....	1	....	....	1
Vermont,	....	1	....	....	....	....	1
Massachusetts,	2	....	....	3	....	....	5
Connecticut,	1	1	....	2	....	....	4
Rhode Island,	2	1	....	....	....	....	3
Virginia,	28	1	....	25	10	....	64
Kentucky,	21	9	3	44	53	....	130
Illinois,	10	2	21	22	8	....	63
Michigan,	....	....	2	2	1	....	9
Arkansas,	....	3	....	....	....	....	3
North Carolina,	8	2	....	13	18	....	41
South Carolina,	3	....	2	2	....	....	7
Tennessee,	39	1	8	55	14	....	117
Missouri,	39	2	4	37	57	....	139
Georgia,	2	....	....	....	....	....	2
Maryland,	6	3	....	1	1	....	11
New Jersey,	2	5	5	....	....	....	12
England.	4	1	....	1	....	....	6
Ireland,	9	....	....	1	....	....	10
Scotland,	1	....	....	....	....	....	1
Germany,	6	....	....	3	2	....	11
France,	1	....	....	....	....	....	1
Norway,	1	....	....	....	....	....	1
Canada,	5	1	....	6	....	....	12
New Brunswick,	....	1	....	....	....	....	1
Switzerland,	....	....	....	....	1	....	1
Wisconsin,	1	....	7	5	....	....	13
Delaware,	2	....	....	2	....	....	4
Unknown,	3	....	....	....	....	....	3

TABLE,

SHOWING THE POPULATION OF POLK COUNTY, FOR 1856.

TOWNSHIPS.	No. dwelling houses.	Number of families.	Number of males.	Number of females.	Colored.	Married.	Widowed.	Native voters.	Naturalized voters.	Aliens.	Militia.	Deaf and Dumb.	Blind.	Insane.	Idiotic.	Owners of land.	Paupers.
Des Moines,	562	582	2201	1629	....	1306	107	783	139	93	836	10	....	....	2	526	....
Jefferson,	85	85	273	228	....	163	13	103	1	2	99	....	1	....	1	54	....
Allen,	69	72	222	195	....	13[illegible]	6	80	1	2	75	....	....	....	1	56	....
Camp,	202	202	584	596	....	384	21	234	6	....	212	....	....	1	....	140	....
Beaver,	34	34	116	92	....	64	2	49	1	....	28	....	....	....	....	34	....
Franklin,	33	33	109	97	....	68	3	41	1	....	33	....	....	....	....	27	....
Washington,	20	25	61	62	....	50	....	32	....	....	28	....	....	....	....	21	....
Elkhart,	58	62	186	150	....	119	5	58	4	1	43	....	....	....	....	54	....
Madison,	174	174	545	507	....	183	10	168	22	8	175	....	....	....	1	133	....
Saylor,	105	108	350	305	....	218	6	125	6	7	96	1	....	....	....	60	....
Delaware,	68	68	235	182	....	135	6	85	2	1	81	....	....	....	....	69	....
Four Mile,	94	94	262	230	....	154	10	99	1	....	90	....	....	....	2	72	....
Total,	1504	1539	5144	4273	....	2980	189	1857	184	114	1796	11	1	1	7	1256	....

TABLE,

SHOWING THE AGRICULTURAL STATISTICS OF POLK COUNTY, FOR 1856.

TOWNSHIPS	Acres of improved land.	Acres of unimproved land.	Acres of meadow.	Tons of Hay.	Bushels of grass seed.	Acres of spring wheat.	Bushels harvested.	Acres of winter wheat.	Bushels harvested.	Acres of Oats.	Bushels harvested.	Acres of corn.	Bushels harvested.	Acres of potatoes.	Bushels harvested.
Des Moines, ...	6495	123552	482	660	2	748	11304	4	35	392	10944	2644	122990	51	7128
Jefferson, ...	2884	9700	3	6	....	283	4852	8	146	105	5142	743	46117	6	1906
Allen, ...	2719	7[illegible]91	38	111	3	336	3948	58	60	30[illegible]	10452	1[illegible]66	85020	11	3167
Camp, ...	5351	13629	23	12	1	801	9538	12	155	220	72[illegible]7	2723	149938	33	4890
Beaver, ...	1228	4773	23	27	....	176	3051	....	....	57	1855	465	24065	7	1098
Franklin, ...	790	5266	15	185	....	143	1865	....	....	115	3143	380	15800	9	795
Washington, ...	507	3340	3	11	....	4	20	....	....	37	960	233	9080	5	695
Elkhart, ...	1456	4822	1	1	....	168	2256	52	1255	39	1025	706	24586	13	1143
Madison, ...	3278	813	31	47	6	461	9470	20	229	227	6853	1827	80468	49	4015
Saylor, ...	2575	9022	124	117	....	393	5655	....	....	188	6450	1688	89300	20	2934
Delaware, ...	2886	10816	41	36	5	433	7917	17	163	217	7185	1081	60100	15	3018
Four Mille, ...	2939	9054	83	80	5	534	7499	5	25	247	9775	1211	67500	15	2594
Total, ...	33108	201978	867	1293	22	4480	67375	176	2068	2165	71021	15067	774964	236	33383

TABLE,

SHOWING THE NUMBER AND VALUE OF HOGS, CATTLE, DOMESTIC AND GENERAL MANUFACTURES OF POLK COUNTY, FOR 1856.

TOWNSHIPS.	No. of hogs sold.	Value of hogs sold.	No. of cattle sold.	Value of cattle sold.	Pounds of butter made.	Pounds of cheese.	Pounds of Wool.	Value of domestic Manufactures.	Value of general Manufactures.
Des Moines,	7189	7908	330	10796	28191	364	1187	525	....
Jefferson,	566	3504	213	5092	8490	....	695	458	2000
Allen,	1020	6551	223	6290	9570	183	887	138	....
Camp,	2192	15148	307	7947	13725	395	2288	1564	33000
Beaver,	136	1169	139	4098	430	67	90	275	86
Franklin,	170	959	86	1922	3294	50	269	245	....
Washington,	71	471	95	2256	1250	....	....	....	....
Elkhart,	267	1405	161	3354	4200	530	389	235	....
Madison,	817	5560	42	2924	9090	150	1351	605	2000
Saylor,	909	6763	193	4924	7330	300	633	542	1374
Delaware,	752	5181	114	2541	8811	193	501	443	8739
Four Mile,	817	4871	108	2749	9918	....	1419	2800	200
Total,	8906	59490	2011	54993	104300	2752	9709	7830	47399

TABLE,

SHOWING THE PROFESSIONS, TRADES, OR OCCUPATIONS OF THE INHABITANTS OF POLK COUNTY FOR 1856.

TOWNSHIPS.	Farmers.	Laborers.	Blacksmiths.	Carpenters.	Wagon makers.	Brick layers.	Plasterers.	Stone masons.	Stone cutters.	Builders	Carriage makers.	Machinists.	Engineers.	Millers	Sawyers.	Millwrights.	Painters.	Cabinet makers.
Desmoines, ...	280	195	24	119	9	8	14	23	2	....	....	6	7	18	5	12	13	10
Jefferson, ...	111	4	1	17	....	....	....	....	....	....	....	....	....	....	....	....	....	....
Allen, ...	62	2	1	5	1	1	1	....	....	....	....	....	1	....	1	....	....	....
Camp, ...	214	30	3	13	....	....	....	....	....	....	....	....	2	....	1	1	....	3
Beaver, ...	28	....	1	1	....	....	....	....	....	....	....	....	....	....	1	....	....	....
Franklin, ...	31	....	....	5	....	....	....	....	....	....	....	....	....	....	....	....	....	....
Washington, ...	16	....	2	3	....	....	....	....	....	....	....	....	....	....	....	....	....	....
Elkhart, ...	63	5	2	6	....	....	....	....	....	....	....	....	1	....	2	....	....	....
Madison, ...	134	28	6	17	....	....	....	2	....	....	2	1	2	3	....	2	....	....
Saylor, ...	125	5	2	9	....	....	....	....	....	....	....	1	1	....	2	....	....	....
Delaware, ...	85	8	....	6	1	....	....	....	....	....	....	....	1	....	....	....	....	1
Four-Mile, ...	68	12	6	6	1	....	1	....	....	....	....	3	....	....	....	....	....	....
Total, ...	1217	282	48	207	12	9	16	25	2	....	2	11	15	21	12	15	13	14

TABLE. CONTINUED,

SHOWING THE PROFESSIONS, TRADES OR OCCUPATIONS OF THE INHABITANTS OF POLK COUNTY, FOR 1856.

TOWNSHIPS.	Chair Makers.	Tinners.	Milliners.	Merchant Tailors.	Tailors.	Hatters.	Shoemakers.	Harness Makers	Bakers.	Butchers.	Mechanics.	Manufacturers.	Merchants.	Speculators	Agents.	Drovers.	Traders.	Druggists.
Desmoines,	3	6	2	....	8	....	11	6	5	5	5	3	54	....	1	....	....	6
Jefferson,	....	....	1	....	....	....	....	....	....	....	....	....	....	....	....	....	....	....
Allen,	....	....	....	....	....	....	....	....	....	....	....	....	1	....	....	....	....	....
Camp,	....	....	....	....	1	....	....	....	....	....	1	2	6	....	....	....	....	....
Beaver,	....	....	....	....	1	....	....	....	....	....	1	....	....	....	....	....	....	....
Franklin,	....	....	....	....	....	....	2	....	....	....	....	....	....	....	....	....	....	....
Washington,	....	....	....	....	1	....	....	....	....	....	....	....	2	....	....	....	....	....
Elkhart,	....	....	....	....	....	....	....	....	....	....	....	....	1	....	....	....	....	....
Madison,	1	....	....	....	....	....	2	....	....	....	....	1	4	....	....	....	1	....
Saylor,	1	....	4	....	1	....	1	....	....	....	3	....	2	....	....	....	....	....
Delaware,	....	....	....	....	....	....	....	....	....	....	....	2	....	....	....	....	....	....
Four-Mile,	....	....	....	....	....	....	....	....	....	....	....	....	6	....	....	....	....	....
Total,	5	6	7	....	12	....	16	6	5	5	11	8	76	....	1	....	1	6

TABLE—Continued,

EXHIBITING THE PROFESSIONS, TRADES, OR OCCUPATIONS OF THE INHABITANTS OF POLK COUNTY, FOR 1856

TOWNSHIPS.	Confectioners.	Boarding house keepers.	Hotel keeper.	Clothiers.	Physicians.	Dentists.	Lawyers.	Clergymen.	Teachers.	Musicians.	Printers	Editors.	Artists.	Deguerrean Artists.	Bankers.	Grocers.	Teamsters.	Chandlers.
Des Moines,	....	2	8	....	21	1	35	4	6	1	7	1	2	....	8	1	27	....
Jefferson,					2				4									
Allen,					1				2									
Camp,								1	2								3	
Beaver,			1															
Franklin,									1									
Washington,					2													
Elkhart,					1													
Madison,					1			2	1								1	
Saylor,					1				1								1	
Delaware,					1				1								2	
Four-Mile,			2		1				1									
Total,	....	2	11	....	31	1	35	7	19	1	7	1	2	....	8	1	34	....

TABLE—Continued,

EXHIBITING THE PROFESSIONS, TRADES, OR OCCUPATIONS OF THE INHABITANTS OF MARION COUNTY, FOR 1856.

TOWNSHIPS.	Brick makers	Watch Makers.	Jewellers.	Gun Smiths.	Coopers.	Clerks.	Barbers.	Land brokers	Peddlers.	Chemists.	Cooks.	Stewards	Stage Agents.	Lumbermen.	Candy makers.	Foundrymen.	Nurserymen.	Surveyors.
Des Moines,..	45	2	7	3	...	30	3	2	1	1	3	2	1	1	1	1	2	9
Jefferson, ...	....	....	....	2	....	....	....	....	....	....	....	....	....	....	....	....	....	1
Allen,........	....	....	....	....	....	....	....	....	....	....	....	....	....	1	....	....	....	....
Camp, ...	....	....	....	....	....	....	....	....	....	....	....	....	....	....	....	....	....	....
Beaver, ...	....	....	....	....	....	....	....	....	....	....	....	....	....	....	....	....	....	....
Franklin,.....	....	....	....	....	1	....	....	....	....	....	....	....	....	....	....	....	....	....
Washington,..	....	....	....	....	....	....	....	....	....	....	....	....	....	....	....	....	....	....
Elkhart, ...	....	....	....	....	....	....	....	....	....	....	....	....	....	....	....	....	....	....
Madison,.....	....	....	....	....	....	....	....	....	....	....	....	....	....	....	....	....	....	....
Saylor,.......	2	....	....	....	3	....	....	....	....	....	....	....	....	....	....	....	....	....
Delaware,....	....	....	....	....	....	....	....	....	....	....	....	....	....	....	....	....	....	....
Four-Mile,....	1	....	....	....	2	..	....	....	....	....	....	....	....	....	....	....	....	....
Total,......	48	2	7	5	6	30	3	2	1	1	3	2	1	2	1	1	2	10

TABLE—Continued,

SHOWING THE PROFESSIONS, TRADES, OR OCCUPATIONS OF THE INHABITANTS OF POLK COUNTY, FOR 1856.

TOWNSHIPS.	Porters.	Draftsmen.	Tanners.	Brewers.	Stage drivers.	Miners.	Builders.	Chamber-maids	Seamstresses.	Weavers.	Ferrymen.	Book binders.	Dress makers.	Wheelwrights.	Wool carders.	Pump makers.
Desmoines,	1	1	1	1	13	4	3	6								
Jefferson,									6	1						
Allen,																
Camp,											1					
Beaver,																
Franklin,												1				
Washington,																
Elk hart,										1						
Madison,													2			
Saylor,														2		
Delaware,										1					1	1
Four-Mile,																
Total,	1	1	1	1	13	4	3	6	6	3	1	1	2	2	1	1

TABLE,

SHOWING THE PLACE OF NATIVITY OF THE INHABITANTS OF POLK COUNTY, FOR 1856.

STATES.	NAME OF TOWNSHIPS.												
	Des Moines.	Jefferson.	Allen.	Camp.	Beaver.	Franklin.	Washington.	Ekhart.	Madison.	Saylor.	Delaware.	Four-Mile.	TOTAL.
Ohio,	684	118	68	267	43	52	32	51	245	137	104	100	1901
Indiana,	603	158	138	270	23	39	49	107	211	183	119	132	2032
Pennsylvania,	332	20	24	56	13	22	2	12	43	70	22	43	659
Iowa,	529	67	77	266	46	38	11	66	168	122	76	107	1573
New York,	273	6	2	3	18	3	6	7	28	7	5	8	366
Maine,	11	....	1	3	....	1	....	....	6	3	....	....	25
N. Hampshire,	26	1	....	2	18	....	....	6	3	....	....	....	56
Vermont,	46	1	....	1	6	2	....	3	6	....	1	....	66
Massachusetts	40	1	1	2	1	1	....	6	18	1	1	....	72
Connecticut,	39	....	1	2	....	....	....	1	4	6	2	....	55
Rhode Island,	2	....	....	....	....	....	....	....	....	....	....	....	2
Virginia,	88	35	7	64	11	5	3	7	37	10	13	13	293
Kentucky,	137	26	46	73	7	7	1	19	31	15	2	41	405
Illinois,	118	11	22	95	7	5	6	23	45	33	34	25	424
Michigan,	37	....	....	....	....	19	2	2	3	3	....	....	66
Arkansas,	1	....	....	....	....	....	....	....	....	....	....	....	1
Texas,	2	....	....	....	....	....	....	....	....	....	....	....	2
Alabama,	1	....	....	1	....	....	....	....	....	5	....	....	7
Louisiana,	1	....	....	....	....	....	....	....	....	....	....	....	1
Mississippi,	....	....	1	....	....	....	....	....	3	....	....	....	4
N. Carolina,	26	18	14	10	1	3	10	5	6	20	9	4	126
S. Carolina,	2	....	....	5	....	1	....	....	....	....	3	3	14
Tennessee,	19	4	7	26	....	1	....	4	26	7	6	....	100
Missouri,	52	18	....	5	....	2	....	2	54	2	....	8	143
District Columbia,	1	....	....	....	....	....	....	....	....	....	....	....	1
Georgia,	5	....	....	....	....	....	....	....	1	....	....	....	6
Maryland,	47	2	4	10	2	1	....	3	3	6	3	2	83
New Jersey,	27	1	....	2	....	1	1	2	2	2	2	1	41
England,	60	2	1	....	....	....	....	....	25	11	3	3	105
Ireland,	272	1	....	10	5	....	....	....	10	2	....	1	301
Wales,	10	1	....	....	....	....	....	....	....	....	....	....	11
Scotland,	13	....	....	2	1	....	....	....	2	1	....	....	19
Germany,	129	2	1	2	....	2	....	2	25	7	1	....	171
France,	6	....	....	....	....	....	....	....	1	....	....	....	7
Austria,	1	....	....	....	....	....	....	....	1	....	....	....	2
Russia,	1	....	....	....	....	....	....	....	....	....	....	....	1
Prussia,	6	....	....	....	....	....	....	....	2	....	2	....	10
Norway,	6	....	....	....	....	....	....	4	....	....	....	....	10
Sweden,	7	....	....	....	....	....	....	....	2	....	....	....	9
Holland,	....	....	....	....	1	....	....	....	....	....	....	....	1
Canada,	20	....	1	....	4	....	....	2	4	....	1	....	32
Switzerland,	5	....	....	....	....	....	....	....	26	....	....	....	31
Wisconsin,	5	....	....	2	1	....	....	....	9	....	6	....	23
Delaware,	4	8	....	....	....	1	....	2	2	2	2	....	21
Bavaria,	2	....	....	....	....	....	....	....	....	....	....	....	2
Nova Scotia,	1	....	....	....	....	....	....	....	....	....	....	....	1
Poland,	1	....	....	....	....	....	....	....	....	....	....	....	1
Unknown,	132	....	1	1	....	....	....	....	....	....	....	1	135

TABLE,

SHOWING THE POPULATION, AGRICULTURAL STATISTICS, NUMBER AND VALUE OF HOGS AND CATTLE SOLD, &c., &c., OF POTTAWATTAMIE COUNTY, FOR 1856.

POPULATION.	NAME OF TOWNSHIPS.					
	Kane.	Rockford.	Macedonia.	Walnut Cre'k.	Knox.	TOTAL.
No. dwelling houses..	404	12	23	18	21	592
Number of families,..	415	127	23	19	21	605
Number of males,....	1346	387	79	59	53	1924
Number of females, ..	1084	238	7[illegible]	48	43	1574
Married,..........	803	24[illegible]	57	38	38	1176
Widowed, ...	64	17	4	1	2	88
Native voters,.......	472	117	38	21	23	671
Naturalized voters,...	84	25	2	.....	......	111
Aliens, ...	106	5	.....	......	1	112
Militia,............	368	119	31	17	......	535
Idiotic,............	1	1	1	1	......	4
Owners of land, ...	343	79	27	14	19	482
AGRICULTURAL—						
Acres of improved land	3783	2740	457	250	218	7448
Acres unimprov'd land	36673	14985	5[illegible]99	2594	3133	62564
Acres of meadow,....	.....	.....	4	295	......	299
Tons of hay, ...	.....	511	......	158	......	669
Bushels of grass seed,.	.....	2	......	......	......	2
Acres of spring wheat,	747	259	115	21	......	1142
Bushels harvested,...	9043	2630	787	165	......	12625
Acres of winter wheat,	11	34	.....	......	......	45
Bushels harvested,....	138	717	.....	......	......	855
Acres of oats, ...	291	107	26	17	......	441
Bushels harvested, ...	4877	2965	610	500	......	8952
Acres of corn,.......	1590	1722	187	159	51	3709
Bushels harvested, ...	57670	77385	11780	5560	1950	154145
Acres of potatoes,....	67	9	5	2	......	83
Bushels harvested, ...	9141	3591	855	400	......	13987
HOGS, CATTLE, &c.,—						
Number of hogs sold,.	207	723	111	40	31	1112
Value of hogs sold, ..	1321	5294	725	267	150	7757
Number of cattle sold,	203	291	43	49	6	592
Value of cattle sold,..	5081	4139	1411	1446	185	12262
Pounds of butter made,	13924	6475	3950	1860	.....	26209
Pounds of cheese, ...	1485	1775	......	......	......	3260
Pounds of wool, ...	405	325	......	......	......	730
Val. domestic man'f's,	102	95	......	......	......	197
Val. gen'l manuf'ures,	13100	......	......	......	......	13100

TABLE,

EXHIBITING THE PROFESSIONS, TRADES OR OCCUPATIONS OF THE INHABITANTS OF POTTAWATTAMIE COUNTY, FOR 1856.

OCCUPATIONS.	TOWNSHIPS.						TOTAL.
	Kane.	Rockford.	Macedonia.	Walnut.	Centre.	Knox.	
Farmers,	228	98	25	24	....	20	395
Laborers,	83	50	....	....	....	....	133
Blacksmiths,	11	3	3	....	....	1	18
Carpenters,	43	3	5	....	....	2	53
Wagon Makers,	3	....	....	....	....	....	3
Plasterers	3	....	1	....	....	....	4
Stone Masons,	7	....	....	....	....	....	7
Carriage Makers,	1	....	....	....	....	....	1
Machinists,	....	....	1	....	....	....	1
Engineers,	6	....	....	....	....	....	6
Millers,	6	3	2	....	....	....	11
Millwrights,	6	....	....	....	....	....	6
Painters,	6	....	....	....	....	....	6
Cabinet Makers,	2	....	....	....	....	....	2
Chair Makers,	1	....	....	....	....	....	1
Tinners,	8	....	....	....	....	....	8
Milliners,	2	....	....	....	....	....	2
Tailors,	10	....	....	....	....	....	10
Shoemakers,	11	....	....	....	....	....	11
Saddle & Harness Makers,	5	....	1	....	....	....	6
Bakers,	2	1	....	....	....	....	3
Butchers,	3	....	....	....	....	....	3
Merchants,	28	1	....	....	....	1	30
Speculators,	6	....	....	....	....	....	6
Agents,	6	....	....	....	....	....	6
Traders,	....	....	1	....	....	....	1
Druggists,	2	....	....	....	....	....	2
Confectioners,	1	....	....	....	....	....	1
Boarding House Keepers,	1	....	....	....	....	....	1
Hotel Keepers,	3	....	....	....	....	....	3
Physicians,	14	2	....	....	....	....	16
Lawyers,	18	....	....	....	....	....	18
Clergymen,	2	....	....	....	....	....	2
Teachers,	2	2	....	....	....	....	4
Musicians,	1	....	....	....	....	....	1
Printers,	10	2	....	....	....	....	12
Editors,	2	....	....	....	....	....	2

TABLE—Continued,

EXHIBITING THE PROFESSIONS, TRADES, OR OCCUPATIONS OF THE INHABITANTS OF POTTAWATTAMIE COUNTY, FOR 1856.

OCCUPATIONS.	TOWNSHIPS.						
	Kane.	Rockford.	Macedonia.	Walnut.	Centre	Knox.	TOTAL.
Daguerrean Artists,	1	....	....	....	....	....	1
Bankers,	3	....	....	....	....	....	3
Grocers,	6	....	....	....	....	....	6
Teamsters,	12	....	....	....	....	....	12
Brick makers,	6	....	....	....	....	....	6
Jewellers,	1	....	....	....	....	....	1
Gun smiths,	2	....	....	....	....	....	2
Coopers,	3	....	....	....	....	....	3
Clerks,	6	....	....	....	....	....	6
Livery keepers,	3	....	....	....	....	....	3
Register of Land Office,	1	....	....	....	....	....	1
Surveyors,	10	1	....	....	....	....	11
County Treasurers,	1	....	....	....	....	....	1
Potters,	1	....	....	....	....	....	1
Book Binders	1	....	....	....	....	....	1
Bar Tenders,	1	....	....	....	....	....	1
Saloon Keepers,	8	....	....	....	....	....	8
Brewers,	1	....	....	....	....	....	1
Ball Alleys,	1	....	....	....	....	....	1
Sheriffs,	1	....	....	....	....	....	1
Staging	1	1	....	....	....	....	2
Porters,	2	....	....	....	....	....	2
Lumber Dealers,	2	....	....	....	....	....	2
Wood Turners,	1	....	....	....	....	....	1
Peddlers	4	....	....	....	....	....	4
Auctioneers,	1	....	....	....	....	....	1
Dress Makers,	3	....	....	....	....	....	3
Barbers,	2	....	....	....	....	....	2
Hostlers,	2	....	....	....	....	....	2
Students,	1	....	....	....	....	....	1
Wheel Wrights,	1	....	....	....	....	....	1
District Judges,	1	....	....	....	....	....	1
Gardeners,	1	....	....	....	....	....	1
Gamblers,	1	....	....	....	....	....	1
Tanners,	1	....	....	....	....	....	1
Hunters,	....	....	....	....	....	1	1

TABLE,

SHOWING THE PLACE OF NATIVITY OF THE INHABITANTS OF POTTAWATTAMIE COUNTY FOR 1856.

STATES.	TOWNSHIPS.						TOTAL.
	Kane.	Rockford	Macedonia.	Walnut.	Centre.	Knox.	
Ohio,	283	68	15	16	....	21	403
Indiana,	87	142	32	14	....	15	290
Pennsylvania,	162	17	4	16	....	4	203
Iowa,	461	153	24	18	....	18	674
New York,	216	32	20	4	....	....	272
Maine,	16	....	....	....	....	3	19
New Hampshire,	31	2	....	....	....	....	33
Vermont,	37	8	1	....	....	1	47
Massachusetts,	40	4	4	7	....	....	55
Connecticut,	24	2	4	1	....	....	31
Rhode Island,	3	....	3	10	....	....	16
Virginia,	58	19	1	....	....	3	81
Kentucky,	51	17	1	6	....	5	80
Illinois,	183	69	27	6	....	13	298
Michigan,	25	7	2	....	....	....	34
Texas,	5	....	....	....	....	....	5
Alabama,	1	1	....	....	....	....	2
Louisiana,	8	....	....	....	....	....	8
Mississippi,	9	....	....	....	....	....	9
North Carolina,	47	10	2	....	....	....	59
South Carolina,	1	3	....	....	....	....	4
Tennessee,	26	17	1	9	....	4	57
Missouri,	90	35	....	....	....	6	131
Georgia,	1	....	....	....	....	....	1
Maryland,	21	1	1	....	....	....	24
New Jersey,	9	....	....	....	....	1	10
England,	240	61	1	....	....	1	303
Ireland,	46	7	....	....	....	....	53
Wales,	12	....	....	....	....	....	12
Scotland,	40	6	1	....	....	....	47
Germany,	99	8	....	....	....	....	107
France,	6	....	....	....	....	....	6
Austria,	1	....	....	....	....	....	1
Prussia,	1	....	....	....	....	....	1
Norway,	1	....	....	....	....	....	1
Sweden,	2	....	....	....	....	....	2
Indian Territory,	....	1	....	....	....	....	1
Canada,	61	19	1	....	....	....	81
New Brunswick,	....	....	2	....	....	....	2
Denmark,	3	....	....	....	....	....	3
Sioux Nation,	....	2	....	....	....	....	2
West Indies,	1	....	....	....	....	....	1
Wisconsin,	14	2	2	....	....	....	18
Delaware,	5	....	1	....	....	....	6
Portugal,	1	....	....	....	....	....	1
Utah Territory,	1	2	....	....	....	....	3
Nebraska Territory,	1	....	....	....	....	....	1

TABLE,

SHOWING THE POPULATION OF POWESHIEK COUNTY, FOR 1856.

TOWNSHIPS.	No. of dwelling houses.	Number of families.	Number of males.	Number of females.	Colored.	Married.	Widowed.	Native voters.	Naturalized voters.	Aliens.	Militia.	Deaf and Dumb.	Blind.	Insane.	Idiotic.	Owners of land.	Paupers.
Jackson,	305	305	977	824	....	632	36	372	11	13	338	17	1	...	1	242	....
Sugar Creek,	106	107	331	275	...	206	10	122	2	6	113	....	....	....	....	91	1
Washington,	62	62	173	160	....	117	10	62	3	5	47	....	....	....	....	55	....
Bear Creek,	67	67	208	165	....	122	8	68	7	1	73	7	...	....	....	57	....
Jefferson,	47	51	146	138	....	90	6	38	4	9	28	2	....	....	....	40	2
Grinnell,	70	70	269	202	....	162	23	143	8	10	148	...	....	....	....	79	....
Madison,	38	41	118	94	....	77	....	55	26	....	39	....	....	....	....	31	....
Warren,	67	73	194	186	....	146	1	81	9	....	73	....	....	....	2	68	....
Total,	762	576	2416	2044	....	1552	94	941	70	44	859	26	1	....	3	663	3

TABLE,

SHOWING THE AGRICULTURAL STATISTICS OF POWESHIEK COUNTY, FOR 1856.

TOWNSHIPS.	Acres of improved land.	Acres of unimproved land.	Acres of meadow.	Tons of hay.	Bushels of grass seed.	Acres of spring wheat.	Bushels harvested.	Acres of winter wheat.	Bushels harvested.	Acres of oats.	Bushels harvested.	Acres of corn.	Bushels harvested.	Acres of potatoes.	Bushels harvested.
Jackson, ...	5544	16583	143	157	70	1341	16875	500	....	1211	9225	2537	136270	33	4869
Sugar Creek, ..	2202	8473	13	20	...	533	6930	12	220	82	3137	761	41374	16	2171
Washington,...	1439	8326	25	....	..	159	2799	31	....	44	1095	547	29449	11	1757
Bear Creek, ...	1388	10623	8	570	11	231	4023	...	....	166	5256	864	19237	16	2691
Jefferson, ...	1142	3722	1	1	1	72	1188	15	290	94	1810	559	21810	15	1862
Grinnell, ...	889	14360	....	269	...	61	995	...	....	13	650	154	5900	4	800
Madison, ...	645	3631	....	....	...	65	818	...	....	18	476	325	12880	6	1007
Warren, ...	1532	10492	790	27	9	350	4550	218	....	173	6549	679	30196	25	3754
Total, ...	14781	76210	979	1044	91	2812	38178	776	510	1801	28198	6426	297116	126	18911

TABLE,

SHOWING THE NUMBER AND VALUE OF HOGS AND CATTLE SOLD, THE VALUE OF DOMESTIC AND GENERAL MANUFACTURES OF POWESHIEK COUNTY, FOR 1856.

TOWNSHIPS.	Number of hogs sold.	Value of hogs sold.	Number of cattle sold.	Value of cattle sold.	Pounds of butter made.	Pounds of cheese.	Pounds of wool.	Value of domestic manufactures.	Value of gen'l manufactures.
Jackson, ...	1504	10702	434	10107	12389	335	1879	878	80
Sugar Creek, ...	653	2705	267	3776	5622	385	962	1052	220
Washington, ...	341	2550	137	3300	3274	3	388	1007	850
Bear Creek, ...	63	167	126	756	590	20	120	10	....
Jefferson, ...	177	899	96	2232	2935	110	242	178	....
Grinnell, ...	4	24	1	20	100	....	875	....	....
Madison, ...	51	315	43	1351	2510	110	40	30	....
Warren, ...	184	1478	164	1342	3941	373	338	5	45
Total, ...	2977	18840	1268	22884	31361	1336	4844	3160	1195

TABLE,

EXHIBITING THE PROFESSIONS, TRADES OR OCCUPATIONS OF THE INHABITANTS OF POWESHIEK COUNTY, FOR 1856.

Occupations.	NAME OF TOWNSHIPS.								Total.
	Jackson.	Sugar Creek.	Washington.	Bear Creek.	Jefferson.	Grinnell.	Madison.	Warren.	
Farmers,	190	98	62	33	53	54	47	60	597
Laborers,	2	4	....	2	5	53	....	....	66
Blacksmiths,	8	3	3	....	1	3	....	2	20
Carpenters,	41	12	2	3	2	19	4	11	94
Wagon makers,	....	....	1	....	....	1	....	....	2
Bricklayers,	....	....	....	....	....	1	....	....	1
Plasterers,	6	....	....	....	2	....	....	....	8
Stone masons,	3	....	....	....	....	3	....	....	6
Carriage makers,	2	....	....	....	....	1	....	....	3
Machinists,	....	....	....	....	....	1	....	....	1
Engineers,	1	....	....	....	....	....	....	....	1
Millers,	2	4	....	....	....	1	....	....	7
Sawyers,	4	....	....	....	....	....	....	....	4
Millwrights,	2	....	....	....	....	....	....	1	3
Painters,	1	....	....	....	....	1	....	....	2
Cabinet makers,	2	....	....	....	....	2	....	....	4
Tinners,	1	....	....	....	....	....	....	....	1
Milliners,	....	....	....	....	....	....	....	3	3
Tailors,	1	....	....	....	....	2	....	....	3
Shoe makers,	5	....	1	....	....	1	....	....	7
Harness makers,	1	....	....	1	1	1	....	....	4
Butchers,	....	....	....	....	....	1	....	....	1
Merchants,	7	1	1	2	....	10	....	....	21
Speculators,	....	....	....	....	....	1	....	....	1
Agents,	....	....	....	....	....	1	....	....	1
Traders,	3	....	....	....	....	....	....	....	3
Board'g house keep's	....	....	....	....	....	1	....	....	1
Hotel keepers,	2	....	1	....	....	2	....	....	5

TABLE—CONTINUED,

SHOWING THE PROFESSIONS, TRADES OR OCCUPATIONS OF THE INHABITANTS OF POWESHIEK COUNTY, FOR 1856.

OCCUPATIONS.	NAME OF TOWNSHIPS.								
	Jackson.	Sugar Creek.	Washington.	Bear Creek.	Jefferson.	Grinnell.	Madison.	Warren.	TOTAL.
Physicians,	....	....	1	2	....	3	....	....	6
Lawyers,	4	....	....	....	....	4	....	2	10
Clergymen,	6	....	....	....	....	4	....	1	11
Teachers,	3	....	....	....	2	2	....	1	8
Printers,	1	....	....	....	....	....	....	....	1
Artists,	1	....	....	....	....	....	....	....	1
Teamsters,	9	....	....	....	....	....	....	....	9
Brick makers,	1	2	....	....	....	1	....	....	4
Coopers,	2	....	....	....	....	....	....	....	2
Clerks,	5	2	....	1	....	....	....	....	8
Surveyors,	1	....	....	....	....	1	....	....	2
Postmasters,	1	....	....	....	....	....	....	....	1
Clerk of Dist. Court,	1	....	....	....	....	....	....	....	1
Probate Judge,	1	....	....	....	....	....	....	....	1
Wool Carders,	1	....	....	....	....	....	....	....	1
Barbers,	1	....	....	....	....	....	....	....	1
Sextons,	1	....	....	....	....	....	....	....	1
Weavers,	....	....	....	....	2	....	....	....	3
Dress makers,	....	....	....	....	....	3	....	....	3
Stage drivers,	....	....	....	....	....	2	....	....	2
Servants,	....	....	....	....	....	11	....	....	11
Liverymen,	....	....	....	....	....	4	....	....	4
Horse doctors,	....	....	....	....	....	1	....	....	1
Turners,	....	....	....	....	....	1	....	....	1
Lumber merchants,	....	....	....	....	....	2	....	....	2
Gentlemen at ease,	....	....	....	....	....	1	....	....	1
Nurserymen,	....	....	....	....	....	....	....	1	1

TABLE,

SHOWING THE PLACE OF NATIVITY OF THE INHABITANTS OF POWESHIEK COUNTY, FOR 1856.

STATES.	TOWNSHIPS.								TOTAL.
	Jackson.	Sugar Creek.	Washington.	Bear Creek.	Jefferson.	Grinnell.	Madison.	Warren.	
Ohio,	608	151	58	73	36	47	35	117	1125
Indiana,	205	132	68	....	65	9	49	15	543
Pennsylvania,	145	46	13	76	9	51	16	36	392
Iowa,	245	105	52	33	39	25	21	38	558
New York,	70	8	24	45	8	91	19	24	289
Maine,	14	....	....	....	1	54	....	....	69
New Hampshire,	12	....	....	....	2	23	....	2	39
Vermont,	17	1	....	21	4	35	4	1	83
Massachusetts,	8	1	2	7	....	63	1	6	88
Connecticut,	1	....	2	11	23	12	4	3	56
Rhode Island,	....	1	....	....	....	1	1	1	4
Virginia,	95	18	21	22	10	2	5	6	179
Kentucky,	43	33	7	6	14	....	2	1	106
Illinois,	84	35	18	....	39	3	28	19	226
Michigan,	2	6	....	....	....	1	1	....	10
Louisiana,	....	....	....	....	....	1	....	....	1
North Carolina,	45	18	23	....	6	....	1	....	93
South Carolina,	....	....	....	....	....	....	1	....	1
Tennessee,	10	6	1	10	3	....	1	....	31
Missouri,	3	4	2	....	....	....	7	....	16
Georgia,	....	3	....	....	....	....	....	....	3
Maryland,	22	3	2	12	8	13	....	19	74
New Jersey,	36	13	1	18	....	....	3	3	74
England,	15	....	20	2	16	13	....	1	67
Ireland,	16	4	6	24	5	10	3	7	75
Wales,	46	3	....	....	....	....	....	....	49
Scotland,	42	....	....	....	....	....	1	....	43
Germany,	4	13	1	4	1	11	2	11	47
France,	1	....	....	9	....	....	....	....	10
Austria,	2	....	....	....	....	....	....	....	2
Prussia,	2	1	....	....	....	....	....	....	3
On the Ocean,	....	....	1	....	....	....	....	....	1
Canada,	4	....	7	....	....	1	....	4	16
Switzerland,	....	1	....	....	....	....	....	3	4
Wisconsin,	1	....	2	....	....	....	....	....	3
District of Columbia,	1	....	....	....	....	....	....	....	1
Delaware,	1	....	....	....	....	....	....	....	1
Unknown,	1	....	1	....	....	5	7	63	77
California,	....	....	1	....	....	....	....	....	1

TABLE,

SHOWING THE POPULATION, AGRICULTURAL STATISTICS, NUMBER AND VALUE OF HOGS AND CATTLE SOLD, &c., OF RINGGOLD COUNTY, FOR 1856.

POPULATION.	NAME OF TOWNSHIPS.					TOTAL.
	Sand Creek.	Platte.	West Fork.	Lot's Creek.	Mount Ayr.	
No. dwelling houses,	48	65	62	79	19	273
Number of families,	52	67	62	79	19	279
Number of males,	145	190	159	238	72	804
Number of females,	127	162	164	172	43	668
Married,	99	133	115	137	38	522
Widowed,	5	10	7	11	3	36
Native voters,	54	70	63	81	28	296
Naturalized voters,	2	3	1	1	....	7
Militia,	53	63	55	68	22	261
Owners of land,	53	64	60	71	20	268
AGRICULTURAL—						
Acres improved land,	516	1157	1048	1148	392	4261
Acres unimproved land,	9061	8904	12401	3	3427	33796
Acres of meadow,	....	....	2	1	....	3
Tons of hay,	....	305	15	2	128	449
Acres of spring wheat,	13	66	130	36	19	264
Bushels harvested,	130	793	1692	738	180	3533
Acres of winter wheat,	....	....	60	9	....	69
Bushels harvested,	....	....	1068	90	....	1158
Acres of oats,	14	44	165	96	5	324
Bushels harvested,	90	1835	2916	1757	100	6698
Acres of corn,	262	429	658	600	152	2101
Bushels harvested,	3940	9552	10720	14232	1740	40184
Acres of potatoes,	2	8	8	3	2	23
Bushels harvested,	240	705	157	190	165	1457
HOGS, CATTLE, &c.—						
No. of hogs sold,	22	256	337	235	16	866
Value of hogs sold,	85	740	2002	776	45	1648
No. of cattle sold,	38	150	131	155	57	531
Value of cattle sold,	731	3958	3483	4225	1467	13864
Pounds of butter made,	1330	4175	1966	1030	400	8901
Pounds of cheese,	33	51	100	60	....	244
Pounds of wool,	....	120	304	318	....	742
Value domestic manufactures,	...	30	26	134	....	190
Value of general manufactures,	....	....	......	55	....	55

TABLE,

EXHIBITING THE PROFESSIONS, TRADES OR OCCUPATIONS OF THE INHABITANTS OF RINGGOLD COUNTY, FOR 1856.

TOWNSHIPS.	Farmers.	Blacksmiths.	Carpenters.	Wagon makers.	Millers.	Cabinet makers.	Hatters.	Shoemakers.	Merchants.	Physicians.	Clergymen.	Brick makers.	Prairie Brakers.	Constables.	Hunters.	Weavers.	Turners.	Co. Recorders.	Surveyors.	County Clerks.
Sand Creek,	33	2	2	..	..	..	..	..	..	..	1	1	1	1	1	..	..	..	..	..
Platte,	63	1	..	1	2	2	..	2	..	1	..	..	..	..	..	1	..	..	..	..
West Fork,	60	1	..	1	..	..	..	1	..	..	..	..	..	..	1	..	..	..	..	..
Lot's Creek,	66	2	4	..	..	..	..	..	1	..	..	..	..	..	..	..	1	1	..	..
Mount Ayr,	21	..	..	..	..	..	1	1	1	1	..	..	1	..	..	..	..	..	1	1
Total,	243	6	6	2	2	2	1	4	2	2	1	1	2	1	2	1	1	1	1	1

TABLE,

SHOWING THE PLACE OF NATIVITY OF THE INHABITANTS OF RINGGOLD COUNTY, FOR 1856.

STATES.	NAME OF TOWNSHIPS.					TOTAL
	Sand Creek.	Platte.	West Fork	Lot's Creek.	Mount Ayr.	
Ohio,	53	71	60	127	19	330
Indiana,	59	89	89	79	23	339
Pennsylvania,	13	24	9	18	14	78
Iowa,	36	69	49	60	18	232
New York,	25	8	1	5	2	41
Maine,	....	....	....	5	1	6
Vermont,	2	1	....	....	3	6
Massachusetts,	....	....	2	...	4	6
Virginia,	7	10	31	12	2	62
Kentucky,	14	18	12	19	5	68
Illinois,	43	33	19	33	13	141
Michigan,	2	1	....	....	6	9
North Carolina,	....	5	13	4	1	23
South Carolina,	1	....	9	....	....	10
Tennessee,	7	3	20	9	1	40
Missouri,	4	1	1	23	2	31
Georgia,	....	....	...	1	....	1
Maryland,	3	2	4	1	....	10
New Jersey,	....	1	1	2	....	4
England,	1	2	...	....	....	3
Ireland,	1	4	....	1	....	6
Germany,	....	4	3	....	....	7
France,	....	1	....	10	1	12
Canada,	1	4	....	1	....	6
Delaware,	....	1	....	....	....	1

TABLE,

SHOWING THE POPULATION OF SCOTT COUNTY, FOR 1856.

TOWNSHIPS.	No. of dwelling houses.	Number of families.	Number of males.	Number of females.	Colored.	Married.	Widowed.	Native voters.	Naturalized voters.	Aliens.	Militia.	Deaf and Dumb.	Blind.	Insane.	Idiotic.	Owners of land.	Paupers.
Allen's Grove, ...	63	71	229	168	....	136	6	71	11	20	60	....	....	....	....	58	....
Buffalo, ...	149	159	462	421	....	294	25	108	66	52	196	....	....	....	....	68	....
Blue Grass, ...	141	144	527	398	....	282	36	93	60	121	235	....	....	....	....	109	2
Hickory Grove, ..	117	121	396	330	....	258	16	107	26	87	197	....	....	....	....	116	....
Liberty, ...	99	99	339	256	....	197	11	114	14	21	139	2	....	....	....	100	1
Pleasant Valley, .	107	123	387	296	....	211	18	123	12	79	71	1	....	1	....	80	....
Rockingham, ...	42	32	139	128	....	80	8	45	8	8	47	....	....	....	....	37	....
Princeton, ...	56	63	353	267	....	206	11	120	11	19	113	2	7	....	2	32	....
Winfield, ...	196	215	701	534	....	388	39	129	67	167	295	....	....	....	1	100	3
Davenport, ...	....	....	7092	5729	12	4424	293	1270	644	1503	3028	12	2	2	5	994	13
Le Clair, ...	416	438	1278	1091	....	826	63	410	59	107	443	....	....	....	4	358	9
Total, ...	1386	1475	11903	9618	12	7321	526	2590	978	2184	4824	17	9	3	12	2052	28

TABLE,

SHOWING THE AGRICULTURAL STATISTICS OF SCOTT COUNTY, FOR 1856.

TOWNSHIPS.	Acres of improved land.	Acres of unimproved land.	Acres of meadow.	Tons of Hay.	Bushels of grass seed.	Acres of spring wheat.	Bushels harvested.	Acres of winter wheat.	Bushels harvested.	Acres of Oats.	Bushels harvested.	Acres of corn.	Bushels harvested.	Acres of potatoes.	Bushels harvested.
Allen's Grove, ..	4 11	5010	108	189	....	1476	31724	....	....	286	11095	668	33535	17	3079
Buffalo, ...	3474	5306	526	512	....	964	16120	27	540	351	12070	1178	57810	30	3870
Blue Grass, ...	11078	4996	383	570	15	3026	63227	....	....	488	20668	1971	89680	70	7891
Hickory Grove, ..	5727	4352	....	1227	....	1858	44668	....	....	328	13689	905	45943	42	4749
Liberty, ...	2985	4848	144	912	109	1080	21762	....	....	170	6410	647	31070	21	4785
Pleasant Valley,	5197	4230	445	752	126	1541	32448	8	100	262	10759	1747	100578	112	15223
Rockingham, ...	1246	228	173	121	10	265	4640	....	....	123	3790	431	18070	10	1430
Princeton, ...	4254	5084	40	46	6	1431	32115	4	110	327	14436	986	50246	57	6310
Winfield, ...	9442	18159	161	166	8	4362	92591	54	1220	686	25462	1692	81386	89	12089
Davenport, ...	19790	41616	1197	3449	66	4355	122316	75	2890	1730	43539	3495	169779	520	56006
Le Clair, ...	6922	6595	451	570	32	3303	75010	10	240	466	17978	1982	102770	83	12960
Total, ...	74226	100424	3628	8514	372	23661	536621	178	5100	5218	179896	15703	780787	1053	128392

TABLE,

SHOWING THE NUMBER AND VALUE OF HOGS, CATTLE, DOMESTIC AND GENERAL MANUFACTURES OF SCOTT COUNTY, FOR 1856.

TOWNSHIPS.	No. of hogs sold.	Value of hogs sold.	No. of cattle sold.	Value of cattle sold.	Pounds of butter made.	Pounds of cheese.	Pounds of Wool.	Value of domestic Manufactures.	Value of general Manufactures.
Allen's Grove, ...	306	2854	265	9337	12760	600	356	20	....
Buffalo, ...	1482	10813	157	5402	15040	100	366	....	....
Blue Grass, ...	895	6845	214	7635	25954	2427	689	26	....
Hickory Grove, ...	393	3147	109	3617	10970	1535	267	....	....
Liberty, ...	188	1652	110	3789	689	2850	1435	....	....
Pleasant Valley, ..	1232	11752	185	6758	14295	75	....	2283	....
Rockingham, ...	271	2158	206	2234	1815	50	....	....	....
Princeton, ...	728	6884	304	9681	16375	4000	148	71	....
Winfield, ...	402	3701	292	10555	15295	1257	887	465	810
Davenport, ...	480	6130	364	13079	65254	4130	650	70010	252600
Le Clair, ...	1251	11667	310	10019	32350	900	417	200	13200
Total, ...	7628	67603	2516	82106	210797	17924	5215	73075	266610

TABLE,

EXHIBITING THE PROFESSIONS, TRADES OR OCCUPATIONS OF THE INHABITANTS OF SCOTT COUNTY, FOR 1856.

TOWNSHIPS.	Farmers.	Laborers.	Blacksmiths.	Carpenters.	Wagon makers.	Brick layers.	Plasterers.	Stone Masons.	Stone Cutters.	Builders.	Carriage makers.	Machinists.	Engineers.	Millers.	Sawyers.	Millwrights.	Painters.	Cabinet Makers.
Allen's Grove,	81	1	4	1	2	....	....	....	....	....	....	....	....	....	....	....	....	....
Buffalo, ...	222	26	4	11	1	....	....	6	....	....	....	....	1	4	....	....	1	....
Blue Glass, ...	184	65	3	13	....	....	1	1	....	....	1	....	1	....	....	....	....	....
Hickory Grove	252	....	1	6	....	....	....	2	....	....	....	....	....	....	....	....	1	....
Liberty, ...	99	3	4	23	1	....	....	2	....	....	....	....	....	....	1	....	....	....
Pleas't Valley,	74	11	3	9	....	....	....	4	....	....	....	....	1	1	....	....	....	....
Rockingham, .	41	5	2	....	....	....	....	....	....	....	....	....	2	....	....	....	....	....
Princeton, ...	81	....	5	13	....	....	....	4	....	....	....	....	....	....	....	....	....	1
Winfield, ...	217	134	3	13	....	....	1	5	1	....	....	....	....	2	....	....	....	2
Davenport, ...	235	1113	93	417	....	....	33	125	12	....	25	45	35	24	17	14	63	16
Le Clair, ...	249	57	10	55	5	....	7	21	4	....	....	....	4	7	4	2	9	2
Total, ...	1735	1415	132	561	9	....	42	174	17	....	26	45	44	38	22	16	74	21

TABLE—CONTINUED,

SHOWING THE PROFESSIONS, TRADES OR OCCUPATIONS OF THE INHABITANTS OF POLK COUNTY, FOR 1856.

TOWNSHIPS.	Chair Makers.	Tinners.	Milliners.	Merchant Tailors.	Tailors.	Hatters.	Shoemakers.	Harness Makers.	Bakers.	Butchers.	Mechanics.	Manufacturers.	Merchants.	Speculators.	Agents.	Drovers.	Traders.	Druggists.
Allen's Grove,..	...	...	1	...	1	...	1	...	...	1	...	...	...	...	...	...	...	...
Buffalo,........	...	1	...	...	1	...	2	...	...	3	...	...	5	...	...	...	...	...
Blue Grass,....	...	...	...	...	...	...	...	...	...	1	...	...	1	...	...	...	...	...
Hickory Grove,.	...	...	...	...	...	...	1	...	...	...	...	...	1	...	...	...	...	...
Liberty,........	...	...	...	...	...	...	5	1	...	...	...	...	1	...	...	...	...	...
Pleas ant Valley	...	2	...	...	...	1	1	...	...	...	...	1	1	...	...	...	...	...
Rockingham,...	...	...	...	...	1	...	...	...	...	...	...	...	1	...	...	...	...	...
Princeton,......	...	1	...	...	1	...	1	1	...	...	...	...	3	...	...	...	...	...
Winfield,.......	...	...	...	...	1	...	2	...	...	...	...	...	...	...	...	...	...	...
Davenport,.....	...	20	3	...	70	5	86	23	27	36	...	5	208	...	9	...	...	5
Le Clair,.......	...	...	4	...	2	...	11	1	1	5	...	...	34	...	...	...	...	3
Total,........	...	24	8	...	77	6	110	26	28	46	...	6	254	...	9	...	...	8

TABLE—CONTINUED,

EXHIBITING THE PROFESSIONS, TRADES, OR OCCUPATIONS OF THE INHABITANTS OF SCOTT COUNTY, FOR 1856.

TOWNSHIPS.	Confectioners.	Boarding house keepers.	Hotel keepers.	Clothiers.	Physicians.	Dentists.	Lawyers.	Clergymen.	Teachers.	Musicians.	Printers.	Editors.	Artists.	Daguerrean Artists.	Bankers.	Grocers.	Teamsters.	Chandlers.
Allen's Grove,	....	....	....	....	1	....	....	1	3	....	....	....	....	....	....	....	....	....
Buffalo,	....	....	1	....	3	....	....	....	1	....	....	....	....	....	....	....	....	....
Blue Grass,	....	....	....	....	6	....	....	....	1	....	....	....	....	....	....	....	....	....
Hickory Grove,	....	....	1	....	1	....	....	....	1	....	....	....	....	....	....	....	....	....
Liberty,	....	....	2	....	3	....	....	....	....	....	....	....	....	....	....	....	....	....
Pleasant Valley,	....	....	1	....	....	....	....	....	5	....	....	....	....	....	....	....	....	....
Rockingham,	....	....	....	....	....	....	....	....	....	....	....	....	....	....	....	....	....	....
Princeton,	....	....	1	....	2	....	1	....	....	....	....	....	....	....	....	....	....	....
Winfield,	....	....	1	....	2	....	....	1	4	....	....	....	....	....	....	....	....	....
Davenport,	8	....	16	....	38	5	50	17	15	5	28	3	....	2	11	....	13	10
Le Clair,	....	....	7	....	5	....	1	5	6	1	....	....	....	....	1	....	20	....
Total,	8	....	30	....	61	5	52	24	36	6	28	3	....	2	12	....	33	10

TABLE,

SHOWING THE PROFESSIONS, TRADES, OR OCCUPATIONS OF THE INHABITANTS OF SCOTT COUNTY FOR 1856.

TOWNSHIPS.	Brick makers	Watch Makers.	Jewellers.	Gun Smiths.	Coopers.	Clerks.	Dress makers.	Seamen.	Surveyors.	Brewers.	Rope makers.	Weavers.	Dyers.	Pilots.	Steam B. Captains.	Coal Pickers.	Gardeners.	Barbers.
Allen's Grove,							1	1	1									
Buffalo,	1				1					1	1	1	2	4	1	12	1	1
Blue Grass,																		
Hickory Grove,																		
Liberty,																		
Pleasant Valley,			1				4					1						
Rockingham,																		
Princeton,	1				1													
Winfield,	1					1						1						
Davenport,	21		41	4	54	116	7			10	1	6	1	10			16	
Le Clair,		1		2	4	4								6				
Total,	24	1	42	6	60	121	12	1	1	11	2	9	3	20	1	12	17	1

TABLE—CONTINUED,

SHOWING THE PROFESSIONS, TRADES, OR OCCUPATIONS OF THE INHABITANTS OF SCOTT COUNTY, FOR 1856.

TOWNSHIPS	Servants.	Porters.	Horse dealers	Hostlers.	Lumbermen.	Nurserymen.	Mariners.	Students.	Jockies.	Farriers.	Peddlers.	Book keepers.	Cigar makers.	Pattern makers.	Inventors.	Paper hangers.	Furnishers.
Allen's Grove,........	....	....	....	....	....	....	....	....	....	....	....	....	....	....	....	....	....
Buffalo,..............	8	2	....	....	....	....	....	....	....	....	....	....	....	....	....	....	....
Blue Grass,...........	....	....	....	....	....	....	....	....	....	....	....	....	....	....	....	....	....
Hickory Grove,........	....	....	1	....	....	....	....	....	....	....	....	....	....	....	....	....	....
Liberty,..............	....	....	....	....	....	....	....	....	....	....	....	....	....	....	....	....	....
Pleasant Valley,......	....	....	....	1	....	....	....	....	....	....	....	....	....	....	....	....	....
Rockingham,...........	....	....	....	....	1	1	1	1	....	....	....	....	....	....	....	....	....
Princeton,............	....	....	....	....	....	....	1	....	1	1	....	....	....	....	....	....	....
Winfield,.............	....	....	....	....	....	....	....	....	....	....	2	....	....	....	....	....	....
Davenport,............	21	....	....	....	6	....	....	1	....	3	3	4	24	6	1	2	3
Le Clair,.............	....	....	....	2	....	....	....	....	....	....	....	....	....	....	....	....	....
Total,............	29	2	1	3	7	1	2	2	1	4	5	4	24	6	1	2	3

TABLE—Continued,

EXHIBITING THE PROFESSIONS, TRADES, OR OCCUPATIONS OF THE INHABITANTS OF SCOTT COUNTY, FOR 1856.

TOWNSHIPS.	Surveyors.	Carvers	Moulders.	Tanners.	Post Masters.	Auctioneers.	Barbers.	Fishermen.	Cloth Dressers.	Seamstresses.	Boatmen.	Carriage Trimmers.	Livery Men.	Paper Makers.	Boiler Makers.	Architects.	Turners	Professors.
Allen's Grove,																		
Buffalo,																		
Blue Grass,																		
Hickory Grove																		
Liberty,																		
Pleas't Valley,																		
Rockingham,																		
Princeton,																		
Winfield,																		
Davenport,	6	1	15	15	1	2	9	5	1	3	5	2	7	1	2	1	5	1
Le Clair,	1																2	
Total,	7	1	15	15	1	2	9	5	1	3	5	2	7	1	2	1	7	1

TABLE—Continued,

EXHIBITING THE PROFESSIONS, TRADES, OR OCCUPATIONS OF THE INHABITANTS OF SCOTT COUNTY, FOR 1856.

TOWNSHIPS.	Lock Smiths.	Marble Dealers.	Engravers.	Copper Smiths.	Ship Carpenters	Book binders.	Well Diggers.	Contractors.	Cotton Spinners.	Slaters.	Silver Platers.	Screw Cutters.	Plumbers.	Gass Fitters.	Conductors.	Upholsterers.	Soda Makers.	Supt. Rail Road.	Piano Makers	Broom Makers.	Sisters of Charity.	Captain.	Ferrymen.	Bar Keepers.	Plough Makers.
Allen's Grove,																									
Buffalo,																									
Blue Grass,																									
Hickory Grove,																									
Liberty,																									
Pleasant Valley,																									
Rockingham,																									
Princeton,																									
Winfield,																									
Davenport,	2	3	2	2	5	5	3	1	1	2	1	1	3	4	1	2	4	1	2	1	5				
Le Clair,					5			1														1	1	1	1
Total,	2	3	2	2	10	5	3	2	1	2	1	1	3	4	1	2	4	1	2	1	5	1	1	1	1

TABLE,

SHOWING THE PLACE OF NATIVITY OF THE INHABITANTS OF SCOTT COUNTY FOR 1856.

STATES.	NAME OF TOWNSHIPS.											
	Allen's Grove.	Buffalo.	Blue Grass.	Hick'ry Gr've	Liberty.	Pleas'nt Val'y	Rockingham.	Princeton.	Winfield.	Davenport.	Le Clair.	TOTAL.
Ohio,	45	100	66	70	91	43	40	60	141	898	189	1743
Indiana,	13	43	28	36	16	11	4	19	27	178	73	448
Pennsylvania,	37	51	109	57	75	110	26	217	142	1220	608	2652
Iowa,	88	222	166	142	94	123	75	130	219	1730	433	3422
New York,	94	58	45	90	100	159	21	47	42	1119	266	2041
Maine,	2	1	....	21	....	1	1	....	3	83	12	124
N. Hampshire,	1	1	....	1	6	3	....	....	....	65	13	90
Vermont,	4	7	....	3	21	42	4	2	1	118	59	261
Massachusetts	1	2	8	4	9	8	3	2	1	203	32	273
Connecticut,	7	....	11	7	16	30	5	2	2	150	13	243
Rhode Island,	1	1	....	....	....	....	....	3	7	31	2	45
Virginia,	3	23	51	8	30	9	11	1	42	167	25	370
Kentucky,	2	5	9	6	9	3	7	....	3	93	27	164
Illinois,	3	20	19	9	16	22	6	89	7	210	123	474
Michigan,	1	4	....	2	8	2	....	1	2	48	7	75
Alabama,	....	1	....	....	....	....	....	1	1	6	1	10
Louisiana,	....	....	....	1	....	....	....	....	5	25	1	32
Mississippi,	....	....	....	1	....	....	....	1	....	3	1	9
N. Carolina,	1	6	1	1	....	....	2	....	....	19	1	31
S. Carolina,	1	....	....	1	....	....	....	....	1	4	....	7
Tennessee,	....	2	2	....	1	2	....	2	....	19	5	33
Missouri,	7	23	5	4	1	....	7	1	5	210	8	271
District Columbia,	....	....	....	....	....	....	....	....	....	14	1	15
Minnesota,	....	....	....	....	....	....	....	....	....	....	2	2
South America,	....	....	....	....	....	....	....	....	....	3	....	3
Georgia,	....	....	....	....	....	....	....	7	1	....	2	10
Maryland,	4	8	4	5	2	3	3	....	10	74	21	134
New Jersey,	....	1	4	8	9	10	1	2	12	159	12	218
England,	6	23	9	17	19	18	13	11	42	461	87	706
Ireland,	20	27	45	14	16	24	14	38	144	1537	135	2014
Wales,	....	1	4	1	....	....	....	....	....	17	....	23
Scotland,	4	10	13	4	2	12	1	2	65	141	4	258
Germany,	15	234	307	188	29	42	11	23	247	3347	114	4557
France,	1	....	1	....	2	....	1	....	1	86	13	105
Austria,	....	....	1	7	3	....	....	....	....	102	1	114
Russia,	....	....	....	3	....	....	....	....	....	1	1	5
Prussia,	9	1	....	....	....	....	1	....	....	1	15	27
Norway,	....	....	....	....	....	....	....	....	....	2	....	2
Sweden,	....	....	....	2	....	....	....	....	....	12	3	17
Holland,	....	....	....	....	....	....	1	....	....	4	3	8
On the Ocean,	....	....	....	....	....	1	....	....	....	....	....	1
Canada,	22	6	5	3	11	3	4	1	46	161	9	271
New Brunswick,	....	....	....	....	....	....	....	....	1	3	....	4
Switzerland,	....	....	4	8	8	....	3	....	15	26	29	93
Denmark,	5	....	....	....	....	....	....	....	....	2	....	7
Hanover,	....	....	....	....	....	....	....	....	....	2	3	5
Saxony,	....	....	....	....	....	....	....	....	....	....	2	2
West Indies,	....	....	....	....	....	....	....	....	....	20	....	20
Wisconsin,	....	3	....	....	....	1	1	4	....	18	7	34
Delaware,	....	....	4	1	1	1	3	4	....	17	4	35
Poland,	....	....	1	....	....	....	....	....	....	....	2	3
East Indies,	....	....	....	....	....	....	....	....	....	2	....	2

TABLE,

SHOWING THE POPULATION, AGRICULTURAL STATISTICS, NUMBER AND VALUE OF HOGS AND CATTLE SOLD, &C., &C., OF SHELBY COUNTY FOR 1856.

POPULATION.	TOWNSHIPS.		
	Round.	Galland's Grove.	TOTAL.
Number of dwelling houses,	33	52	85
Number of families,	38	52	90
Number of males,	105	139	244
Number of females,	83	129	212
Married,	66	92	158
Widowed,	5	11	16
Native voters,	44	54	98
Naturalized voters,	1	5	6
Aliens,	1	......	1
Militia,	40	44	84
Blind,	1	......	1
Owners of land,	46	43	89
AGRICULTURAL STATISTICS.			
Acres of improved land,	797	637	1434
Acres of unimproved land,	5739	4978	10717
Acres of meadow,	1	......	1
Acres of spring wheat,	120	122	242
Bushels harvested,	1733	1774	3507
Acres of winter wheat,	8	2	10
Bushels harvested,	86	20	106
Acres of oats,	19	19	38
Bushels harvested,	327	444	771
Acres of corn,	346	322	668
Bushels harvested,	12300	1523[illegible]	27530
Acres of potatoes,	11	10	21
Bushels harvested,	1560	1405	2965
HOGS, CATTLE, &C.			
Number of hogs sold,	214	173	387
Value of hogs sold,	999	1191	2190
Number of cattle sold,	109	48	157
Value of cattle sold,	2345	1165	3510
Pounds of butter made,	2850	4130	6980
Pounds of cheese,	.....	330	330
Pounds of wool,	250	......	150
Value of domestic manufactures,	134	24	158

TABLE,

EXHIBITING THE PROFESSIONS, TRADES OR OCCUPATIONS OF THE INHABITANTS OF SHELBY COUNTY, FOR 1856.

OCCUPATIONS.	TOWNSHIPS. Round.	Galland's Grove.	TOTAL.
Farmers, ...	49	39	88
Laborers, ...	1	16	17
Blacksmiths, ...	1	3	4
Carpenters, ...	1	....	1
Stone Masons, ...	....	1	1
Tailors, ...	....	1	1
Shoemakers, ...	....	1	1
Physicians, ...	....	1	1
Clergymen, ...	....	1	1
Teachers, ...	....	1	1
Surveyors, ...	....	1	1
Wheel wrights, ..	....	1	1
Wool carders, ...	....	1	1

TABLE,

SHOWING THE PLACE OF NATIVITY OF THE INHABITANTS OF SHELBY COUNTY, FOR 1856.

STATES.	TOWNSHIPS. Round.	Galland's Grove.	TOTAL.
Ohio, ...	39	30	69
Indiana, ...	58	38	96
Pennsylvania, ...	12	8	20
Iowa, ...	36	64	100
New York, ...	9	29	38
New Hampshire,	....	3	3
Vermont, ...	1	1	2
Massachusetts, ...	....	1	1
Connecticut, ...	2	2	4
Virginia, ...	4	2	6
Kentucky, ...	11	9	20
Illinois, ...	6	33	39
Michigan, ...	1	1	2
Louisiana, ...	....	1	1
North Carolina, ..	4	5	9
South Carolina, ..	....	1	1
Tennessee, ...	....	3	3
Missouri, ...	1	15	16
New Jersey, ...	1	....	1
England, ...	2	9	11
Ireland, ...	....	1	1
Scotland, ...	....	1	1
Canada, ...	1	5	6
Denmark, ...	....	5	5
Unknown, ...	....	1	1

TABLE.

SHOWING THE POPULATION OF SAC COUNTY, FOR 1856.

TOWNSHIPS.	No. dwelling houses	Number of families.	Number of males.	Number of females.	Married.	Native voters.	Naturalized voters
Sac,....................................	21	21	72	53	38	28	1
Jackson,..................................	21	20	72	54	45	34	4
Total,..................................	42	41	144	107	83	62	5

TABLE,

EXHIBITING THE PROFESSIONS, TRADES, OR OCCUPATIONS, OF THE INHABITANTS OF SAC COUNTY, FOR 1856.

TOWNSHIPS.	Farmers.	Blacksmiths.	Plasterers.	Cabinet makers.	Mechanics.	Merchants.	Clergymen.	Surveyors.	County Judges.
Sac,............................	27	....	....	1	2	....	....	1	....
Jackson,..........................	19	1	1	1	....	2	1	....	1
Total, ...	46	1	1	2	2	2	1	1	1

TABLE,

SHOWING THE PLACE OF NATIVITY OF THE INHABITANTS OF SAC COUNTY FOR 1856.

TOWNSHIPS.	Ohio.	Indiana.	Pennsylvania.	Iowa.	New York.	Vermont.	Massachusetts.	Connecticut.	Rhode Island.	Virginia.	Kenntucky.	Illinois.	Michigan.	North Carolina.	England.	Scotland.	Germany.	Cananda.
Sac,........................	28	40	8	14	15	..	..	..	..	..	8	6	2	..	..	2	..	2
Jackson, ...	35	11	3	18	13	2	1	2	3	7	6	11	1	3	1	..	7	2
Total,	63	51	11	32	28	2	1	2	3	7	14	17	3	3	1	2	7	4

TABLE,

SHOWING THE POPULATION, AGRICULTURAL STATISTICS, NUMBER AND VALUE OF HOGS AND CATTLE SOLD, &c., &c., OF STORY COUNTY, FOR 1856.

POPULATION.	NAME OF TOWNSHIPS.						TOTAL.
	Nevada.	Union.	Franklin.	Indian Creek.	Washington.	La Fayette.	
No. dwelling houses,.	172	89	58	97	41	45	502
Number of families,..	180	89	63	101	42	45	520
Number of males,....	516	245	191	326	118	164	1560
Number of females, ..	458	214	132	271	114	119	1308
Married,............	326	179	117	208	83	98	1011
Widowed, ...	31	10	6	14	.....	4	65
Native voters,.......	222	80	77	132	50	45	606
Naturalized voters,...	14	13	3	3	.....	1	34
Aliens, ...	5	7	4	1	.....	20	37
Militia,.............	216	61	69	213	43	60	662
Blind,..............	.....	1	.....	.....	.....	.....	1
Idiotic,.............	1	.....	.....	.....	.....	.....	1
Owners of land, ...	151	77	69	85	34	41	457
AGRICULTURAL—							
Acres of improved land	2247	1381	1880	1783	636	557	8484
Acres unimprov'd land	11909	10820	7111	13343	5049	3813	52045
Acres of meadow,....	.....	5	9	.....	.....	.....	14
Tons of hay, ...	124	235	.....	.....	.....	.....	359
Acres of spring wheat,	95	102	120	132	28	.....	477
Bushels harvested,...	1211	1182	1652	2931	479	.....	7455
Acres of winter wheat,	.....	49	12	6	.....	.....	67
Bushels harvested,....	.....	410	30	.....	.....	.....	440
Acres of oats, ...	38	62	49	22	23	.....	194
Bushels harvested, ...	980	1792	1215	940	510	.....	5437
Acres of corn,.......	932	617	711	810	412	.....	3483
Bushels harvested, ...	28530	16785	25570	34800	10455	.....	116140
Acres of potatoes,....	1	9	14	12	5	.....	40
Bushels harvested, ...	200	656	1448	1410	731	.....	4445
HOGS, CATTLE, &c.,—							
Number of hogs sold,.	241	231	287	93	27	.....	879
Value of hogs sold, ..	1071	1131	1584	625	431	.....	4842
Number of cattle sold,	150	71	78	48	45	.....	392
Value of cattle sold,..	4882	1730	2667	1498	1210	.....	11987
Pounds of butter made,	3095	1540	5035	400	1232	.....	11302
Pounds of cheese,....	.....	129	40	.....	.....	.....	169
Pounds of wool, ...	84	162	301	121	72	.....	740
Val. domestic man'f's,	.....	26	245	.....	.....	.....	271
Val. gen'l manuf'ures,	.....	15	150	.....	.....	.....	165

TABLE,

EXHIBITING THE PROFESSIONS, TRADES, OR OCCUPATIONS OF THE INHABITANTS OF STORY COUNTY, FOR 1856.

OCCUPATIONS.	TOWNSHIPS.						TOTAL.
	Nevada.	Union.	Franklin.	Indian Creek.	Washington.	La Fayette.	
Farmers,	146	88	58	89	38	27	446
Laborers,	18	....	....	....	2	....	20
Blacksmiths,	16	2	....	6	....	....	24
Carpenters,	26	4	2	12	2	9	55
Wagon makers,	1	....	....	1	....	....	2
Plasterers,	2	....	....	....	....	....	2
Stone masons,	....	....	....	4	....	2	6
Engineers,	2	....	....	3	....	....	5
Millers,	2	1	....	2	....	....	5
Sawyers,	1	....	....	....	....	1	2
Millwrights,	....	1	....	....	....	....	1
Painters,	1	....	....	....	....	....	1
Cabinet makers,	....	....	....	2	....	....	2
Chair makers,	....	1	....	....	....	....	1
Tinners,	1	....	....	....	....	....	1
Merchant tailors,	....	....	....	....	....	1	1
Tailors,	1	....	....	....	....	....	1
Shoe makers,	2	....	....	1	....	....	3
Saddle and harness makers,	1	....	....	1	....	....	2
Merchants,	6	1	....	7	2	1	17
Traders,	....	1	....	....	....	....	1
Hotel keepers,	1	....	....	....	....	....	1
Physicians,	2	....	2	3	1	1	9
Lawyers,	3	....	....	....	....	....	3
Clergymen,	1	....	....	1	1	....	3
Teachers,	2	....	....	....	....	1	3
Musicians,	....	....	....	....	....	1	1
Teamsters,	1	....	....	....	....	....	1
Clerks,	2	....	....	....	....	....	2
Potters,	1	....	....	1	....	....	2
Surveyors,	3	....	1	....	1	1	6
County Judges,	1	....	....	....	....	....	1
County Clerks,	1	....	....	....	....	....	1
County officers,	1	....	....	....	....	....	1
Turners,	....	....	....	....	....	1	1
Broom makers,	....	....	....	....	....	1	1
Prairie breakers,	....	....	....	....	....	1	1
Hunters,	....	....	....	....	....	1	1

TABLE,

SHOWING THE PLACE OF NATIVITY OF THE INHABITANTS OF STORY COUNTY, FOR 1856.

STATES.	TOWNSHIPS.						
	Nevada.	Union.	Franklin.	Indian Creek.	Washington.	La Fayette.	TOTAL.
Ohio,	224	35	73	148	58	45	583
Indiana,	280	120	110	149	66	48	773
Pennsylvania,	52	11	32	41	3	7	146
Iowa,	109	48	36	79	30	13	315
New York,	50	21	2	22	8	20	123
Maine,	1	3	....	....	....	....	4
New Hampshire,	14	1	....	4	1	2	22
Vermont,	9	1	2	2	....	20	34
Massachusetts,	5	4	....	3	....	1	13
Connecticut,	4	5	....	....	....	3	12
Rhode Island,	....	....	....	....	1	....	1
Virginia,	23	9	8	48	9	10	107
Kentucky,	22	16	12	13	6	6	75
Illinois,	85	89	19	23	30	31	277
Michigan,	2	2	1	4	3	2	14
Louisiana,	....	....	....	1	....	....	1
North Carolina,	6	4	4	11	4	2	31
South Carolina,	....	....	2	2	....	....	4
Tennessee,	11	2	4	22	2	....	41
Missouri,	11	1	...	1	....	....	13
Georgia,	....	....	....	....	....	1	1
Maryland,	16	15	2	4	2	2	41
New Jersey,	3	....	1	1	1	2	8
England,	5	2	....	1	....	....	8
Ireland,	16	10	8	5	....	6	40
Scotland,	....	1	....	1	....	....	2
Germany,	3	....	7	2	3	1	16
France,	1	....	....	....	....	....	1
Prussia,	....	....	....	....	2	....	1
Norway,	....	56	1	....	....	50	107
Holland,	1	....	....	....	....	....	1
Canada,	12	1	....	8	....	8	29
Switzerland,	....	....	2	....	....	....	2
Wisconsin,	....	1	....	2	....	....	3
Delaware,	4	1	....	....	1	....	6
Bavaria,	....	....	....	....	1	....	1
Nova Scotia,	....	....	....	....	1	....	1
Unknown,	5	....	2	....	....	3	10

TABLE,

SHOWING THE POPULATION OF TAMA COUNTY, FOR 1856..

TOWNSHIPS.	No. dwelling houses.	Number of families.	Number of males.	Number of females.	Colored.	Married.	Widowed.	Native voters.	Naturalized voters.	Aliens.	Militia.	Deaf and Dumb.	Blind.	Insane.	Idiotic.	Owners of land.	Paupers.
Buchingham,.......	65	84	230	204	....	160	8	100	10	4	101	....	....	....	....	88	....
Richland,..........	75	75	208	174	....	144	9	81	11	1	77	1	....	....	....	76	....
Indian Village,.....	67	67	161	228	...	131	7	106	5	....	90	....	....	....	....	76	....
Gennesse,..........	24	24	57	73	...	39	2	20	1	5	19	....	....	....	....	20	....
Carleton,..........	68	69	213	195	...	138	9	84	7	....	59	1	....	....	....	72	....
Toledo,............	149	153	419	318	1	280	6	190	14	....	179	....	....	....	....	116	....
Columbia,..........	24	26	52	67	....	49	1	26	4	6	32	....	....	....	....	30	....
Otter Creek,.......	52	50	128	138	....	101	7	48	2	2	48	....	....	....	....	38	....
Howard,...........	85	92	205	268	....	167	12	92	3	5	77	....	....	....	....	81	....
Salt Creek,.........	30	32	102	80	....	58	2	35	1	7	36	....	....	1	....	31	....
Total,...........	639	672	1775	1745	1	1267	63	782	58	30	718	2	....	1	....	628	....

TABLE,

SHOWING THE AGRICULTURAL STATISTICS OF TAMA COUNTY, FOR 1856.

TOWNSHIPS.	Acres of improved land.	Acres of unimproved land.	Acres of meadow	Tons of Hay.	Bushels of grass seed.	Acres of spring wheat.	Bushels harvested.	Acres of winter wheat.	Bushels harvested.	Acres of Oats.	Bushels hatvested.	Acres of corn.	Bushels harvested.	Acres of potatoes.	Bushels harvested.
Buckingham, ...	1607	15778	13	983	....	108	1693	....	....	87	3020	516	17930	17	2310
Richland, ...	1514	10698	6	2	....	85	1493	....	....	40	1065	801	31000	14	2241
Indian Village, ..	1541	8261	....	602	....	134	2790	....	....	79	2835	640	28115	15	1875
Genesee, ...	644	2861	1	....	....	61	651	....	....	31	850	302	11140	12	2806
Carleton, ...	1300	9875	14	547	....	109	1631	....	....	38	1010	501	17531	12	1956
Toledo, ...	2350	15140	95	6	....	249	5079	4	85	175	4672	888	43294	19	3158
Columbia, ...	413	358	....	....	....	33	469	....	....	12	158	202	7645	5	581
Otter Creek, ...	438	1878	....	....	....	51	971	....	....	10	620	161	3665	4	760
Howard, ...	2632	12840	....	....	....	195	3354	....	....	82	1790	730	26005	21	3425
Salt Creek, ...	755	4758	....	215	....	26	420	....	....	14	670	264	7175	10	773
Total, ...	13194	82447	129	2355	...	1051	18551	4	85	567	16690	5005	193500	130	19885

TABLE,

SHOWING THE NUMBER AND VALUE OF HOGS AND CATTLE SOLD, THE VALUE OF DOMESTIC AND GENERAL MANUFACTURES OF TAMA COUNTY, FOR 1856.

TOWNSHIPS.	Number of hogs sold.	Value of hogs sold.	Number of cattle sold.	Value of cattle sold.	Pounds of butter made.	Pounds of cheese.	Pounds of wool.	Value of domestic manufactures.	Value of gen'l manufactures.
Buckingham, ...	124	996	66	2511	4285	100	169	....	....
Richland, ...	202	1145	51	1413	6713	....	80	....	....
Indian Village, ...	178	1573	102	2176	9260	....	112	43	....
Genesee, ...	63	461	27	925	1823	26	43	....	....
Carleton, ...	137	1065	66	2435	4496	60	196	....	....
Toledo, ...	377	2256	124	4072	10930	1178	778	381	150
Columbia, ...	37	282	65	3055	1670	650	....	....	....
Otter Creek, ...	17	21	10	321	1000	200	7	....	....
Howard, ...	109	815	126	3451	8140	20	154	136	....
Salt Creek, ...	40	243	74	1014	1367	50	50	700	....
Total, ...	1284	8858	711	21373	45684	2284	1589	1260	150

TABLE,

EXHIBITING THE PROFESSIONS, TRADES, OR OCCUPATIONS OF THE INHABITANTS OF TAMA COUNTY, FOR 1856.

OCCUPATIONS.	TOWNSHIPS.										
	Buckingham.	Richland.	Indian Village.	Genesee.	Carleton.	Toledo	Columbia.	Otter Creek.	Howard.	Salt Creek.	TOTAL.
Farmers,	97	53	69	25	71	110	29	54	78	[illegible]	613
Laborers,	5	10	1		14	5	3	6	2	5	51
Blacksmiths,	1	1	3	3	1	8			1		17
Carpenters,	8	5	13	4	5	28	2	1	3	8	77
Wagon makers,						2					2
Plasterers,						2					2
Stone masons,			2		1	2			2		7
Machinists,						2					2
Engineers,			3	1		2			1		7
Millers,		1				1					2
Sawyers,	1		2			3	2		1	1	10
Millwrights,									7		7
Painters,		1				3					4
Cabinet makers,	2		1			4			1		8
Tinners,						1					1
Milliners,		1							1		3
Tailors,				1	2	3	1			1	8
Shoe makers,		1	2			3	1		2		9
Saddle and harness makers,						2					2
Bakers,						1					1
Mechanics,						2		3			5
Merchants,	1	1	1			9			1	1	14
Hotel keepers,			1						1		2
Physicians,	2	1	1		1	7		2		1	15
Lawyers,						4					4
Clergymen,	1					6					7
Teachers,	6					2	1				9
Printers.						1	1		1		3
Grocers,			1								1
Teamsters,			1	1							2
Brick makers,		1				1					2
Jewellers,				1							2
Coopers,	1	1	1			1					4
Clerks						2					2
Surveyors,	1										1
Furnace makers,		1									1
Weavers,		1									1
Peddlers,		2									2
County Treasurers,						1					1
County Clerks,						1					1
Wheelwrights,							1				[illegible]
Tailoresses,							1	1			[illegible]

TABLE,

SHOWING THE PLACE OF NATIVITY OF THE INHABITANTS OF TAMA COUNTY, FOR 1856.

STATES.	NAME OF TOWNSHIPS.										TOTAL.
	Buckingham.	Richland.	Indian Village.	Genesee.	Carleton.	Toledo.	Columbia.	Otter Creek.	Howard.	Salt Creek.	
Ohio,	104	82	104	27	69	239	25	77	153	49	929
Indiana,	25	82	34	1	54	112	1	33	73	7	422
Pennsylvania,	....	29	24	11	49	53	14	9	42	28	259
Iowa,	28	51	53	15	53	48	14	26	65	11	364
New York,	53	16	71	31	71	88	5	20	37	9	401
Maine,	3	8	....	1	....	....	....	....	....	....	12
New Hampshire,	2	15	1	1	....	5	11	....	2	....	37
Vermont,	8	3	5	....	9	15	1	....	2	....	43
Massachusetts,	10	2	5	....	5	17	1	2	....	3	45
Connecticut,	15	3	6	....	1	17	13	7	....	8	70
Rhode Island,	1	....	1	....	1	....	....	....	....	....	3
Virginia,	8	12	13	4	18	18	1	13	9	3	99
Kentucky,	6	16	1	....	5	19	....	1	11	1	60
Illinois,	30	80	34	3	23	18	10	16	15	8	187
Michigan,	13	....	4	11	11	20	....	11	27	1	98
Arkansas,	....	....	....	....	....	1	....	....	....	2	3
Alabama,	....	....	....	....	1	....	....	....	....	....	1
Mississippi,	....	....	....	....	....	....	....	....	2	....	2
North Carolina,	....	3	....	....	2	8	1	....	4	....	18
South Carolina,	....	....	1	....	1	....	....	....	....	....	2
Tennessee,	....	3	4	....	....	1	....	....	1	12	21
Missouri,	....	3	....	....	2	1	....	....	....	7	13
Maryland,	....	....	7	1	11	9	3	1	6	5	43
New Jersey,	4	1	7	....	2	2	....	8	5	1	30
England,	13	4	2	....	9	22	3	7	5	2	67
Ireland,	1	10	1	6	1	2	....	2	2	1	26
Wales,	....	....	....	....	....	....	....	....	1	....	1
Scotland,	35	....	....	4	....	5	....	....	....	....	44
Germany,	6	5	5	....	6	12	14	4	8	10	70
France,	1	....	3	....	....	....	....	1	....	....	5
Austria,	....	....	....	....	....	....	....	27	....	9	36
Prussia,	58	....	....	....	....	....	....	....	....	....	58
Norway,	....	2	....	....	....	....	....	....	....	....	2
Sweeden,	....	....	....	....	....	....	....	....	....	1	1
Canada,	2	2	....	14	4	....	2	....	....	3	27
Switzerland,	....	....	....	....	....	....	....	1	1	....	2
Wisconsin,	7	....	3	....	....	1	....	....	....	1	12
Unknown,	1	....	....	....	....	....	....	....	....	....	1
Dist. Columbia,	....	....	....	....	....	3	....	....	....	....	3
Minnesota,	....	....	....	....	....	1	....	....	....	....	1
Delaware,	....	....	....	....	....	....	....	....	2	....	2

TABLE,

SHOWING THE POPULATION, AGRICULTURAL STATISTICS, NUMBER AND VALUE OF HOGS AND CATTLE SOLD, &c., OF TAYLOR COUNTY, FOR 1856.

POPULATION.	TOWNSHIPS.							
	Washington.	Jefferson.	Jackson.	Polk.	Benton.	Clayton.	Ross.	TOTAL.
No. dwelling houses,	66	39	26	50	76	49	41	347
Number of families,	66	43	27	51	75	49	42	352
Number of males,	238	123	132	159	221	135	119	1132
Number of females,	196	93	105	140	209	107	97	947
Married,	147	80	72	94	148	90	87	718
Widowed,	10	3	7	4	7	6	4	41
Native voters,	86	44	44	52	96	55	47	424
Naturalized voters,	3	......	......	2	2	3	1	11
Aliens,	......	......	4	1	......	6	2	13
Militia,	80	39	29	41	82	60	38	369
Blind,	......	......	......	......	......	......	1	1
Owners of land,	75	40	32	40	58	42	39	326
AGRICULTURAL—								
Acres of improved land,	1142	809	936	684	1492	763	602	6428
Acres of unimproved land,	11369	7227	6768	5466	8402	8732	4581	52545
Acres of meadow,	1	7	17	2	16	......	1	44
Tons of hay,	3	......	19	......	2	201	......	226
Acres of spring wheat,	34	2	89	95	52	44	56	373
Bushels harvested,	259	100	779	591	416	567	526	3238
Acres of winter wheat,	30	27	37	81	16	13	3	207
Bushels harvested,	154	387	224	469	90	200	10	1534
Acres of oats,	18	20	159	112	81	73	52	515
Bushels harvested,	148	740	2882	1297	1490	1885	1115	9557
Acres of corn,	560	336	532	510	535	515	382	3370
Bushels harvested,	11640	9696	20140	17935	18096	14275	12640	104422
Acres of potatoes,	10	3	7	8	12	5	4	51
Bushels harvested,	1113	362	874	922	1442	756	185	5634
HOGS, CATTLE, &c.								
No. of hogs sold,	196	233	303	353	177	195	227	1684
Value of hogs sold,	1324	852	1468	1641	555	845	1257	7912
No. of cattle sold,	124	129	90	215	66	163	78	865
Value of cattle sold,	3135	3470	1208	2537	1679	3727	1683	17439
Pounds of butter made,	3420	3535	1868	4615	2840	4105	1978	22411
Pounds of cheese,	......	190	23	1243	......	13	50	1519
Pounds of wool,	517	203	558	630	146	166	205	2425
Val. domestic manufact'r's,	343	259	537	873	140	253	254	2659
Val. general manufactures,	25	......	......	475	......	......	......	500

TABLE

SHOWING THE PROFESSIONS, TRADES OR OCCUPATIONS OF THE INHABITANTS OF TAYLOR COUNTY, FOR 1856.

OCCUPATIONS.	NAME OF TOWNSHIPS.							TOTAL.
	Washington.	Jefferson.	Jackson.	Polk.	Benton.	Clayton.	Ross.	
Farmers,	77	46	37	48	54	65	38	365
Laborers,	....	....	....	....	15	....	6	21
Blacksmiths,	1	1	....	2	5	1	1	11
Carpenters,	2	3	....	....	12	....	....	17
Plasterers,	2	....	....	....	....	....	....	2
Stone Masons,	....	....	....	....	1	3	....	4
Cabinet Makers,	....	....	....	....	....	....	1	1
Milliners,	1	....	....	....	2	....	....	3
Shoe makers,	1	1	....	....	2	....	....	4
Saddle & harness makers,	1	....	....	....	....	....	....	1
Mechanics,	....	....	....	2	1	....	....	3
Merchants,	1	....	....	....	7	....	....	8
Physicians,	....	2	....	1	2	....	....	5
Lawyers,	....	....	....	....	1	....	....	1
Clergymen,	....	....	....	....	1	....	....	1
Teachers,	....	....	....	....	1	....	....	1
Gun Smiths,	....	....	....	1	....	....	....	1
Coopers,	1	1	1	....	....	....	....	3
Clerks,	....	....	....	....	2	....	....	2
Weavers,	....	....	....	1	....	2	....	3

TABLE,

SHOWING THE PLACE OF NATIVITY OF THE INHABITANTS OF TAYLOR COUNTY, FOR 1856.

STATES.	NAME OF TOWNSHIPS.							TOTAL.
	Washington	Jefferson.	Jackson.	Polk.	Benton.	Clayton.	Ross.	
Ohio,	70	30	7	59	43	20	10	239
Indiana,	37	30	35	62	103	47	86	400
Pennsylvania,	89	14	12	5	27	20	7	174
Iowa,	75	61	66	44	58	43	50	397
New York,	6	5	2	2	20	12	1	48
Maine,	....	....	....	....	1	....	....	1
New Hampshire,	2	....	....	....	....	....	....	2
Vermont,	1	....	....	....	1	....	....	2
Massachusetts,	2	3	....	1	....	....	1	7
Connecticut,	2	....	3	....	1	1	2	9
Virginia,	10	3	17	17	9	9	3	68
Kentucky,	31	21	39	12	45	17	24	189
Illinois,	14	17	11	18	20	13	8	101
Michigan,	2	....	2	....	1	....	....	5
Arkansas,	....	....	....	....	....	2	....	2
Texas,	1	....	....	....	....	....	....	1
Alabama,	....	....	....	....	1	3	....	4
Mississippi,	1	....	....	....	....	....	....	1
North Carolina,	2	5	7	4	3	4	....	25
South Carolina,	....	1	3	1	....	....	1	6
Tennessee,	43	2	7	23	19	9	10	113
Missouri,	30	26	22	42	67	23	12	222
Georgia,	3	....	....	....	1	....	....	4
Maryland,	2	....	....	3	1	....	....	6
New Jersey,	....	....	....	....	1	5	....	6
England,	2	1	2	4	1	10	....	20
Ireland,	2	....	1	....	....	1	....	4
Scotland,	....	....	....	....	....	1	....	1
Germany,	....	....	....	2	2	....	1	5
France,	2	....	....	....	1	....	....	3
Norway,	3	....	....	....	....	....	....	3
Canada,	1	....	....	....	2	2	....	5
Switzerland,	....	....	....	....	1	....	....	1
Delaware,	1	2	1	....	1	....	....	5

TABLE,

SHOWING THE POPULATION, AGRICULTURAL STATISTICS, NUMBER AND VALUE OF HOGS AND CATTLE SOLD, &c., &c., OF UNION COUNTY FOR 1856.

TOWNSHIPS.	NAME OF TOWNSHIPS.				
	Jones.	Dodge.	Union.	Platt.	Total.
No. dwelling houses,	35		57	53	145
Number of families,	36		57	53	146
Number of males,	110		178	150	438
Number of females,	100		156	112	368
Married,	71		116	94	281
Widowed,	6		4	2	12
Native voters,	42		72	57	171
Naturalized voters,	2		2	2	6
Aliens,	4			2	[illegible]
Militia,	39		57	38	134
Deaf and dumb,	1				1
Owners of land,	49		54	44	147
AGRICULTURAL—					
Acres improved land,	934		846	812	2592
Acres unimproved land,	8929		10315	9652	28896
Acres of meadow,	10			101	111
Tons of hay,	192		200		392
Bushels of grass seed,			2		2
Acres of spring wheat,	38		42	46	126
Bushels harvested,	250		375	565	1190
Acres of winter wheat,			2	11	13
Bushels harvested,			30	130	160
Acres of oats,	55		75	83	213
Bushels harvested,	1904		1595	1220	4719
Acres of corn,	258		383	46[illegible]	1107
Bushels harvested,	9852		8130	6850	24832
Acres of potatoes,	7		4	5	16
Bushels harvested,	955		743	486	2184
HOGS, CATTLE, &c.—					
No. of hogs sold,	140		17	131	288
Value of hogs sold,	576		134	670	1380
No. of cattle sold,	61		62	111	234
Value of cattle sold,	1685		1538	3111	6334
Pounds of butter made,	2147		2920	3675	8742
Pounds of cheese,	600			200	800
Pounds of wool,	43		84	238	365
Value domestic manufactures,				160	160

TABLE,

EXHIBITING THE TRADES, PROFESSIONS OR OCCUPATIONS OF THE INHABITANTS OF UNION COUNTY, FOR 1856.

OCCUPATIONS.	TOWNSHIPS. Jones.	Union.	Platt.	TOTAL.
Farmers, ...	42	42	52	136
Laborers, ...	1	2	7	10
Blacksmiths, ...	1	5	1	7
Carpenters, ...	1	7	...	8
Wagon Makers,	1	...	...	1
Millers, ...	2	...	...	2
Millwrights, ...	...	...	1	1
Cabinet Makers,	1	...	...	1
Milliners, ...	5	...	..	5
Tailors, ...	1	...	...	1
Shoe makers, ...	2	2	...	4
Harness makers,	...	2	...	2
Merchants, ...	1	2	2	5
Hotel keepers, ..	...	3	...	3
Physicians, ...	1	1	...	2
Lawyers, ...	1	2	...	3
Clergymen, ...	1	1	...	2
Coopers, ...	...	1	...	1
Clerks, ...	1	...	...	1

TABLE,

SHOWING THE PLACE OF NATIVITY OF THE INHABITANTS OF UNION COUNTY, FOR 1856.

STATES.	TOWNSHIPS. Jones.	Union.	Platt.	TOTAL.
Ohio, ...	61	81	37	179
Indiana, ...	43	47	49	139
Pennsylvania, ..	11	40	21	72
Iowa, ...	30	66	48	144
New York, ...	5	14	24	43
Maine, ...	1	...	1	2
New Hampshire,	1	...	...	1
Vermont, ...	4	1	7	12
Massachusetts, ..	...	2	...	2
Connecticut, ...	...	2	...	2
Rhode Island, ..	...	...	1	1
Virginia, ...	13	11	11	35
Kentucky, ...	4	24	6	34
Illinois, ...	7	29	24	60
Michigan, ...	...	1	4	5
North Carolina, .	4	1	3	8
South Carolina, .	1	...	...	1
Tennessee, ...	5	4	4	13
Missouri, ...	...	2	15	17
Maryland, ...	2	3	...	5
England, ...	13	1	1	15
Ireland, ...	...	3	1	4
Germany, ...	5	2	2	9
France, ...	...	...	2	2
Canada, ...	...	...	1	1

TABLE,

SHOWING THE POPULATION OF VAN BUREN COUNTY, FOR 1856.

TOWNSHIPS.	No. of dwelling houses.	Number of families.	Fumber of males.	Number of females.	Colored.	Married.	Widowed.	Native voters.	Naturalized voters.	Aliens.	Militia.	Deaf and Dumb.	Blind.	Insane.	Idiotic.	Owners of land.	Paupers.
Van Buren, ...	291	318	964	906	....	618	65	351	31	14	385	....	....	2	....	253	2
Village, ...	218	218	653	608	...	390	61	237	35	10	248	....	....	....	....	167	....
Union, ...	308	308	902	825	....	576	46	343	18	....	302	1	....	....	....	228	1
Lick Creek, ...	186	186	540	532	....	343	23	186	13	14	152	....	....	....	....	135	....
Cedar, ...	144	153	432	394	....	293	9	146	12	1	127	....	....	1	....	123	....
Harrisburgh, ...	180	180	572	522	....	274	13	56	8	10	12	....	....	1	....	61	2
Washington, ...	258	258	734	663	....	390	41	245	11	10	207	3	....	....	4	150	1
Farmington, ...	468	496	1349	1296	....	900	83	455	67	59	482	1	....	....	....	175	....
Vernon, ...	230	230	639	620	....	417	27	201	10	10	150	1	....	....	3	143	....
Des Moines, ...	170	170	484	467	....	306	29	158	19	.•..	161	....	....	1	....	107	....
Jackson, ...	181	192	543	495	....	338	26	198	7	1	159	1	....	1	....	145	....
Chequest, ...	127	129	413	373	....	232	23	139	10	1	121	1	2	2	....	92	2
Total,	2761	2838	8225	7696	....	5077	446	2705	241	130	2506	8	2	8	7	1779	8

TABLE,

SHOWING THE AGRICULTURAL STATISTICS OF VAN BUREN COUNTY, FOR 1856.

TOWNSHIPS.	Acres of improved land.	Acres of unimproved land.	Acres of meadow.	Tons of hay.	Bushels of grass seed	Acres of spring wheat.	Bushels harvested.	Acres winter wheat.	Bushels harvested.	Acres of oats.	Bushels harvested.	Acres of corn.	Bushels harvested	Acres of potatoes.	Bushels harvested.
Van Buren, ..	5210	20838	689	933	52	7[illegible]4	12263	465	8783	651	21[illegible]76	1463	71580	16	3826
Village, ...	4834	10701	648	635	71	525	675[illegible]	5[illegible]0	9387	599	[illegible]0740	1761	87522	27	2918
Union, ...	10685	11925	1204	1223	164	1576	223[illegible]6	289	5[illegible]35	1501	57167	3536	190705	39	4856
Lick Creek, ...	5166	10657	701	779	85	551	7776	368	9189	773	24064	1727	86[illegible]30	47	5640
Cedar, ...	5648	6187	673	6[illegible]6	71	1[illegible]04	15780	226	3853	976	31367	19[illegible]3	85[illegible]18	23	1966
Harrisburgh, .	8472	8466	1199	1234	602	1762	2[illegible]384	370	7607	1062	37667	2698	1[illegible]3052	41	3849
Washington, ..	7847	9148	988	997	84	9[illegible]7	148[illegible]8	518	8995	9[illegible]3	33560	2[illegible]86	186710	34	3883
Farmington, ..	6558	14912	1124	989	60	917	13599	3[illegible]9	5994	997	30572	2623	91878	29	3066
Vernon, ...	6694	13326	724	764	69	695	9196	453	7303	145[illegible]	36[illegible]3	2200	97448	51	4773
Desmoines, ...	5275	14597	465	555	110	640	8820	231	3402	1073	34686	1937	99056	24	3214
Jackson, ...	6864	14206	461	532	38	798	11013	279	3638	1113	39866	2656	126762	21	2474
Chequest, ...	3849	11892	359	463	27	529	7127	283	3577	509	14856	1664	71755	25	2975
Total, ...	77102	146855	9237	9620	1433	10803	151844	4549	77163	11629	376934	26384	1329506	379	43440

TABLE,

SHOWING THE NUMBER AND VALUE OF HOGS, CATTLE, DOMESTIC AND GENERAL MANUFACTURES OF VAN BUREN COUNTY, FOR 1856.

TOWNSHIPS.	No. of hogs sold.	Value of hogs sold.	No. of cattle sold.	Value of cattle sold.	Pounds of butter made.	Pounds of cheese.	Pounds of Wool.	Value of domestic Manufactures.	Value of general Manufactures.
Van Buren,......	601	4684	181	3702	20585	813	1923	652	45250
Village,.........	812	8550	148	4736	12058	10	1077	1767	14425
Union,...........	2502	21777	803	23448	24450	....	2833	2146	55520
Lick Creek,......	1141	10715	255	5229	19498	230	2564	1784	1000
Cedar,...........	957	7964	174	4060	19485	980	1980	1504	211
Harrisburgh,.....	1643	13427	259	6538	23978	3170	2506	516	5275
Washington,.....	971	9299	278	6363	19095	212	3040	2162	22520
Farmington,.....	938	7975	250	4273	28806	2690	2979	673	600
Vernon,....	1042	9145	563	7454	22463	5755	2697	1248	11958
Desmoines,......	946	8182	281	6486	14197	3892	2045	2938	4000
Jackson,.........	1263	10282	368	9361	18577	3644	1357	1818	....
Chequest,........	731	6369	200	4263	17265	712	1873	1441	1200
Total,.........	13547	118369	3760	85913	240457	22108	26874	18659	161959

TABLE,

EXHIBITING THE PROFESSIONS, TRADES, OR OCCUPATIONS OF THE INHABITANTS OF VAN BUREN COUNTY, FOR 1856.

TOWNSHIPS.	Farmers.	Laborers.	Blacksmiths.	Carpenters.	Wagon makers.	Brick layers.	Plasterers.	Stone Masons.	Stone Cutters.	Machinists.	Engineers.	Millers.	Sawyers.	Millwrights.	Painters.	Cabinet Makers	Chair makers.	Tinners.
Van Buren, ..	134	63	14	19	10	2	2	6	10	...	6	4	....	1	3	6	2	6
Village, ...	109	62	14	9	2	....	2	....	3	...	3	1	1	...	....	....	1	....
Union, ...	143	117	9	30	6	....	3	2	....	....	1	4	2	...	....	3	2	2
Lick Creek, ..	167	2	2	12	1	....	....	1	....	....	...	1	1	2	....	....	...	....
Cedar, ...	176	2	1	5	1	....	....	....	....	....	1	2	....	1	....	....	....	....
Harrisburgh, .	75	2	3	3	....	....	....	....	....	....	....	....	....	....	....	....	....	....
Washington, .	132	26	10	20	1	3	2	7	1	...	1	3	1	...	2	1	....	....
Farmington, .	235	40	25	48	12	2	7	5	8	...	5	15	2	7	6	4	....	4
Vernon, ...	153	15	5	9	4	....	2	2	....	....	....	1	1	1	1	5	1	1
Des Moines, ..	102	....	3	5	1	....	1	1	....	...	....	....	3	....	....	1	....	....
Jackson, ...	185	....	....	....	....	....	....	....	....	9	....	...	....	....	....	....	....	....
Chequest, ...	102	12	....	....	....	....	....	....	....	16	....	....	....	...	....	....	....	....
Total, ...	1713	341	86	160	38	7	19	24	22	25	17	31	11	12	12	20	6	13

TABLE—CONTINUED,

SHOWING THE PROFESSIONS, TRADES, OR OCCUPATIONS OF THE INHABITANTS OF VAN BUREN COUNTY, FOR 1856.

TOWNSHIPS.	Milliners.	Tailors.	Hatters.	Shoemakers.	Harness Makers.	Butchers	Manufacturers.	Merchants.	Speculators.	Traders.	Druggists.	Boarding H. keep'rs.	Hotel keepers.	Clothiers.	Physicians.	Dentists.	Lawyers.	Clergymen.
Van Buren,....	3	6	1	8	7	2	....	20	3		2	....	4	....	6	....	9	5
Village,........	....	1	....	2	....	....	....	8	....	....	....	2	1	....	4	....	1	1
Union,.........	1	1	....	7	2	....	....	24	....	....	....	....	2	....	5	....	....	6
Lick Creek,....	2	1	....	1	1	....	....	....	....	....	....	....	1	....	1	....	....	2
Cedar,.........	....	....	....	1	....	....	....	....	....	....	....	....	....	....	1	....	....	1
Harrisburg,....	....	....	....	....	....	....	....	....	....	....	....	....	....	....	1	....	....	1
Washington,....	3	2	....	6	1	1	9	16	....	....	....	....	2	....	3	....	....	4
Farmington,...	1	6	2	10	3	....	3	28	....	1	....	....	2	....	12	1	1	5
Vernon,.......	....	....	....	1	....	....	1	7	....	....	....	....	1	6	3	....	....	1
Des Moines,....	....	....	....	4	1	....	....	3	....	....	....	....	....	....	2	....	....	2
Jackson,.......	....	....	....	....	....	....	....	3	....	....	....	....	....	....	2	....	....	....
Chequest,......	....	....	....	....	....	....	....	4	....	....	....	....	....	....	....	....	....	....
Total,.......	10	17	3	40	15	3	13	113	3	1	2	2	13	6	40	1	11	28

TABLE—Continued,

EXHIBITING THE PROFESSIONS, TRADES, OR OCCUPATIONS OF THE INHABITANTS OF VAN BUREN COUNTY, FOR 1856.

TOWNSHIPS.	Teachers.	Printers.	Artists.	Grocers.	Teamsters.	Brick Makers.	Jewellers.	Gun Smiths.	Coopers.	Clerks.	Ostlers.	Clerks of Courts.	Justices of the Peace.	Stage drivers	Horticulturists.	Barberers.	Ferrymen.	Weavers.
Van Buren, ...	10	5	2	4	4	3	1	1	4	12	1	1	1	4	1	1	2	1
Village, ...	2							1	4	3							1	
Union, ...	2				2				1	6								
Lick Creek, ...	1				1				1									
Cedar, ...									1									
Harrisburgh, ...																		
Washington, ...	8				4	1			2									1
Farmington, ...	5	1		2	17	3			14	15				2			1	4
Vernon, ...						1			1									
Des Moines, ...	1			1						2								
Jackson, ...	1									2								
Chequest, ...																		
Total, ...	30	6	2	7	28	8	1	2	28	43	1	1	1	6	1	1	4	6

TABLE—Continued,

EXHIBITING THE PROFESSIONS, TRADES, OR OCCUPATIONS OF THE INHABITANTS OF VAN BUREN COUNTY, FOR 1856.

TOWNSHIPS.	Clock makers.	Students.	Livery keepers.	County Judges.	Contractors.	Potters.	Loafers.	Surgeons.	Supervisors.	Colliers.	Constables.	Wool carders.	Wheel wrights.	Peddlers.	Coal diggers.	Tailoresses.
Van Buren,	1	5	1	1	1	2	9	1				1				
Village,								1	1	1	1	1				
Union,													1	1		
Lick Creek,															1	3
Cedar,																
Harrisburgh,													1			
Washington,																2
Farmington,						5	1			4		2				
Vernon,						2							1			
Des Moines,																
Jackson,		1														1
Chequest,																
Total,	1	6	1	1	1	9	10	2	1	5	1	4	3	1	1	6

TABLE— Continued,

SHOWING THE PROFESSIONS, TRADES OR OCCUPATIONS OF THE INHABITANTS OF VAN BUREN COUNTY FOR 1856.

TOWNSHIPS.	Traders.	Broom makers.	Fishermen.	Tanners.	Gentlemen.	Surveyors.	Miners.	Gardeners	Vault makers.	Dyers.	Boatmen.	Pilots.	Post Masters.	Publishers.	Iron Rollers.
Van Buren,															
Village,															
Union,															
Lick Creek,	1	1	1	1	2										
Cedar,	1					1	2								
Harrisburgh,															
Washington,				1				1							
Farmington,						1	2		1	1	3	2	1		
Vernon,				1										1	
Des Moines,		1													1
Jackson,															
Chequest,															
Total,	2	7	1	3	2	2	4	1	1	1	3	2	1	1	1

TABLE,

SHOWING THE PLACE OF NATIVITY OF THE INHABITANTS OF VAN BUREN COUNTY FOR 1856.

STATES.	NAMES OF TOWNSHIPS.												Total
	Van Buren.	Village.	Union.	Lick Creek.	Cedar.	Harrisburgh.	Washington.	Farmington.	Vernon.	Des Moines.	Jackson.	Chequest.	
Ohio,	483	380	461	307	108	209	303	538	266	261	256	264	3836
Indiana,	105	106	113	55	104	70	67	137	114	48	189	43	1151
Pennsylvania,	206	109	240	120	115	233	189	207	146	88	48	66	1767
Iowa,	492	330	492	360	250	259	400	772	387	209	245	220	4416
New York,	100	28	65	38	15	70	46	113	21	28	15	18	557
Maine,	10	2	2	1	....	2	3	4	6	10	....	3	43
N. Hampshire,	8	1	2	....	2	1	4	13	7	5	....	....	43
Vermont,	18	2	11	....	3	1	5	22	6	7	13	4	92
Massachusetts,	10	2	7	3	1	7	14	42	3	....	2	2	93
Connecticut,	20	2	3	2	....	5	1	10	2	14	2	....	61
Rhode Island,	....	....	1	....	....	....	1	4	5	1	1	....	13
Virginia,	89	69	109	47	24	86	77	119	137	111	77	48	993
Kentucky,	33	24	65	32	50	15	94	74	62	30	57	17	548
Illinois,	47	39	49	23	42	39	46	89	18	33	36	15	476
Michigan,	6	....	2	....	2	2	....	1	4	1	1	5	24
Arkansas.	2	....	....	1	....	....	....	1	....	....	....	....	4
Texas,	....	....	....	....	....	....	3	....	....	....	....	....	3
Alabama,	....	....	....	....	15	1	....	....	....	....	....	....	16
Louisiana,	....	....	1	....	....	....	....	6	....	....	....	....	7
Mississippi,	....	....	....	....	....	....	....	....	1	....	....	....	1
N. Carolina,	4	7	7	2	30	3	6	13	7	2	5	....	86
S. Carolina,	3	1	....	1	5	1	1	2	....	....	....	....	14
Tennessee,	16	6	12	11	8	19	15	23	....	11	8	4	133
Missouri,	28	19	6	3	9	5	23	44	16	13	6	9	181
Georgia,	1	....	....	....	....	....	....	....	1	....	....	....	2
Maryland,	40	22	24	11	12	9	13	43	7	12	8	9	210
New Jersey,	16	4	2	1	5	6	7	35	4	7	3	11	101
England,	30	6	17	10	11	7	25	85	11	20	9	4	235
Ireland,	39	56	27	23	7	14	21	39	12	20	4	4	266
Wales,	....	....	....	....	....	....	1	....	....	....	....	....	1
Scotland,	8	2	....	5	2	....	....	17	9	....	....	....	43
Germany,	23	8	2	10	....	19	15	156	5	2	4	27	271
France,	7	20	....	....	....	4	....	3	....	....	2	....	36
Austria,	1	....	....	....	....	....	....	1	....	....	....	....	2
Prussia,	2	....	....	....	....	2	6	1	....	7	....	....	18
Sweden,	4	8	....	....	....	....	....	....	....	....	5	5	22
On the Ocean,	....	....	....	....	....	....	....	1	....	....	....	....	1
Canada,	2	7	....	....	1	2	5	18	4	1	1	1	42
New Brunswick,	2	....	....	....	....	....	....	....	1	....	....	....	3
Switzerland,	....	1	1	....	....	....	3	4	1	9	....	....	19
Denmark,	....	....	....	....	....	....	....	1	....	....	....	....	1
West Indies,	....	....	....	....	1	....	....	....	....	....	....	....	1
Wisconsin,	1	....	3	....	1	3	....	....	1	....	....	....	9
Delaware,	3	....	2	6	3	....	3	6	4	....	39	7	73
Oregon,	1	....	....	....	....	....	....	....	....	....	....	....	1
District Columbia,	....	....	1	....	....	....	....	....	1	1	2	....	5
Minnesota,	....	....	....	....	....	....	....	1	....	....	....	....	1

TABLE,

SHOWIG THE POPULATION OF WAPELLO COUTY, FOR 1856.

TOWNSHIPS.	No. dwelling houses.	Number of families.	Number of males.	Number of females.	Colored	Married.	Widowed.	Native voters.	Naturalized voters.	Aliens.	Militia.	Deaf and dumb.	Blind.	Insane.	Idiotic.	Owners of land.	Paupers.
Adams,	191	207	582	555	1	81	17	218	6	6	193	....	1	3	....	173	3
Green,	162	162	502	420	....	140	4	135	9	1	135	....	....	....	....	90	....
Dahlonega,	116	126	327	412	....	235	23	142	13	2	135	....	....	1	....	92	....
Pleasant,	156	160	485	472	....	150	21	174	8	4	148	....	....	....	1	118	....
Center,	350	337	9[illegible]4	861	1	602	39	304	21	....	267	....	....	....	1	187	....
Richland	166	166	463	458	....	316	26	172	10	4	132	....	1	....	1	146	....
Polk,	131	137	405	347	....	246	7	151	11	12	96	....	....	....	....	95	....
Keokuk,	83	94	237	199	4	143	6	70	11	4	67	....	....	....	....	68	....
Highland,	78	81	266	222	....	161	10	98	2	....	98	....	....	....	....	72	....
Washington,	226	226	672	592	....	445	34	222	8	11	233	....	1	....	2	160	....
Columbia,	291	321	874	803	....	618	40	380	19	14	351	....	....	....	1	73	....
Competine,	113	115	371	328	....	226	7	125	5	1	117	1	....	....	....	74	....
Cass,	84	90	252	233	....	147	16	85	2	....	80	....	....	....	....	55	....
Agency,	193	193	503	500	....	352	29	202	3	....	94	....	....	....	....	163	7
Total,	2140	2415	6344	6402	6	3862	279	2478	128	59	2146	1	3	4	6	1566	10

TABLE,

SHOWING THE AGRICULTURAL STATISTICS OF WAPELLO COUNTY FOR 1856.

TOWNSHIPS.	Acres of improved land.	Acres of unimproved land.	Acres of meadow.	Tons of hay.	Bushels of grass seed.	Acres spring wheat.	Bushels harvested.	Acres winter wheat.	Bushels harvested.	Acres of oats.	Bushels harvested.	Acres of corn.	Bushels harvested.	Acres of potatoes.	Bushels harvested.
Adams, ...	5358	1322	369	235	17	773	8102	133	1245	648	16216	2469	102435	30	4323
Green, ...	3350	8033	97	62	....	257	2174	154	1594	218	6043	857	65555	15	1503
Dahlonega, ...	5100	8770	405	184	33	684	2730	107	198	627	24079	2867	159710	32	4440
Pleasant, ...	7055	10540	426	380	41	856	5539	106	400	752	25013	2815	149865	25	4130
Center, ...	6740	27908	736	402	58	541	3726	93	1051	587	16096	2749	138130	38	4740
Richland, ...	109	2346	434	153	94	1053	3912	88	98	653	16664	2745	149660	34	4985
Polk, ...	2573	1062	81	70	16	405	1918	185	904	239	6451	1206	74806	26	2502
Keokuk, ...	2116	6987	252	215	5	110	1020	63	722	151	3741	641	35920	10	1103
Highland, ...	5179	1393	253	129	53	593	2956	45	406	318	12578	2107	103917	15	2765
Washington, ...	5113	8335	592	487	25	620	7197	261	765	541	16840	2123	93270	11	2656
Columbia, ...	6718	8241	408	207	32	622	2651	92	426	545	11640	2115	102527	12	1489
Competine, ...	4118	5542	288	236	90	840	5937	21	140	435	14177	1915	80200	16	2207
Cass, ...	1835	4673	69	39	1	190	1166	112	736	1513	3810	795	54000	19	2168
Agency, ...	5617	8553	683	1099	63	363	3599	83	1435	512	20987	1714	78820	19	3060
Total, ...	60973	93696	5094	3902	531	6918	52628	1544	10130	7741	194338	27119	1388825	307	42071

TABLE,

SHOWING THE NUMBER AND VALUE OF HOGS AND CATTLE SOLD, AND THE VALUE OF DOMESTIC AND GENERAL MANUFACTURES OF WAPELLO COUNTY, FOR 1856.

TOWNSHIPS.	Number of hogs sold.	Value of hogs sold.	No. of cattle. sold.	Value of cattle sold.	Pounds of butter made.	Pounds of cheese.	Pounds of Wool.	Value of domestic manufactures.	Value of general manufactures.
Adams, ...	1182	7871	251	4576	14769	1252	3206	2036	8439
Green, ...	1583	5581	105	1232	6020	....	1622	1569	52
Dahlonega, ...	3017	25464	534	17559	11090	885	2105	3724	4500
Pleasant, ...	2044	17003	414	13764	17310	1020	2706	2036	....
Center, ...	1759	13214	964	8668	6561	358	1783	1216	....
Richland, ...	1899	16280	335	5256	17252	2575	1710	1742	90
Polk, ...	767	5157	121	2948	9640	190	1351	1630	883
Keokuk, ...	454	3491	71	1481	5685	....	1165	1321	515
Highland, ...	2066	16429	199	4915	7158	478	1515	1226	50
Washington, ...	1455	12541	383	11168	7596	587	1729	1449	1230
Columbia, ...	1606	15629	158	3955	9500	112	1967	4658	14000
Competine, ...	1138	8916	84	2390	11506	150	1431	1063	....
Cass, ...	485	3174	151	3902	8510	....	680	634	3432
Agency, ...	5347	23904	666	6028	13597	908	1515	1626	10900
Total, ...	24802	176654	4436	86842	146194	8515	25485	26030	44091

TABLE,

SHOWING THE PROFESSIONS, TRADES, OR OCCUPATIONS OF THE INHABITANTS OF WAPELLO COUNTY FOR 1856.

TOWNSHIPS.	Farmers.	Laborers.	Blacksmiths.	Carpenters.	Wagon makers.	Brick layers.	Plasterers.	Stone masons.	Stone cutters	Engineers.	Millers.	Sawyers.	Millwrights.	Painters.	Cabinet makers.	Chair makers.	Tinners.	Milliners.
Adams, ...	214	7	6	11	2	....	3	....	....	1	1	....	....	....	1	1	....	7
Green, ...	66	....	1	3	....	....	....	1	....	....	....	....	....	....	....	....	....	....
Dahlonega, ...	160	....	....	....	....	....	....	....	....	....	....	....	....	....	1	....	....	3
Pleasant, ...	157	20	1	6	2	....	....	....	....	....	....	....	....	....	....	....	....	1
Center, ...	122	8	7	23	4	....	7	4	2	1	4	....	....	....	6	....	....	5
Richland, ...	225	20	3	2	2	....	....	1	....	1	2	....	....	....	....	2	....	....
Polk, ...	127	20	3	....	....	....	....	1	....	....	2	....	....	....	....	2	....	....
Keokuk, ...	75	....	....	....	....	....	....	....	....	....	....	....	....	....	....	....	....	....
Highland, ...	131	1	1	1	....	1	....	....	....	....	....	....	....	....	....	....	....	....
Washington, ..	123	37	5	14	1	....	....	3	....	1	4	....	....	....	....	....	....	2
Columbia, ...	104	77	....	57	5	4	6	6	....	5	1	3	2	3	4	1	2	1
Competine, ...	107	44	3	8	....	....	....	....	....	....	....	....	....	....	1	....	....	....
Cass, ...	61	19	9	5	....	....	....	....	....	....	....	....	....	....	....	....	....	1
Agency, ...	66	1	7	15	4	....	3	1	....	3	....	....	....	1	2	....	2	6
Total, ...	1738	254	46	145	20	5	18	17	2	12	14	3	2	4	15	6	4	26

TABLE—Continued,

SHOWING THE PROFESSIONS, TRADES, OR OCCUPATIONS OF THE INHABITANTS OF WAPELLO COUNTY, FOR 1856.

TOWNSHIPS.	Tailors.	Shoemakers.	Harness makers.	Bakers.	Butchers.	Mechanics.	Merchants	Agents.	Traders.	Druggists	Hotel Keepers.	Physicians.	Lawyers.	Clergyman.	Teachers.	Printers.	Artists.
Adams,	....	3	1	....	....	2	6	....	....	1	....	5	....	1	6	....	....
Green,	....	....	1	....	....	....	1	....	....	....	....	2	....	....	....	1	....
Dahlonega,	1	....	1	....	....	....	4	....	....	....	2	1	....	1	....	....	....
Pleasant,	....	1	....	....	....	....	....	....	....	....	....	1	....	....	....	....	....
Center,	3	....	3	2	1	....	16	....	4	....	2	10	12	4	1	....	....
Richland,	1	2	....	....	....	1	....	....	....	....	....	1	....	....	....	....	....
Polk,	1	....	....	....	....	1	....	....	....	....	....	....	....	....	....	....	....
Keokuk,	....	....	....	....	....	....	....	....	....	....	....	....	....	....	....	....	....
Highland,	....	1	1	....	....	1	....	....	....	....	....	2	....	....	3	....	....
Washington,	....	....	....	....	....	....	....	1	2	....	1	6	....	....	....	....	....
Columbia,	3	5	2	....	....	....	13	....	....	1	2	5	2	1	1	3	1
Competine,	....	1	....	....	....	....	2	....	....	....	....	....	....	....	....	....	....
Cass,	....	....	....	....	....	....	....	....	....	....	....	2	....	1	....	....	....
Agency,	3	3	3	1	1	....	13	....	....	....	2	4	1	1	9	....	....
Total,	10	16	12	3	2	5	55	1	6	2	9	39	15	9	20	4	1

TABLE—Continued,

SHOWING THE PROFESSIONS, TRADES, OR OCCUPATIONS OF THE INHABITANTS OF WAPELLO COUNTY, FOR 1856.

TOWNSHIPS.	Grocers.	Teamsters	Brick makers.	Jewellers.	Gun Smiths.	Coopers.	Clerks.	Potters.	Wheelwrights.	Peddlers.	Miners.	Literature.	Barbers.	Carders.	Livery keepers.	Cutlers.
Adams,	....	....	3	....	1	....	4	....	....	....	1	....	....	....	....	....
Greene,	....	....	....	....	....	....	....	....	....	....	....	....	....	....	....	....
Dahlonega,	....	3	....	....	....	1	4	4	....	....	....	1	....	....	....	....
Pleasant,	....	....	....	....	....	....	....	1	1	1	....	....	....	....	....	....
Center,	....	1	7	1	1	1	7	1	....	....	....	....	1	1	2	1
Richland,	....	1	....	....	....	1	....	....	....	....	....	....	....	....	....	....
Polk,	....	....	....	....	....	1	....	....	....	....	....	....	....	....	....	....
Keokuk,	....	....	....	....	....	....	....	....	....	....	....	....	....	....	....	....
Highland,	....	....	....	....	....	....	....	....	....	....	....	....	....	....	....	....
Washington,	....	1	2	....	....	3	1	....	....	....	....	....	....	....	....	....
Columbia,	....	23	3	....	....	4	9	....	....	....	1	....	1	....	....	....
Competine,	....	....	3	....	....	1	....	....	....	....	....	....	....	....	....	....
Cass,	....	4	....	....	....	1	....	....	....	....	....	....	....	....	....	....
Agency,	1	....	1	....	1	3	2	....	....	....	....	....	....	....	....	....
Total,	1	33	19	1	3	15	27	6	1	1	2	1	2	1	2	1

TABLE—Continued,

EXHIBITING THE PROFESSIONS, TRADES, OR OCCUPATIONS OF THE INHABITANTS OF WAPELLO COUNTY, FOR 1856.

TOWNSHIPS.	Stage drivers.	Stove makers.	Supervisors.	Tanners.	Contractors.	Lumberers.	Shingle makers.	Pork Packers.	Surveyors.	Ferrymen.	Hedge planters.	Stage Agents.	Basket makers.	Drovers.
Adams,	...	...	...	...	...	...	...	...	...	...	...	...	...	...
Green,	...	...	...	...	...	...	...	...	...	...	...	...	...	...
Dahlonega,	...	...	...	...	...	...	...	...	...	...	...	...	...	...
Pleasant,	...	...	...	...	...	...	...	...	...	...	...	...	...	...
Center,	2	1	1	1	...	...	...	...	...	1	...	...	1	1
Richland,	...	...	...	...	...	...	...	...	...	...	...	...	...	...
Polk,	...	...	...	...	...	...	...	...	...	...	...	...	...	...
Keokuk,	...	...	...	...	...	...	...	...	...	...	...	...	...	...
Highland,	...	...	...	...	...	...	...	...	...	...	...	...	...	...
Washington,	...	...	...	...	1	...	...	...	...	...	...	...	...	...
Columbia,	1	...	...	...	...	1	1	1	1	1	1	1	...	...
Competine,	...	...	...	...	...	...	...	...	...	...	...	...	...	...
Cass,	...	...	...	...	...	...	...	...	...	...	...	...	...	...
Agency,	...	...	...	...	...	...	...	...	...	...	...	...	...	...
Total,	3	1	1	1	1	1	1	1	1	2	1	1	1	1

TABLE,

SHOWING THE PLACE OF NATIVITY OF THE INHABITANTS OF WAPELLO COUNTY, FOR 1856.

STATES.	NAME OF TOWNSHIPS.														
	Adams.	Green.	Dahlonega.	Pleasant.	Center.	Richland.	Polk.	Keokuk.	Highland.	Washington.	Columbia.	Competine.	Cass.	Agency.	TOTAL.
Ohio,	194	325	148	170	305	256	163	113	91	218	565	126	205	195	3074
Indiana,	212	132	159	115	257	138	142	58	114	295	196	159	49	181	2207
Pennsylvania,	41	27	48	70	79	74	19	48	35	105	120	41	21	99	827
Iowa,	299	254	179	310	436	222	175	131	92	323	329	177	122	267	3313
New York,	31	3	22	6	37	11	15	6	24	22	...	5	7	22	211
Maine,	2	....	....	1	3	....	7	...	1	1	2	...	1	6	24
New Hampshire,	1	....	1	....	7	....	...	...	...	2	42	...	...	1	54
Vermont,	8	....	....	1	6	3	2	...	...	...	15	...	2	3	40
Massachusetts,	2	....	4	1	14	....	5	...	...	2	5	1	1	4	39
Connecticut,	1	....	2	....	8	1	9	...	...	4	6	1	...	1	33
Rhode Island,	1	....	....	....	...	2	...	...	...	...	...	1	...	...	4
Virginia,	50	15	30	52	83	32	30	11	35	53	118	44	31	33	617
Kentucky,	128	20	34	55	89	27	50	7	21	66	49	42	11	33	632
Illinois,	45	31	36	55	95	37	30	8	39	56	66	55	8	38	599
Michigan,	5	....	....	3	4	2	1	...	...	1	9	...	...	1	26
Arkansas,	2	....	....	....	....	....	...	...	...	1	...	...	...	...	3
Alabama,	....	....	....	....	....	....	...	...	...	1	...	1	...	...	2
Louisiana,	....	....	1	....	1	....	...	3	...	...	1	1	...	...	7
Mississippi,	....	....	....	....	....	....	...	...	...	1	...	...	...	...	1
Florida,	...	....	....	....	4	....	...	...	...	...	...	...	...	...	4
North Carolina,	19	21	7	7	25	23	7	1	5	19	9	8	3	10	164
South Carolina,	8	4	....	2	2	3	2	...	...	6	1	...	2	...	30
Tennessee,	30	26	15	54	21	14	8	3	21	31	9	12	2	20	266
Missouri,	10	7	9	7	13	5	3	1	1	2	13	1	3	13	88
Georgia,	1	....	....	....	3	....	...	...	...	...	...	...	...	...	4
Maryland,	10	8	19	10	13	16	3	1	...	15	13	2	2	42	154
New Jersey,	4	15	6	5	12	4	1	1	5	3	9	1	...	3	69
England,	17	6	....	2	28	12	...	2	2	17	18	...	...	2	106
Ireland,	1	6	8	25	85	31	3	35	1	7	25	6	...	3	236
Wales,	....	....	....	....	....	1	...	...	...	7	1	...	...	...	9
Scotland,	....	....	....	....	....	....	...	2	...	...	...	...	...	...	2
Germany,	5	10	4	1	63	....	20	3	...	2	15	11	7	16	157
France,	....	....	8	....	....	....	...	...	...	...	1	1	...	...	10
Austria,	....	....	....	....	2	....	...	...	...	...	...	...	...	...	2
Prussia,	....	....	1	....	4	....	...	...	...	...	...	...	...	1	6
Sweden,	....	....	....	....	5	....	57	...	...	...	3	...	5	...	70
Holland,	....	12	....	....	4	....	...	1	...	...	17	...	...	...	34
Canada,	6	....	...	....	6	....	...	1	...	2	18	1	...	2	36
New Brunswick,	....	....	....	....	....	2	...	...	...	...	...	...	...	...	2
Switzerland,	3	....	....	....	3	....	...	...	...	...	1	...	...	...	7
Saxony,	....	....	....	....	1	....	...	...	...	...	...	...	...	...	1
Wisconsin,	....	....	....	....	9	....	...	...	...	...	...	1	2	6	18
Delaware,	....	....	4	5	3	2	1	...	...	1	2	...	...	...	18
Poland,	....	....	....	....	8	....	...	...	...	...	...	...	...	...	8
Dis. Columbia,	....	....	....	....	3	....	...	...	...	1	1	1	..	1	7
Minnesota,	....	....	....	....	....	....	...	...	...	...	1	..	...	...	1
Unknown,	1	....	....	....	....	3	...	...	1	...	...	...	1	...	6

TABLE,

SHOWING THE POPULATION OF WASHINGTON COUNTY, FOR 1856.

TOWNSHIPS.	No. dwelling houses.	Number of families.	Number of males.	Number of females.	Colored.	Married.	Widowed	Native voters.	Naturalized voters.	Aliens.	Militia.	Deaf and Dumb.	Blind.	Insane.	Idiotic.	Owners of land	Paupers.
Washington, ...	128	134	459	315	....	351	23	171	8	11	168	....	....	....	1	116	....
Town of Washington,	168	203	626	500	....	365	44	292	4	23	313	4	....	....	3	178	....
Clay,............	107	111	366	282	4	217	9	151	4	....	111	2	1	....	....	95	2
Brighton,..........	192	216	576	533	....	399	31	250	....	2	213	2	....	....	....	168	1
Marion, ...	87	87	296	252	....	172	6	83	11	15	89	....	....	....	....	88	....
Crawford,..........	162	180	496	446	2	308	36	200	7	10	189	....	....	....	....	189	....
Oregon, ...	86	86	267	226	....	166	7	89	2	9	95	....	....	....	....	69	2
Franklin,..........	76	79	258	211	....	146	15	103	8	....	83	....	....	....	....	80	1
Dutch Creek,.......	136	151	498	382	....	238	19	153	42	20	184	1	....	....	1	121	....
Seventy Six, ...	28	33	71	64	....	60	5	34	1	1	25	....	....	....	....	29	....
Cedar,............	102	115	365	287	....	205	19	128	5	2	105	1	....	....	2	105	2
Jackson,..........	66	66	205	202	....	127	8	73	1	....	53	2	....	....	....	55	....
Highland, ...	59	60	155	148	....	99	7	51	3	....	46	....	....	....	....	46	....
Iowa, ...	144	148	454	365	....	273	17	130	25	30	135	2	....	....	1	147	....
English River,......	173	178	508	458	....	336	15	176	21	7	173	....	....	....	....	143	....
Lime Creek, ...	145	157	429	413	....	292	30	157	13	15	164	....	....	1	2	135	....
Total, ...	1859	2004	6029	5084	6	3703	291	2241	155	145	2146	14	1	1	10	1764	8

TABLE,

SHOWING THE AGRICULTURAL STATISTICS OF WASHINGTON COUNTY, FOR 1856.

TOWNSHIPS.	Acres of improved land.	Acres of unimproved land.	Acres of meadow	Tons of Hay.	Bushels of grass seed.	Acres of spring wheat.	Bushels harvested.	Acres of winter wheat.	Bushels harvested.	Acres of Oats.	Bushels hatvested.	Acres of corn.	Bushels harvested.	Acres of potatoes.	Bushels harvested.
Washington, ...	4127	8222	300	227	4	1012	10711	24	313	410	14005	1520	79686	22	2701
T. of Washington,	895	1033	61	78	2	180	2095	...	....	119	3805	342	15200	5	415
Clay, ...	5200	4719	760	438	44	678	5603	91	917	607	21044	1798	89770	31	3863
Brighton, ...	4306	8379	494	369	14	802	8118	61	667	506	16412	1069	92105	21	2730
Marion, ...	3585	8509	256	189	12	646	6406	119	1864	379	9835	1141	53210	33	3315
Crawford, ...	6080	5840	354	463	137	1438	19399	4	75	591	20784	1929	95700	14	1290
Gregon, ...	3234	4671	108	105	....	556	7050	23	169	344	9905	1245	72725	25	2347
Franklin, ...	3653	8467	103	105	10	665	9082	13	142	307	12485	1153	72980	15	2339
Dutch Creek, ...	4513	20132	443	443	79	799	10233	81	356	465	14406	1768	68530	42	4690
Seventy Six, ...	706	2981	27	18	....	98	1720	33	420	33	932	165	6850	3	282
Cedar, ...	5726	10237	173	383	66	947	11650	35	478	489	22106	1769	110315	29	4461
Jackson, ...	2060	5602	58	48	2	285	4604	33	445	175	6608	747	38500	14	1950
Highland, ...	1522	6238	284	61	....	139	1781	16	275	102	4769	268	15480	6	688
Iowa, ...	5755	11748	387	774	51	824	9986	19	184	551	17604	1824	108482	37	6190
English River, ..	4966	18471	519	249	92	531	6318	15	185	397	13974	1683	88980	13	2231
Lime Creek, ...	3559	5095	235	136	29	491	6558	19	272	366	14793	1469	79840	26	3953
Total, ...	59357	130344	4562	4094	542	10091	121314	586	6762	5841	203467	20890	1088353	336	43445

TABLE,—SHOWING THE NUMBER AND VALUE OF HOGS, CATTLE, DOMESTIC AND GENERAL MANUFACTURES OF WASHINGTON COUNTY, FOR 1856.

TOWNSHIPS.	No. of hogs sold.	Value of hogs sold.	No. of cattle sold.	Value of cattle sold.	Pounds of butter made.	Pounds of cheese.	Pounds of Wool.	Value of domestic Manufactures.	Value of general Manufactures.
Washington, ...	912	8323	91	2212	12018	72	1153	461	....
Washington Town,	314	2610	65	1430	810	200	75	300	....
Clay, ...	1196	11364	506	10705	16297	56620	2230	1230	8000
Brighton, ...	1962	13060	175	4751	13108	1105	1401	728	....
Marion, ...	1018	8159	271	6341	8213	1022	639	487	2700
Crawford, ...	1241	11568	205	4736	17520	260	2540	150	....
Oregon, ...	749	7066	44	1201	9395	150	804	322	....
Franklin, ...	829	6763	146	4408	7195	7100	586	806	....
Dutch Creek, ...	1152	7231	222	4518	10471	3490	1796	713	50
Seventy-Six, ...	217	1558	43	1115	890	320	65	....	....
Cedar, ...	1127	951	202	6417	12975	80	1233	734	53
Jackson, ...	367	3000	47	1311	5095	432	311	262	46
Highland, ...	135	1121	71	3284	1660	....	156	....	....
Iowa, ...	1524	14296	215	5150	17570	766	1804	1004	17087
English River, ...	1153	10426	244	5214	7200	417	1186	779	4000
Lime Creek, ...	936	6197	171	4289	9520	2670	563	372	560
Total, ...	15232	113993	2718	67082	149937	74704	16642	8388	32496

TABLE,

SHOWING THE PROFESSIONS, TRADES, OR OCCUPATIONS OF THE INHABITANTS OF WASHINGTON COUNTY, FOR 1856

TOWNSHIPS.	Farmers.	Laborers.	Blacksmiths.	Carpenters.	Wagon makers.	Brick layers.	Plasterers.	Stone masons.	Stone cutters.	Carriage makers.	Machinists.	Engineers.	Millers	Sawyers.	Millwrights.	Painters.	Cabinet makers.	Chair makers.
Washington, …	144	39	1	3	…	1	…	…	…	…	…	…	…	…	…	…	…	1
Town of Wash'n,	28	74	12	59	7	7	9	3	…	…	3	2	…	2	…	8	8	…
Clay, …	105	9	1	9	…	…	…	1	…	…	…	1	1	1	…	…	…	…
Brighton, …	122	56	6	21	3	…	2	2	…	…	…	2	8	…	…	…	2	2
Marion, …	116	18	…	4	…	…	…	3	…	…	…	1	3	…	…	…	…	…
Crawford, …	162	36	3	12	…	…	2	…	…	…	…	…	…	…	…	1	…	…
Oregon, …	78	…	1	4	…	…	…	…	…	…	…	1	…	…	…	…	…	…
Franklin, …	108	16	2	6	…	1	…	1	…	…	…	…	…	…	…	…	1	…
Dutch Creek, …	186	29	3	11	…	…	1	2	…	…	…	1	4	…	…	…	…	1
Seventy-Six, …	35	…	1	2	…	…	…	…	…	…	…	…	…	…	…	…	…	…
Cedar, …	117	…	3	8	…	…	…	…	…	…	1	…	…	…	…	…	…	…
Jackson, …	87	…	…	3	…	…	…	…	…	…	…	…	…	…	1	…	…	…
Highland, …	40	4	1	4	…	…	…	2	…	…	…	…	…	…	2	…	…	…
Iowa, …	192	…	3	6	…	…	…	…	…	1	…	3	2	3	…	…	…	…
English River, .	150	4	4	24	1	…	2	1	…	…	…	…	1	7	…	…	1	…
Lime Creek, …	127	10	4	6	…	…	…	…	2	…	…	…	2	3	…	…	1	…
Total, …	1797	295	45	182	11	9	16	15	2	1	4	11	21	16	3	9	13	4

TABLE—Continued

EXHIBITING THE PROFESSIONS, TRADES, OR OCCUPATIONS, OF THE INHABITANTS OF WASHINGTON COUNTY, FOR 1856.

TOWNSHIPS.	Tinners.	Milliners.	Tailors.	Shoe makers.	Harness makers.	Bakers.	Butchers.	Mechanics.	Merchants.	Agents.	Drovers.	Traders.	Druggists.	Hotel keepers.	Clothiers.	Physicians.	Dentists.	Lawyers.
Washington,			1	1					1									
Town of Wash'n,	9	11	5	6	3	1	1		24	1			5	4		8	1	9
Clay,			1								1				1			
Brighton,	1		2	2	3				12			1	2	2		3		2
Marion,					2				1									
Crawford,		2		2	1				3							3		
Oregon,									2									
Franklin,					2													1
Dutch Creek,				2					4							2		
Seventy-Six,																		
Cedar,																		
Jackson,																1		
Highland,									1							1		
Iowa,		2							3									1
English River,			1	5	1				4				1	1		4		
Lime Creek,			1	5	2			1	5					1		2		
Total,	10	15	11	23	14	1	1	1	60	1	1	1	8	8	1	24	1	13

TABLE—Continued,

SHOWING THE PROFESSIONS, TRADES, OR OCCUPATIONS OF THE INHABITANTS OF WASHINGTON COUNTY, FOR 1856.

TOWNSHIPS.	Clergymen.	Teachers.	Musicians.	Artists.	Grocers.	Teamsters.	Brick makers.	Jewellers.	Coopers.	Clerks.	Lumbermen.	Students.	Notary publics.	Spinners.	Carders.	Professors.	Cooks.	County Treasurers.
Washington, ...	1	....	....	....	....	....	4	....	....	....	1	1	....	....	....	....	....	....
Town of Wash'n,	5	4	....	1	....	4	1	2	....	11	....	3	1	1	1	1	1	1
Clay, ...	....	....	....	....	....	....	....	....	....	....	....	....	....	....	....	....	....	....
Brighton, ...	2	2	....	....	....	2	....	1	....	3	1	....	....	....	....	....	....	....
Marion, ...	....	2	....	....	....	....	1	....	1	....	....	....	....	....	....	....	....	....
Crawford, ...	4	1	....	....	....	....	....	....	....	....	....	....	....	....	....	....	....	....
Oregon, ...	....	....	....	1	....	....	....	....	1	....	....	1	....	....	....	....	....	....
Franklin, ...	....	....	....	....	....	....	....	....	2	....	....	....	....	....	....	....	....	....
Dutch Creek, ...	2	2	....	....	....	....	....	....	....	1	....	3	....	....	....	....	....	....
Seventy-Six, ...	....	....	....	....	....	....	....	....	....	....	....	....	....	....	....	....	....	....
Cedar, ...	....	....	....	....	....	....	....	....	....	....	....	....	....	....	....	....	....	....
Jackson, ...	....	1	....	....	....	....	....	....	....	....	....	....	....	....	....	....	....	....
Highland, ...	....	....	....	....	....	1	....	....	....	....	....	....	....	....	....	....	....	....
Iowa, ...	....	3	....	....	....	....	1	....	1	1	....	....	....	....	....	....	....	....
English River, ..	3	....	....	....	1	1	....	....	2	1	....	....	....	....	....	....	....	....
Lime Creek, ...	....	....	1	....	....	1	....	....	2	1	....	....	....	....	....	....	....	....
Total, ...	17	15	1	2	1	9	7	3	9	18	2	8	1	1	1	1	1	1

TABLE—Continued,

SHOWING THE PROFESSIONS, TRADES OR OCCUPATIONS OF THE INHABITANTS OF WASHINGTON COUNTY, FOR 1856.

TOWNSHIPS.	Horse doctors.	Sheriffs.	Surveyors.	Liverymen.	Engine Makers.	Seamstresses.	Dairymen	Dress makers.	Wheelwrights.	Mail carriers.	Broom makers.	Railroad contract'rs	Hedgers.	Lime burners.	Tanners.	Jobbers.	Peddlers.	Diggers.
Washington,																		
Town of Wash'n,	1	1	1	1	1													
Clay,						3	6	1	1									
Brighton,										1								
Marion,											1							
Crawford,																		
Oregon,																		
Franklin,						1												
Dutch Creek,												4	1					
Seventy-Six,																		
Cedar,																		
Jackson,																		
Highland,														1	1			
Iowa,								1										
English River,	1															1	1	1
Lime Creek,						1			1		1							
Total,	2	1	1	1	1	5	6	2	2	1	2	4	1	1	1	1	1	1

TABLE,

SHOWING THE PLACE OF NATIVITY OF THE INHABITANTS OF WASHINGTON COUNTY, FOR 1856.

STATES.	NAME OF TOWNSHIPS.																
	Washington.	Town of Washington.	Clay.	Brighton.	Marion.	Crawford.	Oregon.	Franklin.	Dutch Creek.	Seventy-Six.	Cedar.	Jackson.	Highland.	Iowa.	English River.	Lime Creek.	TOTAL.
Ohio, ...	167	360	196	374	148	252	94	143	237	74	223	131	64	160	313	184	3120
Indiana, ...	64	56	34	86	57	41	87	38	53	4	48	28	26	61	75	100	858
Pennsylvania,....	102	187	62	114	51	195	99	103	153	10	47	99	30	68	38	31	1389
Iowa, ...	174	178	181	292	129	207	89	82	169	11	130	59	58	218	253	140	2370
New York,.......	17	61	28	33	11	18	11	15	28	8	12	8	25	35	15	83	408
Maine,...........	....	5	1	8	....	2	11	....	1	3	1	....	9	2	7	10	60
New Hampshire..	....	2	1	2	....	3	....	1	1	....	....	....	1	1	....	....	12
Vermont, ...	....	5	18	14	1	4	....	6	2	1	9	5	1	7	27	15	115
Massachusetts, ...	....	7	5	14	2	3	1	....	12	2	....	3	....	2	11	16	78
Connecticut,......	1	8	13	8	1	3	....	2	8	3	2	6	1	1	....	6	63
Rhode Island,....	....	2	....	1	....	1	....	....	....	....	....	....	....	....	....	....	4
Virginia,.........	115	55	21	34	11	27	7	24	19	9	55	24	3	35	63	62	564
Kentucky, ...	34	32	18	30	16	10	11	15	16	1	29	10	33	10	17	25	307
Illinois, ...	20	42	11	30	8	12	11	10	14	...	41	15	4	22	54	78	372
Michigan,........	....	1	....	1	....	....	....	....	8	....	....	....	....	4	10	5	29
Arkansas, ...	....	....	1	3	....	....	....	....	....	....	....	....	....	....	....	1	5
Alabama, ...	....	2	....	....	....	....	....	....	1	....	1	....	....	....	....	....	4
Louisiana,.......	....	....	....	....	....	19	2	....	....	....	....	....	....	1	....	....	22
Mississippi, ...	....	....	1	....	....	....	....	....	1	....	....	....	....	1	....	....	3
North Carolina,..	1	....	14	5	2	8	....	2	1	....	1	....	1	1	....	7	43
South Carolina,...	2	....	....	2	....	....	....	....	1	....	....	....	....	1	1	....	7
Tennessee, ...	9	5	15	16	2	43	36	1	1	....	....	....	10	7	....	5	150
Missouri,.........	....	2	....	3	....	2	....	....	6	....	3	....	2	2	3	11	34
Chili, ...	....	....	....	....	....	....	....	....	....	....	1	....	....	....	....	....	1
Minnesota, ...	....	....	....	....	....	....	....	....	1	....	....	....	....	....	....	....	1
Georgia, ...	2	....	....	2	....	....	....	1	....	....	....	....	....	1	....	....	6
Maryland,........	26	15	2	9	4	6	4	3	11	4	21	8	5	9	1	15	143
New Jersey,......	....	3	5	13	1	11	1	3	3	....	10	2	5	10	....	....	67
England,.........	2	9	15	4	1	10	3	1	11	1	1	....	2	1	....	4	65
Ireland,..........	18	30	1	6	6	36	11	2	23	2	1	6	12	14	1	10	179
Wales, ...	....	1	....	....	....	....	....	....	....	....	....	....	....	2	....	....	3
Scotland,.........	3	6	....	....	....	....	....	8	2	....	4	....	....	1	....	....	24
Germany,........	2	4	....	4	5	4	....	....	55	....	1	2	7	43	72	31	230
France, ...	14	21	....	....	41	3	14	....	12	....	2	....	....	76	3	....	186
Austria, ...	....	....	....	....	....	....	....	....	7	....	....	....	....	....	....	....	7
Russia,...........	....	....	....	....	2	....	....	....	....	....	....	....	....	....	....	....	2
Prussia,..........	....	....	....	....	....	....	....	....	8	....	....	....	....	9	2	1	20
Sweden, ...	....	....	....	....	....	....	....	....	....	....	....	....	....	1	....	....	1
On the Ocean,....	....	....	....	....	....	....	....	....	1	....	....	....	....	1	....	1	3
Canada,..........	....	15	....	1	37	5	....	8	5	...	....	....	....	3	....	....	74
New Brunswick, .	....	1	....	....	....	....	....	....	1	....	....	....	....	....	....	....	2
Switzerland,......	....	7	....	....	12	3	....	1	....	....	....	....	1	1	....	1	26
Hanover,.........	....	....	....	....	....	....	....	....	....	....	....	....	....	6	....	....	6
Saxony, ...	....	....	....	....	....	....	....	....	....	....	....	....	....	1	....	....	1
Wisconsin, ...	1	....	4	....	....	....	1	....	3	2	1	....	....	....	....	....	12
Unknown, ...	....	4	....	....	....	14	....	....	....	....	....	....	....	....	....	....	18
Delaware,........	....	....	1	....	....	....	....	....	....	....	7	1	1	1	....	....	11
Bavaria, ...	....	....	....	....	....	....	....	....	4	....	1	....	....	....	....	....	5
Baden,...........	....	....	....	....	....	....	....	....	1	....	....	....	....	....	....	....	1
Poland, ...	....	....	....	....	....	....	1	....	1	....	....	....	....	....	....	....	2

TABLE,

SHOWING THE POPULATION OF WAYNE COUNTY, FOR 1856.

TOWNSHIPS.	No. of dwelling houses.	Number of families.	Number of males.	Number of females.	Colored.	Married.	Widowed.	Native voters.	Naturalized voters.	Aliens.	Militia.	Deaf and Dumb.	Blind.	Insane.	Idiotic.	Owners of land.	Paupers.
Wright,.........	75	77	192	181	....	139	7	77	....	2	71	1	2	....	1	73	....
Union,.........	62	70	225	203	....	137	6	92	....	1	56	....	....	....	1	64	....
Washington,.....	52	52	165	133	....	103	6	43	3	5	38	....	....	....	....	43	....
Richmond,.......	21	21	70	58	....	36	5	24	....	....	18	....	....	....	1	22	....
Clay,...........	27	27	68	57	....	46	3	32	....	....	25	1	....	....	....	26	....
Benton,.........	85	85	261	259	....	168	4	86	7	....	77	....	....	....	....	74	4
Corydon,........	84	89	239	231	1	177	4	101	1	1	86	....	....	....	....	93	....
South Fork,.....	44	46	149	117	....	78	6	42	....	1	34	....	....	....	....	35	....
Monroe,.........	61	67	222	175	....	143	3	79	2	1	86	....	....	....	....	68	....
Medicine,.......	87	87	257	222	....	179	5	82	....	1	79	....	....	....	....	73	....
Jackson,........	34	33	99	58	....	52	4	27	1	6	30	....	....	....	....	31	....
Grand River,....	56	56	158	163	....	102	7	59	2	....	53	....	....	....	1	51	....
Jefferson,......	43	43	116	105	....	72	6	50	....	....	47	....	....	....	....	39	....
Total,.........	731	753	2221	1962	1	1432	63	794	16	18	700	2	2	....	4	692	4

TABLE,

SHOWING THE AGRICULTURAL STATISTICS OF WAYNE COUNTY, FOR 1856.

TOWNSHIPS.	Acres of improved land.	Acres of unimproved land.	Acres of meadow.	Tons of hay.	Bushels of grass seed	Acres of spring wheat.	Bushels harvested.	Acres winter wheat.	Bushels harvested.	Acres of oats.	Bushels harvested.	Acres of corn.	Bushels harvested.	Acres of potatoes.	Bushels harvested.
Wright, ...	2076	6478	48	186	13	330	2692	136	216	311	5180	842	24750	16	1041
Union, ...	969	7929	92	6	....	78	332	7	48	56	1200	537	13385	12	1155
Washington, ..	1706	8684	....	....	....	91	839	....	.....	149	4228	1010	21950	2	850
Richmond, ...	938	2855	....	....	....	.....	......	....	.....	24	470	177	3400	2	265
Clay, ...	645	3549	....	....	....	30	200	....	.....	26	1035	239	5140	1	80
Benton, ...	3076	9233	34	6	....	170	1298	74	251	250	6795	1141	32462	35	1657
Corydon, ...	1563	12508	17	8	....	82	335	17	105	80	1603	579	14180	15	1413
South Fork, ..	766	5547	1	....	....	68	559	19	50	78	1527	353	11605	....	304
Monroe, ...	2811	12119	3	1	....	121	735	168	321	245	8205	829	28716	10	1149
Medicine, ...	1671	9186	1	1	....	79	451	7	44	98	2775	1249	20355	2	175
Jackson, ...	785	7073	2	....	....	27	214	24	230	40	1360	372	9580	5	368
Grand River, .	1677	8383	82	25	9	93	624	29	285	435	9125	736	24920	6	572
Jefferson, ...	1073	6304	....	....	....	14	65	5	50	83	990	563	7810	5	486
Total, ...	19756	99849	280	233	22	1187	8344	486	1600	1875	44493	8617	218253	111	10515

TABLE,

SHOWING THE NUMBER AND VALUE OF HOGS AND CATTLE SOLD, THE VALUE OF DOMESTIC AND GENERAL MANUFACTURES OF WAYNE COUNTY, FOR 1856.

TOWNSHIPS.	No. of hogs sold.	Value of hogs sold	Number of cattle sold.	Value of cattle sold.	Pounds of butter made.	Pounds of cheese.	Pounds of wool.	Value of domestic manufactures.	Value of general manufactures.
Wright, ...	223	1809	87	2438	4911	88	461	300	....
Union, ...	55	374	62	1032	2263	50	179	94	....
Washington, ...	129	908	58	1354	4260	50	210	986	....
Richmond, ...	8	39	22	529	884	....	52	52	....
Clay, ...	74	291	24	592	1525	50	43	50	....
Benton, ...	456	5405	181	3943	4912	218	861	679	....
Corydon, ...	151	2292	105	3072	3813	70	166	78	....
South Fork, ...	75	378	5	135	....	....	88	112	....
Monroe, ...	618	4110	151	4140	4779	80	286	326	....
Medicine, ...	77	499	137	1319	6490	800	292	105	25
Jackson, ...	100	346	59	1413	2238	....	42	140	....
Grand View, ...	233	1039	220	2688	4920	....	574	697	....
Jefferson, ...	84	514	16	614	870	292	297	170	18
Total, ...	2283	18003	1127	23269	41865	1698	3551	3789	43

TABLE,

EXHIBITING THE PROFESSIONS, TRADES, OR OCCUPATIONS OF THE INHABITANTS OF WAYNE COUNTY, FOR 1856.

OCCUPATIONS.	NAME OF TOWNSHIPS.													Total.
	Wright.	Union.	Washington	Richmond.	Clay.	Benton.	Corydon.	South Fork.	Monroe.	Medicine.	Jackson.	Grand River.	Jefferson.	
Farmers,	73	39	42	28	30	83	70	29	87	48	53	45	41	668
Laborers,	...	...	...	...	1	...	1	...	1	3	...	...	...	6
Blacksmiths,	1	2	...	...	...	4	1	...	1	1	...	...	3	13
Carpenters,	6	8	2	...	...	2	8	2	1	3	1	1	3	37
Wagon makers,	...	...	...	...	...	1	...	...	...	...	...	...	...	1
Plasterers,	...	...	...	...	...	...	1	...	...	...	...	...	...	1
Engineers,	...	...	...	...	...	...	...	1	1	...	...	...	...	2
Millers,	...	3	...	...	...	1	...	...	...	...	...	...	...	4
Sawyers,	...	1	...	...	...	...	...	3	...	...	...	...	...	4
Painters,	...	...	...	...	...	...	...	...	...	1	...	...	1	2
Cabinet makers,	...	...	...	...	...	2	...	...	...	...	...	...	...	2
Milliners,	...	...	...	...	...	...	...	...	1	...	...	...	...	1
Shoemakers,	...	1	...	...	1	...	1	1	...	2	...	1	...	7
Saddle and harness makers,	...	...	...	...	...	...	1	...	...	...	...	...	...	1
Mechanics,	...	...	...	...	...	...	...	...	...	...	1	...	...	1
Merchants,	...	3	...	...	...	1	7	...	...	1	...	1	...	13
Speculators,	...	...	...	...	...	...	...	...	...	...	...	...	1	1
Hotel keepers,	...	...	...	...	...	...	1	...	...	...	...	...	...	1
Physicians,	1	2	...	...	...	...	3	...	1	1	...	1	1	10
Lawyers,	...	...	...	...	...	...	4	...	...	...	...	1	...	5
Clergymen,	...	1	...	...	1	...	1	...	...	...	...	1	...	4
Teachers,	...	...	...	2	1	...	...	...	...	...	...	...	...	3
Musicians,	...	...	...	...	...	...	...	...	...	1	...	...	...	1
Grocers,	...	...	...	...	...	...	1	...	...	...	...	...	...	1
Brick makers,	...	...	...	...	...	...	...	...	...	...	...	1	...	1
Coopers,	...	2	...	...	1	...	...	1	...	...	...	...	...	4
Wheelwrights,	...	...	...	...	...	1	...	...	1	...	...	...	...	2
Peddlers,	...	...	...	...	...	...	1	...	...	...	...	...	...	1
Lumbermen,	...	...	...	...	...	...	1	...	...	...	...	...	...	1
Tailoresses,	...	...	...	...	...	...	...	...	1	...	...	...	...	1

TABLE,

SHOWING THE PLACE OF NATIVITY OF THE INHABITANTS OF WAYNE COUNTY, FOR 1856.

STATES.	TOWNSHIPS.													TOTAL.
	Wright.	Union.	Washington.	Richmond.	Clay.	Benton.	Corydon	South Fork.	Monroe.	Medicine.	Jackson.	Grand River.	Jefferson.	
Ohio,	22	160	52	31	29	99	105	82	83	69	49	43	37	811
Indiana,	135	93	70	31	22	98	67	82	43	111	28	24	30	784
Pennsylvania,	15	8	6	16	4	18	50	10	58	11	7	9	5	217
Iowa,	74	56	50	16	17	102	75	35	69	83	19	71	27	694
New York	2	5	13	4	7	1	12	....	7	17	1	5	7	81
Maine,	....	....	...	....	....	....	....	1	...	....	...	...	...	1
N. Hampshire,	....	....	1	....	....	....	....	1	....	8	1	...	...	11
Vermont,	....	1	....	1	....	2	2	4	....	1	...	...	...	11
Massachusetts,	....	....	1	..	1	....	....	....	....	2	...	2	4	11
Connecticut,	1	....	2	1	....	....	....	...	1	...	2	...	...	7
Virginia,	30	23	28	7	16	107	71	66	17	16	5	9	8	403
Kentucky,	35	6	12	4	...	17	23	2	8	46	5	66	43	267
Illinois,	37	20	8	10	6	38	34	14	29	77	9	26	36	344
Michigan,	....	....	8	6	3	....	....	....	3	7	...	...	...	27
Arkansas,	....	....	1	....	....	....	....	....	....	....	...	...	...	1
Alabama,	....	....	....	....	....	....	1	....	....	....	...	...	...	1
Mississippi,	....	....	1	....	....	....	....	....	....	....	...	...	...	1
North Carolina,	7	22	6	1	2	7	2	2	100	2	...	1	7	159
South Carolina,	....	2	....	....	....	....	....	....	....	1	...	...	...	3
Tennessee,	3	9	12	....	9	5	11	4	17	10	11	22	7	120
Missouri,	7	12	11	....	....	....	5	7	3	8	1	30	6	90
Georgia,	....	....	....	....	....	....	....	....	....	....	...	...	1	1
Maryland,	....	3	....	....	6	4	....	....	1	6	1	1	2	24
New Jersey,	....	1	....	....	....	2	1	1	....	....	...	3	...	8
England,	5	3	2	....	....	7	1	2	....	....	12	...	1	33
Ireland,	....	4	4	....	....	....	4	....	5	1	...	6	...	24
Wales,	....	...	4	....	....	....	....	....	....	....	...	...	...	4
Scotland,	....	....	....	....	....	....	....	....	....	....	2	...	...	2
Germany,	....	....	4	....	3	10	2	....	3	1	...	...	...	23
Holland,	....	....	....	....	....	....	....	....	....	1	...	...	...	1
Canada,	....	....	1	....	....	....	....	....	....	....	...	3	...	4
Switzerland,	....	....	1	....	....	....	....	....	....	....	...	...	...	1
Unknown,	....	....	....	....	....	1	....	3	....	....	4	...	...	8
Delaware,	....	....	....	....	....	2	1	....	....	1	...	...	...	4
Kansas Ter.,	....	....	....	....	....	....	1	....	....	....	...	...	...	1
Wisconsin,	....	....	....	....	....	....	1	....	....	....	...	...	...	1

TABLE,

SHOWING THE POPULATION OF WEBSTER COUNTY, FOR 1856.

TOWNSHIPS.	No. dwelling houses.	Number of families.	Number of males	Number of females.	Colored.	Married.	Widowed.	Native voters.	Naturalized voters.	Aliens.	Militia.	Deaf and dumb.	Blind.	Insane.	Idiotic.	Owners of land.	Paupers.
Webster,	170	171	515	460	....	298	10	195	9	....	10	....	1	....	....	130	....
Wakonsa,	112	112	452	277	....	240	14	209	83	9	280	....	....	....	....	....	....
Hardin,	27	27	74	62	....	34	1	16	2	12	14	....	....	....	....	28	....
Clear Lake,	13	16	40	40	....	24	....	15	1	9	5	....	....	....	....	29	....
Boone,	46	48	186	102	....	106	6	103	4	4	89	....	....	....	....	55	....
Cass,	47	47	154	140	....	100	11	65	5	...	61	....	....	....	....	52	....
Yell,	63	63	189	160	....	126	4	63	5	...	46	....	....	....	....	47	....
Humbolt,	8	8	30	13	....	8	1	12	3	1	14	....	....	....	....	2	....
Washington,	35	39	117	77	....	67	4	49	4	4	47	....	....	....	....	50	....
Total,	521	531	1757	1331	....	10 3	51	727	116	39	566	....	1	....	....	393	....

TABLE,

SHOWING THE AGRICULTURAL STATISTICS OF WEBSTER COUNTY FOR 1856.

TOWNSHIPS.	Acres of improved land.	Acres of unimproved land.	Acres of meadow.	Tons of hay.	Bushels of grass seed.	Acres spring wheat.	Bushels harvested.	Acres winter wheat.	Bushels harvested.	Acres of oats.	Bushels harvested.	Acres of corn.	Bushels harvested.	Acres of potatoes.	Bushels harvested.
Webster,.........	1518	16268	15	120	3	101	1090	2	37	61	1370	568	17114	16	814
Wakonsa,.........	....	......	....	....	....	....	......	....	.....	....	.....	.....	......	....	....
Hardin,..........	599	3734	1	325	1	11	93	13	150	18	260	317	8590	15	992
Clear Lake,.......	142	1833	....	....	....	....	......	....	.....	....	.....	41	475	1	95
Boone,............	500	12997	50	83	....	19	330	....	.....	13	445	392	11780	5	960
Cass,.............	934	5700	2	....	....	65	918	2	50	39	1040	392	15045	12	1947
Yell,.............	....	......	....	....	....	....	......	....	.....	....	.....	.....	......	....	....
Humbolt,.........	6	189	....	62	....	....	......	....	.....	....	.....	25	500	2	300
Washington, ...	734	3654	1	485	....	44	597	....	.....	13	300	398	10265	5	1505
Total,..........	4433	44375	69	1075	4	240	3028	17	236	144	3415	2133	63769	56	6613

TABLE,

OWING THE NUMBER AND VALUE OF HOGS AND CATTLE SOLD, AND THE VALUE OF DOMESTIC AND GENERAL MANUFACTURES OF WEBSTER COUNTY FOR 1856.

TOWNSHIPS.	Number of hogs sold.	Value of hogs sold.	Number of cattle sold.	Value of cattle sold.	Pounds of butter made.	Pounds of cheese.	Pounds of wool.	Value of domestic manufactures.	Value of gen'l manufactures.
Webster,	215	2159	158	3265	6306	285	48	4	300
Wakonsa,	....	....	....	....	....	....	....	....	....
Hardin,	404	3061	76	1346	526	52	78	76	600
Clear Lake,	3	27	4	200	150	....	....	....	....
Boone,	58	488	78	2174	725	....	45	....	....
Cass,	120	1644	191	2402	4170	80	9	82	....
Yell,	....	....	....	....	....	....	....	....	....
Humbolt,	5	25	7	600	1825	....	....	....	....
Washington,	84	845	77	2456	5605	50	223	79	350
Total,	889	8249	591	12443	19307	467	403	241	1250

TABLE,

EXHIBITING THE PROFESSIONS, TRADES, OR OCCUPATIONS OF THE INHABITANTS OF WEBSTER COUNTY, FOR 1856.

OCCUPATIONS.	NAME OF TOWNSHIPS.									TOTAL.
	Webster.	Wakonsa.	Hardin.	Clear Lake.	Boone.	Cass.	Yell.	Humbolt.	Washington.	
Farmers,	128	134	26	14	41	57	62	15	64	541
Laborers,	1	45			15				1	62
Blacksmiths,	4	2	1	1	3		5		1	17
Carpenters,	12	25	3		13	4	3		4	64
Wagon makers,		1			2					3
Plasterers,	1									1
Stone mrsons,		10								10
Machinists,	1				1					2
Engineers,		3			3					6
Millers,	7	4			1		1		2	15
Sawyers,	1				2					3
Millwrlghts,					1	2				3
Cabinet makers,	1	1			3		2			7
Tinners,		4								4
Milliners,						3				3
Tailors,	2	1	3			1	1			8
Shoe makers,	2	3	1			1			1	8
Saddle & harness makers,									1	1
Mechanics,					1					1
Merchants,	6	6	1	1	6		1			21
Speculators,			1							1
Agents,		24			1					25
Hotel keepers,		1			3					4
Physicians,	3	2			4					9
Lawyers,		10			1					11
Clergymen,	1					1			1	3
Teachers,					1	1			1	3
Printers,		1								1
Daguerrean artists,					1					1
Bankers,		8			2	1				11
Teamsters,		2				1				3
Jewellers,	1	1								2
Coopers,	1	2		1	2	1				7
Clerks,	2	5								7
Surveyors,	2	4			1			1		8
Moulders,	1									1
United States Registers,		1								1
United States Receivers,		1								1
Stage drivers,		1			1					2
Nurserymen,		1								1
Drovers,		1								1
Livery keepers,		1								1
Trappers,		1								1
Wheelwrights,		1								1
Ship carpenters,					1					1
Seamen,					1					1
Traders,					1					1
Lumbermen,					1					1
Weavers,						1				1
Dyers,						1				1

TABLE,

SHOWING THE PLACE OF NATIVITY OF THE INHABITANTS OF WEBSTER COUNTY, FOR 1856.

STATES.	NAME OF TOWNSHIPS.									TOTAL.
	Webster.	Wakonsa.	Hardin.	Clear Lake.	Boone.	Cass.	Yell.	Humbolt.	Washington.	
Ohio,	47	104	12	12	58	59	82	9	17	400
Indiana,	34	68	17	11	29	11	84	1	18	273
Pennsylvania,	38	79	2	4	29	58	17	7	8	289
Iowa,	6	70	28	6	23	28	52	3	31	247
New York,	15	112	2	8	35	31	2	1	38	244
Maine,	1	27	....	6	3	....	....	....	1	38
N. Hampshire,	1	4	....	1	....	....	....	....	....	6
Vermont,	2	30	....	1	8	4	1	....	2	48
Massachusetts,	3	12	....	1	18	5	1	1	....	41
Connecticut,	....	6	....	....	3	4	2	....	7	22
Rhode Island,	....	....	....	....	....	1	....	....	....	1
Virginia,	16	11	1	2	13	8	6	1	7	60
Kentucky,	21	4	6	....	8	2	9	1	7	58
Illinois,	9	28	3	11	31	50	20	9	39	200
Michigan,	....	3	....	4	3	7	....	....	....	17
Louisiana,	....	1	....	....	....	....	....	....	....	1
N. Carolina,	3	2	....	....	6	2	6	....	5	24
S. Carolina,	1	1	....	....	....	....	....	....	....	2
Tennessee,	6	3	6	9	2	7	15	....	1	49
Missouri,	3	5	....	....	....	....	20	2	1	31
Georgia,	....	1	....	....	....	....	....	....	....	1
Maryland,	3	3	3	....	....	....	4	....	1	14
New Jersey,	3	....	....	....	5	3	1	3	....	15
England,	5	4	....	....	4	1	....	....	2	16
Ireland,	1	95	....	2	6	8	....	1	5	118
Wales,	....	....	....	....	....	....	....	....	1	1
Scotland,	1	5	....	....	1	4	....	2	....	13
Germany,	....	40	....	....	1	2	11	....	....	54
France,	....	....	....	....	....	1	....	....	....	1
Russia,	....	....	....	....	....	....	....	....	1	1
Norway,	....	1	1	....	....	....	....	....	....	2
Sweden,	....	2	54	....	....	....	14	....	....	70
On the Ocean,	....	1	....	....	....	....	....	....	....	1
Canada,	....	7	....	1	3	3	....	1	2	17
New Brunswick,	....	....	....	....	....	1	....	....	....	1
Saxony,	....	....	....	....	....	....	....	1	....	1
Unknown,	755	....	....	....	....	1	....	....	....	756
Delaware,	1	....	1	....	....	1	1	....	....	4
Wisconsin,	....	....	....	1	2	2	1	....	....	6

TABLE,

SHOWING THE POPULATION OF WINNESHEIK COUNTY, FOR 1856.

TOWNSHIPS.	No dwelling houses.	Number of familes	Number of males	Number of females.	Colored.	Married.	Widowed.	Native voters.	Naturalized voters.	Aliens.	Militia.	Deaf and dumb.	Blind.	Insane.	Idiotic.	Owners of land.	Paupers.
Decorah, ...	108	108	334	248	....	227	7	37	25	85	123	....	....	....	1	102	....
Freeport Village, .	34	34	132	109	....	96	1	56	5	6	62	....	....	....	....	39	....
Decorah Village, .	126	126	484	281	....	208	8	196	21	65	295	....	....	....	....	190	....
Summit, ...	85	87	295	229	....	177	7	76	28	17	94	....	....	....	....	82	....
Bloomfield, ...	109	123	347	302	....	234	11	125	8	13	111	....	....	....	....	114	....
Military, ...	158	158	394	374	....	313	5	49	59	86	135	....	....	....	1	164	1
Washington, ...	239	258	614	528	....	438	7	21	78	....	....	....	....	....	....	139	1
Glenwood, ...	110	110	293	259	....	212	15	30	20	55	93	....	1	....	3	102	....
Canoe, ...	87	87	258	213	....	168	4	91	19	16	107	....	....	....	....	90	....
Burr Oak, ...	186	186	435	387	....	284	12	139	23	....	....	....	....	1	2	116	....
Fremont, ...	101	101	280	241	....	201	5	29	8	3	86	....	....	....	....	97	....
Pilot Grove, ...	51	54	158	115	....	100	3	49	11	....	33	....	....	....	....	3	....
Blufton, ...	41	42	104	92	....	79	2	31	10	....	....	....	....	....	....	32	....
Total, ...	1435	1474	4128	3378	....	2737	87	929	315	356	1140	...	1	1	7	1270	2

TABLE,

SHOWING THE AGRICULTURAL STATISTICS OF WINNESHEIK COUNTY, FOR 1856.

TOWNSHIPS	Acres of improved land.	Acres of unimproved land.	Acres of meadow	Tons of Hay.	Bushels of grass seed.	Acres of spring wheat.	Bushels harvested.	Acres of winter wheat.	Bushels harvested.	Acres of oats	Bushels hatvested.	Acres of corn.	Bushels harvested.	Acres of potatoes.	Bushels harvested.
Decorah, ...	1486	9940	....	....	....	8	240	....	....	....	....	....	....	....	....
Freeport Vil., .	125	215	....	....	....	....	....	....	....	....	....	....	....	....	....
Decorah Vil., .	34	415	....	....	....	....	....	....	....	....	....	....	....	....	....
Summit, ...	5511	10945	240	1047	52	1498	35174	....	....	708	47415	897	37930	42	3485
Bloomfield, ...	3891	11911	13	11	2	858	15505	45	1010	181	6502	491	17840	23	2773
Military, ...	2898	22106	1132	1717	....	1027	19344	....	....	194	6262	357	14030	41	4707
Washington, ...	2168	12808	100	50	....	472	10236	....	....	126	4302	341	12605	24	4111
Glenwood, ...	1012	10359	15	21	....	416	7671	....	....	44	1415	242	10061	31	2467
Canoe, ...	3018	8152	168	294	2	470	9338	....	....	115	4856	409	16391	28	2753
Burr Oak, ...	2806	16045	43	1143	74	1099	12474	13	96	288	7214	895	24770	66	6111
Fremont, ...	1704	18168	228	918	....	1274	10234	....	....	148	6552	247	5800	7	524
Pilot Grove, ...	205	975	....	....	....	6	156	....	....	....	....	46	990	1	125
Blufton, ...	172	4502	....	691	....	173	....	....	....	....	....	15	....	....	....
Total, ...	25031	117542	1939	5892	130	7303	120362	58	1106	1807	84518	3941	140417	265	27056

TABLE,

SHOWING THE NUMBER AND VALUE OF HOGS, CATTLE, DOMESTIC AND GENERAL MANUFACTURES OF WINNESHEIK COUNTY, FOR 1856.

TOWNSHIPS.	No. of hogs sold.	Value of hogs sold.	No. of cattle sold.	Value of cattle sold.	Pounds of butter made.	Pounds of cheese.	Pounds of Wool.	Value of domestic Manufactures.	Value of general Manufactures.
Decorah, }	....	....	....	....	....	....	....	....	....
Freeport Vill'ge, }	....	....	....	....	....	....	....	....	....
Decorah Village, }	....	....	....	....	....	....	....	....	....
Summit, ...	465	6363	194	6141	5600	....	1504	85	....
Bloomfield, ...	131	816	114	5189	12327	2203	1325	785	240
Military, ...	148	1136	160	7034	16810	....	154	908	1845
Washington, ...	94	4858	101	3967	6709	1650	645	....	....
Glenwood, ...	108	806	79	1601	5026	190	318	....	20
Canoe, ...	104	1257	51	1909	8056	885	258	....	100
Burr Oak, ...	235	2692	219	10053	14481	3040	1418	420	950
Eremont, ...	100	1276	39	1706	330	....	50	....	....
Pilot Grove, ...	....	....	16	765	554	....	....	....	....
Blufton, ...	27	431	14	460	2690	....	....	....	....
Total, ...	1408	19636	987	38825	72583	7968	5672	2198	3155

TABLE,

SHOWIG THE PROFESSIONS, TRADES, OR OCCUPATIONS OF THE INHABITANTS OF WINNESHEIK COUNTY FOR 1856.

TOWNSHIPS.	Farmers.	Laborers.	Blacksmiths.	Carpenters.	Wagon makers.	Plasterers.	Stone masons.	Machinists.	Engineers.	Millers.	Sawyers.	Millwrights.	Painters.	Cabinet makers.	Tinners.	Milliners.	Tailors.	Hatters.	Shoe makers.	Harness makers.	Butchers.
Decorah,	133	4	2	1	...	...	...	...	...	1	...	...	...	1	...	...	1	...	...	...	...
Freeport Village,	7	4	4	16	2	...	1	...	...	4	2	...	...	1	...	...	3	...	2	1	...
Decorah Village,	30	31	7	40	1	1	10	...	1	2	2	...	2	2	2	1	2	...	6	7	1
Summit,	102	11	2	3	11	...	...	...	...	...	...	...	...	...	...	2	1	...	1	...	...
Bloomfield,	128	14	6	12	1	...	2	...	1	1	1	...	...	...	...	...	...	...	1	...	...
Military,	131	16	...	...	...	...	...	...	...	...	1	...	...	...	...	...	1	...	...	...	...
Washington,	57	...	4	2	...	...	...	...	...	1	...	...	1	...	...	...	...	...	7	...	...
Greenwood,	77	40	...	...	...	...	...	...	...	1	...	...	...	...	...	...	...	...	...	...	...
Canoe,	64	16	1	8	...	...	1	...	...	6	1	1	...	1	...	...	...	...	2	...	...
Burr Oak,	177	...	4	10	1	...	2	2	1	1	1	1	...	...	...	...	...	1	3	1	...
Fremont,	83	...	1	4	...	...	1	...	...	...	...	...	...	...	...	...	...	...	...	...	...
Pilot Grove,	62	...	...	2	...	...	...	...	...	...	...	...	...	...	...	...	...	...	...	...	...
Blufton,	31	...	1	2	...	...	2	...	...	2	...	1	...	...	...	...	...	...	...	...	...
Total,	1082	136	32	100	16	1	19	2	3	19	8	3	3	5	2	3	8	1	22	9	1

TABLE—Continued,

EXHIBITING THE PROFESSIONS, TRADES, OR OCCUPATIONS OF THE INHABITANTS OF WINNESHIEK COUNTY, FOR 1856.

TOWNSHIPS.	Manufacturers.	Merchants.	Speculators.	Agents.	Traders.	Boarding House Keepers	Hotel Keepers.	Physicians.	Lawyers.	Clergymen.	Teachers.	Printers.	Editors.	Artists.	Bankers.	Grocers.	Teamsters.	Watch makers.	Jewelers.	Gun Smiths.	Coopers.	Clerks.
Decora,	...	1	...	...	...	...	...	1	...	...	...	...	...	...	...	...	...	3	...	...	...	...
Freeport Vill.,	...	6	...	...	...	...	...	1	...	1	2	...	...	...	...	...	...	...	...	1	2	...
Decora Vill'ge	...	23	...	18	...	...	1	5	8	...	...	3	1	1	8	1	5	...	...	1	...	11
Summit,	...	3	...	...	...	...	1	1	...	1	3	...	...	...	...	...	...	...	...	...	...	2
Bloomfield,	1	2	...	...	...	...	...	3	...	...	...	...	...	...	...	...	...	...	...	...	...	...
Military,	...	1	...	...	2	...	...	1	...	...	...	...	...	...	...	...	...	...	...	...	...	...
Washington,	...	10	1	...	...	...	...	1	...	...	...	...	...	...	...	...	...	...	...	...	1	...
Glenwood,	...	...	...	...	...	...	...	1	...	...	...	...	...	...	...	...	...	...	...	...	...	...
Canoe,	...	...	...	...	...	...	...	...	...	1	1	...	...	...	...	...	...	...	...	...	...	...
Burr Oak,	...	4	...	...	...	1	...	...	...	...	...	...	...	...	...	...	...	...	1	...	...	...
Fremont,	2	...	...	...	...	...	...	...	...	...	...	...	...	...	...	...	...	...	...	...	...	...
Pilot Grove,	...	...	...	...	...	...	...	...	...	...	...	...	...	...	...	...	...	...	...	...	...	...
Blufton,	...	1	...	...	...	...	...	...	...	...	...	...	...	...	...	...	...	...	...	...	2	...
Total,	3	51	1	18	2	1	2	14	8	3	6	3	1	1	8	1	5	3	1	2	5	13

TABLE—Continued,

SHOWING THE PROFESSIONS, TRADES, OR OCCUPATIONS OF THE INHABITANTS OF WINNESHIEK COUNTY, FOR 1856.

TOWNSHIPS.	Lumber men.	County Judges.	County Recorder.	Plough makers.	Surveyors.	Constables.	Domestic.	Barbers.	Lime burners.	Sheriff.	Registers.	Land Office Receivers.	Livery Stable Keepers.	Justices.	Postmasters.	Pilots.	Mariners.	Miners.	Prairie breakers.	Colliers.	Founders.	Moulders.
Decora,	1	...	...	...	...	...	...	...	...	...	...	...	...	...	...	...	...	...	...	...	...	...
Freeport Vill'ge	...	...	...	...	...	...	...	...	...	...	...	...	...	...	...	...	...	...	...	...	...	...
Decora Village,	...	1	1	1	2	1	2	1	1	1	1	1	2	1	...	...	...	...	...	...	...	...
Summit,	...	...	...	...	...	...	...	...	...	...	...	...	...	...	1	...	...	...	...	...	...	...
Bloomfield,	1	...	...	...	...	...	...	...	...	...	...	...	...	...	...	1	1	...	...	...	...	...
Military,	...	...	...	...	...	...	...	...	...	...	...	...	...	...	...	...	...	1	...	...	...	...
Washington,	...	...	...	...	...	...	...	...	...	...	...	...	...	...	...	...	...	...	...	...	...	...
Glenwood,	...	...	...	...	...	...	...	...	...	...	...	...	...	...	...	...	...	...	...	...	...	...
Canoe,	...	...	...	...	1	...	...	...	...	...	...	...	...	...	...	...	...	...	...	...	...	...
Burr Oak,	...	...	...	...	...	...	...	...	...	...	...	...	...	...	...	...	...	...	1	1	...	...
Fremont,	...	...	...	...	...	...	...	...	...	...	...	...	...	...	...	...	...	...	...	...	1	1
Pilot Grove,	...	...	...	...	...	...	...	...	...	...	...	...	...	...	...	...	...	...	...	...	...	...
Blufton,	...	...	...	...	...	...	...	...	...	...	...	...	...	...	...	...	...	...	...	...	...	...
Total,	2	1	1	1	3	1	2	1	1	1	1	1	2	1	1	1	1	1	1	1	1	1

TABLE,

SHOWING THE PLACE OF NATIVITY OF THE INHABITANTS OF WINNESHEIK COUNTY, FOR 1856.

STATES.	NAME OF TOWNSHIPS.													
	Decora.	Freeport Vill'e.	Decora Vill'e.	Summit.	Bloomfield.	Military.	Washington.	Glenwood.	Canoe.	Burr oak.	Fremont.	Pilot Grove.	Blufton.	TOTAL.
Ohio,	21	7	87	43	131	19	46	29	58	31	22	23	8	525
Indiana,	3	5	24	40	65	...	52	1	8	5	28	35	4	260
Pennsylvania,	28	38	36	56	38	24	37	14	41	45	47	15	7	426
Iowa,	75	20	60	62	73	125	85	75	44	21	54	7	11	712
New York,	41	73	186	70	100	94	59	57	71	131	11	54	42	989
Maine,	2	1	7	....	3	2	1	....	4	3	...	...	...	23
New Hampshire,	1	1	4	4	2	3	5	....	15	3	6	6	2	52
Vermont,	16	....	4	29	13	9	15	8	19	51	3	22	2	191
Massachusetts,	7	3	10	4	7	5	2	3	5	13	...	14	6	79
Connecticut,	3	23	5	7	16	2	1	1	3	22	1	6	4	94
Rhode Island,	1	2	...	....	1	1	2	1	....	3	...	...	...	11
Virginia,	6	13	40	3	25	1	7	....	4	17	1	10	3	130
Kentucky,	1	1	1	2	1	....	....	....	5	...	1	...	2	14
Illinois,	33	3	49	9	32	4	86	28	35	34	14	36	29	342
Michigan,	8	1	17	5	3	3	8	6	8	7	5	...	...	71
Alabama,	....	....	2	....	....	....	....	....	....	...	...	...	...	2
Louisiana,	....	....	1	....	....	....	....	....	2	...	...	...	...	3
Mississippi,	1	....	3	....	....	....	....	....	....	...	...	...	...	4
North Carolina,	2	1	....	....	....	....	....	1	1	6	1	4	...	16
Tennessee,	....	....	....	....	2	....	....	....	1	2	...	...	...	5
Missouri,	....	9	....	....	....	....	....	....	1	...	...	...	...	10
Georgia,	....	....	1	....	....	....	....	....	1	...	...	...	...	2
Maryland,	....	....	4	1	1	....	4	....	1	1	...	...	...	12
New Jersey,	....	....	4	1	2	....	3	5	4	7	2	...	...	28
England,	10	11	22	1	5	1	7	6	18	13	4	21	16	135
Ireland,	30	1	38	19	15	15	44	42	23	20	10	7	27	291
Scotland,	2	....	3	1	....	1	7	1	....	3	...	...	...	18
Germany,	2	....	12	1	1	25	223	5	8	3	5	2	...	290
France,	....	....	2	2	1	....	33	1	1	...	18	...	...	58
Austria,	....	....	....	....	....	....	164	....	....	...	...	...	...	164
Russia,	....	....	3	....	....	....	....	....	....	...	...	...	...	3
Prussia,	....	....	....	....	....	8	5	....	4	...	...	...	...	17
Norway,	230	17	90	58	1	340	174	225	41	30	228	...	17	1451
Sweden,	....	....	....	....	....	....	11	....	....	...	...	...	...	11
Canada,	10	8	24	84	73	38	19	10	20	57	4	3	3	348
New Brunswick,	....	....	....	1	....	....	....	....	....	...	...	...	...	1
Switzerland,	....	....	....	....	....	....	39	....	....	...	...	...	...	39
Denmark,	....	....	....	....	....	....	1	....	....	...	...	...	...	1
West Indies,	....	....	....	....	....	....	1	....	....	...	...	...	...	1
Wisconsin,	49	8	20	20	46	48	23	32	19	15	56	6	13	355
Delaware,	....	....	....	1	2	....	....	....	....	...	...	2	...	5
Minnesota,	....	....	....	....	....	....	....	1	....	...	...	...	...	1
Poland,	....	....	....	....	....	....	....	....	6	...	...	...	...	6
Dis. Columbia,	....	....	....	....	....	....	1	....	....	...	...	...	...	1
Unknown,	....	....	....	....	....	....	24	....	....	285	...	...	...	309

TABLE,

SHOWING THE POPULATION, AGRICULTURAL STATISTICS, THE NUMBER AND VALUE OF HOGS AND CATTLE SOLD, THE VALUE OF DOMESTIC AND GENERAL MANUFACTURES, OF WRIGHT COUNTY, FOR 1856.

POPULATION.	NAME OF TOWNSHIPS.				TOTAL.
	Troy.	Eagle Grove.	Liberty.	Pleasant.	
No. dwelling houses,	18	16	18	34	86
Number of families,	17	18	18	38	91
Number of males,	40	39	35	115	229
Number of females,	35	34	42	87	198
Married,	28	37	30	69	164
Widowed,	1	......	......	3	4
Native voters,	17	21	14	56	108
Naturalized voters,	1	......	1	3	5
Aliens,	......	......	......	1	1
Militia,	17	13	13	51	94
Owners of land,	15	20	5	43	83
AGRICULTURAL—					
Acres of improved land,	125	231	70	443	869
Acres of unimproved land,	2070	2454	1120	9684	15328
Acres of meadow,	446	......	......	......	446
Tons of hay,	60	211	......	378	649
Acres of spring wheat,	......	23	......	14	37
Bushels harvested,	......	......	......	260	260
Acres of oats,	......	......	25	31	56
Bushels harvested,	......	......	......	1450	1450
Acres of corn,	63	118	......	322	503
Bushels harvested,	600	675	......	4510	5785
Acres of potatoes,	......	4	......	7	11
Bushels harvested,	......	55	......	735	790
HOGS, CATTLE, &c.					
No. of hogs sold,	......	......	19	33	52
Value of hogs sold,	......	......	60	92	152
No of cattle sold,	12	......	6	31	49
Value of cattle sold,	450	......	245	798	1493
Pounds of butter made,	200	609	4	2825	3[illegible]38
Pounds of cheese,	......	......	......	100	100
Pounds of wool,	......	......	......	20	20

TABLE,

EXHIBITING THE PROFESSIONS, TRADES, OR OCCUPATIONS OF THE INHABITANTS OF WRIGHT COUNTY, FOR 1856.

TOWNSHIPS.	Farmers.	Laborers.	Bl'ksmiths	Carpent'rs	Sawyers.	Tailors.	Shoem'k'rs.	Agents.	Physicians.	Lawyers.	Clerks.
Troy,	18	....	1	1	....	1	1	....	....	....	...
Eagle Grove,	18	1	....	2	....	....	....	....	....	....	...
Liberty,	15	....	....	....	....	1	....	....	1	....	....
Pleasant,	52	1	2	3	1	....	1	1	2	1	1
Total,	103	2	3	6	1	2	2	1	3	1	1

TABLE,

SHOWING THE PLACE OF NATIVITY OF THE INHABITANTS OF WRIGHT COUNTY, FOR 1856.

STATES.	TOWNSHIPS.				TOTAL.
	Troy.	Eagle Grove.	Liberty.	Pleasant.	
Ohio,	11	15	14	46	86
Indiana,	5	14	10	26	55
Pennsylvania,	8	4	2	16	30
Iowa,	7	10	10	24	51
New York	15	9	8	24	56
Maine,	1	2	3	3	9
N. Hampshire,	....	5	....	3	8
Vermont,	....	1	....	5	6
Massachusetts,	....	7	....	5	12
Connecticut,	2	....	1	5	9
Rhode Island,	....	....	1	.. .	1
Virginia,	1	....	1	1	3
Kentucky,	1	....	1	....	2
Illinois,	19	....	3	16	38
Michigan,	....	....	8	15	23
Arkansas,	....	....	1	....	1
Louisiana,	....	....	....	1	1
North Carolina,	....	1	....	1	2
Tennessee,	....	3	3	1	7
Missouri,	....	1	6	1	8
Maryland,	1	....	....	1	2
England,	1	....	2	....	3
Ireland,	....	....	2	3	5
Germany,	2	....	....	1	3
Canada,	1	....	1	3	5
Wisconsin,	....	1	....	....	1

INDEX.

CORRECTIONS.

On page 9, instead of "showing the number of hogs, cattle, domestic and general manufactures," read "showing the agricultural statistics."

On page 157, instead of "Harrison," read "Hardin."

www.ingramcontent.com/pod-product-compliance
Lightning Source LLC
LaVergne TN
LVHW011149110826
845150LV00006B/1197

* 9 7 8 1 4 2 5 5 4 6 3 4 2 *